More praise f

THE
BOOK OF
PSALMS

"One of the best outcomes of Alter's translation is a sense of an abrupt, muscular intensity; he restores to the Psalms a kind of strangeness that emanates from an encounter with a culture we recognize yet is distinctly alien to us, far removed in time and frame of mind."
—Mark Doty, *Los Angeles Times*

"Alter stands out for his combination of scholarly accuracy with a poet's ear."
—*Angels on Earth*

"Every reader of this translation will be led towards fresh thoughts and will discover favorites that inspire the imagination in new, rich ways."
—Walter Brueggemann, *Christian Century*

"In his compelling and swiftly moving translations, Alter has thrust the reader back to the place where the monotheistic religions were born out of even more ancient beginnings."
—*Jewish Book World*

"Alter is amazingly successful. . . . [His] translations of many famous passages are primordially spare and dignified, the work of a scholar with an unusually sure ear for verse."
—Christopher Tayler, *Saturday Guardian*

"Alter's translation . . . offers both clarity and fidelity to the meaning, meter, and nuances of the original Hebrew."
—*Library Journal*

"The achievement of this new translation is to present the Book of Psalms as a wonder of ancient literature."
—*The Tablet*

ALSO BY ROBERT ALTER

THE
BOOK OF
PSALMS

A Translation with Commentary

ROBERT ALTER

W · W · *Norton & Company* NEW YORK LONDON

Copyright © 2007 by Robert Alter

For information about permission to reproduce selections from this book,
write to Permissions, W. W. Norton & Company, Inc.,
500 Fifth Avenue, New York, NY 10110

For information about special discounts for bulk purchases, please contact
W. W. Norton Special Sales at specialsales@wwnorton.com or 800-233-4830.

Manufacturing by LSC Harrisonburg
Book design by Margaret M. Wagner
Production manager: Andrew Marasia

Library of Congress Cataloging-in-Publication Data

Bible. O.T. Psalms. English. Alter. 2007.
The book of Psalms : a translation with commentary / Robert Alter. —
1st ed.
p. cm.
Includes bibliographical references.
ISBN 978-0-393-06226-7 (hardcover)
1. Bible. O.T. Psalms—Commentaries. I. Alter, Robert. II. Title.
BS1424.A48 2007
223'.2077—dc22
2007013485

ISBN 978-0-393-33704-4 pbk.

W. W. Norton & Company, Inc.
500 Fifth Avenue, New York, N.Y. 10110
www.wwnorton.com

W. W. Norton & Company Ltd.
15 Carlisle Street, London W1D 3BS

9 0

IN MEMORY OF TOM ROSENMEYER

(1920–2007)

staunch friend, scrupulous reader,

exemplary guide to antiquity

CONTENTS

ACKNOWLEDGMENTS

THE draft of this book was carefully scrutinized by two finely discerning readers of poetry, Carol Cosman and Michael André Bernstein. They labored heroically to prevent me from doing undue violence to the English language in my pursuit of fidelity to the Hebrew, and in most instances they succeeded. The eminent classicist T. G. Rosenmeyer read the revised draft and raised helpful questions pertaining to rigor and consistency. As with my translation of *The Five Books of Moses*, I have palpably benefited from the historically informed and philologically acute suggestions of my colleague in biblical studies, Ron Hendel. Steve Forman, my editor at W. W. Norton for more than a decade, raised a variety of helpful questions about the notes and the translation. Editorial assistance for this project was paid for through funds from the Class of 1937 Chair in Comparative Literature at the University of California, Berkeley. Janet Livingstone once again was patient and efficient in deciphering my handwriting (a reflection of my continuing attachment to archaic things) and converting it into orderly electronic text. I would like to thank Rabbi Israel Stein for catching many errors of reference and typographical errors in the hardcover edition and also for his intelligent interpretative suggestions. Beyond all these, I feel a kind of gratitude to the ancient Hebrew poets who have left us these wonderful poems that have been a joy for me to live with and attempt to convey in English.

INTRODUCTION

I. HISTORICAL CONTEXTS

THROUGH the ages, Psalms has been the most urgently, personally present of all the books of the Bible in the lives of many readers. Both Jewish and Christian tradition made it part of the daily and weekly liturgy. Untold numbers have repeatedly turned to Psalms for encouragement and comfort in moments of crisis or despair. The inner world of major Western writers from Augustine, Judah Halevi, and George Herbert to Emily Dickinson and Paul Celan was inflected by the reading of Psalms. But for all the power of these Hebrew poems to speak with great immediacy in many tongues to readers of different eras, they are in their origins intricately rooted in an ancient Near Eastern world that goes back to the late Bronze Age (1600–1200 BCE) and that in certain respects is quite alien to modern people.

The prose narratives of the Hebrew Bible, despite the sundry links with the surrounding literatures that scholarship has identified, are formally innovative in striking ways. Indeed, it is arguable that at least as a set of techniques and conventions, they constitute the most original literary creation of the biblical writers. Psalms, on the other hand, or psalm-like cultic hymns and celebrations of the gods, were common in Egypt and Mesopotamia, and in Syro-Canaanite literature. We know this literature chiefly through the trove of texts found at the site of Ugarit, on the Mediterranean coast of present-day Syria, dating roughly from 1400 to 1200 BCE—several centuries earlier than the main body of biblical writings. As previously unknown texts in the various ancient Near Eastern languages have been unearthed and deciphered over the past century, it has become clear that the psalmists not only adopted the formal system of poetry (about which more is said later) from the antecedent literature of the region but also tapped their predecessors for verbal formulas, imagery, elements of mythology, and even entire sequences of lines of poetry. Some scholars have gone so far as to claim that a few psalms are essentially Hebrew translations of pagan poems, though a comparison with the proposed originals suggests rather that what the psalmists did was to adapt, briefly cite, or even polemically transform the polytheistic poems, which is, after all, what poets everywhere do with their predecessors—both building on them and emphatically making something new out of them.

In any case, the imaginative and verbal affiliation of many of the psalms with the pagan literary tradition—particularly the Canaanite tradition—that came before them is quite strong, and surely would have surprised pious readers of the canonical book over the centuries. Although God is often entreated in Psalms as a compassionate God, healer of broken hearts, and sustainer of the lowly, a good many of these poems represent the deity as a warrior god on the model of the Canaanite Baal riding through the skies with clouds as his chariot, brandishing lightning bolts as his weapons. Famously, a triadic line in one of the Ugaritic texts is virtually replicated in Psalm 92:10, with little more than the name of the god changed: "Look, your enemies, O Baal, / look, your enemies you will smash, / look, you will destroy your foes."

The council of the gods, a regular feature of Canaanite mythology, makes an appearance in a number of psalms and with it the notion of either lesser gods over whom YHWH the God of Israel presides, or of a celestial entourage ("the sons of God") that serves Him. At the great temporal remove from which we read these texts, it is hard to know to what extent such residues of polytheism were literally embraced as items of belief or were simply used as vivid poetic resources. Some of the psalms seem to reflect an ambiguous oscillation between those two possibilities. Another theme drawn from Canaanite mythology that recurs frequently in Psalms, the cosmogonic conquest of a monstrous sea god—intimating chaos—by a warrior god—associated with order—is on the whole more firmly assimilated into a monotheistic outlook. Although the various names of the primordial sea monster—Leviathan, Rahab, Yamm, Tanin—conquered by God do appear here, the originally mythological conflict is characteristically figured in more naturalistic terms as God's subduing the breakers of the sea. In Psalm 104 the fearsome Leviathan is actually reduced to an aquatic pet with whom YHWH can play.

Many of the psalms, then, derive some of their poetic force from the literary antecedents on which they draw. But the Hebrew poems were manifestly framed for Israelite purposes that were in many regards distinctive and at best no more than loosely parallel to the polytheistic texts that served as poetic precedents.

When were the various psalms composed and to what ends? The dating of individual psalms has long been a region of treacherous scholarly quicksand. The one safe conclusion is that the writing of psalms was a persistent activity over many centuries. The Davidic authorship enshrined in Jewish and Christian tradition has no credible historical grounding. It was a regular practice in the later biblical period to ascribe new texts to famous figures of the past. Although many psalms include the name David in the superscription supplied by the editors, the meaning of the Hebrew particle l^e that usually prefixes the name is ambiguous. It is conventionally translated as "of," and in ancient seals and other objects that have been discovered, it does serve as a possessive. But l^e also can mean "for," "in the manner of," "suitable to," and so forth. The present translation seeks to preserve this ambiguity by translating *mizmor l^edawid* as "a David psalm." David was no doubt identified by the editors of the collection as the exemplary psalmist because in his story, as told in 1 and 2 Samuel, he appears as a poet and the player of a stringed instrument, and at the end of the narrative is given the epithet "the sweet singer of Israel." But the editors themselves ascribed psalms to different poets—Asaph, Ethan the Ezrahite, Heyman the Ezrahite, the Korahites, and others. One cannot categorically exclude the possibility that a couple of these psalms were actually written by David, though it is difficult to gauge the likelihood (and some scholars altogether doubt David's historicity).

In any case, a few of the psalms might be as early as the Solomonic court, or even the pre-monarchic period. Many of these poems appear to have been written at some indeterminate point during the four centuries of the First Commonwealth (approximately 996 to 586 BCE). Many others offer evidence in their themes and language of composition in the period of the Return to Zion (that is, after 457 BCE). One famous instance, Psalm 137, which begins with the words "By Babylon's streams," was clearly written when the pain of exile was fresh, not long after the national trauma of 586 BCE. There is no way to date what may be the latest psalms, and the texts found at Qumran indicate that some sort of psalm writing was still a literary activity in the last two centuries before the Christian era. But the extravagant scholarly hypothesis that many of the psalms were composed in the Hasmonean period in the second century BCE is now generally rejected—among other reasons because the Septuagint, the Greek translation of the Bible completed during the third century BCE, already has virtually the same contents (with the exception of one additional psalm) as the canonical Hebrew collection passed down to us. These poems, then, were produced by many different poets over more than half a millennium, probably beginning during or even before the tenth century BCE, though the precise dating of most individual psalms remains elusive. It seems unlikely that any of the psalms is later than the fifth or fourth century BCE. By the late first century CE, the Book of Psalms was considered such a cornerstone of the scriptural canon that in Luke 24:44 it is mentioned together with the Torah and the Prophets as one of the three primary categories of the sacred writings.

Many but by no means all the psalms were composed for use in the temple cult, though it is worth noting that the elaborate instructions for the conduct of the cult in Leviticus and elsewhere include all sorts of regulations for the preparation and offering of sacrifices but no mandate for songs or liturgical texts. (The post-exilic Chronicles does represent David appointing Levitical singers.) Such songs, however, were part of the rituals celebrated throughout the region, and their attractiveness as an enhancement to the cult, with the words performed by singers to orchestral accompaniment (as many of the palms indicate) was irresistible. What should be resisted is the inclination of many scholars, beginning in the early twentieth century, to turn as many psalms as possible into the liturgy of conjectured temple rites—to recover what in biblical studies is called the "life-setting" of the psalms. Perhaps the chief offender among these conjectures is a purported enthronement rite, marking an annual festival in which God was crowned as king. Although Mesopotamian analogies have been cited as evidence, there is simply no indication in the biblical corpus or in the archaeological record that such a ritual existed in ancient Israel, and surely the

Israelites were not such literalists as to be incapable of acclaiming God's kingship without a cultic ceremony of enthronement.

Some psalms nevertheless offer strong evidence of their use as liturgical texts. Several psalms, for example Psalm 118, bear indications that three distinct groups of participants in the temple service—"Israel," "the house of Aaron," and "those who fear the LORD"—were called on to chant the refrain "forever is His kindness." Several other psalms follow the progress of pilgrims climbing Mount Zion, then entering the gates of the sacred precincts. Some psalms celebrate a national victory or pray for God's intercession in a time of national danger. Many of the psalms, however, have an individual rather than a collective focus—prayers of thanksgiving after a person has escaped a deadly illness or some other danger, and supplications imploring God to intervene on behalf of someone threatened by enemies or ailments. At least the thanksgiving psalms would probably have accompanied a cultic act, the offering of a thanksgiving sacrifice. It is conceivable, though not entirely demonstrable, that there were professional psalm poets in the vicinity of the temple from whom a worshipper coming to Jerusalem could have purchased a psalm that he would recite to express his own particular need. Such compositions might have provided a nucleus for the different collections of psalms that were put together in the canonical anthology. There are, however, other psalms that show no evident connection with any temple ritual. The most clear-cut instances of this category are the psalms that are general reflections on the nature of human existence or on the role of morality in human affairs (most of these would also probably not have been performed to musical accompaniment). Still other psalms have a political or public subject that has no obvious link with worship, such as the royal psalms (including one composed to celebrate a king's wedding) and the psalms in praise of Zion.

From all this, one may reasonably infer that the psalm was conceived in the ancient period as a fairly flexible poetic form. Sung and played in the temple service, it could be a liturgical text in the strict sense. It could also accompany individual ritual acts of thanksgiving, confession, and supplication, or perhaps express these various themes outside a ritual context. (Jonah in Jonah 2 and Hannah in 1 Samuel 2 are assigned psalms by the redactor to recite at critical moments in their life stories that have no connection with a cult.) The psalm could serve as a poetic

vehicle for philosophic reflection or didactic instruction or the commemoration of national history or for the celebration of the monarch
and the seat of the monarchy. Psalm 137, announcing its own composition in Babylonian exile, is an instructive instance of how far the literary concept of psalm could be pushed. It amounts to an anti-psalm,
declaring from the beginning that it is impossible to sing Zion's songs
"on foreign soil." Yet the editors thought it appropriate for inclusion in
the Book of Psalms, alongside poems that were explicitly framed for use
in the temple ritual. The case of this poem should alert us to the limits
of one of the most common scholarly modes of analysis of Psalms, the
form-criticism that identifies distinct genres of psalms (supplication,
thanksgiving, Wisdom psalm, royal psalm, historical psalm, Zion psalm,
psalm of praise). Though these generic categories are sometimes useful
for understanding the thrust of a particular text, there is more fluidity of
genre than they allow, with many psalms being hybrids or switching
genre in mid-course and at least a few psalms, such as Psalm 137, standing outside the system of genre. What can be concluded from all this
variegated evidence is that the psalm was a multifaceted poetic form
serving many different purposes, some cultic and others not, and that it
played a vital role in the life of the Israelite community and of individ-
uals within that community throughout the biblical period.

II. ASSEMBLING THE BOOK

THE anthology that became the Book of Psalms was put together in the
Second Temple period, perhaps in the fifth century BCE but probably no
later than the fourth century BCE. The decision to assemble the dis-
parate psalms in a book may have been motivated by the redaction of
the Torah in the fifth century BCE as a canonical book intended for public reading. We have no precise knowledge about the identity of the editors, though the usual suspects—priestly circles in Jerusalem—seem
plausible candidates, because they would have had a particular interest
in making the psalms authoritatively available for use in worship.

The canonical collection is divided into five books, 1–41, 42–72,
73–89, 90–106, 107–150. The end of each book is marked by a brief
prose doxology praising God that is not part of the psalm after which it

is inserted. The fifth book lacks this doxological coda, perhaps because Psalm 150 as a whole, a string of exhortations to praise God in song, was thought to serve that purpose. The first three books seem to have originally been independent collections of psalms, and in all likelihood what is now the fourth and fifth books was at first a single additional book. Psalms 1 and 2 are usually considered to be a prologue to the Book of Psalms as a whole and not part of the collection that constitutes the first book of Psalms. Two duplications of psalms (Psalms 14 and 53, Psalm 40:14–18 and Psalm 70) in different books of the collection offer evidence that these were originally separate anthologies that evolved independently. Further evidence for the independence of the precanonical collections is the conclusion of the second book with the words, "the prayers of David son of Jesse are ended," a formula that is then contradicted by psalms in the next three books, many of which are in fact ascribed to David. The division into five books was clearly in emulation of the Five Books of Moses. Perhaps this division was merely a formal device to help confer canonical status on Psalms, following the precedent of the recently canonized Torah. Some scholars have inferred that it was motivated by a practical need to facilitate the public reading of Psalms in coordination with the public reading of the Torah according to a triennial cycle, although the crucial consideration for such reading would be not the number of books (three would have worked better than five) but the number of psalms, 150, allowing for approximately a psalm each week over the three-year cycle. (The number was not absolutely fixed at 150 but rather hovered somewhere around 150 because a few of the psalms that are now separate units may be the result of the joining together of two psalms, and Psalms 9 and 10 were originally a single psalm.)

There are also a few smaller groupings of psalms, such as the psalms attributed to Asaph, the "songs of ascents" (the meaning of that term is in dispute), and the hallelujah psalms at the end of the collection (the term *hallelujah*, "praise God," appears only in the fourth and fifth books and is a sign that they once were a single collection distinct from the other three books). It is possible that these shorter sequences of psalms were once small separate scrolls that were incorporated into the books where they now appear, which in turn were put together to make the five-part Book of Psalms.

The title given to this book by Hebrew tradition reflects a particular view of what was its essential subject. The Hebrew term for "psalm" is *mizmor*, which means "something sung," cognate with the verb *zamer*, "to sing" or "to hymn." It is possible but by no means certain that this verb designates singing accompanied by a musical instrument. It is definitely singing associated with praise or jubilation; one would never use it for the chanting of a dirge. The noun *mizmor*, whether or not attached to the name David, appears in the heading of a large number of the psalms. And yet the book as a whole has never been called *Mizmorim*, "Psalms," but *Tehilim*, "Praises" (a rabbinic plural of the noun *tehilah* that appears in the collection with some frequency in the singular). Now, the two preponderant genres in the book are psalms of thanksgiving, which overlap significantly with psalms of praise, and supplications, but there are more supplications than psalms of thanksgiving or praise. Nevertheless, the idea of calling the book *Tehilim*, "Praises," reflects an insight into what is going on in most though not all of the poems. Again and again, the psalmists tell us that man's ultimate calling is to use the resources of human language to celebrate God's greatness and to express gratitude for His beneficent acts. This theme is sometimes given special urgency by being joined with an emphasis on the ephemerality of human life: Only the living can praise God. There are moments of such praise, or at least expressions of readiness to turn to praise, even in many of the psalms of supplication. The editorial decision to conclude the book with six psalms of praise, each of the last five beginning with "hallelujah" (two words in the Hebrew—an imperative verb "praise" and its object Yah, "God"), all coming to a grand orchestral climax in the last psalm, is surely an effort to define the whole collection as a gathering of songs of praise. Despite the variegated character of the sundry psalms, it is a definition to a large extent justified by the poems themselves.

III. THE POETRY OF *PSALMS*

IT HAS BEEN generally understood since the eighteenth century, and among some Jewish scholars still earlier, that biblical poetry is based on a parallelism of meaning between the two halves of the line (or, in the minority of lines that are triadic, among the three parts of the line). There is no requirement of rhyme (very occasionally one encounters an ad hoc rhyme) and no regular meter of the kind manifested in Greek and Latin poetry, though some Bible scholars in recent decades have made misguided attempts to impose such a meter by counting syllables or other proposed phonetic units. The best account of the formal system of biblical poetry is the concise article by Benjamin Hrushovski (now Harshav) under the rubric "Prosody, Hebrew," in the *Encyclopedia Judaica*. Hrushovski calls the system "semantic-syntactic-accentual parallelism." That is to say, between the two halves of the line there may be some equivalence of meaning ("semantic"), an equivalent number of stressed syllables ("accentual"), and a parallelism of syntax. Some lines may manifest a neat parallelism in all three categories, but that is not obligatory. As to the parallelism of meaning that has chiefly absorbed the attention of scholars since the idea was first expounded by the Anglican bishop Robert Lowth in the eighteenth century, such parallelism is prevalent, but many divergences are allowed, in the same way, for example, that Shakespeare often permits himself to modify or swerve from strict iambic pentameter in his deployment of blank verse. Finally, much of the force of ancient Hebrew poetry derives from its rhythmic compactness, something one could scarcely guess from the existing English versions. A typical line of biblical poetry has three beats in each verset (I borrow this term for the half lines from Hrushovski, who uses it instead of "hemistich" or "colon" to avoid confusion with other systems of prosody). Some lines exhibit a three-beat four-beat pattern; sometimes a verset may have only two beats. Typically, given the compact structure of biblical words, there are usually only one or two unaccented syllables between the accented ones. In the next section, I will consider the implications of this prosodic system for translating the Hebrew poems.

Although, as systems of prosody go, biblical poetics remains relatively conservative with the passage of time, it is worth noting that over the six centuries or more during which the canonical psalms were composed, some evolution in the system is observable. The oldest stratum of biblical poetry, as evidenced in the Song of Deborah (Judges 5), shows a fondness for patterns of incremental repetition. These occur in Psalms as well, whether because the poem is old or because the poet has chosen to use an archaizing device. Here is an instance of incremental repetition in a verse I alluded to earlier without quoting: "For, look, Your enemies, O LORD, / for, look, Your enemies *perish* . . ." (92:10). The increment in the repetition is italicized. The archaic poetic style here can be attributed to the adoption by the psalmist, as we noted, of a line from an old Canaanite poem. At the other end of the historical spectrum, in the Second Temple period semantic parallelism is somewhat weakened. Many lines show no parallelism of meaning between versets; in numerous instances, this lack is compensated for by a semantic parallelism between two whole lines in sequence, though this is not invariably the case. One observes, for example, such interlinear parallelism in Psalm 27:3:

> Though a camp is marshaled against me,
> my heart shall not fear.
> Though battle is roused against me,
> nonetheless do I trust.

Since the pioneering work of Bishop Lowth, scholars have been inclined to imagine semantic parallelism as a deployment of synonyms between the two versets. Sometimes this is actually the case. Thus, Psalm 6:2 reads, "LORD, do not chastise me in Your wrath, / do not punish me in Your fury." The two versets are neatly parallel in meaning, term for term, and the syntax is parallel as well (in the Hebrew the verb comes at the end of each clause). The only divergence in the strict symmetry between the two clauses is that the first verset begins with the vocative "LORD." The immediately following verse of this psalm, on the other hand, exhibits a far more prevalent use of semantic parallelism: "Have mercy on me, LORD, for I am wretched. / Heal me, for my limbs are stricken." This is synonymity with a difference, or, one should say, with a development. The general plea "Have mercy on me" (*honeini*) becomes the physically concrete "Heal me" (*refa'eini*), and a general condition of misery ("for I am wretched") is translated into the somatically specific "for my limbs are stricken." This is how poetic parallelism usually works in the Bible. Poets in any language are rarely content simply to repeat the same thing in different words. If the more common or general term for a concept appears in the first verset, as is usually the

enters the watery depths; then, in the second verset, he discovers that the current (perhaps in this instance an undertow) is sweeping him away. In the third line, first he cries for help to the point of exhaustion; then, in the second verset, he notes the concrete physical consequence of all this desperate shouting—a hoarse throat. Although some psalms are laden with stereotypical language in which both the parallelism within the line and the poem as a whole are relatively static, the strong forward thrust in many of these lines of poetry as well as from line to line means that this is by and large a highly dynamic poetic system in which ideas and images are progressively pushed to extremes and themes brought to a crisis and a turning point. It is a formal aspect of the poetry of Psalms that helps make it an abiding resource for readers, whether they are in the grip of stark despair or on the crest of elation.

For all these features of the poetry of Psalms that are common to the general system of poetics in the Bible, there are also ways in which the kind of poetry deployed here is distinct from what we see in other poetic texts of the Bible. As poetry often framed for use in worship, it flaunts its own traditionalism. It rarely seeks startling effects, and again and again it deliberately draws on a body of familiar images. In Job, one encounters an astonishing inventiveness in the use of figurative language; that is often true in the Prophets as well. In Proverbs, didactic points are frequently made through sharp thrusts of wit in the metaphors. But the psalmists, to a large extent composers of liturgical and devotional texts, have no desire to surprise or disorient the pilgrims and supplicants and celebrants for whose use the texts are intended. If a person is threatened with death, the danger is represented, as we have seen, by the depths of the sea, swirling waves, waters that come up to the neck, and the "originality" of the poem inheres in the imaginativeness and freshness with which the poet reworks familiar images, as is strongly evident in Psalm 69, from which I have quoted. This notion of putting a fresh spin on stock images is common in other bodies of poetry: One might recall, for example, the Renaissance tradition of love sonnets from Petrarch to Spencer, in which the fair beloved is both fire and ice, her hair pure gold, her lips coral, and so forth. In similar fashion, God in the psalms of thanksgiving is a rock and a fortress, a shield and a buckler, a sheltering wing and a hiding place on an evil day. (Psalm 91 strikingly illustrates how great poetry can be created out of such stock images.) Each genre of psalms draws on its own reservoir of conventional images. In the many supplications that are also complaints, the speaker's enemies, even if their enmity is in the civic realm, lay snares and dig pits for the speaker's feet, speak words like piercing arrows with a tongue that is a sharpened sword and drips poison like serpents. In the psalms of praise, because the subject is God, figurative language is often less central, but God is represented in stereotypical phrases performing the same acts—keeping truth forever, making heaven and earth, rendering justice to the oppressed, giving bread to the hungry, and, in a mythological register, riding on the clouds, crushing Leviathan, subduing the waves of the sea.

The reliance of these poems, however, on a repertoire of traditional images and stereotypical phrases does not preclude the creation of fresh and moving poetry. Granted, there are poems in the collection that are largely a stringing together of psalmodic clichés. What is remarkable is the poetic beauty and eloquence of many of the psalms, qualities that have made this book one of the primary models for lyric poetry in the Western tradition, leading many English Renaissance poets to use the verse rendering of Psalms as a basic exercise for the composition of poetry. Some of the poetic power of the psalms derives from their strategically effective use of fairly simple archetypal imagery. Thus, the first psalm sets up a strong antithesis between the just man, likened to a fruit-bearing tree deeply rooted alongside streams of water, and the wicked, who are like chaff driven by the wind. The similes are grounded in a familiar agricultural world in which the difference between what is rooted and perennially productive and what is a mere waste product that is blown away would be clear to everyone, but these images still speak to us. In many of the psalms, the simple directness of statement in the use of traditional figurative language becomes affectingly eloquent, as readers through the ages have attested. Here, for example, is the initial verse of Psalm 27 (two lines of poetry exhibiting a compact three-beat two-beat rhythm in the Hebrew):

> The LORD is my light and my rescue.
>> Whom should I fear?
> The LORD is my life's stronghold.
>> Of whom should I be afraid?

God as light for someone plunged in darkness and God as a fortress for someone under assault are recurrent metaphors in Psalms. But the succinctness with which these familiar terms are set here opposite the speaker's declaration that he has nothing to fear, coupled with the reinforcing effect of the interlinear parallelism, gives these lines striking expressive power. One sees why such psalms have meant so much to countless people in their own hour of uncertainty and dread.

Often, the sequencing of observation and poetic statement produces the most moving effects. Memorably, the speaker in Psalm 8 looks up at the night sky and reflects:

> When I see Your heavens, the work of Your fingers,
>> the moon and the stars You fixed firm,
> "What is man that You should note him,
>> and the human creature, that You pay him heed,
> and You make him little less than the gods,
>> with glory and grandeur You crown him?" (verses 4–6)

The first line here incorporates a reminiscence of the creation of the celestial bodies in Genesis 1 with an elegantly apt variation on a biblical idiom. Instead of "the work of Your hands," we have "the work of Your fingers," in keeping with the delicate tracery of the stars. In the next two lines, the speaker's exclamation of astonishment hurtles downward in the cosmic hierarchy from the heavens above, where the celestial beings (perhaps *'elohim* here is an ellipsis for "sons of God") would dwell, to man down below. The synonymous parallelism of the middle line ("What is man . . .") is counterpointed by the focusing parallelism of the line that follows ("You make him little less . . . , / with glory and grandeur You crown him.") The idea that humankind is to have dominion over the created world is prominent in the first creation story, but in the last line of this sequence, it is poetically realized in a little fanfare of royal imagery.

Poetically effective sequencing may be combined with the semantic dynamics to which lines of parallelistic verse lend themselves. Psalm 90:4 offers a remarkable expression of the overwhelming disparity between the divine perspective of eternity and the fleeting temporal experience of ephemeral man: "For a thousand years in Your eyes / are like yesterday gone, / like a watch in the night." This triadic line offers

us a vision of time from God's end of the telescope. In a pattern of
diminution, it takes us from a thousand years to a yesterday that has
already vanished to a single watch in the night, barely four hours. And
Psalm 90 as a whole uses a poetic strategy frequently observable in
these poems by repeating key words with a thematic point. In this meditation on temporality, the psalmist rings the changes on "years" and
"days," "morning" and "evening," all the way to the plea just before the
end, "Give us joy as the days You afflicted us, / the years we saw evil"
(90:15).

Finally, though much of the figurative language is manifestly taken
from a traditional repertoire, there are moments of striking metaphoric
inventiveness. Water, as we saw in the case of the first psalm, is a potent
metaphor in this culture existing often precariously in a semi-arid climate. It is understandable that Jeremiah should represent God as the
source of living waters. What the poet in Psalm 42:2–3 does with this
traditional background is nevertheless utterly arresting:

> As a deer yearns for streams of water,
>> so I yearn for You, O God.
> My whole being thirsts for God,
>> for the living God.

The thirsting reflects a distinctive aspect of Psalms. These poems, even
if many of them were written to be used in the temple cult, exhibit an
intensely spiritual inwardness. Yet that inwardness is characteristically
expressed in the most concretely somatic terms. Here is another example of the psalmist's longing for God articulated as thirst:

> God, my God, for You I search.
>> My throat thirsts for You,
> my flesh yearns for You
>> in a land waste and parched, with no water. (63:2)

The King James Version, and most modern translations in its footsteps,
has the "soul" thirsting for God, but this is almost certainly a mistake.
The Hebrew *nefesh* means "life breath" and, by extension, "life" or
"essential being." But by metonymy, it is also a term for the throat (the

passage through which the breath travels) or, sometimes, for the neck. As the subject of the verb "thirst" and with the interlinear parallelism with "flesh," *nefesh* here surely has its physical meaning of "throat." The very physicality, of course, makes the metaphor of thirsting all the more powerful.

Let me offer one last example of the force of figurative language in Psalms within a framework of traditional language. God, as we noted in a verse quoted from Psalm 27, is associated with light—in that instance, because light, archetypically, means safety and rescue to those plunged in fearful darkness, but also because radiance is a mythological property of deities and monarchs. Psalm 104 is a magnificent celebration of God as king of the vast panorama of creation. It begins by imagining God in the act of putting on royal raiment: "Grandeur and glory You don" (*hod wehadar lavashta*). The psalmist then goes on: "Wrapped in light like a cloak, / stretching out the heavens like a tent-cloth" (verse 2). What makes the familiar figure of light for the divinity so effective is its fusion with the metaphor of clothing. The poet, having represented God donning regalia, envisages Him wrapping Himself in a garment of pure light (the Hebrew verb used here is actually in the active mode, "wrapping"). Then, associatively continuing the metaphor of fabrics, he has God "stretching out the heavens like a tent-cloth," the bright sky above becoming an extension of the radiance that envelopes God. This is a small but vivid instance of the imaginative energy that produces poetry of the highest order in Psalms. The figurative invention is not meant to startle or disorient the reader, who is invited to participate in the mood of exaltation of the psalmist, but it is fresh enough, and tightly enough woven into a texture of related images, that it serves to convey a strong vision of God as king of creation and of the luminous enchantment of the created world. These poems retain their eloquence and liveliness after two and a half millennia or more, for believers and simply for people who love poetry.

IV. THE CHALLENGE OF TRANSLATING *PSALMS*

IT IS A constant challenge to turn ancient Hebrew poetry into English verse that is reasonably faithful to the original and yet readable as poetry.

Perhaps the most pervasive problem is the intrinsic structural compactness of biblical Hebrew, a feature that the poets constantly exploit musically and otherwise. Biblical Hebrew is what linguists call a synthetic language, as opposed to analytic languages such as English. Pronominal objects of verbs are usually indicated by an accusative suffix attached to the verb. The pronominal subject of verbs is usually indicated by the way the verb is conjugated, without need to introduce the pronoun, unless it is added for emphasis. Thus, "He will guard you" is a single word, *yishmorkha*. Instead of using possessive pronouns, nouns are declined with possessive suffixes. And the verb "to be" has no present tense, instead being merely implied by the juxtaposition of a subject noun and a predicate noun (hence the King James Version constantly italicizes *is* because there is no literal equivalent in the Hebrew text). Thus, "The LORD is my shepherd" is only two words, four syllables, in the Hebrew: YHWH *ro'i*.

There is no way of consistently getting this terrific rhythmic compactness into English, but I am convinced that a more strenuous effort to approximate it is called for than the existing translations have made. The King James Version is often (though not invariably) eloquent, but it ignores the rhythms of the Hebrew almost entirely. The various modern English versions are only occasionally eloquent and sometimes altogether flat-footed and, more often than not, arythmic. Thus, the concluding verset of Psalm 104:1, quoted with a transliteration of the Hebrew in the last paragraph of the preceding section, reads in the King James Version as follows: "thou art clothed with honour and majesty." This is dignified, though "honour" for *hod* is wrong. What is notable is that the 1611 version has seven words for the three in the Hebrew, and no equivalent for the strong alliterative effect of the Hebrew. The New Jewish Publication Society translation, "You are clothed in glory and majesty," is simply a modernization of the King James Version. The Revised English Bible has "clothed in majesty and splendour," which does eliminate two words, "You are," but at the cost of diminishing the active sense of God's putting on the royal raiment. In my translation I render the verb as "You don," the monosyllable allowing a phrase of just two syllables that brings the whole verset close to the Hebrew rhythm: "Grandeur and glory You don."

The question of syntax here and throughout these poems also

deserves a comment. Biblical syntax is more flexible than English syntax, often adjusting the order of terms for emphasis or for other expressive purposes. The object of the verb can precede it, as it does in the verset we are considering, or follow it, as it does repeatedly in the next several lines of Psalm 104. The syntactic fronting of *hod wehadar*, "grandeur and glory," is a way of highlighting these accoutrements of majesty that the God of creation dons. The reversal of normal English word order is, it seems to me, idiomatically viable because traditional English poetry makes abundant use of syntactic inversions; and, given that all biblical poetry incorporates a more archaic stratum of the ancient language than one encounters in the prose, the appropriate English style and diction for representing it should have a slightly antique coloration.

Let me offer as a test case for the issue of rhythm a single line that, in the King James Version, has probably become the most famous set of words from the whole Book of Psalms. The initial line—there are two in the verse—of Psalm 23:4 grandly reads in the 1611 translation: "Yea, though I walk through the valley of the shadow of death, I will fear no evil." This beautiful line has understandably moved readers for four centuries, but it is the stately beauty of a leisurely prose amble, not of a line of poetry (or, if one prefers, the beauty of a proto-Whitmanesque line of poetry rather than of biblical poetry). The Hebrew sounds like this: *gam ki-'elekh begey' tsalmawet / lo'-'iyra' ra'*. If we ignore the Masoretic hyphenation, the Hebrew comes to eight words, eleven syllables. The King James Version weighs in with seventeen words, twenty syllables. My version reads, "Though I walk in the vale of death's shadow, / I fear no harm." When I showed the line in draft to a discriminating friend, he objected that I had flagrantly done it this way simply to be different from the King James Version. I had to explain, and add the explanation to my notes, that I was impelled by the desire to get a better approximation of the Hebrew rhythm—more concise, with the intimation of dachtylic cadence in the first verset, and actually matching the cinched effect of the Hebrew's four stark syllables in the second verset.

This preoccupation with rhythm, which will be self-evidently justified to any serious reader of poetry and probably seem odd to anyone else, is inseparable from the underlying aspiration of this translation. I do not want to make the poetry of Psalms sound like Shakespeare or

Keats or Whitman or Yeats. Milton, one of the great virtuosos of English poetry (and one of the very few who actually read biblical Hebrew), translated a small selection of psalms into rhyming couplets, abab rhymes, *terza rima*, and other intricate patterns. It is an astonishing performance, and less far removed from the literal sense of the Hebrew than one might imagine. But it is nothing like biblical poetry. What I have aimed at in this translation—inevitably, with imperfect success— is to represent Psalms in a kind of English verse that is readable as poetry yet sounds something like the Hebrew—emulating its rhythms wherever feasible, reproducing many of the effects of its expressive poetic syntax, seeking equivalents for the combination of homespun directness and archaizing in the original, hewing to the lexical concreteness of the Hebrew, and making more palpable the force of parallelism that is at the heart of biblical poetry. The translation is also on the whole quite literal—something that the King James Version has probably conditioned English readers to expect—in the conviction that the literal sense has a distinctive poetic force and that it is often possible to preserve it in workable literary English. Where English usage has compelled me to depart from a literal rendering, I have noted the divergence in my commentary.

An observation about the concreteness of language is in order here. Biblical Hebrew uses few abstractions. In most instances a term anchored in physical existence, some metonymy or synecdoche, serves in place of an abstraction. There is no real biblical word for "progeny" or "posterity"; poets and prose writers as well prefer to say "seed," which also means "semen" and, by metonymy, the product of semen. It should also be observed that the Hebrew word for "seed" is two syllables, as against the two polysyllabic Greco-Latinate equivalents just cited. Wherever possible, the translation resists substituting an abstraction for the concrete term in the Hebrew. I have tried to avoid ponderous Latinate terms such as "iniquity" and "transgression," which misrepresent the tone and sound of the Hebrew equivalents if not their denotations; I have preferred instead more everyday terms such as "wrongdoing" and "crime." What is at stake in this preference is not just a matter of phonetics or aesthetics but a world view that informs these poems. We are all accustomed to think of Psalms, justifiably, as a religious book, but its religious character is not the same as that of the Christian and Jewish traditions that variously evolved over the centuries after the Bible. The psalmists are constantly concerned with the relationship between man and God, or Israel and God, which is more than sufficient to qualify their poetry as religious. But this relationship is often imagined in social, political, and even physical terms rather than in the framework of what Protestant theology calls "salvation history." "Crime" is frequently a more apt English equivalent for the Hebrew *'awen* than "iniquity" because what triggers the indignation of the supplicant is the bribing of judges, defamation, theft, conspiracy to murder, and other violations of the law. Another Hebrew term, *ḥet'*, which repeatedly figures in both older and modern English versions as "sin," is translated here as "offense." I do not mean to say that there is no notion of sin in Psalms, but the fraught theological connotations of the English term are not quite right. Etymologically, *ḥet'* comes from a verb that means "to miss the mark." In the prose narratives, it is the word used in political contexts for the rebellion of a vassal people against its overlord and, in court settings, for when a subject person causes displeasure to his superior. Giving offense to God as king is connotatively different from sinning, with the associations of that English term with spiritual degradation leading to contrition, self-flagellation, and penance.

The two most notable instances of resistance to inappropriately theological language in this translation are the pointed absence in it of "soul" and "salvation." The avoidance of these terms, which many English readers may automatically associate with Psalms, is not the result of contrariness on my part but reflects a commitment to philological fidelity and to the notions of reality manifested in the Hebrew words. *Nefesh*, as I observed above, has a core meaning of "life breath," but the Vulgate generally rendered it as *anima*, and that in turn predisposed the King James translators to represent it as "soul." It covers so many different meanings that it is impossible to translate in all contexts with the same English equivalent, something I attempt to do with all the Hebrew terms that will allow it. The possessive "my *nefesh*" is often chiefly an intensive form of the first-person-singular pronoun and, given the lack of any analogous term in English, is usually rendered here simply as "I." When *nefesh* is the object of a verb such as "to save," the reasonable English translation is "life." Because it is the very breath that quickens a person with life, it sometimes carries the sense of "essential being," and in these cases it is usually rendered here as "being." I am aware that "my being" is more awkward than "my soul," but "soul" strongly suggests a body-soul split—with implications of an afterlife—that is alien to the Hebrew Bible and to Psalms in particular. (There are indications of a Hades-like underworld, Sheol, a shadowy realm of nonbeing into which the dead descend, but this remains far from the distinct afterworld of later Judaism and Christianity.) As such, "soul" is a word that has to be avoided if we are not to get a misleading idea of what the psalmists are saying.

As previously noted, *nefesh* often occurs in Psalms as an anatomical term for the part of the body between the head and the shoulders. This usage is widely recognized by modern scholars, though in my view it is more frequently applied in Psalms than is generally allowed. Here is an instance where there is scant disagreement: Psalm 69 begins with these words in the King James Version: "Save me, O God; for the waters are come in unto my soul." This image of internal seepage is picturesque if mystifying, but what the Hebrew really says, in a vivid depiction of threatened drowning, is "for the waters have come up to my neck." Most modern versions have seen this, but in Psalm 44:26, where the King James Version has "For our soul [*nafsheinu*] is bowed down to the dust: our belly cleaveth unto the earth," modern translators opt for a simple "we" instead of "soul," missing the strong physical parallelism with "belly" (a word that in the New Jewish Publication Society translation vanishes into the prim generality of "body"). The present translation renders this line as "For our neck is bowed to the dust, / our belly clings to the ground," in fidelity to the poet's strong concrete image of a person thrust into a prostrate position on the ground from neck to belly.

"Salvation" is the term that the translators in 1611 chose to represent the Hebrew *yeshu'ah*, and it has shown more than a little persistence in the various modern versions. "Salvation" is a heavily fraught theological term, pulling in its tow all sorts of associations of eschatological redemption or radical spiritual transformation and sublime elevation of the individual sinner. In Christianity, it also strongly implies a particular Savior (whose name is derived from this verbal stem); in post-biblical Judaism as well, the Hebrew word *yeshu'ah* comes to designate a global process of messianic redemption. But in Psalms this noun and its cognate verb *hoshi'a* are strictly directed to the here and now. *Hoshi'a* means to get somebody out of a tight fix, to rescue him. When the tight fix involves the threat of enemies on the battlefield, *yeshu'ah* can mean "victory," and *hoshi'a* "to make victorious"; more commonly, both the noun and the verb indicate "rescue." It will no doubt take getting used to for some readers to feel comfortable with "the God of my rescue" instead of "the God of my salvation," but that is precisely the sort of readjustment of mind-set that this translation aims to effect. The relationship between man and God is as urgent as readers of Psalms in English have always imagined, but it is not enacted in the kind of theological theater that has conventionally been assumed. The psalms of supplication, where rescue is the central issue, are poems emerging from the most pressing sense of personal or collective crisis. The speakers in these poems, however, do not seek some transport to a different spiritual realm, some radical transformation of their inward self. Instead, they implore God to extricate them from terrible straits, confound their enemies, restore them to wholeness and safety. Notions of the heavens opening and flights of angels in glorious raiment bearing redeemed souls on high have their own excitements, but they are not within the purview of these Hebrew poets. This translation is an effort to reground Psalms in the order of reality in which it was conceived, where the spiritual was realized through the physical, and divine purposes were implemented in social, political, and even military realms.

One special issue of translation deserves comment: how to render in English the various Hebrew names of the deity. The proper name for the God of Israel is indicated by the four consonants YHWH, which almost all modern scholars think was pronounced "Yahweh." I have decided not to use "Yahweh" for several reasons. Though this may well have been the original pronunciation, there remains, at least in my stubborn view, a margin of uncertainty about it. Some Jewish readers would be uncomfortable with it because all communities of practicing Jews still observe the prohibition on pronouncing the tetragrammaton. In the late-biblical period, only the High Priest in the Holy of Holies on the Day of Atonement was allowed to utter the ineffable name. When several centuries later the Hebrew text of the Bible was assigned vowel markings, YHWH was vocalized as though it were *'adonai*, "Master" or "Lord," and was pronounced as *'adonai*. The King James Version in most instances honored this precedent by translating the name as "the Lord," using smaller upper-case font for the last three letters to indicate that there was some-

scribal transmission that any text copied by scribes from century to century accumulates errors over time. A copyist's eye can easily skip over a letter, a word, even a whole phrase. He may inadvertently duplicate a letter occurring at the end of one word at the beginning of the next word in the text (what is called "dittography"), or, alternately, he may mistakenly drop a letter that actually belongs because he has just copied the same letter in a preceding word (what is called "haplography"). Consonants can get reversed, or even words or phrases. The standard Hebrew text of the Bible, the Masoretic text (from *masoret* or *mesorah*, meaning "tradition") was fixed by a school of Jewish grammarians and editors in Tiberias between the sixth and ninth centuries CE. They also added vowel points and cantillation marks (the latter serving to parse the syntax) to the ancient unpunctuated consonantal text. The evidence suggests that they were scrupulous in the work they did, but a millennium or more had passed since the original composition of most of the texts, and in that period a host of errors had crept in, and they themselves were hardly immune to error in their editorial decisions. The biblical texts found among the Dead Sea Scrolls as well as the versions that appear to have been used by the ancient translators of the Bible into Greek, Aramaic, Syriac, and Latin all show local divergences from the Masoretic text, though it is often not easy to determine which is more authoritative than the others, and any translator, as I can attest from experience, might be tempted to "improve" the text when it is difficult.

Textual errors cluster far more heavily in biblical poetry than in the prose. A straightforward explanation for this difference offers itself. Biblical poetry uses a specialized poetic vocabulary incorporating many words that never occur in prose and in some instances are rare or archaic. When a copyist is confronted with an unfamiliar word or idiom, he runs the risk of scrambling it or substituting a more familiar term. Let us imagine for a moment that the poetry of T. S. Eliot was composed before the invention of the printing press and so was exposed to the vagaries of scribal transmission. What would a poor scribe do when he encountered in "Sweeney Among the Nightingales" the following line: "Swelling to maculate giraffe"? Many speakers of English, apart from zoologists and perhaps other scientists, have never seen or heard the word "maculate." Our hypothetical scribe would be doing a perfectly natural thing if he replaced this puzzler, either unconsciously or because he thought he was correcting an error, with the familiar "immaculate," though by so doing he would have his version say the opposite of what the poet wrote and would entirely lose the image of the giraffe's spots. Moving on to "Gerontion," he would be perplexed by "Spawned in some estimanet of Antwerp" because "estimanet" is a French word (a shabby tavern), and he might be tempted to make sense of it by substituting "estimate," thus reducing the whole line to gibberish. A similar borrowing from French a few lines down in the same poem, "Rocks, moss, stonecrop, iron, merds" (the last word from *merde*, here plural without the *e*, used to mean "turds") would produce further incomprehension, and the scribe, a sensible man, might therefore replace it with the blander, if context-appropriate, "mud."

There is abundant evidence that slips or blunders of this sort occurred again and again in the copying of the psalms, rendering some phrases or whole lines or even sequences of lines almost unintelligible. I don't mean to exaggerate. Many psalms, including some of the most famous, such as the first, the twenty-third, and the last psalm in the collection, are beautifully transparent in the original from beginning to end, inspiring considerable confidence that there was no slip between the pen of the poet and the pens of the long line of scribes. But there are also many instances in which the meaning of the text as it stands is quite opaque, with no easy path of reconstruction back to what the poet might have originally written.

Psalms 9 and 10 are a striking illustration of these textual problems. In the Septuagint, these appear as a single psalm. Internal evidence for their unity is the fact that together they form an alphabetic acrostic. Psalm 9 begins with the initial letters of the alphabet in proper order, though it lacks a line beginning with *dalet*, the fourth letter of the Hebrew alphabet. The acrostic vanishes in the last two verses of Psalm 9, reappears at the beginning of Psalm 10, only to vanish again, then resurfaces toward the end of the psalm, which has lines beginning respectively with the last four letters of the Hebrew alphabet (verses 12–17), though interspersed with lines that are not part of the acrostic pattern. This scrambling of the acrostic is accompanied by a slide into incoherence in 9:21 and 10:3–6. It is reasonable to infer that something happened here to the text more extensive than a scribal inadvertence. Perhaps a purportedly authoritative manuscript used by the line of scribes that led to the Masoretic text was damaged—by moisture, fire, or otherwise. With bits missing and the continuity of the acrostic no longer in clear sight, some later editor may not have realized that these two segments of the text were the halves of a single psalm. Moreover, at least in the four verses I have just cited, there may have been missing or illegible elements in the text, and a desperate scribe might have copied the incoherent fragments or, in an effort to make sense of them, created nonsense on the order of "spawned in an estimate of Antwerp."

What is a translator to do with these many places where the text has been corrupted? The standard scholarly resource is to emend the text in an effort to restore it as it originally read. Some scholars have not hesitated to reconstruct clauses or whole lines and sequences of lines, but such extensive emendation usually looks more like an exercise in ingenuity than a reliable means of recovering the original text. This translation is relatively conservative in adopting emendations, and some biblical scholars may look askance at this cautiousness. Small-scale emendations seemed the safest: reversals of consonants, single-letter changes as in evident dittography or haplography or in the confusion of *dalet* and *resh*—letters that look similar in Hebrew script. I was especially encouraged to follow such divergences from the Masoretic text when they were confirmed by one or more of the ancient translations, or by the Qumran texts, or by variant Hebrew manuscripts. Where no plausible modest emendation of an unintelligible word or phrase suggested itself, I have done what most previous translators of the Bible have done, which is to try to make some sense out of the Hebrew words as they stand by an interpretive stretch. Occasionally, when the stretch seemed too extravagant and no viable emendation was available, I have actually reproduced the incoherence of the Hebrew in my translation, duly explaining the difficulties in my commentary. These moments will be a perhaps disconcerting novelty for English readers of Psalms, but they are intended to remind the audience of this translation that there are spots and patches where unfortunately we do not have the text that the poets originally wrote. We must nevertheless be grateful that such problems, though persistent, are not pervasive, and that a large part of these remarkable poems remains eminently readable despite all the textual vicissitudes of many centuries.

A NOTE ON TRANSLITERATION

GIVEN the phonetic differences between Hebrew and English, any effort to convey the sound of the Hebrew in the Latin alphabet is bound to be an approximate and rather awkward procedure. The accepted scholarly system of transliteration works well enough for those who actually know the Hebrew letters and are familiar with their equivalences in the system, but its profusion of diacritical marks is likely to be forbidding to general readers, and the system is not an easy guide to pronunciation unless one knows both languages. I have limited myself to three diacritical marks: ' for *aleph*, which was probably a lightly aspirated sound in the biblical period but has become a "silent" letter; ' for *ayin*, a consonant pronounced as a strong glottal stop in the biblical period but also no longer articulated by modern speakers; and a dot under an *ḥ* to indicate *ḥet*, a light fricative, something like the *j* in Spanish words. (*Kh* is used for *khaf*, which is a stronger fricative, something like the German *ch* in words such as *noch*.) I do not double the English consonant to reflect a *dagesh* in a Hebrew consonant—for example, *diber* for the word that means "spoke," and not *dibber*—because the so-called doubled Hebrew consonant is basically a grammatical concept and is not audible in anyone's pronunciation today. I use a *v* for the letter *bet* when it lacks the *dagesh*, which is how everyone now pronounces it. To avoid confusion with the *v*, I represent the sixth letter of the Hebrew alphabet as a *w*. In the biblical period, it would in fact have been pronounced as a *w*, though in modern Hebrew it has become a *v*. The vowel *a* in the transliteration is pronounced *ah*, as the letter *a* would be pronounced in most French words (for example, *pas*). The vowel *i* in the transliteration is a shorter version of the *ee* in "beet," as *i* would be pronounced in most French words (for example, *tique*). I did not want to confuse matters further by introducing indications of accent, but the rough rule of thumb is that the last syllable is generally the accented one in Hebrew words. It would have been nice to obviate all this clumsiness by using Hebrew font for all Hebrew words in the notes, but that would have excluded readers unfamiliar with the Hebrew alphabet. What is offered here is a crude approximation, necessary in order to comment on particular Hebrew words and their configurations and sometimes to say something about the sound of the poetry in the original. I hope it will be more helpful than annoying, and for its inadequacies I beg the reader's indulgence.

THE
BOOK OF
PSALMS

1

Happy the man who has not walked in the wicked's counsel,   1
     nor in the way of offenders has stood,
        nor in the session of scoffers has sat.
But the Lord's teaching is his desire,   2
     and His teaching he murmurs day and night.

---

1. *walked . . . stood . . . sat.* It is easy to understand why the ancient editors set this brief, eloquent psalm at the head of the collection. In content, it is a Wisdom psalm, affirming the traditional moral calculus (to which Job will powerfully object) that it pays to be good, whereas the wicked will be paid back for their evil. (Wisdom literature is an international genre in the ancient Near East. It reflects, in an approximately philosophical manner, on the uses of human life, and one of its major thrusts is the didactic inculcation of the principles of proper living. It tends to be universal rather than national in its perspective.) In style, this psalm is a lovely instance of the force of familiar imagery favored by the psalmists. Walking on a way is a traditional metaphor for pursuing a set of moral choices in life. In this verse, that idea is turned into an elegant narrative sequence in the triadic line—first walking, then standing, then sitting, with the attachment to the company of evildoers becoming increasingly more habitual from one verset to the next. Nahum Sarna raises the interesting possibility that the first word of the psalm, *'ashrei,* "happy," may pun on *'ashurim,* "steps," and hence reinforce the walking metaphor.

2. *murmurs.* The verb *hagah* means to make a low muttering sound, which is what one does with a text in a culture where there is no silent reading. By extension, predominantly in post-biblical Hebrew, it has the sense of "to meditate."

3 And he shall be like a tree planted by streams of water,
    that bears its fruit in its season,
        and its leaf does not wither—
and in all that he does he prospers.

4 Not so the wicked,
    but like chaff that the wind drives away.

5 Therefore the wicked will not stand up in judgment,
    nor offenders in the band of the righteous.

6 For the LORD embraces the way of the righteous,
    and the way of the wicked is lost.

---

3. *like a tree planted by streams of water.* These words inaugurate the second traditional image of the poem. In a semi-arid climate, everyone recognized that a tree had to be near a water source to flourish, and this becomes a standard metaphor for perdurable success, fruitfulness, blessing. All this is succinctly invoked in the bearing of fruit and the evergreen leaf of the second and third versets. The image of the windblown chaff then makes a neat contrast to the rooted, well-watered, leafy tree.

in all that he does he prospers. The masculine verb could refer to the man or the tree, but "prosper" (*yatsliaḥ*), despite its occasional application to horticulture, is a verb that probably jibes better with a person than with a plant.

5. *the wicked will not stand up in judgment.* These words glance back at the beginning of the psalm, though "stood" there and "stand up" here are two entirely different Hebrew verbs. Against the self-destructive sitting in the sessions of scoffers, the court of judgment is a place where the wicked will have no leg to stand on (like chaff).

6. *embraces.* The Hebrew, literally "knows," is a verb often used for intimate connection, including, when the subject is a man and the object is a woman, the sexual one.

the way of the wicked. In a kind of envelope structure, this phrase loops back to "the way of offenders" at the beginning. Now we see the fate of oblivion to which such a way is condemned.

2

Why are the nations aroused,   1
       and the peoples murmur vain things?
Kings of the earth take their stand,   2
       and princes conspire together
            against the LORD and against His anointed.
"Let us tear off their fetters,   3
       let us fling away their bonds!"
He Who dwells in the heavens will laugh,   4
       the Master derides them.
Then will He speak to them in His wrath,   5
       in His burning anger dismay them:

---

1. *Why are the nations aroused.* This is one of many psalms that seems to have been composed in response to a specific historical situation, but attempts to identify the circumstances or to date them have been unavailing. What one can make out is an alliance of nations intending to attack Judea, or perhaps merely to rebel against their condition of subjugation to it (see verse 3).

2. *Kings of the earth.* The hyperbolic sweep of biblical poetic idiom already transposes what might well have been a local political uprising into something like a grand global confrontation.

    His anointed. The term *mashiah* clearly is used here in its political sense as the designation of the legitimate current heir to the Davidic dynasty, without eschatological implications.

6   "And I—I appointed My king
           on Zion, My holy mountain."
7   Let me tell as is due of the LORD.
           He said to me: "You are My son.
             I Myself today did beget you.
8   Ask of me, and I shall give nations as your estate,
           and your holdings, the ends of the earth.
9   You will smash them with a rod of iron,
           like a potter's jar you will dash them."
10   And now, O you kings, pay mind,
           be chastened, you rulers of earth.

---

6. *I appointed My king / on Zion, My holy mountain.* The geo-theological para-dox of these words runs through many of the psalms. Zion is a modest moun-tain on the crest of which sits a modest fortified town, the capital of a rather small kingdom, surrounded by vast empires. Yet, the poet boldly imagines it as God's chosen city, divinely endorsed to be queen of nations and the splendor of humankind.

7. *Let me tell.* As the next two versets make clear, the speaker now is God's cho-sen king . . . who reigns on Mount Zion.
    I Myself . . . did beget you. Despite Christological readings of this verse over the centuries, it was a commonplace in the ancient Near East, readily adopted by the Israelites, to imagine the king as God's son. The Hebrew emphasis of this concept seems to be more political than theological.

8. *nations . . . / . . . the ends of the earth.* The large sweep of the initial threat from "kings of the earth" is picked up.

9. *smash them with a rod of iron.* The rod, *shevet,* would be the ruler's scepter, but here it becomes a battle mace, pulverizing the enemies that thought to assault Judea.

10. *And, now, O you kings, pay mind.* This is another variety of envelope struc-ture. The poem began by asking the nations and their kings why they were so stirred up. It closes by enjoining them to keep in mind the LORD's overwhelm-ing power, which is the guarantee of Zion's continuing dominion.

Worship the LORD in fear,   11
  and exult in trembling.
With purity be armed,   12
  lest He rage and you be lost on the way.
For His wrath in a moment flares up.
  Happy, all who shelter in Him.

---

12. *With purity be armed.* The two Hebrew words *nashqu bar* are the first of a long series of textual cruces in Psalms. As they stand, they make little sense, and the most elaborate efforts have been undertaken—none very convincing—to make the text mean something by extensive reconstructive surgery. The present translation hews to the Masoretic text, merely revocalizing *bar* (son? wheat?) as *bor*, "purity." The usual sense of the verb *nashqu* is "to kiss," but it also means "to bear [or, wield] arms" (compare its use in Psalm 78:9, 1 Chronicles 12:2, 2 Chronicles 17:17). As an idiom, to arm oneself with purity is not otherwise attested to in the Bible, but it might make sense here as a counterpoint to the implied raising of arms against Zion at the beginning of the psalm.

3

1 A David psalm, when he fled from Absalom his son.
2   LORD, how many are my foes,
              many, who rise up against me.
3   Many, who say of my life:
              "No rescue for him through God."   selah
4   And You, LORD, a shield are for me,
              my glory, Who lifts up my head.

---

1. *A David psalm.* The traditional rendering is "a psalm of David," which tends to imply authorship. The Hebrew preposition *l^e* is ambiguous: It could mean "of" or "by"; it often means "belonging to;" Another common meaning is "for"; or it might refer to something as loose as "in the manner of." The choice of translation is intended to preserve these ambiguous possibilities.

   when he fled from Absalom his son. Such ascriptions have no historical authority. Because the psalm is spoken by someone beset by relentless enemies, it would have seemed plausible to the editor to tie it in to this moment of David's flight after Absalom had usurped the throne (2 Samuel 16).

3. *selah.* Though there is general agreement that this is a choral or musical notation, there is no way of determining the meaning or the etymology.

4. *You, LORD, a shield are for me.* Remarkably, this is the only metaphor in the entire poem (unless one chooses to include the borderline case of "glory" in the next verset). The palpable strength of this psalm resides in its sheer simplicity and directness. The speaker, a man beleaguered by bitter foes, is first mocked by them when they tell him no god will rescue him. Ignoring the mockery, he cries out to the LORD for help (verse 5), sure he will be answered. Surrounded by enemies, he can sleep undisturbed (verse 6).

With my voice I cry out to the LORD,   5
      and He answers me from His holy mountain.   selah
I lie down and I sleep.   6
      I awake, for the LORD has sustained me.
I fear not from myriads of troops   7
      that round about set against me.
Rise, LORD! Rescue me, my God,   8
      for You strike all my foes on the cheek,
            the teeth of the wicked You smash.
Rescue is the LORD's!   9
      On Your people Your blessing.   selah

---

8. *Rise, LORD! Rescue me, my God.* As though answering the mocking foes to whom he never speaks directly, the speaker exhorts God to extend him the very rescue (verbal stem *y-sh-ʿ*) that the enemies had said would be denied him. And the rescuing act is to be manifested by bashing in the very mouths ("strike all my foes on the cheek / the teeth of the wicked You smash") that had uttered the jeering words he quoted.

9. *Rescue is the LORD's! / On Your people Your blessing.* Though it is pleasing to have "rescue" reiterated at the end, the line doesn't scan, and the sudden appearance of a national perspective at the conclusion of an exclusively first-person poem looks odd. One may suspect that this is a textual tag from somewhere else introduced in redaction, perhaps because of the initial words, "Rescue is the LORD's."

4

1   For the lead player, with stringed instruments, a David psalm.

2   When I call out, answer me, my righteous God.

               In the straits, You set me free.

                   Have mercy upon me and hear my prayer.

3   Sons of man, how long will My glory be shamed?

               You love vain things and seek out lies.   selah

4   But know that the Lord set apart His faithful.

         The Lord will hear when I call to Him.

---

1. *lead player.* The Hebrew *menatseah* probably means "leader," evidently the person directing the music.

     with stringed instruments. This identification, as is the case with all the musical terms in Psalms, is no more than a guess. The literal sense of the Hebrew is "melodies," but the verbal stem is often associated with plucking strings.

2. *When I call out, answer me.* This phrase, or some variation on it, is an identifying formula for the psalm of supplication and often appears, as here, at the beginning of the psalm.

4. *But know that the Lord set apart His faithful.* Here the situation rather than the language is a formula for the supplication. The speaker, beset by mocking enemies who say he is beyond hope (compare Psalm 3), affirms that God will confound them by answering the cry of those who are faithful to Him.

Quake, and do not offend.   5
      Speak in your hearts on your beds, and be still.   selah
Offer righteous sacrifices   6
      and trust in the LORD.
Many say, "Who will show us good things?"   7
      Lift up the light of Your face to us, LORD.
You put joy in my heart,   8
      from the time their grain and their drink did abound.
In peace, all whole, let me lie down and sleep.   9
      For You, LORD, alone, do set me down safely.

---

5. *Quake . . . Speak in your hearts . . . be still.* The syntax of this entire verse is
choppy, and the semantic logic behind it remains somewhat obscure. If in fact
the text as we have it reflects what the psalmist wrote, the sense would be as
follows: The auditors of the poem are exhorted to tremble as an act of conscience that will dissuade them from acts of transgression, then commune with
themselves in the solitude of their beds and speak no more. The verse thus
moves from a state of troubled agitation ("quake") to silence at the end.

7. *Lift up the light of Your face.* The spelling of the verb n^e*sah* deviates from the
normative n^e*sa'*, but the image of God's lifting up the light of His face as a gesture of divine favor (as in the Priestly Blessing) is so common in biblical idiom
that one is compelled to construe the verb here as "lift up."

8. *from the time their grain and their drink did abound.* Although the flourishing
of crops is understandably a cause for joy in an agricultural society, it must be
said that the syntactic link between the initial clause and this one is obscure,
and one suspects the text has been damaged. Among the difficulties are the
odd temporal indication in "from the time" and the third-person plural references ("their grain and their drink").

9. *In peace, all whole, let me lie down and sleep.* This prayer for tranquil sleep at
the end of the psalm may be a deliberate counterpoint to the image of those
who quake, then speak to themselves on their beds. Restful sleep as a restorative manifestation of the speaker's trust in God's protection is a recurrent motif
in Psalms. It is the precise antithesis to the tormented "blank nights" without
rest of which Job speaks.

5

<table>
<tr><td>1</td><td>To the lead player, on the nehilot, a David psalm.</td></tr>
<tr><td>2</td><td>Hearken to my speech, O LORD,
        attend to my utterance.</td></tr>
<tr><td>3</td><td>Listen well to my voice crying out, my king and my God,
        for to You I pray.</td></tr>
<tr><td>4</td><td>LORD, in the morning You hear my voice,
        in the morning I lay it before You and wait.</td></tr>
<tr><td>5</td><td>For not a god desiring wickedness are You,
        no evil will sojourn by You.</td></tr>
<tr><td>6</td><td>The debauched take no stand in Your eyes,
        You hate all the wrongdoers.</td></tr>
</table>

---

1. *the* nehilot. This particular musical instrument has defied identification and hence is offered here in transliteration.

2. *Hearken to my speech, O L*ORD. These initial words are another formula for beginning a psalm of supplication.

4. *in the morning I lay it before You.* The idiom suggests sacrifice, but instead of sacrifice it is a prayer of supplication that the speaker lays before God. The reference in verse 8 to entering God's house is an indication that the supplicant has come into the temple to offer his prayer.

6. *The debauched. . . .* For the moment, all we can conclude is that the speaker emphatically dissociates himself from this crowd of reprobates with whom God has no truck. From verse 10, we infer that these sinister figures have been actively menacing the speaker, so the poem is an entreaty to God to extricate him from their vicious plots and confound them.

You destroy the pronouncers of lies,   7
      a man of blood and deceit the Lord loathes.
As for me—through Your great kindness I enter Your house,   8
      I bow to Your holy temple in the fear of You.
Guide me, O Lord, in Your righteousness.   9
      On account of my foes, make my way straight
      before me.
For there is nothing right in their mouths,   10
      within them—falsehood.
An open grave their throat,
      their tongue, smooth-talking.
Condemn them, O God.   11
      Let them fall by their counsels for their many sins.
      Cast them off, for they have rebelled
      against You.

---

7. *a man of blood and deceit.* Here we begin to get some concrete sense of the nature of these plotters of evil: They are prepared to do violence to the speaker, to deceive and despoil him.

8. *As for me.* The Hebrew pronoun *wa'ani* sets out the speaker in strong contrast to the evildoers.

10. *An open grave their throat.* This startling image suggests how lethal are the intent and the effect of the smooth-talking deceivers. The smoothness (the Hebrew idiom is literally "they smooth with their tongue") intimates a kind of slippery slope of language into the open grave of the throat.

11. *Cast them off.* The Masoretic cantillation marks place this (one word in the Hebrew) at the end of the previous clause, but the whole line scans much better—and makes better sense—if the word is set at the beginning of the third verset of a triadic line.

12   Let all who shelter in You rejoice,
                let them sing gladly forever—protect them!
                        and those who love Your name exult in You.
13   For You bless the just man, O Lord.
                Like a shield You crown him with favor.

---

12. *sing gladly.* The choice of this verb might express not only a state of exulta-
tion but the poetic prayer that the speaker has laid before God.

13. *Like a shield You crown him with favor.* The "favor" vouchsafed the man who
has come into God's temple in prayer with a clean conscience is theologically
self-evident. The comparison of this condition of favor (*ratson*) with a shield
picks up at the end the supplicant's urgent sense that he needs protection
against malefic and bloody-minded enemies.

6

For the lead player, on stringed instruments, on the eight-stringed   1
lute, a David psalm.
   LORD, do not chastise me in Your wrath,   2
       do not punish me in Your fury.
   Have mercy on me, LORD, for I am wretched.   3
       Heal me, for my limbs are stricken.
   And my life is hard stricken.   4
       —and You, O LORD, how long?
   Come back, LORD, deliver my life,   5
       rescue me for the sake of Your kindness.

---

2. *do not chastise me . . . / do not punish me.* This psalm is another variation of the supplication pattern. The speaker is in dire straits not because he is beset by enemies (though, as we shall see, they do come into the picture) but because God has "chastised" him—which would have been a typical ancient interpretation of illness.

3. *for my limbs are stricken.* Here the condition of acute physical infirmity is made explicit. The two versets of this line reflect one prevalent pattern of biblical poetry: a general statement in the first verset ("I am wretched") followed by a more concrete image in the second verset ("my limbs are stricken").

4. *and You, O LORD, how long?* This cry of desperation to God is a recurrent verbal formula in the supplications.

6   For death holds no mention of You.
        In Sheol who can acclaim You?
7   I weary in my sighing.
        I make my bed swim every night,
           with my tears I water my couch.
8   From vexation my eye becomes dim,
        is worn out, because of all my foes.
9   Turn from me, all you wrongdoers,
        for the LORD hears the sound of my weeping.

---

6. *For death holds no mention of You.* The speaker, gravely ill, fears he is on the brink of death, and that is why he offers this prayer. It is man's calling in the biblical world to celebrate or acclaim God's greatness. Hence in the psalms of supplication the speakers often remind God in their entreaty for life that the dead—those who go down to the underworld, Sheol—cannot praise God.

8. *From vexation my eye becomes dim, / is worn out, because of all my foes.* The syntax of this line is arranged in an elegant chiasm: a (vexation) b (becomes dim), b́ (is worn out) á (because of all my foes). The tendency of the second verset to intensify an image or idea in the first verset is strikingly reflected in the move from "becomes dim" to the violent and hyperbolic "is worn out," which more literally means "is torn out."

because of all my foes. Now, somewhat surprisingly, enemies appear. The most plausible way to understand their introduction in the poem is that the supplicant imagines that malicious enemies are exulting over his deathly illness. It is of course conceivable that the physical wretchedness invoked at the beginning of the poem is not a symptom of illness but a somatic consequence of being harassed by enemies, but such a construction does not accord well with the assertion that the physical misery is God's chastisement.

The LORD hears my plea,   10
    the LORD will take my prayer.
Let all my enemies be shamed and hard stricken,   11
    let them turn back, be shamed in an instant.

---

10. *The LORD hears my plea, / the LORD will take my prayer.* This line is another neat illustration of how the two versets of a line are typically deployed. "My plea" (*teḥinati*) and "my prayer" (*tefilati*) make a clear semantic parallelism, reinforced by the phonetic-morphological similarity of the two terms. The two verbs, on the other hand, form a miniature narrative sequence: first God "hears" (or "has heard"), in the perfective mode of the verb, the plea or supplication. Then, as a result of hearing it in all its desperate sincerity, He "will take" (or "accept") it, in the imperfective mode of the verb that here has the force of a future tense.

11. *Let all my enemies be shamed.* Presumably, they will be shamed for crowing in triumph over the gravely ill supplicant when God restores him to health.

    hard stricken. This verb pointedly looks back to the use of the same term in verses 3 and 4. In the speaker's return to health, he and his enemies will change places.

7

1 A David *shiggayon*, which he sang to the LORD regarding Cush the
  Benjamanite.
2 LORD, my God, in You I sheltered.
        Rescue me from all my pursuers and save me.
3 Lest like a lion they tear up my life—
        rend me, with no one to save me.
4 LORD, my God, if I have done this,
        if there be wrongdoing in my hands.
5 If I paid back my ally with evil,
        if I oppressed my foes without reason—

---

1. shiggayon. Like so many of the technical terms in Psalms, it is unclear exactly
what subcategory of psalm is indicated. Because the probable verbal root of this
noun suggests emotional excess, it might mean something such as "rhapsody,"
though that is not necessarily borne out by the body of the poem. The reference to Cush the Benjamanite in the heading of the psalm is equally enigmatic.

3. *Lest . . . they tear up.* The Hebrew at this point switches from plural enemies
to a singular, a fluidity common in biblical idiom.

4. *if I have done this.* The two "if" clauses are a formula for making a vow, the
sense being "I swear I have not done this."

may the enemy pursue and overtake me   6
   and trample to earth my life
      and make my glory dwell in the dust.   selah
Rise up, O Lord, in Your anger,   7
   Loom high against the wrath of my enemies.
      Rouse for me the justice You ordained.
A band of nations surrounds You,   8
   and above it to the heights return.
The Lord will judge peoples.   9
   Grant me justice, Lord, as befits my righteousness
      and as befits my innocence that is in me.
May evil put an end to the wicked;   10
   and make the righteous stay unshaken.
He searches hearts and conscience,
   God is righteous.

---

7. *Rise up, O Lord in Your anger.* This psalm's treatment of the supplication gives special prominence to martial imagery. The enemy pursues and would tear its quarry to pieces; the leonine metaphor is common in ancient Near Eastern martial poetry. Now God is enjoined to rise up to a towering height in angry deployment against the battalions of enemies.

8. *A band of nations.* The language of this verse is obscure, and one suspects that the text is defective. It is unclear whether the band of nations consists of the assembled foes or God's terrestrial allies.

9. *that is in me.* The Hebrew ʿalai literally means "upon me" and does not sound idiomatic.

10. *May evil put an end to the wicked.* The Hebrew is rather crabbed, hence the meaning is in doubt. Another possible construction: "May the evil of the wicked come to an end."
  conscience. The literal sense of the Hebrew is "kidneys." The kidneys were thought to be the seat of conscience.

11   My shield—upon God,
                rescuing the upright.
12   God exacts justice for the righteous
                and El utters doom each day.
13   If a man repent not, He sharpens His sword,
                He pulls back his bow and aims it.
14   And for him, He readies the tools of death,
                lets fly His arrows at the fleers.
15   Look, one spawns wrongdoing,
                grows big with mischief,
                        gives birth to lies.
16   A pit he delved, and dug it,
                and he fell in the trap he made.

---

11. *My shield—upon God.* The translation replicates the odd use of the preposition in the Hebrew.

13. *If a man repent not.* This and the next several verses spell out what is implied in the negative second half of the previous verse ("El utters doom"). Although Psalms repeatedly divides the world into the doomed wicked and the righteous who will flourish, it also allows for the possibility that those bent on evil may turn back (the literal meaning of the verb rendered as "repent") to the way of righteousness.

14. *He readies the tools of death.* Some interpreters understand all the lethal acts enumerated here to refer to the evildoers, but it seems more plausible to see them as images of the doom that God prepares for the wicked.

15. *spawns . . . grows big . . . gives birth.* In the midst of battle imagery, the actions of the wicked are likened to the birth process in order to stress the idea that there is a quasi-biological causality in which evil acts, like seed quickening in the womb, will inevitably lead to disastrous consequences. The nature of these consequences is spelled out in the next verse, which moves antithetically from womb to pit. One detects a satiric intention in comparing the fierce evildoer to a parturient woman.

His mischief comes down on his head,   17
      on his skull his outrage descends.
I acclaim the LORD for His righteousness,   18
      let me hymn the LORD's name, Most High.

---

17. *His mischief comes down on his head, / on his skull his outrage descends.* In biblical idiom, it is often *blood* that comes down on the head of the person who has shed blood. This biblical metonymy for murder is thus a hidden echo in this line, as we move from "mischief" (*'amal*) in the first verset to a term more directly associated with violence, *ḥamas*, "outrage," in the second verset.

18. *I acclaim . . . let me hymn.* This concluding formula actually belongs to the psalm of thanksgiving (*todah*, a noun cognate with the verb translated here as "acclaim"). Such crossovers of genre are fairly common in Psalms. The poem began with a supplication for help from a man pursued by murderous enemies. Now, having conjured up a whole series of images of how the wicked will come to a terrible end through their own nefarious plots, the speaker can conclude by celebrating God in thanks.

8

1   For the lead player, on the *gittith*, a David psalm.

2   L<small>ORD</small>, our Master,

how majestic Your name in all the earth!

Whose splendor was told over the heavens.

3   From the mouth of babes and sucklings

You founded strength

---

1. *the* gittith. This is another musical instrument that has eluded persuasive identification.

2. *Master . . . majestic.* The alliteration seeks to mirror the strong alliterative effect between the two Hebrew words *'adonenu* and *'adir*.

    was told. The Masoretic text has *tenah*, which appears to be an imperative of the verb "to give," and does not make much sense in context. I have revocalized it as *tunah*, yielding "was told." The beauty of the night sky, which the psalmist contemplates in verse 4, speaks out God's glory wordlessly.

3. *From the mouth of babes and sucklings.* The meaning of this phrase, however proverbial it has become, has not been satisfactorily explained. One distant possibility: God draws strength from consciously aware humankind, made in His image, even from its weakest and youngest members, against the inhuman forces of chaos. Perhaps the innocence of infants is imagined as a source of strength.

on account of Your foes
        to put an end to enemy and avenger.
When I see Your heavens, the work of Your fingers,   4
        the moon and the stars You fixed firm,
"What is man that You should note him,   5
        and the human creature, that You pay him heed,
and You make him little less than the gods,   6
        with glory and grandeur You crown him?

---

to put an end to enemy and avenger. Because this is a psalm celebrating creation, there is plausibility in the identification proposed by some scholars between this implacable foe and the primordial sea monster, who, in Canaanite myth, must be subdued by the god of order so that the world can come into stable being. Imagery taken from that cosmogonic battle between gods is borrowed by a good many psalms.

4. *the work of Your fingers.* The "work of Your hands," as in verse 7, is a common idiom, but this variation of it is unique, probably meant to suggest the delicate tracery of the starry skies.

5. *What is man . . .* At the exact center of the poem, we find a poetic parallelism not based on any semantic development or focusing from verset to verset (as, for example, in the immediately preceding line) but rather on balanced synonymity, producing a stately emphasis through the equivalence between the two halves of the line.

6. *the gods.* The ambiguous Hebrew *'elohim,* which could refer to gods or celestial beings but probably not in this context to the single deity, sets humankind in a hierarchical ladder: God at the very top, the gods or celestial beings below Him, then man, and below man the whole kingdom of other living creatures.
   with glory and grandeur You crown him. All these terms appropriate to royalty establish the image of man ruling over nature, with all things "under his feet," a common ancient Near Eastern image of subjugation.

7   You make him rule over the work of Your hands.
                All things You set under his feet.
8   Sheep and oxen all together,
                and also the beasts of the field,
9   birds of the heavens and fish of the sea,
                what moves on the paths of the seas."
10 LORD, our Master,
                how majestic Your name in all the earth!

8–9. *Sheep and oxen . . . birds of the heavens and fish of the sea.* The language of this compact but embracing catalog is a deliberate recasting in somewhat different words of the first creation story (even "fish of the sea" is a slight variation on *degat hayam* in Genesis 1, the phrase used here being *degey hayam*), but the audience of the poem is surely meant to hear in all this a beautiful poetic reprise of Genesis 1. The eye moves downward vertically in the poem from the heavens to the divine beings who are God's entourage to man's feet and, below those, to the beasts of the field and then to what swims through the sea (which no longer harbors a primordial sea beast). The last term in the catalog is a neat poetic kenning for sea creatures, "what moves on the paths of the seas."

10. LORD, *our Master, / how majestic Your name in all the earth!* Although biblical literature, in poetry and prose, exhibits considerable fondness for envelope structures, in which the end somehow echoes the beginning, this verbatim repetition of the first line as the last, common in other poetic traditions, is unusual. It closes a perfect circle that celebrates the harmony of God's creation. The "all" component of "all the earth," which at first might have seemed like part of a formulaic phrase, takes on cumulative force at the very end of the poem. God's majesty is manifest in all things, and the creature fashioned in His image has been given dominion over all things. The integrated harmony of the created world as the poet perceives it and the integrated harmony of the poem make a perfect match.

9

For the lead player, 'almut laben, a David psalm. ¹

This psalm and the next one are a striking testimony to the scrambling in textual transmission that, unfortunately, a good many of the psalms have suffered. The Septuagint presents Psalms 9 and 10 as a single psalm, and there is formal evidence for the fact that it was originally one poem. Psalm 9 in the Hebrew begins as an alphabetical acrostic: verses 2 and 3, *aleph* (four times); verse 4, *bet*; verse 6, *gimmel* [*dalet*, the next letter, is missing]; verse 7, *heh*; verses 8–11, *waw*; verse 12, *zayin*; verse 14, *ḥet*; verse 16, *tet*; verse 18, *yod*; verse 19, *kaf*. It is notable that some lines of poetry have been interspersed between the acrostic lines, unlike other acrostic psalms in which the sequential letters of the alphabet occur in consecutive lines. Then Psalm 10 begins with the next letter of the alphabet, *lamed*, after which the acrostic disappears, to surface near the end of the psalm with the last four letters of the alphabet—verse 12 (*qof*), verse 14 (*resh*), verse 15 (*shin*), and verse 17 (*taw*). Now, what accompanies this confusion is a whole series of points, especially in the second half of the psalm, at which the text is not intelligible and is in all likelihood defective. Something along the following lines seems to have happened to our psalm: At some early moment in the long history of its transmission, a single authoritative copy was damaged (by decay, moisture, fire, or whatever). Lines of verse may have been patched into the text from other sources in an attempt to fill in lacunae. Quite a few phrases or lines were simply transcribed in their mangled form or perhaps poorly reconstructed. When the chapter divisions of the Bible were introduced in the late Middle Ages, the editors, struggling with this imperfect text, no longer realized that it was an acrostic and broke it into two separate psalms. The result of this whole process, alas, is that we are left with a rather imperfect notion of what some of the text means.

1. 'almut laben. This is another opaque musical term. The second word seems to say "to the son," but it may be a reversal of letters, *n-b-l*, for *nevel*, a kind of lyre.

2   I acclaim the LORD with all my heart,
        let me tell of all His wonders.   א

3   Let me rejoice and be glad in You,
        let me hymn Your name, Most High,

4   when my enemies turn back,   ב
        when they stumble and perish before You.

5   For You upheld my justice, my right,
        You sat on the throne of the righteous judge.

6   You rebuked the nations, destroyed the wicked,   ג
        their name You wiped out forever.

7   The enemy—ruins that are gone for all time,   ה
        and the towns you smashed, their name is lost.

8   But the LORD is forever enthroned,
        makes His throne for justice unshaken.

9   And He judges the world in righteousness,
        lays down law to the nations in truth.

10 Let the LORD be a fortress for the downcast,   ו
        a fortress in times of distress.

11 And those who know Your name will trust You,
        for You forsook not Your seekers, O LORD.

12 Hymn to the LORD Who dwells in Zion,   ז
        tell among the peoples His deeds.

13 For the Requiter of blood recalled them,
        He forgot not the cry of the lowly.

---

2. *I acclaim the* LORD. The initial verb, '*odeh*, announces the status of the poem as a thanksgiving psalm (*todah*, the cognate noun)—in this case because God has caused the speaker to triumph over his enemies.

7. *The enemy—ruins that are gone for all time.* The syntax here seems confused, and "ruins that are gone" (or "ended") is odd as an idiom. This entire verset looks textually suspect.

ח   Grant me grace, O Lord,   14
              see my torment by my foes,
                     You Who raise me from the gates of death.
   So that I may tell all Your praise   15
              in the gates of the Daughter of Zion.
                   Let me exult in Your rescue.
ט   The nations sank down in the trap that they made,   16
              in the snare that they made their foot was caught.
   The Lord is known for the justice He did.   17
             By his own handiwork was the
             wicked ensnared.   *higayon* selah
י   The wicked will turn back to Sheol,   18
             All the nations forgetful of God.

---

15. *So that I may tell all Your praise / in the gates of the Daughter of Zion.* The poet develops here a familiar idea in Psalms: Those who descend to the underworld (verse 14) cannot tell God's praise, so after God has raised the speaker from the gates of death—presumably because enemies were threatening to destroy him—he is able to stand in the gates of Jerusalem and publicly celebrate God's greatness. The gates of the city were a place of assembly and, especially relevant to the imagery of God as judge in this poem, a place where justice was conducted. The personification of Jerusalem as Daughter of Zion is common in the Prophets.

17. *The Lord is known for the justice He did.* The translation assumes an ellipsis in the Hebrew. The literal sense of the four Hebrew words in sequence here is: "The Lord is known justice He did."

18. *The wicked will turn back to Sheol.* This stands in contrast to the fate of the speaker, who has been raised from the gates of death. The form of the Hebrew *le she'ola* is anomalous, because it incorporates both the preposition "to" at the beginning and the directional suffix that means "to" at the end.

19   For not forever will the poor man be forgotten,
                the hope of the lowly not lost forever.   כ

20   Arise, O Lord, let not man flaunt his strength,
                let nations be judged in Your presence.

21   O Lord, put fear upon them,
                let the nations know they are mortal.   selah

---

19. *the hope of the lowly not lost forever.* The Hebrew seems to say "will be lost forever," but this may not be a scribal omission because the "not forever" of the first verset could be doing double duty for the second verset as well.

10

ל Why do You stand far off, O Lord,   1
          turn away in times of distress?
In the wicked man's pride he pursues the poor,   2
          but is caught in the schemes he devised.
For the wicked did vaunt in his very lust,   3
          grasping for gain—cursed, blasphemed the Lord.
The wicked sought not in his towering wrath—   4
          "There is no God" is all his schemes.

---

1. *Why do You stand far off, O Lord?* This note of distress does not match the mood of thanksgiving of the first half of the psalm. It is possible that material from other sources was spliced into the text at this point.

2. *he devised.* The Hebrew here switches from singular to plural. The scheming of the wicked against the vulnerable poor reflects a recurrent theme in Psalms of a plea for social justice.

3. *the wicked did vaunt . . . / grasping for gain—cursed, blasphemed the Lord.* The translation seeks to rescue some meaning from the received text, but the whole verse as it stands is not very intelligible.

4. *The wicked sought not in his towering wrath.* Syntax and idiom are confusing. The text that has come down to us again looks suspect.

5   His ways are uncertain in every hour,
                   Your judgments are high up above him.
                         All his foes he enflames.
6   He said in his heart, "I will not stumble,
                   for all time I will not come to harm."
7   His mouth is full of oaths,   פ
                   beneath his tongue are guile and deceit,
                         mischief and misdeed.
8   He waits in ambush in a sheltered place,
                   from a covert he kills the blameless,
                         for the wretched his eyes look out.   ע
9   He lies in wait in a covert like a lion in his lair,
                   lies in wait to snatch up the poor,
                         snatch the poor as he pulls with his net.
10   The lowly bow down,
                   and the wretched fall into his traps.
11   He said in his heart, "God has forgotten,
                   has hidden His face, never more to see."

---

5. *His ways are uncertain.* The textual difficulties continue through this patch of the poem. The meaning of the verb *yaḥilu* (rendered as "are uncertain") is uncertain. "Your judgments are high up above him" is literally "Height Your judgments before him". The meaning of the verb *yafiaḥ* ("enflames") is no more than an educated guess, and it could even be a noun, "witness."

6. *I will not come to harm.* The Hebrew (literally, "that is not in harm [or, evil]") is crabbed and unclear.

9. *as he pulls with his net.* At this point the poet abandons the lion simile and represents the evildoer as a human schemer lying in wait with a net to entangle his victim.

10. *The lowly.* Instead of the enigmatic *widkeh* (the *qeri*, the marginal notation of how to sound the word, here is *yidkeh*, "he will be low") of the Masoretic text, this translation assumes the original reading was either *nidkeh* or *wᵉdakh*, either of which means "the lowly."

ק   Rise, O LORD, raise Your hand,   12
             forget not the lowly.
   Why has the wicked despised God,
             has said in his heart, "You shall not seek out"?   13

ר   For You have seen mischief
             and have looked on vexation.   14
   The wretched leaves his fate in Your hands.
             It is You Who help the orphan.

ש   Break the arm of the wicked,   15
             and seek out evil,
                   let wickedness not be found.
   The LORD is king for all time,   16
             nations are lost from His land.

ת   The desire of the poor You have heard, O LORD,   17
             You make their heart firm, Your ear listens.
   To do justice for the orphan and the wretched,   18
             and let none still oppress man in the land.

---

14. *The wretched leaves his fate in Your hands.* The Hebrew is far less smooth than this. A literal representation of the sequence of Hebrew words would be: "to give in Your hands upon You the wretched leaves." This could scarcely be the original form of the text.

17. *The desire of the poor.* The conclusion of the psalm, formally signaled by the initial letter *taw,* the last letter of the Hebrew alphabet, returns to the thanksgiving theme that was sounded at the beginning and thus appears to be part of the original poem.

18. *let none still oppress man in the land.* The very last words of the psalm once more are not entirely transparent in the Hebrew. The concluding phrase in the Hebrew is literally "from the land," which seems better suited to a verb such as "wipe out" or "drive out" than "oppress," but the Hebrew verb used means rather "to oppress" or "to terrorize."

1 For the lead player, for David.
      In the LORD I sheltered.
            How could you say to me,
                  "Off to the hills like a bird!
2 For, look, the wicked bend back the bow,
            they fix to the string their arrow
                  to shoot from the gloom at the upright.

---

1. *How could you say to me.* Unusually, this psalm begins with a triadic verset, and one in which the three parts are linked by sequentiality rather than semantic parallelism. The speaker of this personal psalm at the outset announces that he trusts in God's sheltering protection. Thus he has no need to flee to the hills like a bird, as his friends have enjoined him.

Off to the hills like a bird. The literal sense is: wander [to] your hill [or, mountain], bird. The translation follows the Septuagint, which reads *har kemo tsipor* instead of the Masoretic *harkhem tsipor* ("your hill, bird").

2. *the wicked bend back the bow.* The archery imagery picks up the image of the fleeing bird of the previous line: the bowmen aim at the bird in flight. Here and elsewhere in this psalm the poet favors archaic-poetic grammatical forms: *yidrekhun* instead of the standard *yidrekhu* for "bend back," and *bemo* instead of the standard *b^e* for "from" (or "in").

the upright. Literally, "the straight of heart."

The foundations destroyed,
      what can a righteous man do?"   3
The LORD in His holy palace,
      The LORD in the heavens His throne—   4
His eyes behold,
      His look probes the sons of man.
The LORD probes the righteous and wicked,   5
      and the lover of havoc He utterly hates.

---

3. *what can a righteous man do?* It makes sense to view everything from "Off to the hills . . ." through to the end of this verse as the words of the fearful and despairing friends of the speaker. With the vicious and destructive enemies prevailing, they say, there is no recourse for the helpless righteous person except flight.

4. *The LORD in His holy palace.* These words mark the turning point of the poem. The terrestrial landscape may be littered with the depredations of the wicked, who imagine they will continue to have the upper hand, but above it all God looks down, sorting out the evil from the good and preparing retribution for those who deserve it. Given this context, and given the parallelism with the second verset, "His holy palace" here must refer to God's celestial abode and not to the Temple in Jerusalem.

look. The literal meaning is "eyelids," a parallel term to "eyes" in the first verset, but in English one cannot see with the eyelids.

5. *He utterly hates.* The adverb "utterly" is added to pick up the intensive equivalent of the first-person pronoun in *nafsho* (literally, "His life" or "His essential being").

6   He rains fiery coals on the wicked,
                sulphur and gale-winds their lot.
7   For righteous the LORD is,
                righteous acts He does love.
                        The upright behold His face.

---

6. *He rains fiery coals on the wicked.* This whole line, of course, alludes to the destruction of Sodom and Gomorrah in Genesis 19, which figures as a canonical demonstration of God's determination to administer justice and not allow evil to go unpunished. *Paḥim*, the word rendered as "coals," everywhere else means "traps" or "pitfalls," but this translation assumes, following one ancient Greek version, that the original reading was *peḥamey*, which in fact means "coals [of]." The Masoretic text puts a syntactic pause at "coals," then has "fire and sulfur." This makes the second verset inordinately long. It is much more likely that a scribe reversed the *mem* and *yod* of *peḥamey* ("coals of," which is then attached to *'esh* "fire"), yielding *paḥim*.

      gale-winds. The Hebrew *ruaḥ zilʿafot* is literally "raging wind," the second term being a derivative form from *zaʿaf*, "rage."

      their lot. Literally, "the portion of their cup."

7. *The upright behold His face.* With the wicked disposed of in the previous verse, the psalm ends on this positive note of the upright beholding God—even as God from the heavens beholds all humankind. In the Hebrew, the noun is singular and the verb is plural; presumably one of the two (probably the verb) should be adjusted. The Masoretic text reads "their face," with no obvious antecedent for the plural, but variant Hebrew versions have "His face."

12

1
To the lead player, on the eight-stringed lyre, a David psalm.
   Rescue, O Lord! For the faithful is gone,
         for vanished is trust from the sons of man.
   Falsehood every man speaks to his fellow,
         smooth talk, with two hearts they speak.
   The Lord will cut off all smooth-talking lips,
         the tongue that speaks of big things,

2. *Rescue, O Lord! For the faithful is gone.* Although this psalm falls into the general category of supplication, it reflects a subgenre in which the speaker scans his society in a harsh light of moral castigation. Poetry is thus marshaled for a purpose similar to that of the literary prophets, and one might describe such a poem as a prophetic supplication.

for vanished is trust from the sons of man. To the despairing speaker, it looks as though all humankind has turned treacherous. The noun 'emunim is an abstraction and hence refers to the quality, not the people, as many translations have it.

3. *with two hearts they speak.* This vivid image for duplicity is especially effective, because it opposes the organ of speech ("smooth talk" is literally "lips of smooth things") to the organ of intention and understanding, which is itself divided.

4. *The Lord will cut off all smooth-talking lips.* Although "cut off" is a standard verb for "destroy," it has a violent concreteness here because one gets an image of lips being cut off or cut away.

5   those who said, "Let us make our tongue great,
                 our own lips are with us—who is master to us?"
6   "From the plunder of the poor, from the wretched men's groans,
                 now will I rise," says the LORD.
7   "I will set up for rescue a witness for him."
              The LORD's sayings—pure sayings,
                    silver tried in a kiln in the earth
                          refined sevenfold.
8   You, LORD, will guard him,
                 will keep him from this age for all time.

---

5. *Let us make our tongue great.* The idea is to make speech a weapon (the root of the verb used, *g-b-r*, suggests "warrior" and "warfare"). Some take this to mean, "Let us become great by our tongue," but that would require the preposition *b^e* ("in," "through," or "by"), whereas the preposition used here is *l^e* ("to," or "for" but also sometimes the prefix of a direct object). Or the letter *lamed* here might be a mistaken scribal duplication of the *lamed* that immediately follows it.

our own lips are with us—who is master to us? These clauses continue the idea that language serves as a weapon or rather an army for the wicked.

6. *From the plunder of the poor.* God's speech signals the turning point of the poem, when the exploiters of lying language will at last be confounded.

7. *I will set up for rescue a witness for him.* This verset has been variously construed, or misconstrued. It might make sense to understand the difficult term *yafiaḥ* not as a verb but as a noun, "witness," at least conjecturally. That particular meaning is a plausible one in light of what has preceded: The persecuted man has been surrounded by an army of liars, but now God will provide someone to bear true witness for him and thus rescue him from his plight.

kiln. The term *'alil* appears only here, and the understanding of it as "kiln" goes back to the Aramaic translation of Onkelos in Late Antiquity. The meaning, however, is not certain; it should be said that the rabbis construed it as an adverb, "clearly." In any case, there is a pointed contrast between the LORD's sayings, pure as refined silver, and the lying words of cheating men.

8. *guard him . . . keep him.* The Hebrew uses first a plural, then a singular object of the verb.

All around go the wicked,
      they have dug deep pits for the sons of men.

9

---

9. *All around go the wicked*. This whole line, which reverts to the triumphalist wicked, looks tacked on, because the declaration of God's guarding the just in the previous line is a characteristic upbeat psalm ending. The dubiety of the line is reinforced by the first two words of the second verset, *kerum zulot*, which make no evident sense and can be understood only through an exegetical somersault (for example, the New Jewish Publication Society, "when baseness is exalted"). Some emendation seems necessary, and the present translation, conjecturally, presupposes that the final *mem* of *kerum* should be moved forward to begin the next word, thus yielding an intelligible *karu*, "dug," a verb often associated in Psalms with the wicked. The object of the verb might then be *metsulot*, depths, or perhaps *metsudot*, traps, though if such a word once stood here, it has been lost in scribal transmission.

13

1 To the lead player, a David psalm.
2   How long, O LORD, will You forget me always?
             How long hide Your face from me?
3   How long shall I cast about for counsel,
          sorrow in my heart all day?
             How long will my enemy loom over me?
4   Regard, answer me, LORD, my God.
          Light up my eyes, lest I sleep death,
5   lest my enemy say, "I've prevailed over him,"
          lest my foes exult when I stumble.

---

2. *How long, O LORD, will You forget me always?* The cry of desperation—"How long?"—from a person whose anguish seems protracted indefinitely is a recurrent feature of the psalms of supplication. The apparent logical contradiction between "how long" and "always" actually makes psychological sense: From the speaker's tormented perspective, it feels as though God is forgetting him forever.

4. *Light up my eyes, lest I sleep death.* The antithesis between light for the eyes and the implied darkness of death is striking, and the poet uses a jolting elliptical form, "lest I sleep death" (not "the sleep of death") that is worth preserving in translation.

5. *lest my enemy say.* As elsewhere in the supplications, the pain of imagined death is made more bitter by the imagined schadenfreude of the enemy, who will delight in this death.

But I in Your kindness do trust,   6
        my heart exults in Your rescue.
Let me sing to the LORD,
        for He requited me.

---

6. *But I in Your kindness do trust.* This affirmation of faith in God's readiness to stand by the supplicant and rescue him from his distress is a turning point in mood, and perhaps even in genre, in this short poem. The speaker, no longer fearing that God will forget him forever, is suddenly sustained by a sense of trust in God, and he conjures up God's intervention on his behalf almost as though it were an accomplished fact. In this way, the poem that began as desperate supplication concludes on a note of celebration, in the manner of a thanksgiving psalm, "Let me sing to the LORD, for He requited me." The fluidity of genres of many of the psalms is an expression of their psychological dynamism—they express not one static attitude but an inner evolution or oscillation of attitudes. Perhaps the prayer itself served as a vehicle of transformation from acute distress to trust.

14

1 For the lead player, for David.
    The scoundrel has said in his heart,
        "There is no God."
    They corrupt, they make loathsome their acts.
        There is none who does good.
2   The LORD from the heavens looked down
          on the sons of humankind
    to see, is there someone discerning,
        someone seeking out God.

---

1. *The scoundrel has said in his heart, / "There is no God."* The thrust of this line is more moral than theological. The concern is not a philosophical question of God's existence but the scoundrel's lack of conscience, his feeling that he can act with impunity, because he thinks he need not fear divine retribution. This psalm, then, is a "prophetic" psalm, lacking any element of supplication because the speaker who denounces the society he observes does not put himself forth as victim.

2. *The LORD from the heavens looked down / on the sons of humankind / to see.* These three versets are remarkable for involving enjambments from verset to verset (a rare maneuver) and avoiding semantic parallelism, which appears only at the end ("discerning, / . . . seeking out"). Thus, the eye is drawn downward in a miniature narrative sequence, following the divine gaze, from the heavens to the human sphere. The illusion of the scoundrel that there is no God examining human actions is here spectacularly refuted.

All turn astray,   3
          altogether befouled.
There is none who does good.
          There is not even one.
Do they not know,   4
          all wrongdoers?
Devourers of my people devoured them like bread.
          They did not call the LORD.
There did they sorely fear,   5
          for God is with the righteous band.
In your plot against the poor you are shamed,   6
          for the LORD is his shelter.

---

3. *There is none who does good. / There is not even one.* The sentence repeated
from verse 1 is less a refrain than a dumfounded pronouncement by the dismayed speaker, who cannot find a single good person—"There is not even one."
The brevity of the versets here (two beats, four syllables in each in the Hebrew)
as well as elsewhere in the poem should be noted. In the face of such dismaying, pervasive corruption, the speaker is moved to register a response in stark,
brief statements, without ornamentation.

4. *devoured them like bread.* The words "them like" do not appear in the Hebrew
and are added for clarity.

5. *sorely fear.* The Hebrew is literally "feared a fear."

6. *In your plot against the poor you are shamed.* The Hebrew is crabbed because
a necessary preposition seems to be missing, so the translation is somewhat
conjectural.

7   Oh, may from Zion come Israel's rescue
               when the LORD restores His people's condition.
    May Jacob exult,
               May Israel rejoice.

---

7. *Oh, may from Zion come Israel's rescue.* Although "my people" has been mentioned in the poem, it was chiefly an indication of the populace that is subjected to the depredations of the wicked. The national perspective, then, with the reference to some sort of restoration—perhaps after defeat or exile—of the nation, a restoration that will emerge from its capital, looks like a formulaic tag, of the sort that sometimes ends the psalms of Zion, which has been added here editorially as a conclusion.

15

A David psalm.
  LORD, who will sojourn in Your tent,
          who will dwell on Your holy mountain?
  He who walks blameless
          and does justice
                  and speaks the truth in his heart.

---

1. LORD, *who will sojourn in Your tent, / who will dwell on Your holy mountain?*
The reference, of course, is to Mount Zion, but this line need not be understood literally, as some scholars propose, as a kind of entrance quiz for people
coming into the temple—that is, a set of questions posed by priests or Levites
to the arriving pilgrims. Those who deserve to be in God's special place are the
people who exhibit the moral virtues that the psalm will enumerate. Though
the two versets in fact refer synonymously to the same place, there is a progression in the language. The first verset uses a verb of temporary residence,
gur, "sojourn," appropriately paired with "tent," originally the characteristic form
of nomadic habitation, whereas the second verset uses "dwell" (*sh-k-n*), and by
mentioning God's holy mountain invokes the solid structure of the temple.

2. *He who walks blameless.* The answer to the opening question is a catalog of
moral attributes. It is noteworthy that these are presented as an objective list
of items without figurative elaboration; there is not a single metaphor in the
poem. The enumerated virtuous acts all pertain to a person's moral obligations
to others. Neither cult nor covenant is involved.

3   Who slanders not with his tongue
                nor does to his fellow man evil
                        nor bears reproach for his kin.

4   The debased in his eyes is repugnant
                but to LORD-fearers he accords honor.
    When he vows to his fellow man,
              he does not revoke it.

5   His money he does not give at interest
                and no bribe for the innocent takes.
    He who does these
             will never stumble.

---

3. *Who slanders not with his tongue.* This verset is absent in the text of Psalms discovered at Qumran. But the previous line is a stately triad; thus, there is poetic logic in this line's being triadic as well.

nor reproach bears for his kin. The translation reproduces the cryptic formulation of the Hebrew. The meaning might be: When his kin behave badly, he does not pass over the misdeed in silence because of the kinship.

4. *When he vows to his fellow man, / he does not revoke it.* The Masoretic text here is problematic. It appears to read: "he vows to do evil / and will not revoke it," which is hardly an attribute one would attach to the moral person. But three ancient translations—the Septuagint, the Syriac, and the Peshitta—read here instead of *lehara'*, "to do evil," *lere'eihu*, "to his fellow man," which merely reverses the order of the consonants. It is the sort of error a scribe could have easily made.

5. *no bribe for the innocent takes.* The evident meaning is that he takes no bribe to declare the innocent guilty.

He who does these / will never stumble. This brief line succinctly—indeed, almost abruptly—summarizes the happy fate of the person who follows the moral path traced by the poem.

16

A David *michtam*.   1
   Guard me, O God,
         for I shelter in You.
  I said to the LORD,   2
      "My Master You are.
            My good is only through You."
  As to holy ones in the land   3
      and the mighty who were all my desire,

---

1. michtam. What sort of composition is indicated by this term remains uncertain. The Septuagint translators thought it was an inscription incised in stone.

   Guard me, O God, / for I shelter in You. The subject of this psalm, a confession of faith, is unusual. Some scholars, because of the apparent references to pagan worship in verses 3 and 4, have imagined that the poem is the self-dedication of a Canaanite convert to the worship of YHWH, but this is by no means a necessary inference, and it must be said that much of verses 3 and 4 is obscure. In any case, a native Israelite could easily have been immersed in pagan practices.

2. *is only through You.* The textual difficulties of this whole segment of the poem begin here, because the Hebrew *bal-ʿaleikha* is unclear.

3. *holy ones . . . mighty.* Any translation here is guesswork. These terms might refer to local deities, as many interpreters have supposed, or they might indicate Canaanite (?) potentates who were idol worshippers.

   who were all my desire. The "were" is an interpretive addition, on the assumption that the speaker at a point in the past had attachments to paganism. But the phrase in context is enigmatic.

4   let their sorrows abound—
              another did they betroth.
     I will not pour their libations of blood,
              I will not bear their names on my lips.
5   The LORD is my portion and lot,
              it is You Who sustain my fate.
6   An inheritance fell to me with delight,
              my estate, too, is lovely to me.
7   I shall bless the LORD Who gave me counsel
              through the nights that my conscience would lash me.
8   I set the LORD always before me,
              on my right hand, that I not stumble.

---

4. *let their sorrows abound.* Again, the translation is conjectural.

another did they betroth. The translation assumes, with other interpreters, that "another" refers to another god and that the verb *maharu* means to espouse or betroth, but neither reading is certain.

I will not pour their libations of blood. At last, the text becomes transparent. This is a clear affirmation that the speaker will distance himself from pagan rites.

6. *inheritance . . . estate.* Given the emphasis of the previous verse on the LORD as the speaker's portion and lot, the inheritance he now celebrates is probably not a reference to real estate but to his being happy in his sense of sustaining connection (see the next verse) with the God of Israel.

7. *conscience.* The Hebrew says "kidneys," thought to be the seat of conscience. It is not clear how peoples of the ancient Near East arrived at the ascription of sundry functions to the various internal organs.

So my heart rejoices and my pulse beats with joy,   9
     my whole body abides secure.
For You will not forsake my life to Sheol,   10
     You won't let Your faithful one see the Pit.
Make me know the path of life.   11
     Joys overflow in Your presence,
       delights in Your right hand forever.

---

9. *my pulse beats with joy.* The Masoretic text has *kevodi*, "my glory," but some manuscripts show *keveidi*, "my liver." Elsewhere I have translated this word as "heart," but that inner organ already appears in the immediately preceding phrase, and to keep the strong somatic imagery of the line, the translation here substitutes "pulse," yielding the sequence heart-pulse-body. Though the prevalent meaning of *basar* is "flesh," it does appear frequently in Leviticus in the sense of "body."

11. *Joys overflow in Your presence.* The literal sense of the Hebrew is "a satiety of joys in Your presence."

17

1   A David prayer.
    Hear, O LORD, a just thing.
        Listen well to my song.
            Hearken to my guileless prayer.
2   From before You my judgment will come,
    Your eyes behold rightness.
3   You have probed my heart, come upon me by night,
    You have tried me, and found no wrong in me.
        I barred my mouth to let nothing pass.

---

1. *A David prayer.* This is one of several times in Psalms in which *tefilah*, prayer, is used instead of the anticipated *mizmor*, psalm. The generic distinction is not clear because this poem is essentially a psalm of supplication. The speaker is beset by enemies who threaten to destroy him as he entreats God to confound his foes and rescue him. Perhaps the note of inwardness in the first part of the poem, in which the speaker proclaims the integrity of his prayer (*tefilah* is the term he uses), and his having met the challenge of God's probing are what qualify this text as prayer.

my guileless prayer. The literal sense of the Hebrew is "my prayer without lips of deceit."

3. *come upon me by night.* This succinct phrase suggests some sort of nocturnal inner wrestling, a dark night of the soul.

found no wrong in me. "Wrong" is merely implied in an ellipsis.

I barred my mouth. The Hebrew verb is the one used for a muzzle. The speaker not only has stood God's inward testing but refused to allow any word of doubt or bad faith to pass the barrier of his lips.

As for human acts—by the word of Your lips! 4
      I have kept from the tracks of the brute.
Set firm my steps on Your pathways, 5
      so my feet will not stumble.
I called You, for You will answer me, God. 6
      Incline Your ear, O hear my utterance.
Make Your mercies abound, O rescuer of those who shelter 7
      from foes at Your right hand.
Guard me like the apple of the eye, 8
      in the shadow of Your wings conceal me
from the wicked who have despoiled me, 9
      my deadly enemies drawn round me.
Their fat has covered their heart. 10
      With their dewlaps they speak haughty words.

---

4. *As for human acts—by the word of Your lips!* The meaning of the Hebrew is uncertain. Perhaps the idea is that whereas the speaker seals his lips, God's words determine human events or guide humankind.

6. *Incline Your ear, O hear.* These verbs pick up the imperative verbs of listening from the beginning of the poem.

7. *Make Your mercies abound.* The translation follows the Masoretic text. A small emendation of *ḥasadekha,* "Your mercies," to *ḥasidekha* would yield "Set aside Your faithful ones."

10. *Their fat has covered their heart.* "Heart," if it is indeed the intended object, is only implied. The heart is the seat of understanding and feeling; fat over the heart (presumably, a token of the offensive prosperity of the wicked) insulates it from perception and feeling.
    With their dewlaps. The Masoretic text reads *pimo,* a grammatically archaic form meaning "their mouth." Because of the prominent fat image in the first verset, this translation emends that word to *pimatam* (or, in an undeclined form, simply *pimah*), a term that refers to folds of fat under the chin.

11   My steps now they hem in,
                their eyes they cast over the land.
12   He is like a lion longing for prey,
                like the king of beasts lying in wait.
13   Rise, LORD, head him off, bring him down,
                save my life from the wicked with Your sword,
14   from men, by Your hand, from men,
                from those fleeting of portion in life.
    And Your protected ones—fill their bellies,
                let their sons be sated,
                        and let them leave what is left for their young.

---

11. *My steps.* The Hebrew text says "our steps."

their eyes they cast over the land. The Hebrew is somewhat obscure. A very literal rendering would be: their eyes they set to incline in the land. Given the predatory nature of their activity, made explicit in the next verse, the most probable sense to extract from these words without emendation is that they look all about the land for objects of prey.

14. *from men, by Your hand, from men, / from those fleeting of portion in life.* This line employs the strategy of incremented repetition that is common in the oldest stratum of biblical poetry—as, for example, in the Song of Deborah. The idea of the line is to remind God that these bloody-minded enemies are mere mortals, and of a sort whose actions warrant that their fate of mortality be instantly fulfilled. The reference to God's hand is motivated by the fact that this hand wields a sword.

Your protected ones. Literally, "Your hidden ones"—that is, those concealed in the shadow of God's wings (verse 8).

fill their bellies. This reference at the end to food may suggest that the wicked, while fattening themselves, have been starving out the righteous in beleaguering them.

let them leave what is left for their young. This verset is either a kind of gloss on the two preceding verses or envisages a third generation: God's protected ones, their sons, the infants of the sons.

As for me, in justice I behold Your face,
      I take my fill, wide awake, of Your image.   15

---

15. *As for me, in justice.* The appearance of the noun *tsedeq,* "justice," at the end of the poem makes a neat envelope structure, for the speaker began his prayer by asking God to hear "a just thing" (also *tsedeq*). The envelope structure is reinforced by the occurrence of "behold" here and in verse 2.

    I take my fill, wide awake, of Your image. The speaker has just invoked full bellies and sated sons, but now at the end it is God's image—not in a dream vision but in complete wakefulness—that sates him. The sensual concreteness of this concluding clause is so striking that it led Judah Halevi, the great medieval Hebrew poet, to adopt it for a homoerotic poem in which the speaker awakes and sees his beloved friend's face by his side.

18

1   For the lead player, for the LORD's servant, for David, who spoke
to the LORD the words of this song on the day the LORD saved him
from the grasp of all his enemies and from the hand of Saul.

2   And he said:

I am impassioned of You, LORD, my strength!

---

1. *For the lead player, for the* LORD's *servant, for David.* The superscription of this
psalm is extraordinarily long. Perhaps this reflects an editorial desire to fit this
into the biography of David, from which in fact the entire psalm was borrowed.
It is essentially the same poem as the one that appears as the twenty-second
chapter of 2 Samuel. Still, there are many small differences between the two
versions. Those that throw some light on the reading of our psalm are noted in
the comments below. The textual evidence suggests that the version in 2
Samuel 22 is the older one: Certain unusual forms have been regularized or
glossed here, and there are also signs of some errors in scribal copying. Because
David is represented in his narration as a poet, it is even conceivable, though
in no way demonstrable and perhaps unlikely, that this particular psalm might
have been composed by him.

2. *I am impassioned of You,* LORD, *my strength!* This clause lacks a parallel verset
to make it a line of poetry, and it is absent from the text in 2 Samuel. The verb
for "impassioned" (*raḥam* in the *qal* conjugation) is an Aramaic usage that
appears only here in the Bible.

The Lord is my crag and my bastion, 3
   and my deliverer, my God, my rock where I shelter,
    my shield and the horn of my rescue, my
    fortress.
Praised I called the Lord 4
   and from my enemies I was rescued.
The cords of death wrapped round me, 5
   and the torrents of perdition dismayed me.
The cords of Sheol encircled me, 6
   the traps of death sprung upon me.
In my strait I called to the Lord, 7
   to my God I cried out.
He heard from His palace my voice, 8
   and my outcry before Him came to His ears.

---

3. *The Lord is my crag and my bastion.* This is of course a victory poem, bristling with martial imagery. At the same time, it exhibits considerable overlap with the thanksgiving psalm: the experience of near death attested to by the speaker, the celebration of God's saving power, the occurrence of the verbs *hodah,* "acclaim," and *zamer,* "hymn," at the end.

8. *He heard from His palace.* The outcry of the beleaguered warrior ascends all the way to the highest heavens, thus launching a downward vertical movement that is followed through the narrative sweep of the next several verses.

9   The earth heaved and shuddered,
        the mountains' foundations were shaken.
    They heaved, for smoke rose from His nostrils
        and fire from His mouth consumed,
           coals blazed up around Him.

10   He tilted the heavens, came down,
        dense mist beneath His feet.

11   He mounted a cherub and flew,
        and He soared on the wings of the wind.

12   He set darkness His hiding-place round Him,
        His abode water-massing, the clouds of the skies.

---

9. *The earth heaved and shuddered.* The seismic imagery of this line begins a powerful anthropomorphic representation of God, drawing freely on pre-Israelite mythological poetry. The heaving of the earth functions as a kind of preliminary artillery barrage before God's direct assault on the speaker's enemies.

for smoke rose from His nostrils / and fire from His mouth consumed, / coals blazed up around Him. God Himself is imagined as a kind of erupting volcano. In an intensifying narrative sequence through this triadic line, first we see the smoke from the nostrils, then consuming flame from the mouth, and God is altogether so incandescent that everything around him ignites.

10. *He tilted the heavens.* The heavens are imagined as a flat slab. God tilts them to begin His downward course, and our eye is thus led downward here to God's feet at the end of the line.

11. *He mounted a cherub and flew, / and He soared on the wings of the wind.* The cherub is a fierce winged beast, the charger ridden by the sky god in Canaanite mythology (not the dimpled darling of Renaissance painting). The verb "soar" here is one point where the text of Psalms seems better than that of 2 Samuel, which has "was seen"—a word that differs by one consonant (*resh* instead of the similar-looking *dalet*).

12. *water-massing.* The translation follows 2 Samuel 22, which has *ḥashrat-mayim*, as against *ḥeshkat-mayim* here ("darkness of water"). This appears to be an instance in which the copyist substituted a familiar term for a rare one that he may not have understood. The mistake would have been triggered by the graphic similarity between *resh* and *kaf*.

From the brilliance before Him His clouds moved ahead—   13
        hail and fiery coals.
The Lord thundered from on high.   14
          Elyon sent forth His voice—
              hail and fiery coals.
He let loose His arrows, and scattered them,   15
          lightning bolts shot, and He panicked them.
The channels of water were exposed,   16
          and the world's foundations laid bare
from the Lord's roaring,
          from the blast of Your nostrils' breath.
He reached from on high and took me,   17
          pulled me out of the many waters.
He saved me from my daunting enemy   18
          and from my foes who were stronger than I.
They came at me on my day of disaster,   19
          but the Lord became my support
and brought me out to a wide-open space,   20
          set me free, for His pleasure I was.

---

14. *Elyon.* This is the designation of a Canaanite deity ("the Most High") that has been co-opted by the monotheistic poet. It is preserved here in its Hebrew form in the translation to suggest the archaic effect of the original.

   hail and fiery coals. This recurrence of the phrase used at the end of the previous verse looks suspiciously like an inadvertent scribal repetition. It is entirely absent from 2 Samuel 22.

16. *The channels of water were exposed.* 2 Samuel 22 has "the channels of the sea" (a difference of only one letter in the Hebrew), which makes stronger sense as an image of the sea dried up or driven back by God's fiery descent.

17. *pulled me out of the many waters.* Although it is enemies on the battlefield who threaten the speaker, the image of drowning in the depths of the sea recurs in thanksgiving psalms as a metaphoric representation of near death.

20. *brought me out to a wide-open space.* The "wide-open space," *merḥav*, is the antithesis to the "strait" (*tsar*, as in verse 7) in which the speaker felt trapped.

21 The Lord dealt with me by my merit,
　　　　for my cleanness of hands He requited me.
22 For I kept the ways of the Lord
　　　　and did no evil before my God.
23 For all His laws were before me.
　　　　From His statutes I did not swerve.
24 And I was blameless before Him,
　　　　and I kept myself from crime.
25 And the Lord requited me for my merit,
　　　　for my cleanness of hands in His eyes.
26 With the faithful You deal faithfully,
　　　　with a blameless man, act without blame.
27 With the pure one, You deal purely,
　　　　with the perverse man, deal in twists.
28 For it is You Who rescues the lowly folk
　　　　and haughty eyes You bring low.
29 For You light up my lamp, O Lord,
　　　　my God illumines my darkness.
30 For through You I rush at a barrier,
　　　　through my God I can vault a wall.
31 The God, His way is blameless,
　　　　the Lord's utterance unalloyed.
32 For who is god except the Lord,
　　　　and who the Rock except our God?
33 The God who girds me with might
　　　　and keeps my way blameless,
34 makes my legs like a gazelle's,
　　　　and stands me on the heights,

---

21. *The Lord dealt with me by my merit.* These words initiate a confession of virtue that continues for six verses. The explanation for God's spectacular intervention to rescue the speaker from his implacable and powerful enemies is that he has been careful to follow God's precepts.

trains my hands for combat,
        makes my arms bend a bow of bronze. 35
You gave me Your shield of rescue,
        Your right hand did sustain me, 36
          and Your battle-cry made me many.
You lengthened my strides beneath me,
        and my feet did not trip. 37
I pursued my enemies, caught them,
        turned not back till I wiped them out. 38
I smashed them, they could not rise,
        they fell beneath my feet. 39
You girt me with might for combat.
        You laid low my foes beneath me, 40
and You made my enemies turn back before me,
        my foes, I demolished them. 41
They cried out—there was none to rescue,
        to the LORD—He answered them not. 42

---

35. *trains my hands for combat.* This follows the quickening and steadying of the legs in the previous line. The second verset here, in a nice focusing development, then shows the warrior's arms bending a bow of bronze.

36. *Your battle-cry made me many.* The version here has ʿ*anwatkha* ("Your humility"?), which does not make evident sense. The text in 2 Samuel has ʿ*anotkha*; one of the meanings of ʿ*anot* is a crying out. (The consonantal text is the same in both readings.) The likely sense is that the warrior's use of a battle-cry, probably incorporating the name YHWH, terrified the enemy and made his own force seem many even if it may have been outnumbered. In sequence, then, God gives his protected warrior three formidable implements of war—a bow, a shield, and a battle-cry incorporating the divine name.

41. *turn back before me.* The literal sense of the Hebrew is "gave to me [their] nape."

43   I crushed them like dust in the wind,
               like mud in the streets I ground them.
44   You saved me from the strife of peoples,
               You set me at nations' head,
                     a people I knew not served me.
45   At the mere ear's report they obeyed me,
               aliens cringed before me.
46   Aliens did wither,
               filed out from their forts.
47   The LORD lives and blessed is my Rock,
               exalted the God of my rescue.
48   The God who grants vengeance to me
               and crushes peoples beneath me,
49   frees me from my enemies,
               yes, from those against me You raise me,
                     from a man of violence You save me.

---

43. *I crushed them like dust in the wind.* The wind image is a little odd, and some manuscripts of this psalm read, as does 2 Samuel 22, "like dust of the earth."

44. *the strife of peoples, / . . . nations' head, / a people I knew not served me.* All this might conceivably fit David's creation of a mini-empire, but perhaps it is no more than formulaic language for military victory.

45. *aliens cringed before me.* The meaning of the Hebrew verb is somewhat conjectural.

46. *filed out from their forts.* Both the verb and the noun are in doubt, so the translation is an educated guess. The verb *ḥ-g-r* could mean to come out or slip out, and the noun suggests something like "enclosure."

Therefore I acclaim You among nations, O LORD,   50
          and to Your name I would hymn,
making great the rescues of His king,   51
               keeping faith with His anointed,
                    for David and his seed forever.

---

50. *Therefore I acclaim You . . . / and to Your name I would hymn.* Having completed the account of the glorious victory that God has granted him, the speaker now moves to a formal conclusion, in keeping with the convention of the thanksgiving psalm, announcing that he has here celebrated God's greatness.

51. *making great the rescues of His king.* The version in 2 Samuel has "tower of rescues" (*migdol yeshu'ot*) instead of *magdil yeshu'ot* here. The image of a tower is more striking, and it picks up the fortress metaphors of the beginning of the poem.

19

1 To the lead player. A David psalm.
2   The heavens tell God's glory,
               and His handiwork sky declares.
3   Day to day breathes utterance
               and night to night pronounces knowledge.
4   There is no utterance and there are no words,
               their voice is never heard.

---

2. *The heavens tell God's glory.* The locus of contemplation of the speaker in this poem resembles that of the speaker in Psalm 8: He contemplates the splendid design of the heavens overhead and sees in it a manifestation of God's beautiful work as creator. But the imagery and the movement of cosmic vision here immediately swerve in a very different direction from that of Psalm 8.

3. *Day to day . . . night to night.* In the complementary parallelism of this line, we get a sense that the splendor of the creation is steadily manifested through the whole diurnal cycle, from the brilliance of sunlight to the lovely illumination of moon and stars. But as the poem proceeds, it focuses on the sun.

    breathes. The literal, or at least etymological, sense of the Hebrew verb *yabi'a* is to "well forth," though it is used a few times in the biblical corpus in the extended sense of "express," the meaning it bears in post-biblical Hebrew.

4. *There is no utterance and there are no words.* This seeming contradiction of verses 2 and 3 is, of course, only the underlining of a moving paradox. The heavens speak, but it is a wordless language, what the great twentieth-century Hebrew poet H. N. Bialik, in a poem akin to this one, would call "the language of images." Thus the psalmist can go on from this affirmation of speechlessness and silence to the declaration in the next verse of speech going out to the ends of the earth.

Through all the earth their voice goes out,   5
   to the world's edge, their words.
For the sun He set up a tent in them—
    and he like a groom from his canopy comes,   6
     exults like a warrior running his course.
From the ends of the heavens his going out   7
   and his circuit to their ends,
     and nothing can hide from his heat.

---

5. *For the sun He set up a tent in them.* The poet now proceeds to a grandly mythological image of the sun—residing in a celestial pavilion, emerging from it at dawn like a bridegroom from his wedding canopy, and then, in a switch of imagery, racing across the sky to the west like a warrior dashing across the battlefield. Some interpreters have viewed this section of the poem as a pagan hymn to a solar deity simply borrowed by the monotheistic poet from a poem written in Egypt by Judeans or Samaritans influenced by Egyptian religion. It makes better sense to view it as a monotheistic adaptation of mythological imagery. (The contemporary American scholar Nahum Sarna even suggests it may be a polemic against paganism.) Because the only plausible antecedent for the verb "set up" is God, the poet does seem to be saying that it is God who has ordained the circuit of the sun, and that the images in which we cast this daily celestial road of light—the bridegroom emerging from his canopy, the warrior racing on his way—are but poetic expressions of how the heavens tell God's glory day after day.

7. *and nothing can hide from his heat.* The Hebrew conceals a neat pun, for the word that means "heat," *ḥamah,* is also another name for the sun.

8   The Lord's teaching is perfect,
                    restoring to life.
       The Lord's pact is steadfast,
                    it makes the fool wise.
9   The Lord's precepts are upright,
                    delighting the heart.
       The Lord's command unblemished,
                    giving light to the eyes.
10   The Lord's fear is pure,
                    outlasting all time.
       The Lord's judgments are truth,
                    all of them just.

---

8. *The Lord's teaching is perfect.* With these words, the psalm switches gears, from a celebration of the splendor of the heavens to praise for the life-sustaining perfection of God's commandments. There has been some debate among scholars as to whether in fact Psalm 19 might be a splicing together of two unrelated poems belonging to different genres. Because cut and paste is a standard technique of literary composition in the Bible, one can say minimally that the redactor—or, perhaps, redactor-poet—saw the two parts of the poem as constituting a single whole. Sarna, pursuing the idea of a polemic response to pagan solar poetry, notes that the sun god, Shamash, is often associated with justice and truth or enlightenment. (In the Greek tradition, precisely this linkage appears in the figure of Apollo.) This poem, Sarna proposes, is a pointed transference of those attributes from the sun god to YHWH, the one God.

More desired than gold,   11
                 than abundant fine gold,
and sweeter than honey,
                 quintessence of bees.
Your servant, too, takes care with them.   12
                 In keeping them—great reward.
Unwitting sins who can grasp?   13
                 Of unknown actions clear me.
From willful men preserve Your servant,   14
                 let them not rule over me.
Then shall I be blameless
                 and clear of great crime.

---

11. *More desired than gold, / . . . and sweeter than honey.* Till this point, the general quality of perfection of God's teaching and its restorative force have been stressed. But with the images of this verse, the divine precepts are represented as sensually luscious—an object of desire and a source of sweetness.

quintessence of bees. Both halves of this compound term for honey, *nofet* and *tsufim*, mean "honey." As elsewhere in biblical usage, when two synonyms are combined, as here, in a construct form ("*x* of *y*"), the semantic effect is to create a hyper-intensification—the sweetest of imaginable honeys. The English equivalent offered here may sound like a turn of phrase one might encounter in the poetry of Wallace Stevens, but it offers a good semantic match for the Hebrew.

13. *Unwitting sins.* The speaker, having affirmed the supreme value of God's commandments, is impelled to confess that, even with the best of intentions, an imperfect human being can scarcely be sure of never having violated any of them. So he requests God's indulgence for any unwitting transgressions of the laws he holds dear.

15   Let my mouth's utterances be pleasing
                    and my heart's stirring before You,
                            LORD, my rock and redeemer.

---

15. *Let my mouth's utterances*. This verse forms an apt formal coda to the psalm, or at least to its second half, and has appropriately been adopted as the conclusion to the silent prayer recited three times daily in Jewish worship.

my heart's stirring. The root of the noun *higayon* suggests murmuring (the same verb prominently used in Psalm 1), but that English term is avoided here because of the unfortunate suggestion of cardiac irregularity.

20

To the lead player, a David psalm.   1
   May the LORD answer you on the day of distress,   2
       the name of Jacob's God make you safe.
   May He send help to you from the sanctum,   3
       and from Zion may He sustain you.

---

2. *May the* LORD *answer you.* The "you" in the Hebrew here and throughout the poem is in the masculine singular. Verses 7 and 10 make clear that the person addressed is the king. In genre, then, this text is a royal psalm, the first in a series of such psalms in the canonical collection that are prayers for the welfare of the anointed king. The language of this particular royal psalm is repeated through many phases in a pagan hymn written on papyrus and composed in second-century BCE Egypt in Aramaic. The pagan hymn may have borrowed from this one, or both may have drawn on an earlier Canaanite polytheistic poem.

   the name of Jacob's God make you safe. This is the first of three references to "the name of God" in the poem. The usage may reflect a growing belief in the later biblical period that God's name in itself was an efficacious agent, and also a kind of intermediary, between the deity and Israel. The verb *s-g-b*, "make you safe," is cognate with *misgav*, "fortress"—etymologically, an elevated place.

3. *the sanctum . . . Zion.* The theo-geographical logic is that Jerusalem is both the capital city, where the king and his government are headquartered, and the location of God's sanctuary.

4   May He recall all your grain-offerings,
             and your burnt-offerings may He relish.   selah

5   May He grant you what your heart would want,
             and all your counsels may He fulfill.

6   Let us sing gladly for Your rescue
             and in our God's name our banner raise.
                May the LORD fulfill all your desires.

7   Now do I know
             that the LORD has rescued His anointed.
    He has answered him from His holy heavens
             in the might of His right hand's rescue.

---

4. *your burnt-offerings may He relish.* The verb *yedashneh* is somewhat obscure. Perhaps it means "to regard as *dashen*, rich, ripe, full of nutrients." If so, this is a linguistic survival (not necessarily a theological one) of the pre-monotheistic idea that the gods took pleasurable nourishment from the sacrifices offered them.

5. *what your heart would want.* The literal sense is "according to your heart."

6. *our banner raise.* The translation is an educated guess, assuming that the verb *nidgol* is cognate with the noun *degel*, banner.
    May the LORD fulfill all your desires. This verset looks out of place because it does not belong with the exulting exhortation to sing out and raise banners, and it makes this the only triadic line in the poem. Perhaps it is an inadvertent scribal duplication of the second verset of verse 5, which it more or less repeats.

7. *Now do I know.* These words signal the turning point of the poem, when the speaker is flooded with certainty that God has in fact rescued the king from his straits.
    in the might of His right hand's rescue. The language strongly suggests that the "distress" of the king is a military threat.

They—the chariots, and they—the horses,   8
        but we—the name of the LORD our God invoke.
They have tumbled and fallen   9
        but we arose and took heart.
O LORD, rescue the king.   10
        May He answer us on the day we call.

---

8. *They—the chariots, and they—the horses.* The whole line is a neat instance of a strong periodic sentence in which the verb that gives everything meaning—"invoke"—is withheld until the very end. "They" are the enemies of the Israelite king, who foolishly "invoke" or depend on their chariots and horses, instruments of power that are no match for the name of the LORD.

10. *O LORD, rescue the king.* The Masoretic cantillation marks place a full stop at "rescue," thus turning "king" into a vocative in apposition with "LORD." This construction, however, produces an uncharacteristically unbalanced line (two beats in the first verset and four in the second). In keeping with all the indications in the poem that this is a royal psalm, it makes better sense to have "the king" here at the end as the direct object of the verb "rescue." One should note that the psalm exhibits a neatly concise envelope structure, beginning "answer you on the day of distress" and here concluding with "answer us on the day we call."

21

1 To the lead player, a David psalm.
2   LORD, in Your strength the king rejoices,
            and in Your rescue how much he exults!
3   His heart's desire You gave to him,
            and his lips' entreaty You did not withhold.   selah
4   For You met him with blessings of bounty,
            You set on his head a crown of pure gold.
5   Life he asked You—You gave him,
            length of days for time without end.
6   Great is his glory through Your rescue.
            Glory and grandeur You bestowed upon him.

---

2. *in Your strength the king rejoices.* The poem announces itself at its very beginning as a royal psalm. There is no definite article in the Hebrew before "king," but biblical poetry fairly often elides the article. "Strength" (*'oz*) has a military sense in many psalms, as does the parallel term "rescue" (*yeshu'ah*), which implies something like extricating a person or an army from enemies who appeared to have the upper hand.

5. *length of days for time without end.* The formulation is intended as a hyperbole—what the king has been granted is not immortality but a long life. That life had run the danger of being cut off prematurely by the threatening enemies from whom God has rescued him.

6. *Great is his glory through Your rescue.* The king, beleaguered by powerful enemies, emerges victorious in battle through God's help. As a result, he suddenly grows in regal stature, now a figure of kingly glory and grandeur in his triumph.

For You granted him blessings forever,   7
    cheered him with joy in Your presence.
For the king puts his trust in the LORD,   8
    through Elyon's kindness he will not fail.
Your hand will find out your enemies,   9
    your right hand find out your foes.
You will make them like a fiery kiln   10
    . in the hour of Your wrath.
The LORD will devour them in His anger,
    and fire will consume them.
Their fruit from the land You destroy   11
    and their seed from among humankind.
For evil they plotted against you,   12
    devised schemes they could not fulfill.

---

8. *through Elyon's kindness he will not fail.* It is also possible to construe this clause to mean "through Elyon's kindness [or, keeping faith] that will not fail."

9. *Your hand will find out your enemies.* Until this point, the second-person-singular pronoun has been addressed to God, and the king has been referred to in the third person. From this point, it is the king who is addressed, although in verse 10 God is invoked in the third person as agent of destruction. All the verbs refer to future acts of routing the enemies, whereas in the first half of the poem the victory is invoked as a recently accomplished fact. Perhaps the poet means to say that the king, already empowered, will go on to future triumphs of this nature, though the possibility suggests itself that two different psalms (verses 2–8, verses 9–13) have been spliced together.

10. *in the hour of Your wrath.* The Hebrew appears to say, literally, "in the hour of your face," but "face" is sometimes used elliptically to mean grim or hostile face, angry aspect—and that meaning makes sense here. The cantillation marks of the Masoretic text put "LORD" (YHWH) together syntactically with "wrath" ("in the hour of Your wrath, O LORD"). That construction, however, introduces confusion by having two different referents for "you" in the same sentence. It is preferable to understand YHWH as the subject of the first verb in the next clause, "devour."

13   For you will make them turn back,
            with your bowstring you aim at their face.
14   Loom high, O Lord, in Your strength.
            Let us sing, let us hymn Your might.

---

13. *make them turn back.* The literal anatomical reference is to the back of the shoulder. The idiom does not occur elsewhere, but it clearly refers to making the enemy turn around and flee. (The verb *tashit*, to put, make, grant, which occurs four times in the psalm, is one that the poet—or, if there were two, both poets—favored.) The aimed bows of the second verset are what makes the enemy flee.

14. Lord, *in Your strength.* This phrase marks the closing of the envelope structure, for the psalm began with "Lord, in Your strength." The poem then concludes with the thanksgiving formula, "Let us sing, let us hymn."

22

To the lead player, on *ayeleth hashahar*, a David psalm.   1
   My God, my God, why have You forsaken me?   2
         Far from my rescue are the words that I roar.
   My God, I call out by day and You do not answer,   3
        by night—no stillness for me.
   And You, the Holy One—enthroned in Israel's praise.   4
   In You did our fathers trust,   5
        they trusted, and You set them free.
   To You they cried out, and escaped,   6
        in You they trusted and were not put to shame.

---

1. ayeleth hashahar. The name elsewhere means "morning star" (or, literally, "dawn doe"). One assumes it refers to a musical instrument of some sort or, alternately, to a melody.

2. *My God, my God, why have You forsaken me?* These famous words are the ones pronounced by Jesus in his last agony—though in Aramaic, not in the original Hebrew. That moment in Matthew is a kind of *pesher*, or fulfillment interpretation, of this psalm, because there are other details here (for example, verses 16–19) that could be connected with the crucifixion.

4. *And You, the Holy One—enthroned in Israel's praise.* This whole verse looks oddly out of place. Indeed, it lacks the parallelism and the rhythmic regularity of a line of poetry.

7   But I am a worm and no man,
                  a disgrace among men, by the people reviled.
8   All who see me do mock me—
                  they curl their lips, they shake their head.
9   Who turns to the LORD, He will set him free.
                  He will save him, for He delights in him.
10   For You drew me out from the womb,
                  made me safe at my mother's breasts.
11   Upon You I was cast from birth,
                  from my mother's belly You were my God.
12   Do not be far from me,
                  for distress is near,
                              for there is none to help.

---

7. *But I am a worm and no man.* This impulse of self-revilement puts the speaker in contrast to the meritorious forefathers, who trusted in God and were rescued by Him. The speaker wonders: Could I possibly be worthy of God's intervention in my state of utter abasement?

9. *Who turns to the* LORD. After the assertion of desperate doubt, the speaker affirms the sustaining idea that those who put their full faith in the LORD will be answered by Him.

10. *For You drew me out from the womb.* Having stated the general principle, the speaker now thinks retrospectively about how in his own life God has sustained him from birth onward—a palpable proof that his present state of abjection will not continue.

11. *from birth.* The Hebrew uses one of two terms for the uterus ("womb," "belly") that alternate in these lines.

12. *Do not be far from me / for distress is near.* The far-near polarity, first announced in "Far from my rescue are the words that I roar," defines the urgent plea that runs through the poem.

Brawny bulls surrounded me,   13
    the mighty of Bashan encompassed me.
They gaped with their mouths against me—   14
    a ravening roaring lion.
Like water I spilled out,   15
    all my limbs fell apart.
My heart was like wax,
    melting within my chest.
My palate turned dry as a shard   16
    and my tongue was annealed to my jaw,
      and to death's dust did You thrust me.

---

13. *Brawny bulls.* The Hebrew adjective *rabim* usually means "many" but some-times "big" or "large." The latter meaning makes better sense here, especially in parallel with another epithet for powerful beasts (or men), "the mighty of Bashan" (Bashan being famous for the breeding of bulls).

14. *a ravening roaring lion.* To the modern eye, this might look like a contradic-tory image. But the sequence works as follows: First the crowd of enemies is likened to a herd of brawny bulls; then the poet focuses on the gaping mouths, presumably imagined as human mouths (because bulls gore but are not car-nivorous). In the final step, these rapacious men ready to swallow him are likened to lions.

15. *Like water I spilled out.* This verse and the next describe the psychological impact of sheer terror and impotence induced by the menacing foes.
    melting within my chest. The literal sense of the Hebrew is "melting within my innards."

16. *My palate turned dry as a shard.* The translation adopts an emendation pro-posed by many interpreters, medieval and modern, reading *ḥiki*, "my palate," for the Masoretic *koḥi*, "my vigor" (a simple reversal of letters in the consonan-tal text). Palate and tongue recur as parallel terms in biblical poetry.

17   For the curs came all around me,
           a pack of the evil encircled me,
                they bound my hands and my feet.

18   They counted out all my bones.
           It is they who looked, who stared at me.

19   They shared out my garments among them
           and cast lots for my clothes.

20   But You, O Lord, be not far.
           My strength, to my aid O hasten!

21   Save from the sword my life,
           from the cur's power my person.

---

17. *curs.* Though the Hebrew is the ordinary word for dog, because dogs were not domesticated in ancient Israel (though they had long been domesticated elsewhere) and roamed about in packs as scavengers, the biblical term is wholly negative. Hence a pejorative English equivalent seems justified.

    they bound my hands and my feet. The received Hebrew text—literally "like a lion my hands and feet"—makes no sense. The translation adopts one proposed emendation—reading *karkhu*, "they bound," for *ka'ari*, "like a lion"—though there is admittedly no ancient textual warrant for this reading.

18. *They counted.* The received text has "I counted," which is puzzling. The small emendation is made in the interest of coherence and on the basis of the parellelism with the second verset.

20. *My strength.* The Hebrew term *'eyalut* is an unusual epithet for the deity. Some have argued that it brings out the etymology of the ordinary word for God, *'el.* It has even been suggested that the term may play on *ayeleth* in the superscription of this psalm.

21. *from the cur's power.* The literal sense is "from the cur's hand," but because dogs don't have hands, the translation here adopts the extended sense of "hand."

Rescue me from the lion's mouth.   22
        And from the horns of the ram You answered me.
Let me tell Your name to my brothers,   23
        in the assembly let me praise You.
Fearers of the LORD, O praise Him!   24
        All the seed of Jacob revere Him!
                And be afraid of Him, all Israel's seed!
For He has not spurned nor has despised   25
        the affliction of the lowly,
and has not hidden His face from him;
        when he cried out to Him, He heard.
For You—my praise in the great assembly.   26
        My vows I fulfill before those who fear Him.
The lowly will eat and be sated.   27
        Those who seek Him will praise the LORD.
           May you be of good cheer forever.
All the far ends of earth will remember   28
        and return to the LORD.
All the clans of the nations
        will bow down before You.

---

22. *You answered me.* This is how the received text reads, though we might have expected an imperative parallel to "rescue me"—that is, "answer me." Because the rest of the psalm is devoted to praising rather than imploring God, perhaps the verb in the past tense is intended as a compact turning point: God has indeed answered the speaker's prayer.

26. *My vows I fulfill.* This phrase refers regularly in Psalms to a votive offering that the speaker, his prayers having been answered, offers in the temple. Thus "my praise in the great assembly" invokes the crowd of worshippers in the temple.

27. *May you be of good cheer forever.* The Hebrew says literally, "May your heart live forever." The conjectural translation depends on a recurrent idiomatic use of "heart" in expressions that refer to mood, good or bad.

29   For the Lord's is the kingship—
          and He rules over the nations.
30   Yes, to Him will bow down
          all the netherworld's sleepers.
   Before Him will kneel
          all who go down to the dust
             whose life is undone.
31   My seed will serve Him.
          It will be told to the Master for generations to come.

---

30. *Yes to Him will bow down / all the netherworld's sleepers / . . . all who go down to the dust.* The received text seems to say, "They ate and bowed down," *'akhlu wehistaḥawu,* which does not make much sense. The translation adopts a commonly proposed emendation that involves merely a respacing of the consonants and one change in a vowel, *'akh lo hishtaḥawu.* This inclusion of the dead among God's worshipful subjects is unusual because a reiterated theme in Psalms is that the dead, mute forever, cannot praise God. Perhaps the poet, having imagined God's dominion extending to the far ends of the earth, also wants to extend it downward—against common usage—into the very underworld. The Masoretic text continues to be incoherent here, reading *kol-dishney-'arets,* "all the fats (?) of the earth." The translation assumes a widely accepted emendation, *kol-yesheiney-'arets* (the last word, *'arets,* means both "earth" and "netherworld").

whose life is undone. Again, the Hebrew is enigmatic—literally: "and his life he did not cause to survive." This sounds unidiomatic, but in all probability the reference is to the condition of death. Beginning with this phrase, everything in the Hebrew through the end of the next verse (and the psalm) is opaque, bearing the look of a word salad tossed by a bewildered scribe.

31. *My seed.* The Masoretic text simply says, unidiomatically, "seed," but there are manuscripts that show "my seed."

to generations to come. The received text places *yavo'u* (literally, "they will come") at the beginning of the next verse. But *dor yav'o,* "a generation to come," makes good sense. (The *waw* at the end that turns it into a plural, *yav'ou,* is probably a dittography from the *waw* at the beginning of the next word, *weyagidu,* "they will proclaim.")

They will proclaim His bounty to a people aborning,
      for He has done.   32

---

32. *to a people aborning*. Again, the Hebrew is a little strange—literally, "a people born." The translation is based on my inference that the reference is to futurity, parallel to "a generation to come."

   for He has done. The abruptness reflects the Hebrew. What God has done, in any case, would have to be His bounty or kindnesses (Hebrew *tsedaqot*) to those who fear Him.

23

1 A David psalm.
    The LORD is my shepherd,
        I shall not want.
2 In grass meadows He makes me lie down,
        by quiet waters guides me.
3 My life He brings back.
        He leads me on pathways of justice
          for His name's sake.

---

1. *The LORD is my shepherd*. Although the likening of God or a ruler to a shepherd is a commonplace in this pastoral culture, this psalm is justly famous for the affecting simplicity and concreteness with which it realizes the metaphor. Thus, in the next line the shepherd leads his sheep to meadows where there is abundant grass and riverbanks and where quiet waters run that the sheep can drink.

2. *makes me lie down*. The verb used here, *hirbits*, is a specialized one for making animals lie down; hence the sheep-shepherd metaphor is carefully sustained.

3. *My life He brings back*. Though "He restoreth my soul" is time-honored, the Hebrew *nefesh* does not mean "soul" but "life breath" or "life." The image is of someone who has almost stopped breathing and is revived, brought back to life.
    pathways of justice. With this phrase, the speaker glides from the sheep metaphor to speaking of himself in human terms.

Though I walk in the vale of death's shadow,   4
       I fear no harm,
             for You are with me.
Your rod and Your staff—
       it is they that console me.
You set out a table before me   5
       in the face of my foes.
You moisten my head with oil,
       my cup overflows.

---

4. *in the vale of death's shadow.* The intent of the translation here is not to avoid the virtually proverbial "in the shadow of the valley of death" but rather to cut through the proliferation of syllables in the King James Version, however eloquent, and better approximate the compactness of the Hebrew—*begey tsalmawet.* Though philologists assume that the Masoretic *tsalmawet* is actually a misleading vocalization of *tsalmut*—probably a poetic word for "darkness" with the *ut* ending simply a suffix of abstraction—the traditional vocalization reflects something like an orthographic pun or a folk etymology (*tsel* means "shadow," *mawet* means "death"), so there is justification in retaining the death component.

I fear no harm. The imbalance between this extremely brief verset and the relatively long first verset, equally evident in the Hebrew, gives these words a climactic effect as an affirmation of trust after the relatively lengthy evocation of the place of fear.

You are with me. / Your rod and Your staff. At this crucial moment of terror in the valley of the shadow, the speaker turns to God in the second person, though the rod and staff are carried over from the shepherd image.

5. *You moisten my head with oil.* The verb here, *dishen*, is not the one that is used for anointment, and its associations are sensual rather than sacramental. Etymologically, it means something like "to make luxuriant." This verse, then, lists all the physical elements of a happy life—a table laid out with good things to eat, a head of hair well rubbed with olive oil, and an overflowing cup of wine.

6   Let but goodness and kindness pursue me
              all the days of my life.
       And I shall dwell in the house of the LORD
              for many long days.

---

6. *for many long days.* This concluding phrase catches up the reference to "all the days of my life" in the preceding line. It does not mean "forever"; the viewpoint of the poem is in and of the here and now and is in no way eschatological. The speaker hopes for a happy fate all his born days, and prays for the good fortune to abide in the LORD's sanctuary—a place of security and harmony with the divine—all, or perhaps at least most, of those days.

24

A David psalm.
>The LORD's is the earth and its fullness, 1
>>The world and the dwellers within it.
>For He on the seas did found it, 2
>>and on the torrents set it firm.
>Who shall go up on the mount of the LORD, 3
>>and who shall stand up in His holy place?

---

1. *The LORD's is the earth and its fullness.* The cosmological proclamation of this and the next verse looks like an editorial introduction to the structure of question and response that makes up the rest of the psalm.

2. *For He on the seas did found it.* This is one of many psalms that invoke the creation story—harking back to Canaanite mythology—of the deity who establishes the world by subduing the threatening power of the sea and setting a firm limit between land and sea.

3. *Who shall go up on the mount of the LORD.* These questions and responses, as scholarship has long recognized, are liturgical in nature. (Compare the parallel questions in Psalm 15.) One can easily imagine a procession of pilgrims ascending the temple mount while a chorus chants these questions, perhaps with an antiphonal response.

4   The clean of hands and the pure of heart,
                who has given no oath in a lie
                        and has sworn not in deceit.
5   He shall bear blessing from the LORD
                and bounty from his rescuing God.
6   This is the generation of His seekers,
                those who search out your presence, Jacob.   selah
7   Lift up your heads, O gates,
                and rise up, eternal portals,
                        that the king of glory may enter.
8   Who is the king of glory?
                The LORD, most potent and valiant,
                        The LORD Who is valiant in battle.

---

4. *given no oath in a lie.* The Masoretic text reads *nafshi*, which would yield the literal meaning of "has not borne My self [name?] in a lie." Several manuscripts, however, read *nafsho*, "his self," to "bear oneself" meaning to take an oath. There is really no place in this question-and-response structure for God's speaking in the first person.

7. *Lift up your heads, O gates.* Scholarly consensus views verses 7–10 as an originally separate poem. It is formally linked with the previous poem by the liturgical questions and responses, but now the questions are directed not to the moral fitness of worshippers coming up the temple mountain but rather to the identity of the king of glory who is entering the gates of the temple. Many scholars have proposed that this second set of questions refers to a different procession, in which the Ark of the Covenant is brought into the temple. If in fact the Ark was sometimes carried out to the battlefield, as it is in the early chapters of 1 Samuel, that would provide a special motivation for the reference here to God as a warrior.

Lift up your heads, O gates,   9
          and lift up, eternal portals,
                    that the king of glory may enter.
Who is he, the king of glory?   10
          The LORD of armies, He is the king of glory.   selah

---

9. *Lift up your heads, O gates, / and lift up, eternal portals.* In a manner appropriate to the liturgical occasion, as a refrain the language of the two preceding verses is repeated almost verbatim. (It is in keeping with the original biblical occasion of this psalm that later Jewish tradition should have adopted it to be sung when the Torah scroll is about to be returned to the Ark and carried around the congregation.) There is one small variation in the repetition here: The verb "lift up," *se'u*, is identical in both halves of the line, whereas in verse 7 it is used in two different conjugations (*se'u* and *hinas'u*).

10. *Who is he, the king of glory? / The LORD of armies, He is the king of glory.* In this repetition of verse 8, the pronoun "he" (*hu'*) is added for climactic emphasis, whereas "the LORD of armies" is a kind of generalizing substitution for "most potent and valiant . . . valiant in battle." Whether or not this second part of the psalm was framed to celebrate a ceremonial bearing of the Ark into the temple, it clearly envisages a triumphant return of YHWH as warrior god to His terrestrial abode. Many psalms sound this military note: The temple within the lofty walled city of Jerusalem is not only the cultic place where Israel is joined with God through harmonious worship but also the citadel from which Israel prevails against its enemies.

25

¹ For David.
> To You, O L<small>ORD</small>, I lift my heart.

א
ב

² > > My God, in You I trust. Let me be not shamed,
> > > let my enemies not gloat over me.

ג

³ > Yes, let all who hope in You be not shamed.
> > Let the treacherous be shamed, empty-handed.

ד

⁴ > Your ways, O L<small>ORD</small>, inform me,
> > Your paths, instruct me.

This is one of nine alphabetical acrostics in the Book of Psalms, a form used elsewhere in biblical poetry only in Lamentations. The acrostic may have been favored by psalmists as an aid to memory because of the liturgical use of their texts. The sixth letter of the alphabet, *waw*, is missing here, as is the nineteenth letter, *qof*.

1. *I lift my heart.* The Hebrew noun used is *nefesh*, meaning "essential self" or "life breath." The clear meaning of the idiom is to pray fervently or plead.

3. *be not shamed . . . be shamed.* In the Hebrew, the positive and negative use of the verb trace a perfect chiasm, because the first verset ends with *yeivoshu*, "be shamed," or "know shame," and the second verset begins with the same word.

4. *inform me . . . instruct me.* Though the genre of this psalm is a supplication, instead of the usual central emphasis on the acute distress of the speaker (of which there are some strong expressions in the poem), this text stresses the speaker's sense of having erred (verse 7) and his desire for guidance from God about the way he should follow.

ה   Lead me in Your truth and instruct me,   5
               for You are the God of my rescue.
                    In You do I hope every day.

ז   Recall Your mercies, O LORD,   6
           and your kindnesses—they are forever.

ח   My youth's offenses and my crimes recall not.   7
           In Your kindness, recall me—You;
                 for the sake of Your goodness, O LORD.

ט   Good and upright is the LORD.   8
           Therefore He guides offenders on the way.

י   He leads the lowly in justice   9
           and teaches the lowly His way.

כ   All the LORD's paths are kindness and truth   10
           for the keepers of His pact and His precepts.

ל   For the sake of Your name, O LORD,   11
           may You forgive my crime, which is great.

מ   Whosoever the man who fears the LORD,   12
           He will guide him in the way he should choose.

נ   His life will repose in bounty,   13
           and his seed will inherit the earth.

---

7. *recall me—You.* This startling juxtaposition of "me" (*li*) and "You" (*'atah*) is striking in the Hebrew, which otherwise would not idiomatically require the introduction of the second-person pronoun after the imperative verb.

8. *He guides offenders on the way.* The poet may be playing with the etymology of *hata'im* "offenders," which suggests missing the target and hence, by implication, straying from the right way. The word for "guide," *yoreh*, could also be a pun on "shoot," as Rabbi Israel Stein has suggested to me.

13. *His life will repose in bounty.* The subject of this sentence is the ubiquitous *nefesh*, life or essential self. The orientation of vision is toward existence in the here and now. He who fears God will go to sleep each night (the verb *talin*, "repose") enjoying the good things of this world, and his offspring will have a secure inheritance.

14	The Lord's counsel is for those who fear Him, and His pact He makes known to them.	ס
15	My eyes at all times to the Lord, for He draws my feet from the net.	ע
16	Turn to me and grant me grace, for alone and afflicted am I.	פ
17	The distress of my heart has grown great. From my straits bring me out.	צ
18	See my affliction and suffering and forgive all my offenses.	ר
19	See my enemies who are many and with outrageous hatred despise me.	ר
20	Guard my life and save me. Let me be not shamed, for I shelter in You.	ש
21	May uprightness, wholeness, preserve me, for in You do I hope.	ת

15. *for He draws my feet from the net.* The metaphor, frequently used in Psalms, is taken from the nets used to trap birds and small game.

18. *See my affliction and suffering.* This verse and the next one begin with the letter *resh*. It is a plausible scholarly conjecture that instead of the verb *re'eh* ("see") at the head of the verse as we have it, there was originally another verb, beginning with the missing letter *qof* (perhaps *qeshov*, "hearken to").

20. *Let me be not shamed.* The repetition, just before the end, of this phrase from verse 2 marks an envelope structure—a form, as we have seen, that is abundantly used in Psalms.

21. *uprightness, wholeness.* The King James Version's "uprightness and integrity" is a good literal rendering of the Hebrew *tom-wayosher* but is unfortunately arhythmic. Because *tom* and *yosher* are synonyms, the two terms combined may in any case be a hendiadys—two nouns bracketed to convey a single concept—yielding the sense here of "absolute integrity."

Redeem, God, Israel from all its straits.   22

---

22. *Redeem, God, Israel from all its straits.* This concluding verse lacks poetic parallelism and does not scan as a line of poetry. The national theme, moreover, has until this point not been evident in the psalm, which is spoken from the perspective of an individual. For both these reasons, one suspects that the verse was added by an editor as a conclusion from a repertory of stock verses.

26

1   For David.
    Judge me, O Lord.
            For I have walked in my wholeness,
                And the Lord I have trusted.
                    I shall not stumble.
2   Test me, O Lord, and try me.
            Burn pure my conscience and my heart.
3   For Your kindness is before my eyes
        and I shall walk in Your truth.

---

1. *Judge me, O Lord.* Although the explicit mention of thanksgiving, *todah*, in verse 7 has led some interpreters to classify this as a thanksgiving psalm, it is rather a profession of innocence. The speaker expresses his readiness to withstand God's searching gaze into his innermost parts (verse 2) in the confident knowledge that he has lived an upright life (verses 3–5) and hence is fit to celebrate God in His sanctuary (verses 6–8).

For I have walked in my wholeness / . . . I shall not stumble. The simple, and conventional, metaphor of walking secure is beautifully expressive in this poem. It is picked up at the end, again in an envelope structure, when the speaker proclaims, "My foot stands on level ground."

2. *my conscience.* As elsewhere, the literal sense of the Hebrew is "kidneys," thought to be the seat of conscience.

3. *kindness . . . truth.* This is a clear instance of what some biblical scholars call a breakup pattern. The phrase "kindness and truth" *ḥesed-we'emet*, meaning something like "steadfast kindness," is split between the two versets, standing as bookends at the beginning and end of the line.

I have not sat with lying folk   4
               nor with furtive men have dealt.
I despised the assembly of evildoers,   5
               nor with the wicked have I sat.
Let me wash my palms in cleanness   6
               and go round Your altar, LORD,
to utter aloud a thanksgiving   7
               and to recount all Your wonders.
LORD, I love the abode of Your house   8
               and the place where Your glory dwells.
Do not take my life's breath with offenders   9
               nor with blood-guilty men my life,
in whose hands there are plots,   10
               their right hand full of bribes.
But I shall walk in my wholeness.   11
               Redeem me, grant me grace.

---

4. *I have not sat with lying folk.* The avoidance of the company of the wicked articulated in this verse and the next one stands in implicit contrast to enjoying the company of the righteous in the temple ceremony. These two verses approximately correspond to the profession of innocence at the beginning of Psalm 1.

6. *Let me wash my palms in cleanness, / and go round Your altar,* LORD. Some scholars have conjectured that these words were the text of a temple ceremony in which the celebrant proclaimed his innocence, ritually washing his hands while he marched around the altar. Although the existence of such a ritual is a distinct possibility, one wonders whether the whole conjecture might be an instance of what A. N. Whitehead, in a very different context, called "misplaced concreteness." Washing the palms could simply be an apt metaphor for innocence.

9–10. *blood-guilty men . . . / in whose hands there are plots.* The "lying folk" and "evildoers" referred to in general terms earlier in the poem are now given criminal specificity: they are murderers, schemers, and bribe takers. The speaker has done well to keep a distance from them.

12   My foot stands on level ground.
              In the chorus I bless the LORD.

---

12. *In the chorus I bless the* LORD. As a concrete expression of the sweetness of being able to stand in the place where God's glory dwells, the speaker at the conclusion of the psalm praises God among the many singers (in the Hebrew, "chorus" is in the plural) taking part in the joyous temple rite.

27

For David.
1
    The LORD is my light and my rescue.
              Whom should I fear?
    The LORD is my life's stronghold.
              Of whom should I be afraid?
    When evildoers draw near me to eat my flesh—
              my foes and my enemies are they—
                    they trip and they fall.
    Though a camp is marshaled against me,
              my heart shall not fear.
    Though battle is roused against me,
              nonetheless do I trust.

---

1. *The* LORD *is my light and my rescue. / Whom should I fear?* This psalm is a supplication in which, as elsewhere, a speaker in great distress implores God to intervene on his behalf. The distinction of emphasis is that the poem begins with a confident affirmation of God as the source of help under all grave threats. This positive note is continued through verses 2 and 3, 5 and 6, and, most extravagantly, in verse 10. But this sense of trust, in a psalm that manifests powerful psychological verisimilitude, does not preclude a feeling of fearful urgency in the speaker's plea to God (see verses 9 and 13).

3. *Though a camp is marshaled . . . / Though battle is roused.* It is not entirely clear whether the speaker is literally under assault by armed enemies seeking to kill him or whether the martial imagery is a metaphor for other kinds of hostility. In verse 12, at any rate, the voracious foes attempt to destroy him by underhanded judicial proceedings rather than military means.

4   One thing do I ask of the LORD,
                    it is this that I seek—
     that I dwell in the house of the LORD
                    all the days of my life,
     to behold the LORD's sweetness
                    and to gaze on His palace.
5   For He hides me in His shelter
                    on the day of evil.
     He conceals me in the recess of His tent,
                    on a rock He raises me up.
6   And now my head rises
                    over my enemies around me:

---

4. *One thing do I ask of the* LORD. In a casual glance, this verse may look like a non sequitur: the speaker, having expressed his firm confidence in God as his rescuer in distress, suddenly declares that his most cherished desire is to spend all his time in the temple. But, as we have seen in other psalms, the privilege of enjoying God's presence in the Jerusalem sanctuary is a consequence of having followed the ways that God dictates to man. And the temple itself, within the walled city, is repeatedly seen as a sanctuary in the political sense—a place of secure refuge from threatening foes. There is, then, a logical link between this verse and the next one, in which God provides a shelter and a safe hiding place.

to gaze on. The precise meaning of the verb *baqer* is in dispute, but the cognate noun *biqoret*, used in Leviticus 19:20 in the sense of "observation," suggests it may mean here to take in with the eyes, to enjoy the sight of.

5. *shelter . . . tent.* The two nouns are drawn from the lexicon of nomadic habitation, but here they are used in subtle metaphorical understatement as designations for a much more solid and imposing structure, as the third term in the sequence, "rock," suggests.

5–6. *He raises me up.* / *And now my head rises.* The Hebrew plays on the same verbal stem in two different conjugations—*yeromemeini*, then *yarum*—and the translation seeks to approximate that effect.

Let me offer in His tent
> sacrifices with joyous shouts.
>> Let me sing and hymn to the LORD.
Hear, O LORD, my voice when I call,   7
> and grant me grace and answer me.
Of You, my heart said: 8
> "Seek My face."
>> Your face, LORD, I do seek.
Do not hide Your face from me,   9
> do not turn Your servant away in wrath.
You are my help.
> Abandon me not, nor forsake me,
> O God of my rescue.
Though my father and mother forsook me,   10
> the LORD would gather me in.

---

6. *in His tent.* Here the metaphorical use of "tent" to indicate temple is perfectly clear.

9. *Do not hide Your face from me.* "Face" suggests "presence," but the anthropomorphic concreteness of "face" is palpable. The speaker desperately seeks God's face (a privilege denied Moses). The practical manifestation of God's turning away His face would be abandoning the person to his enemies.

10. *Though my father and mother forsook me, / the LORD would gather me in.* The extravagance of this declaration of trust in God, perhaps the most extreme in the whole Bible, is breathtaking and perhaps even disturbing. In the best of circumstance, the most unconditional, unstinting love and care we experience are from a mother and father. We can imagine, the psalmist says, circumstances in which even that love might fail, but God will be both father and mother to him in the most dire straits.

11   Teach me, O Lord, Your way,
              and lead me on a level path
                    because of my adversaries.
12   Do not put me in the maw of my foes.
              For false witnesses rose against me,
                  outrageous deposers.
13   If I but trust to see the Lord's goodness,
              in the land of the living—
14   Hope for the Lord!
              Let your heart be firm and bold,
                  and hope for the Lord.

---

11. *my adversaries.* This term for enemy, *shorerim* (sometimes *shorim*), appears half a dozen times in Psalms and nowhere else in the biblical corpus. It may be derived from a verbal root that means "to watch" (as enemies gleefully watch one's humiliation). It certainly plays on a more common word for "foes," *tsorerim* (or, as in the next verse here, *tsarim*).

12. *the maw of my foes.* Here *nefesh*, "life breath," shows a secondary meaning, through metonymy—the throat or gullet, through which breath passes.

13. *If I but trust.* This sentence, at least in the textual form passed down to us, seems to be an ellipsis.

14. *Hope for the Lord! / Let your heart be firm and bold.* This last exhortation—whether of the speaker to himself or to an individual member of his audience—is an apt summary of the psychology that informs this psalm. It begins by affirming trust in God and reiterates that hopeful confidence, but the trust has to be asserted against the terrors of being overwhelmed by implacable enemies.

28

For David.
1
    To You, O Lᴏʀᴅ, I call.
                My Rock, do not be deaf to me.
    Lest You be mute to me
              and I be like those gone down to the Pit.
    Hear the sound of my pleading
2
              when I cry out to You,
    when I lift up my hands
              to Your holy shrine.

---

1. *do not be deaf . . . / Lest You be mute.* The Hebrew uses a pun, the first verb being *teḥerash* and the second *teḥesheh.* (Some interpreters actually understand *teḥerash* as "to be silent.") To follow the logic of the punning language, should God turn a deaf ear to the supplicant, He will not answer the supplicant's prayer and hence will be "mute." In an associative logic, the supplicant himself will then perish, becoming forever silent like all the legions of the dead and hence incapable of imploring God or praising him. In this psalm he does both, because, as elsewhere, the supplication turns into a thanksgiving psalm from verse 6 to the end.

2. *when I lift up my hands.* This is, of course, a gesture of prayer, abundantly attested to in a variety of ancient Near Eastern texts and drawings.

3   Do not pull me down with the wicked,
            and with the wrongdoers,
    who speak peace to their fellows
            with foulness in their heart.
4   Pay them back for their acts
            and for the evil of their schemings.
    Their handiwork give them back in kind.
            Pay back what is coming to them.
5   For they understand not the acts of the LORD
            and His handiwork they would destroy and not build.
6   Blessed is the LORD
            for He has heard the sound of my pleading.
7   The LORD is my strength and my shield.
            In Him my heart trusts.
    I was helped and my heart rejoiced,
            and with my song I acclaim Him.

---

3. *who speak peace to their fellows / with foulness in their heart.* The transition between the end of the first verset and the beginning of the second is marked in the Hebrew by a pun: *re'eihem* ("their fellows") and *ra'ah* (literally, "evil"). The translation choice of fellows / foulness is an attempt to replicate this effect.

4. *schemings.* The Hebrew *ma'alalim* is a synonym for "acts," but with a negative connotation.

6. *Blessed is the* LORD */ for He has heard the sound of my pleading.* This line strongly marks the turning point of the poem: the imploring "Hear the sound of my pleading" (verse 2) is now an accomplished fact.

7. *with my song I acclaim Him.* Here the speaker completes the expected gesture of the thanksgiving psalm, announcing that he is giving thanks to God in song.

The LORD is His people's strength   8
        and His anointed's stronghold of rescue.
Rescue Your people   9
        and bless Your estate.
           Tend them, bear them up for all time.

---

8. *The* LORD *is His people's strength.* The Masoretic text reads, "The LORD is their strength," which is puzzling, because there is no obvious antecedent to "their." But the Septuagint, the Peshitta, and some manuscripts show "his people's strength." In the consonantal Hebrew text, this is a difference of just one letter, an added *ʿayin* that an ancient scribe might easily have dropped in copying. This reading then makes a neat parallelism with the second verset.

His anointed's stronghold. The national-political perspective of this entire line was not evident earlier in the poem. Either it is an editorially introduced ending drawn from a repertory of stock phrases used for codas, or the speaker imagines a seamless continuity between divine intervention to aid the individual and the nation.

9. *Tend them, bear them up.* The first of these two verbs is the one used for a shepherd's looking after his flock. It is likely, then, that the second verb, "bear" or "lift up" (the same word used for the hands in prayer in verse 2) also refers to a pastoral context—the act of a shepherd bearing a lamb in his arms.

29

1   A David psalm.
    Grant to the LORD, O sons of God,
            grant to the LORD glory and strength!

---

1. *O sons of God.* This is the first clue of many that have led a whole line of scholars (H. L. Ginsberg, Moshe Held, Mitchell Dahood, Theodore Gaster) to see this psalm as a translation or close adaptation of a Canaanite psalm. It has been variously claimed that in the original text, it was Baal as thunder-god, not YHWH, who imposed his awesome voice over the whole world. None of these arguments is entirely convincing. Though there are parallels to certain wordings here in Ugaritic poetry (the one cache of Syro-Palestinian poetry, several centuries prior to the Bible, that has physically survived), that scarcely proves that this poem is a translation. The same is true of the proposed linguistic and prosodic evidence (too technical to take up here) that has been put forth to support the same claim. Canaanite poetry was the literary tradition that constituted the most immediate background for biblical poetry. It would be surprising if the biblical poets did not make use of images, phrasing, and even mythological elements from the antecedent tradition with which they and their audience were acquainted. The relation of this psalm, and a good many others, to the Syro-Palestinian tradition is roughly like that of *Paradise Lost* to the *Aeneid* and the *Iliad*. Virgil and Homer gave Milton a model, and a repertory of devices and *topoi*, with which he could frame a cosmic epic from his own monotheistic perspective, but he was not merely "transposing" the pagan epic poets into English. As to the address to the "sons of God" at the beginning of the psalm, it should be noted that these celestial creatures appear not infrequently elsewhere in the Bible (here they are *beney 'elim*; more commonly, they appear as *beney 'elohim*). They are best thought of as the flickering literary afterlife of a polytheistic mythology—God's royal entourage on high, His *famalia*, as Rashi called them, invoking a Latin term that had entered Hebrew during the time of the

Grant to the LORD His name's glory.   2
        Bow to the LORD in holy majesty!
The LORD's voice is over the waters.   3
        The God of glory thunders.
            The LORD is over the mighty waters.
The LORD's voice in power,   4
        the LORD's voice in majesty,
the LORD's voice breaking cedars,   5
        the LORD shatters the Lebanon cedars,

Roman empire. Literal belief in them may have survived in popular religion but is unlikely to have been shared by the scribal circles that produced *Psalms*.

Grant to the LORD. The verb for "grant" or "give," *y-h-b*, is a relatively rare synonym (though the standard term in Aramaic) for the more common *n-t-n*. Perhaps it may actually have been called out in its imperative form, *havu*, as here, on ceremonial occasions, having something of the effect of "hail!" The use of the whole phrase at the beginning of the psalm in a pattern of incremental repetition may be evidence of the antiquity of the poem because incremental repetition is a device favored in the oldest stratum of biblical poetry (as, notably, in the Song of Deborah, which might date back as far as 1100 BCE).

3. *The LORD's voice is over the waters.* Though the image is a naturalistic one of thunder—often imagined by the Hebrew poets as God's voice—rumbling over the sea, the line registers a recollection of old Canaanite myths, in which creation is effected through the conquest of a primordial sea monster by the god who rules the land. In the incremental repetition here, the phrase "the mighty waters" has an especially mythological resonance in the Hebrew.

5. *the Lebanon cedars.* Throughout biblical poetry, these trees are the great emblem of proud loftiness. An excessive literalism has led some interpreters to see the mention of the northern mountains of Lebanon and Syria as evidence of a Syrian provenance for the poem. These name places appear equally in the late and distinctly un-Canaanite Song of Songs. Lebanon is not only a place of towering forests but also the northern border of Israel. In verse 8, God's thunder rakes the Wilderness of Kadesh, presumably in the eastern half of the Sinai, so the poet imagines God's power sweeping over the whole land of Israel and beyond from north to south.

6   and He makes Lebanon dance like a calf,
                Sirion like a young wild ox.
7   The LORD's voice hews flames of fire.
8   The LORD's voice makes the wilderness shake,
                the LORD makes the Kadesh Wilderness shake.
9   The LORD's voice brings on the birth-pangs of does
                and lays bare the forests.
                        And in His palace all says glory.
10   The LORD was enthroned at the flood
                and the LORD is enthroned as king for all time.

---

8. *makes the wilderness shake, / the LORD makes the Kadesh Wilderness shake.*
These two versets are a textbook illustration of incremental repetition, with the
added element giving the second verset additional specificity, as is generally
true in the use of poetic parallelism in the Bible.

9. *lays bare the forests.* A commonly proposed emendation turns "forests"
(*ye'arot*) into "gazelles" (*ye'alot*) in the interests of neat parallelism. But then the
verb "lay bare" would have to have something to do with calving, a meaning not
otherwise attested. It is certainly possible to imagine the fearsome assault of
lightning and thunder triggering birth pangs and also devastating the forests.
    And in His palace all says glory. It is probably a mistake to translate *heikhalo*
as "His temple" rather than "His palace," because the context suggests God's
celestial palace, where, while the earth roils in the storm below, everything
bespeaks God's glory. The awesome power manifested on earth in thunder and
lightning is celebrated ceremoniously on high in the divine palace populated by
angelic or quasi-divine courtiers.

10. *The LORD was enthroned at the flood.* The mention of the primordial Flood
is not only a measure of the eternity of God's reign but also of His supreme
dominion over the forces of nature. It is, of course, in a storm that the poet has
imagined God's power in this psalm.

May the LORD give strength to His people.   11
    May the LORD bless His people with peace.

---

11. *May the* LORD *give strength to His people.* Whether or not this line is a stock coda added by an editor, it does pick up a verbal motif from the beginning, as Israeli scholar Yitzhak Avishur has noted. The psalm starts with a verb meaning "to give" or "to grant," an act to be directed from the divine entourage to God, and concludes with the more common synonym for the act of giving, now directed from God to Israel.

30

1 Psalm, song for the dedication of the house, for David.
2   I shall exalt You, LORD, for You drew me up,
          and You gave no joy to my enemies.
3   LORD, my God,
          I cried to You and You healed me.
4   LORD, You brought me up from Sheol,
          gave me life from those gone down to the Pit.
5   Hymn to the LORD, O his faithful,
          acclaim his holy name.

---

1. *song for the dedication of the house.* The consensus of traditional interpreters is that the reference is to the temple (the literal sense of the Hebrew for temple is "house of the sanctuary"), or to a renovated altar or some other structure within it. Some scholars, noting the somewhat odd syntax of the superscription with "psalm" (*mizmor*) separated from "for David" (*leDawid*), suspect that this entire phrase is an editorial interpolation not originally belonging to the psalm.

2. *for You drew me up.* The Hebrew verb *daloh* is the one used for drawing water from a well. Death, then, is imagined as a deep pit from which the speaker has been drawn up by God. In this fashion, at its beginning the poem announces itself as a thanksgiving psalm.

4. *from those gone down to the Pit.* The Masoretic text uses a form that does not correspond to biblical grammar, *miyordi*, which would mean "from my going down." Several ancient versions, however, show *miyordey*, "from those gone down," which is not only grammatical but highlights the idea that the speaker felt he had gone down to death, yet of all who go down there, he alone was raised up.

But a moment in His wrath, 6
      life in His pleasure.
At evening one beds down weeping,
      and in the morning, glad song.
As for me, I thought in my quiet days, 7
      "Never will I stumble."
LORD, in your pleasure You made me stand mountain-strong. 8
      —When You hid Your face, I was stricken.
To You, O LORD, I call, 9
      and to the Master I plead.
"What profit in my blood, 10
      in my going down deathward?
Will dust acclaim You,
      will it tell Your truth?"

---

6. *At evening one beds down weeping, / and in the morning, glad song.* This upbeat vision of life has, of course, been manifested in the recent experience of the speaker.

8. *You made me stand mountain-strong.* The translation is only an educated guess, because the sequence of words in the Hebrew (not the meaning of the individual words) is perplexing. Literally, it would be: You-made-stand my-mountain-of-strength (or, simply, mountain-of-strength). The translation accords with the understanding of Rashi and ibn Ezra.

9. *To You, O LORD, I call.* These words, through to the end of verse 11, appear to be self-quotation: the speaker, now rescued from death, recalls the words of desperate supplication that he addressed to God from his straits.

10. *What profit in my blood, / in my going down deathward?* Here the poet sounds, with powerful compactness, the recurrent theme shared by the psalms of thanksgiving and supplication: man cannot fulfill his vocation of celebrating God if he is engulfed by death. It is living human beings whom God needs to sing His praises. It looks as though the giving of praise to God is imagined as a replacement of the pagan idea in which the sacrifices were thought of as food necessary to the gods.

11 Hear, LORD, and grant me grace.
            LORD, become helper to me.
12 You have turned my dirge to a dance for me,
            undone my sackcloth and bound me with joy.
13 O, let my heart hymn You and be not still,
            LORD, my God, for all time I acclaim You.

---

12. *undone my sackcloth and bound me with joy.* The general synecdoches for
mourning and rejoicing, dirge and dance, of the first verset are focused concretely through the metaphor of clothing in the parallel second verset: The
garment of mourning is undone, or removed, and joy becomes the new garment that God pulls tight or binds (verbal stem '-z-r) around the person He
has rescued.

13. *O, let my heart hymn You.* This translation, following one ancient Greek version, reads *keveidi*, "my liver" ("heart" being the viable English substitution)
instead of *kavod*, "glory." Like many other thanksgiving psalms, this one exhibits
an envelope structure, beginning and ending with the declaration that the
speaker will exalt God for His mercies granted.

Love the Lord, all his faithful,   24
          steadfastness the Lord keeps
                    and pays back in good measure the haughty
                    in acts.
Be strong, and let your heart be firm,   25
          all who hope in the Lord.

---

24. *steadfastness.* A general pattern of biblical noun formations argues that this
term, *'emunim,* is an abstract noun and does not refer—as many translations
have it—to a group of people ("the loyal" or "the steadfast").
   the haughty in acts. Literally, "who does haughtiness."

32

1   A David *maskil*.
    Happy, of sin forgiven,
          absolved of offense.
2   Happy, the man to whom
          the Lord reckons no crime,
              in whose spirit is no deceit.
3   When I was silent, my limbs were worn out—
          when I roared all day long.

---

1. **maskil.** This is clearly a category of song, but its precise nature remains unknown. From the word's use in Amos 5:13, it would appear to be a joyous song, though not all the occurrences in Psalms substantiate that connotation. In this particular psalm, there may also be a punning reference to a homonym that means "discerning person" or "giver of instruction." The word translated as "let me teach you" in verse 8 employs the same root. Hermann Gunkel noted that this psalm contains distinct Wisdom elements, especially from verse 8 onward. As to genre, though it has sometimes been described as a thanksgiving psalm, it is really more of a confession in the perfect tense: the speaker admits he has transgressed, affirms that he has confessed his transgression, and that as a result God has granted him forgiveness.

of sin forgiven, / absolved of offense. The speaker at the outset presents himself through two passive verbs as the object of forgiveness.

3. *When I was silent, my limbs were worn out— / when I roared all day long.* Attempts to resolve the contradiction between silence and roaring here have been unavailing. The text looks suspect. Especially because the second verset is abbreviated, one may guess that a phrase has been dropped out that would have formed a complementary parallelism, such as, "when I roared all day long, my body was wasted."

For day and night   4
       Your hand was heavy upon me.
              My sap turned to summer dust.   selah
My offense I made known to You   5
       and my crime I did not cover.
I said, "I shall confess my sins to the LORD,"
       and You forgave my offending crime.   selah
[For this every faithful man prays to You in time of need: 6
only that the rush of mighty waters should not reach him.]
You are a shelter for me.   7
       From the foe You keep me,
          with glad songs of deliverance
           surround me.   selah
Let me teach you, instruct you the way you should go.   8
       Let me counsel you with my own sight.

---

4. *summer dust.* The Hebrew uses a plural abstraction, impossible in English, that would literally be "summer parchednesses."

6. *For this every faithful man.* It would be misleading to set this verse as poetry because it does not scan and has no true parallelism. One suspects a sentence from another text was introduced through scribal inadvertence. The brackets are meant to indicate that this verse is not part of the poem.

7. *From the foe You keep me.* This may be merely a conventional phrase, for no foes appear earlier in the psalm.
    glad songs of deliverance. The Hebrew *roney palet* looks odd. The first of the two nouns would seem to be a plural (occurring nowhere else) of *ron*, "glad song."

8. *Let me teach you.* After the second selah, an entirely new movement in the poem (or another poem?) begins, in which the speaker, like the figure of the mentor in Proverbs, enjoins the person who listens to heed his counsel.
    with my own sight. This rendering, like all others for this phrase, is no more than an interpretive guess. The Hebrew says literally, "Let me counsel you my eye," which is not a biblical idiom.

9   Be not like a horse, like a mule, without sense,
             the bit and the reins his adornment—
                  to keep him from drawing near you.

10   Many are the wicked's pains,
             but who trusts in the LORD kindness surrounds him.

11   Rejoice in the LORD and exult, O you righteous,
             sing gladly, all upright men!

---

9. *the bit and the reins his adornment— / to keep him from drawing near you.* This is another cryptic moment in the text. The Masoretic text breaks the line after "reins," which makes no clear sense. Perhaps the idea is that the bit and reins, which may seem an ornament, are actually put on the uncomprehending beast simply in order to guide him away from running into people.

33

Sing gladly, O righteous, of the LORD,   1
      for the upright, praise is befitting.
Acclaim the LORD with the lyre,   2
      with the ten-stringed lute hymn to Him.
Sing Him a new song,   3
      play deftly with joyous shout.
For the word of the LORD is upright,   4
      and all His doings in good faith.
He loves the right and the just.   5
      The LORD's kindness fills the earth.

---

1. *Sing, gladly, O righteous.* Hermann Gunkel long ago plausibly identified this psalm as a hymn. The setting is choral; the form of address is collective; and the perspective, in contrast to the individual thanksgiving psalm, is both global and national. The emphasis on music through the first three verses suggests a public performance of the psalm with orchestra and chorus.

3. *Sing Him a new song.* This phrase is, in a sense, the composer's self-advertisement: God is to be celebrated not with a stock item from the psalmodic repertoire but with a freshly composed piece.

    play deftly. This stipulation is surely an indication that the new song must be presented in a technically skilled performance.

6   By the word of the LORD the heavens were made,
          and by the breath of His mouth all their array.

7   He gathers like a mound the sea's waters,
          puts in treasure houses the deeps.

8   All the earth fears the LORD,
          all the world's dwellers dread Him.

9   For He did speak and it came to be,
          He commanded, and it stood.

---

6. *By the word of the* LORD *the heavens were made.* The poet, developing a cue he has introduced at the end of the previous line—"the LORD's kindness fills the earth"—takes us back to the creation story in Genesis 1, for which he offers a kind of poetic interpretation. "Earth" and "heaven" are terms often paired in parallel versets of poetry as well as key terms in the creation story. God's word as the agent of creation is, of course, a recasting of the narrative in Genesis 1, in which God speaks the world into existence.

   by the breath of His mouth. Ostensibly a synonym for "the word of the LORD," this phrase also catches up the image in Genesis of God's breath hovering over the primordial waters.

   all their array. The "heavens and all their array," referring to the stars, is still another phrase borrowed from the first creation story.

7. *He gathers like a mound the sea's waters.* This is a punning double allusion: It recalls God's dividing dry land from water in the creation story and at the same time picks up an image from the dividing of the waters in the Song of the Sea— "streams stood up like a mound" (Exodus 15:8). Both this text and the one in Exodus use the relatively rare noun *ned* for "mound."

   puts in treasure houses the deeps. This psalm shares with Job the mythological image of God's stocking the elemental forces of nature in cosmic caches or storehouses (*'otsarot*).

9. *For He did speak and it came to be, / He commanded, and it stood.* This entire line again picks up the notion from Genesis 1 that God created the world through a series of speech-acts. This was an idea particularly favored by the Priestly writers, the literary circle that at some midpoint in the First Temple period produced the creation story of Genesis 1, a variety of passages that occur later in Genesis, and most of Leviticus.

The LORD thwarted the counsel of nations,   10
      overturned the devisings of peoples.
The LORD's counsel will stand forever,   11
      His heart's devisings for all generations.
Happy the nation whose god is the LORD,   12
      the people He chose as estate for Him.
From the heavens the LORD looked down,   13
      saw all the human creatures.
From His firm throne He surveyed   14
      all who dwell on the earth.
He fashions their heart one and all.   15
      He understands all their doings.
The king is not rescued through surfeit of might,   16
      the warrior not saved through surfeit of power.
The horse is a lie for rescue,   17
      and in his surfeit of might he helps none escape.

---

11. *The LORD's counsel will stand forever.* This line makes an obvious but effective antithesis to the previous line, in which the LORD thwarts the counsel of nations.

13. *From the heavens the LORD looked down, / saw all the human creatures.* The viewpoint of this poem manages to be at once national ("the people He chose as estate for Him") and universalist: The God of creation surveys the deeds of men and women throughout the world.

15. *one and all.* This is the idiomatic force of *yaḥad,* which elsewhere, and invariably in post-biblical Hebrew, means "together."

16. *surfeit of might, / . . . surfeit of power.* The impotence of any material power a human being can command stands in vivid contrast to God's overwhelming power, expressed in the preceding lines, over all the earth. It is noteworthy, moreover, that God is seen in this poem creating the world not through sheer force but through speech—not with a big bang but in a series of carefully measured words.

18   Look, the L<small>ORD</small>'s eye is on those who fear Him,
             on those who yearn for His kindness

19   to save their lives from death
             and in famine to keep them alive.

20   We urgently wait for the L<small>ORD</small>.
             Our help and our shield is He.

21   For in Him our heart rejoices,
             for in His holy name do we trust.

22   May Your kindness, O L<small>ORD</small>, be upon us,
             as we have yearned for You.

---

20. *We urgently wait.* The adverb "urgently" is added to suggest the force of emphasis achieved in the Hebrew through the use of *nafsheinu*—"our life breath," "our very selves"—as an intensive form of the first-person-plural pronoun.

34

For David, when he altered his good sense before Abimelech,   1
who banished him, and he went away.

א   Let me bless the Lord at all times,   2
         always His praise in my mouth.

---

1. *when he altered his good sense before Abimelech*. The superscription refers
directly to 1 Samuel 21:14, where David, surrounded before the city of Gath by
the Philistine king and his men, saves himself by playing the madman. The
same unusual idiom for feigning madness, "altered his good sense" (*shanot 'et
ta'amo*), is used in Samuel. But the Philistine king there is not Abimelech (who
appears in Genesis 20) but Achish. This may be a confusion on the part of the
editor, though Rashi and other medieval commentators try to save the text by
arguing that Abimelech was a hereditary royal title, not a proper name. Why did
the editor detect a link between our psalm and this incident in the David story?
In all likelihood, the connection he saw was the psalm's emphasis on God's rescuing power, even when the just man is threatened with imminent death by his
enemies. Particularly pertinent are these lines near the end of the poem: "Many
the evils of the righteous man, / yet from all of them the Lord will save him. //
He guards all his bones, / not a single one is broken." And perhaps the image
in 1 Samuel 21 of the future king of Israel rolling in the dirt and drooling over
his beard may have been called to the editor's mind by "Near is the Lord to the
broken-hearted, / and the crushed in spirit He rescues."

2. *Let me bless*. The first Hebrew word, *'avarakha*, beginning with an *'aleph*, signals the start of an alphabetical acrostic. Only the sixth letter, *waw*, is missing.
The psalm ends, as does the acrostic in Psalm 25, with a wrap-up verse that
begins with the verb *padah*, "ransom."

3	In the LORD do I glory. Let the lowly hear and rejoice.	ב
4	Extol the LORD with me, let us exalt His name one and all.	ג
5	I sought the LORD and He answered me, and from all that I dreaded He saved me.	ד
6	They looked to Him and they beamed, and their faces were no longer dark.	ה
7	When the lowly calls, God listens and from all his straits rescues him.	ז
8	The LORD's messenger encamps round those who fear Him and sets them free.	ח
9	Taste and see that the LORD is good, happy the man who shelters in Him.	ט
10	Fear the LORD, O His holy ones, for those who fear Him know no want.	י

---

3. *do I glory.* Although this is the proper sense of the verb *hithalel*, it also plays etymologically with the noun for "praise," *tehilah*, which appears in the previous line.

8. *The LORD's messenger encamps.* The idea that God sends a divine emissary to accompany man, guide him, protect him, and, in some instances, scrutinize his actions, is common in biblical literature, with instances occurring as early as Genesis and Exodus. When Abraham dispatches his servant to Mesopotamia to find a bride for Isaac, the servant is persuaded that the LORD's messenger has come along with him to show him the right way.

9. *Taste and see that the LORD is good.* The sensory concreteness of the verb is somewhat startling, perhaps intended to suggest the powerful immediacy of experiencing God's beneficence. It also probably puns on the same root—*t-ʿ-m*—used as a noun in the superscription with the meaning "good sense." If the pun is significant, "tasting" may also mean using good sense.

כ	Lions are wretched, and hunger,	11
	but the LORD's seekers lack no good.	
ל	Come, sons, listen to me,	12
	the LORD's fear will I teach you.	
מ	Whoever the man desiring life,	13
	who loves long days to see good,	
נ	keep your tongue from evil	14
	and your lips from speaking deceit.	
ס	Swerve from evil and do good,	15
	seek peace and pursue it.	
ע	The LORD's eyes are on the righteous	16
	and His ears to their outcry.	
פ	The LORD's face is against evildoers,	17
	to cut off from the earth their name.	
צ	Cry out and the LORD hears,	18
	and from all their straits He saves them.	

---

11. *Lions are wretched, and hunger, / but the LORD's seekers lack no good.* There is a certain smoothness—indeed, a kind of patness—in the formulation of this line and, in fact, in most of the lines of this poem. The language is more formulaic than elsewhere, and the moral calculus invoked is itself a kind of pious formula. All this gives this psalm a measured, choreographed dignity (it is not surprising that this text has been incorporated into the Sabbath morning liturgy). But the expression of God's unwavering protection of the just and His punishment of the wicked is precisely the view against which the Job poet will rebel so vehemently.

12. *Come, sons, listen to me.* This introductory phrase and what follows in the next few verses have a distinct coloration of Wisdom literature.

19   Near is the LORD to the broken-hearted,   ק
              and the crushed in spirit He rescues.
20   Many the evils of the righteous man,   ר
              yet from all of them the LORD will save him.
21   He guards all his bones,   ש
              not a single one is broken.
22   Evil will kill the wicked,   ת
              and the righteous man's foes will bear guilt.
23   The LORD ransoms His servants' lives,
              they will bear no guilt, all who shelter in Him.

---

19. *Near is the LORD to the broken-hearted / and the crushed in spirit He rescues.*
If one is inclined to argue with Job that this psalm puts forth a view of the
implementation of divine justice that disintegrates in the harsh crucible of
experience, the poet nevertheless succeeds, at moments like this, in articulat-
ing a moving vision of hope for the desperate. Part of the spiritual greatness of
Psalms, part of the source of its enduring appeal through the ages, is that it pro-
foundly recognizes the bleakness, the dark terrors, the long nights of despair
that shadow most lives, and, against all this, evokes the notion of a caring presence that can reach out to the broken-hearted.

35

For David.

Take my part, Lord, against my contesters,

        fight those who fight against me.

Steady the shield and the buckler,

        and rise up to my help.

Unsheathe the spear to the haft

        against my pursuers.

Let them be shamed and disgraced,

        who seek my life.

Let them retreat, be abased,

        who plot harm against me.

1

2

3

4

---

1. *Take my part, Lord, against my contesters.* These initial words announce the psalm's status as a supplication. Although military imagery is used in verses 1–4, the Hebrew term for "contesters," *yerivim*, is related to *riv*, a legal disputation. The references to false witnesses and baffling legal interrogations in verse 11 strongly suggest that these implacable enemies are attempting to destroy the supplicant in a trumped-up legal case, with the military imagery being strictly metaphorical.

3. *haft.* The Hebrew *segor* means etymologically "closing" or "seal." But in one of the Qumran scrolls, it has the sense of the join between spear and handle, so "haft" seems a legitimate approximation.

5   Let them be like chaff before the wind,
                with the LORD's messenger driving.
6   May their way be darkness and slippery paths,
                with the LORD's messenger chasing them.
7   For unprovoked they set their net-trap for me,
                unprovoked they dug a pit for my life.
8   Let disaster come upon him unwitting
                    and the net that he set entrap him.
                        May he fall into it in disaster.
9   But I shall exult in the LORD.
                    shall be glad in His rescue.
10   All my bones say,
                    "LORD, who is like You?
        Saving the poor from one stronger than he
                    and the poor and the needy from his despoiler."
11   Outrageous witnesses rose,
                    of things I knew not they asked me.
12   They paid me back evil for good—
                    bereavement for my very self.

---

5. *with the LORD's messenger driving.* This is a neat instance of how the second
verset is used in biblical poetry to intensify and specify an idea put forth in the
first verset. Wind blowing chaff of course scatters it (as in Psalm 1), but this
wind is driven by an agent of divine judgment. Similarly in the next line, it is
risky to make one's way in the dark on a slippery road, but how much more so
when the nocturnal pedestrian is on the run, pursued by God's messenger.

8. *Let disaster come upon him.* In a common idiomatic procedure, the poet slips
from referring to the plural enemies of the supplicant to a single figure who is
presumably representative of them all.
    May he fall into it in disaster. Though the wording sounds odd, the poet has
clearly gone out of his way to build a small envelope structure in this verse, with
"disaster" at the beginning and at the end syntactically surrounding the enemy.

And I, when they were ill, my garment was sackcloth,   13
        I afflicted myself with fasting.
                May my own prayer come back to my bosom.
As for a friend, for a brother,   14
          I went about as though mourning a mother,
            in gloom I was bent.
Yet when I limped, they rejoiced, and they gathered,   15
        they gathered against me,
like strangers, and I did not know.
          Their mouths gaped and they were not still.

---

13. *And I, when they were ill, my garment was sackcloth.* This profession of innocence has a certain Job-like quality. Not only, the speaker says, did he harbor no ill intention toward his persecutors, but when they themselves were in distress, he went into mourning to plead for their recovery.

May my own prayer come back to my bosom. This clause is somewhat cryptic. The least strained interpretation is that the speaker wishes the prayer he once uttered for the restoration of these people who then persecuted him would now be fulfilled for himself. The problem is that the clause appears to be set in the time now past when the speaker was mourning for his supposed friends.

15. *like strangers.* The Masoretic text has *nekhim*, "lame people," which makes no sense. The Syriac version has *kenokhrim*, "like strangers," which nicely catches the idea of purported friends acting hostilely. It is possible that a scribe mistook *nokhrim* for *nekhim* because of the reference to limping at the beginning of the line.

Their mouths gaped. As the next clause and the following verse indicate, this is an image of mouths open to pronounce derisive speech, though there is also a suggestion, picked up later in the psalm (verse 25), of swallowing the hapless object of persecution. The Hebrew shows only the verb *qarʿu*, "they tore open," which can be applied to opening the eyes wide. Here, by the suggestion of context, it may refer to an elided "mouth."

16   With contemptuous mocking chatter
          they gnashed their teeth against me.

17   O Master, how long will You see it?
          Bring back my life from their violence,
             from the lions, my very being.

18   I shall acclaim You in a great assembly,
          in a vast crowd I shall praise You.

19   Let not my unprovoked enemies rejoice over me,
          let my wanton foes not leer.

20   For they do not speak peace
          and against the earth's quiet ones plot words of deceit.

21   They open their mouths wide against me.
          They say, "Hurrah! Hurrah! Our eyes have seen it."

22   You, LORD, have seen, do not be mute.
          My Master, do not keep far from me.

23   Rouse Yourself, wake for my cause,
          my God and my Master, for my quarrel.

24   Judge me by Your justice, LORD my God,
          and let them not rejoice over me.

---

16. *contemptuous mocking chatter.* This translation follows a proposal of the medieval Hebrew commentator David Kimchi that the enigmatic noun *ma'og* is related to the Talmudic *'ugah*, which means "empty talk."

18. *I shall acclaim You in a great assembly.* The reference, as in similar locutions elsewhere, is to pronouncing words of thanksgiving in the temple rite.

22. *You, LORD, have seen.* God's just and omniscient seeing is, of course, neatly contrasted with the evildoers' seeing the desperate plight of their foe and gloating.

23. *my cause . . . my quarrel.* The "quarrel" (*riv*) looks back to the *yerivim* of the beginning of the poem, but the term here has an explicitly legal meaning as it is paired with "cause" (*mishpat*).

Let them not say in their heart,
                "Hurrah for ourselves."
                        Let them not say, "We devoured him."   25
Let them be shamed and abased one and all,   26
                who rejoice in my harm.
Let them don shame and disgrace,
                who vaunted over me.
May they sing glad and rejoice,   27
                who desire justice for me,
and may they always say,
                "Great is the LORD
                        Who desires His servant's well-being"
and my tongue will murmur Your justice,   28
                all day long Your praise.

---

26. *Let them be . . . abased . . . / . . . don shame and disgrace.* This line picks up
a cluster of terms used at the beginning of the poem as the psalm rounds out
toward its conclusion.

27. *May they sing glad and rejoice, / who desire justice for me.* It is important to
note that this is a drama that has four groups of players: God, the supplicant,
his enemies, and his supporters. To be viciously pursued by legal means is an
isolating experience, and Job, who feels he has been condemned without ever
having his day in court, repeatedly complains of his withering isolation. The
speaker of this poem, on the other hand, can imagine at the end a whole crowd
of people who support him and want justice for him; and so he invokes a blessing upon them that is syntactically parallel and thematically antithetical to the
curse he has pronounced on his persecutors.

28. *and my tongue will murmur Your justice.* Thus at the very end, the speaker,
praising God's justice, places himself in a community of the upright who celebrate the presence of the divine order in the lives of humankind.

36

1 For the lead player, for the LORD's servant, for David.
2 Crime's utterance to the wicked
                within his heart:
    "There is no fear of God
                before my eyes."
3 For it caressed him with its eyes
                to find his sin of hatred.
4 The words of his mouth are mischief, deceit,
                he ceased to grasp things, to do good.

---

2. *Crime's utterance to the wicked.* The beginning of this psalm adopts an anomalous rhetorical device. "Crime," as a personified figure, is presented speaking its pernicious speech within the heart of the wicked person. The Masoretic text reads "my heart," which has made interpreters strain to imagine a quasi-prophetic speaker who claims to know what Crime says inwardly to the wicked. More plausibly, a couple of ancient versions read "his heart." In any case, this odd beginning also makes the genre of the psalm difficult to identify. It is not a supplication, but it puts into play the supplication's characteristic contrast between the upright and the evil and also its confidence in God's overarching justice. The translation emends "his eyes" at the end to "my eyes."

3. *For it caressed him with its eyes.* This line continues the personification of Crime, suggesting its seductive power (though the verb here could be construed differently than this translation does). Perhaps "eyes" is deliberately repeated to play against the eyes of the wicked mentioned in the previous verse.

Mischief he plots in his bed,   5
      takes his stand on a way of no good,
          evil he does not despise.
LORD, in the heavens, Your kindness,   6
      and Your faithfulness to the skies.
Your justice like the unending mountains,   7
      Your judgment, the great abyss,
          man and beast the LORD rescues.
How dear is Your kindness, O God,   8
      and the sons of men in Your wings' shadow shelter.
They take their fill from the fare of Your house   9
      and from Your stream of delights You give them drink.
For with You is the fountain of life.   10
      In Your light we shall see light.
Draw down Your kindness to those who know You,   11
      and Your justice to the upright.
Let no haughty foot overtake me,   12
      nor the hand of the wicked repel me.

---

5. *Mischief he plots in his bed, / takes his stand on a way of no good.* The wicked man is the antithetical parallel of the good Israelite enjoined in Deuteronomy to speak God's words when he lies down and when he gets up and when he goes on his way.

7. *like the unending mountains.* The Hebrew, *harerey 'el*, might also be construed as "mountains of God," but most interpreters conclude that *'el* here is a suffix of intensification, yielding something like "the mighty mountains" or "the unending mountains" and thus constituting a cosmic complement to "the great abyss" at the end of the parallel verset.

9. *the fare of Your house / . . . Your stream of delights.* God's unwavering regimen of justice for humankind is experienced in the language of the poem as concrete sensual pleasure. The drinking imagery continues with "the fountain of life" in the next line. The Hebrew for "delights" is *'adanim*, and so it may allude to the streams of Eden.

13   There did the doers of mischief fall.
                    They were toppled and could not rise.

---

13. *There did the doers of mischief fall.* Initially, the use of the deictic "there" is puzzling, but it has an emotional rightness. The poem that began with an intimate recording of the wicked man's malicious speech ends with a confounding of the wicked. But this defeat of the wicked happens at a distance, in the past, in a place from which the speaker is happily removed.

37

For David.

  א   Do not be incensed by evildoers.   1
                  Do not envy those who do wrong.
       For like grass they will quickly wither   2
               and like green grass they will fade.
  ב   Trust in the Lord and do good.   3
               Dwell in the land and keep faith.

---

1. *Do not be incensed by evildoers.* The form of this psalm is an alphabetical acrostic, with the letter ʿ*ayin* missing. (The Septuagint reflects a Hebrew version in which there appears to have been a line, in verse 28, beginning with ʿ*ayin*.) Two lines of verse are assigned to each letter of the alphabet, which explains why this acrostic is twice as long as the previous acrostics in the collection of psalms. This is emphatically a Wisdom psalm, expressing in a variety of more or less formulaic ways the idea that the wicked, however they may seem to prosper, will get their just deserts and the righteous will be duly rewarded. The distinctive note in all this is a plea for equanimity: The good person is enjoined not to get stirred up by the seeming success of the wicked. The verb used at the beginning (repeated later in the psalm) is one that derives etymologically from a root that means "to heat up."

2. *For like grass they will quickly wither.* This simile is a stock image in biblical poetry. It is especially concrete for someone living in the climate of the Near East, where, after the rainy season ends in late spring, there is great heat and no precipitation, so that everything green becomes parched and quickly withers.

3. *keep faith.* The literal sense is "shepherd [or "chase"] trust."

4   Take pleasure in the LORD,
      that He grant you your heart's desire.

5   Direct your way to the LORD.   ג
      Trust Him and He will act,

6   and He will bring forth your cause like the light,
      and your justice like high noon.

7   Be still before the LORD and await Him.   ד
      Do not be incensed by him who prospers,
        by the man who devises schemes.

8   Let go of wrath and forsake rage.   ה
      Do not be incensed to do evil.

9   For evildoers will be cut off,
      but those who hope in the LORD, they shall inherit
      the earth.

10 And very soon, the wicked will be no more.   ו
      You will look at his place—he'll be gone.

11 And the poor shall inherit the earth
      and take pleasure from great well-being.

12 The wicked lays plots for the just   ז
      and gnashes his teeth against him.

13 The Master will laugh at him,
      for He sees that his day will come.

14 A sword have the wicked unsheathed   ח
      and drawn taut their bow,
  to take down the poor and the needy,
      to slaughter those on the straight way.

15 Their sword shall come home in their heart
      and their bows shall be broken.

---

8. *Let go of wrath and forsake rage.* The plea for equanimity in the face of the success of the wicked is especially pronounced here.

ט   Better a little for the just   16
             than wicked men's great profusion.
      For the wicked's arms shall be broken,   17
             but the Lord sustains the just.

י   The Lord embraces the fate of the blameless,   18
             and their estate shall be forever.
      They shall not be shamed in an evil time   19
             and in days of famine they shall eat their fill.

כ   For the wicked shall perish, and the foes of the Lord,   20
             like the meadows' green—gone, in smoke, gone.

ל   The wicked man borrows and will not pay,   21
             but the just gives free of charge.
      For those He blesses inherit the earth   22
             and those He curses are cut off.

מ   By the Lord a man's strides are made firm,   23
             and his way He desires.
      Though he fall, he will not be flung down,   24
             for the Lord sustains his hand.

---

16. *Better a little for the just / than the wicked men's great profusion.* This line of verse takes the explicit form of a didactic proverb ("Better *x* than *y*") and thus clearly reflects the Wisdom character of the psalm.

18. *embraces.* Literally, "knows," a verb sometimes used sexually that implies intimate knowledge and affection as much as cognition.

20. *like the meadows' green—gone, in smoke, gone.* "Meadows' green" (*yeqar karim*) might be a metaphor (literally, "meadows' splendor") for grass, though this translation prefers to see in *yeqar* ("splendor") a simple reversal of consonants for *yeraq*, "green." Some interpreters understand *karim* as its homonym, "sheep," and so imagine that "sheep's splendor" refers to the fat of the animal burned "in smoke" on the altar, but that reading seems rather strained. The entire verset in the Hebrew is notable for its alliteration and assonance—*kiqar karim kalu be'ashan kalu*—and the translation seeks to approximate that effect.

25   A lad I was, and now I am old,
                and I never have seen a just man forsaken
                        and his seed seeking bread,
26   all day long lending free of charge
                and his seed for a blessing.
27   Turn from evil and do good
                and abide forever.
28   For the LORD loves justice
                and will not forsake His faithful.
        They are guarded forever,
                but the seed of the wicked is cut off.
29   The just will inherit the earth
                and abide forever upon it.
30   The just man's mouth utters wisdom
                and his tongue speaks justice.
31   His God's teaching in his heart—
                his steps will not stumble.
32   The wicked spies out the just man
                and seeks to put him to death.
33   The LORD will not forsake him in his hands
                and will not condemn him when he is judged.

---

25. *A lad I was, and now I am old, / and I never have seen a just man forsaken.* The beauty of this line in part explains its presence in Jewish liturgy at the end of the grace after meals, but the questionable moral calculus behind it is precisely what Job argues against so trenchantly. The only way to sustain the idea that no just person is ever in want is to assume that a needy person must somehow be unjust, whatever the appearances to the contrary. This is the very conclusion that Job's friends draw about him: If he is sorely afflicted, he must have done something terribly wrong to deserve it. The Job poet challenges this received wisdom and proposes a more complicated, indeed paradoxical, moral vision.

28. *His faithful / . . . are guarded forever, / but the seed of the wicked is cut off.* This psalm, with its heavy reliance on proverbial wisdom, tends to a good deal of repetitiousness in its formulations.

ק   Hope for the Lord and keep His way   34
       and He will exalt you to inherit the earth;
       you will see the wicked cut off.

ר   I have seen an arrogant wicked man   35
       taking root like a flourishing plant.
      He passes on, and, look, he is gone,   36
       I seek him, and he is not found.

ש   Watch the blameless, look to the upright,   37
       for the man of peace has a future.
      And transgressors one and all are destroyed,   38
       the future of the wicked cut off.

ת   The rescue of the just is from the Lord,   39
       their stronghold in time of distress.
      And the Lord will help them and free them,   40
       He will free them from the wicked and rescue them,
       for they have sheltered in Him.

---

35. *I have seen an arrogant wicked man / taking root like a flourishing plant.* This line picks up the image from the beginning of the poem of the ephemerality of the triumph of evil as the transience of green growing things. It participates in the exhortation to the listener not to be perturbed by the seeming success of the wicked, for this success will soon be reversed.

40. *And the Lord will help them.* The concluding line of the psalm is triadic, instead of the dyadic pattern of the preceding lines. This is a formal device often used in biblical poetry to mark closure or transition.

38

1   A David psalm, to call to mind.
2   LORD, do not rebuke me in Your fury
            nor chastise me in Your wrath.
3   For Your arrows have come down upon me,
            and upon me has come down Your hand.
4   There is no whole place in my flesh through Your rage,
            no soundness in my limbs through my offense.

---

1. *to call to mind.* The Hebrew infinitive *lehazkir* is anomalous in the super-scription of a psalm, appearing here and at the beginning of Psalm 70. It may simply refer to the speaker's intention to bring to mind his suffering in his supplication to God. It might also have a connotation of confession: Compare the words of Pharaoh's chief cupbearer in Genesis 41:9, "My offenses I recall [*mazkir*] today," and those of the widow from Tsorfath to Elijah in 1 Kings 17:18, "You have come to me to call to mind [*lehazkir*] my crime."

2. LORD, *do not rebuke me in Your fury,* / *nor chastise me in Your wrath.* This line, with its symmetrical parallelism, is formulaic in supplications.

3. *Your arrows . . . come down . . . / . . . come down Your hand.* The line takes the form of a neat chiasm (ab͞b͞a), which this translation reproduces.

4. *There is no whole place in my flesh through Your rage.* In most of the Bible, as elsewhere in the ancient Near East, illness was understood to be a punishment by the deity, presumably for some transgression, whether deliberate or unwitting. This psalm goes on to evoke the physical symptoms—festering sores, inward burning, numbness, bodily contortion, dizziness—as well as the social rejection that accompanies the illness.

For my crimes have welled over my head,   5
     like a heavy burden, too heavy for me.
My sores make a stench, have festered   6
     through my folly.
I am twisted, I am all bent.   7
     All day long I go about gloomy.
For my innards are filled with burning   8
     and there is no whole place in my flesh.
I grow numb and am utterly crushed.   9
     I roar from my heart's churning.
O Master, before You is all my desire   10
     and my sighs are not hidden from You.
My heart spins around, my strength forsakes me,   11
     and the light of my eyes, too, is gone from me.
My friends and companions stand off from my plight   12
     and my kinsmen stand far away.
They lay snares, who seek my life and want my harm.   13
     They speak lies, deceit utter all day long.
But like the deaf I do not hear,   14
     and like the mute whose mouth will not open.

---

5. *my crimes have welled over my head.* Literally, "my crimes have passed over my head." The probable implied image is of drowning, abundantly used elsewhere in Psalms. Perhaps the "burden" in the second verset suggests a crushing weight of water bearing down on the head.

13. *They . . . who seek my life.* This sprawling line does not scan in the Hebrew, and the same is true of the English version.

14. *like the deaf I do not hear.* The speaker has already said he was going blind in his illness (verse 11). Here, however, he turns an infirmity to advantage: Whether or not he is literally losing his hearing, he is able in the figurative sense to turn a deaf ear to his mocking enemies and concentrate all his expectant attention on God. Evidently, the situation evoked in this psalm is roughly analogous to that of Job. The man has suffered some terrible illness, including

15 And I become like a man who does not hear
            and has no rebuke in his mouth.
16 For in You, O Lord, I have hoped.
            You will answer, O Master, my God.
17 For I thought, "Lest they rejoice over me,
            when my foot slips, vaunt over me."
18 For I am ripe for stumbling
            and my pain is before me always.
19 For my crime I shall tell,
            I dread my offense.
20 And my wanton enemies grow many,
            my unprovoked foes abound.
21 And those who pay back good with evil
            thwart me for pursuing good.
22 Do not forsake me, Lord.
            My God, do not stay far from me.
23 Hasten to my help,
            O Master of my rescue.

---

repellent malodorous sores visible all over his body. As a result, his friends have kept their distance from him, and others have chosen to revile him.

20. *my wanton enemies.* The Masoretic text reads ʾoyvay ḥayim, literally, "my enemies of life," which some construe as "my mortal enemies," though it is not a biblical idiom as it is worded here. A scroll of Psalms found at Qumran reads ʾoyvay ḥinam, "my wanton enemies" (that is, "enemies for no good reason"), which is nicely idiomatic and makes the parallelism in the two versets here exactly that of 35:19 (where *sheqer* appears in the first verset and *ḥinam* in the second, rather than the other way around as here).

22. *Do not forsake me . . . / . . . do not stay far from me.* This strictly formulaic line just before the end of the psalm is a counterpart to the formulaic line at the beginning.

39

For the lead player, for Jeduthun. A David psalm.   1
   I thought, "Let me keep my ways from offending with my tongue.   2
        Let me keep a muzzle on my mouth
            as long as the wicked is before me."

---

1. *for Jeduthun*. This name appears among the lists of Levite choristers in 1 Chronicles 16:42. It is not entirely certain, however, that this is a proper name here. Some interpreters have conjectured that it might be a musical term.

2. *I thought, "Let me keep my ways from offending with my tongue."* There are elements of the psalm, here at the beginning and later on (see, for example, verse 11, "Take away from me Your scourge") that identify it as a supplication. But the poem takes the distinctive form of a haunting meditation on the ephemerality of human life. Some of the ideas and formulations seem like an anticipation of Ecclesiastes (most notably, the reiterated term *hevel*, "breath," as an image of man's insubstantiality). Other lines sound like Job ("mere handspans You made my days," "You . . . melt like the moth his treasure").
   as long as the wicked is before me. The predominant form of the line in biblical poetry is dyadic—that is, consisting of two parallel members or versets. This poem is unusual in that triadic lines predominate. Each of the first six lines of poetry has three members. The first dyadic line appears when the speaker in a transition summons up his expectations of God (verse 8). The poem returns to triadic lines in verses 12 and 13. This preference for the triadic is a formal expression of a powerful psychological tension: Whereas the dyadic line encourages balance and symmetry, the addition of a third verset is often used to introduce an element of surprise or to destabilize what has gone before it. Here, after the two parallel versets announcing the resolution to be silent, we discover in the third verset, which is a subordinate clause, that this resolution has been taken in the presence of the wicked and caused by that presence.

3   I was mute—in silence.
         I kept still, deprived of good,
              and my pain was grievous.
4   My heart was hot within me.
         In my thoughts a fire burned.
              I spoke with my tongue:
5   Let me know, O Lord, my end
         and what is the measure of my days.
              I would know how fleeting I am.
6   Look, mere handspans You made my days,
         and my lot is as nothing before You.
              Mere breath is each man standing.   selah

---

3. *I kept still, deprived of good.* The Hebrew is *mitov,* literally, "from good," and the translation risks the assumption that the initial *mem* is a *mem* of deprivation.

and my pain was grievous. The third verset introduces a hitherto unannounced datum—the suffering of the speaker.

4. *I spoke with my tongue.* After two parallel versets expressing acute pain, speech bursts out in the destabilizing third verset—the very thing that the speaker had meant to forswear.

6. *mere handspans . . . / as nothing . . . / Mere breath.* Like the Job poet, who so powerfully expresses the fleeting nature of human existence, this psalmist calls on a rich vocabulary of synonyms for ephemerality. The middle term here, "nothing" (*'ayin*), is what human transience must ultimately come to, and it is precisely the word (in a declined form, first person singular) with which the poem ends.

my lot. The Hebrew *ḥeldi* (undeclined form *ḥeled*), which elsewhere means something like "the existing world," is an obvious play on *ḥadel,* "fleeting," in the previous line.

Mere breath is each man standing. The term "standing" (*nitsav*) is enigmatic in context. The possible meaning (assuming that the text is correct) is that though a man seems to stand firm and tall, he is mere breath.

In but shadow a man goes about.   7
      Mere breath he murmurs—he stores
          and knows not who will gather.
And now, what I expect, O Master,   8
      my hope is in You.
From all my sins save me.   9
      Make me not the scoundrel's scorn.
I was mute, my mouth did not open,   10
      for it is You who acted.
Take away from me Your scourge,   11
      from the blow of Your hand I perish.
In rebuke for crime You chastise a man,   12
      melt like the moth his treasure.
          Mere breath all humankind.   selah

---

7. *he stores / and knows not who will gather.* This is an especially Ecclesiastian note. The literal sense of the last word of the line in the Hebrew is "gather them," "them" evidently referring to the things a man stores.

9. *Make me not the scoundrel's scorn.* This could mean do not make me the butt of the scoundrel who would mock me for my suffering, or do not make me an object of scorn as though I were a scoundrel.

13   Hear my prayer, O LORD,
                to my cry hearken,
                        to my tears be not deaf.
        For I am a sojourner with You,
                a new settler like all my fathers.
14   Look away from me, that I may catch my breath
                before I depart and am not.

---

13. *to my tears be not deaf.* This is an interesting use of the third verset in a tri-adic line. The first two versets are strictly parallel in meaning: Hear / hearken my prayer / my cry. "Tears" (in the singular in the Hebrew) is of course a metonymy for weeping, but in itself a tear is mute, unlike the prayer and the cry. God here is entreated in a negative formulation, not to hear but rather to be not deaf.

For I am a sojourner . . . / a new settler. This line is a striking instance of the so-called breakup pattern, in which a hendiadys ("sojourner and settler," meaning "resident alien") is split up with each of the component terms set into one of the two parallel versets. The procedure becomes a way of doubling and emphasizing the term for resident alien, thus underscoring the idea of transience associated with it. "New" has been added to "settler" (*toshav*) in the translation to convey the notion of impermanence clearly implied in the Hebrew idiom.

14. *Look away from me, that I may catch my breath.* The entire line sounds distinctly Jobean, and one wonders whether the Job poet (who in all probability wrote at a moment after the composition of this psalm) may have quoted our text. See Job 10:20–21: "Let me alone so I may catch my breath // before I go on my way, not to return, / into a land of darkness and deathgloom" (translation by Raymond Scheindlin). I follow Scheindlin in rendering the disputed verb *'avli-gah* as "catch my breath." It should also be noted that the verb *ḥ-d-l* (to be fleeting, to come to an end, to stop), which is central to this psalm, appears in the passage from Job in the verset immediately before the first one quoted here.

and am not. The finality of death that darkens the consciousness of the speaker throughout the poem figures climactically in the single Hebrew word for extinction, *we'eyneni*, with which the poem concludes.

40

For the lead player, for David, a psalm.   1
  I urgently hoped for the Lᴏʀᴅ.   2
          He bent down toward me and heard my voice,
  and He brought me up from the roiling pit,   3
          from the thickest mire.
  And He set my feet on a crag,
          made my steps firm.
  And He put in my mouth a new song—   4
          praise to our God.
  May many see and fear
          and trust in the Lᴏʀᴅ.

---

2. *He bent down toward me and heard my voice.* Generically, this psalm is a
hybrid. These opening words, signaling a prayer already answered, are the gesture of a thanksgiving psalm. Verses 13–18 are the urgent plea of a psalm of supplication. In verses 7–11, the speaker assumes a stance resembling that of the
prophets. Indeed, the idea that God wants not sacrifices but truth and adherence to His teaching (verses 7 and 8) is reminiscent of certain famous passages
in Isaiah and Micah.

3. *the roiling pit.* Literally, "the pit of noise." Most interpreters conclude that
the noise is the rushing sound of the confluent waters of the abyss.
  the thickest mire. The Hebrew is *tit hayawen*. On the assumption that the
obscure *yawen* is a synonym of *tit*, which clearly means "mud" or "mire," the
conjunction of two synonyms in construct form would indicate a superlative or
an intensification of meaning.

5   Happy the man who puts
                in the LORD his trust
   and does not turn to the sea monster gods
                and to false idols.

6   Many things You have done—You,
                O LORD our God—Your wonders!
   And Your plans for us—
                none can match You,
   I would tell and I would speak:
                they are too numerous to recount.

7   Sacrifice and grain-offering You do not desire.
                You opened ears for me:
                        for burnt-offering and offense-offering You do
                        not ask.

8   Then did I think: Look, I come
                with the scroll of the book written for me.

---

5. *the sea monster gods.* The noun *rahav* (here in plural form) is one of the designations of the primordial sea beast of Canaanite mythology.

   false idols. The noun here, *satey*, is anomalous, and the common claim that it means "those who turn [to falsehood]" rests on scant philological evidence. This translation, strictly on the basis of the poetic parallel with *rehavim*, "sea monster gods," conjectures that the reference is to false gods or idols.

7. *You opened ears for me.* The phrase literally means, "You dug open ears for [or, to]"—that is, vouchsafed me a new acute power of listening to the divine truth. In later Hebrew, this idiom *karah 'ozen* comes to mean "listen attentively." It is also possible to construe this—because "ears" is not declined in the possessive—as God's listening attentively to the speaker.

   offense-offering. This is the "sin-offering" of the traditional translations.

8. *I come / with the scroll of the book written for me.* Some claim that the book is the book of the Torah, which spells out what God requires of man. It is equally possible, however, that this scroll of the book is a kind of personal-prophetic emblem, a miniature vision of how God dictates His will to the speaker.

To do what pleases You, my God, I desire,   9
    and Your teaching is deep within me.
I heralded justice in a great assembly.   10
    Look, I will not seal my lips.
        LORD, You Yourself know.
Your justice I concealed not in my heart.   11
    Your faithfulness and Your rescue I spoke.
        I withheld not from the great assembly Your
    steadfast truth.
You, LORD, will not hold back   12
    Your mercies from me.
Your steadfast truth
    shall always guard me.
For evils drew round me   13
    beyond count.
My crimes overtook me
    and I could not see—
more numerous than the hairs of my head—
    and my heart forsook me.
Show favor, O LORD, to save me.   14
    LORD, to my help, hasten.
May they be shamed and abased one and all,   15
    who seek my life to destroy it,
may they fall back and be disgraced,
    who desire my harm.

---

9. *deep within me.* Literally, "within my bowels."

13. *crimes overtook me . . . / more numerous than the hairs of my head.* There is a counterpoint between God's wonders, too numerous to count, and the speaker's misdeeds, so numerous that they literally overwhelm him, blind him, make him lose heart. In both instances, the same verb for being numerous, ʿ*atsmu*, is used in the same form.

16   Let them be devastated on the heels of their shame,
              who say of me, "Hurrah! Hurrah!"
17   Let all who seek You
              exult and rejoice in You.
    May they always say, "God is great!"—
              those who love Your rescue.
18   As for me, I am lowly and needy.
              May the Master account it for me.
    My help, he who frees me You are.
              My God, do not delay.

---

18. *As for me, I am lowly and needy.* The speaker, having just conjured up an image of God's rejoicing celebrants who proclaim His greatness, suddenly remembers that he himself is in a far more unhappy condition, miserable and needy, desperately requiring God's help.

May the Master account it for me. The root ḥashav means to plan or to devise (as in verse 6), or to account, to take into consideration. Those who opt for the former meaning here are obliged to imagine a merely implied object of the verb, such as "deliverance," "rescue." Without such strain, one can understand this clause, logically consequent to the preceding clause, to mean: may God take into account my desperate plight of neediness and hasten to my rescue.

41

To the lead player. A David psalm.   1
  Happy who looks to the poor.   2
        On the day of evil may the Lord make him safe.
  May the Lord guard him and keep him alive.   3
      May he be called happy in the land.
        And do not deliver him to his enemies' maw.
  May the Lord sustain him on the couch of pain.   4
      —You transformed his whole bed of illness.
  I said, "Lord, grant me grace,   5
     heal me, though I offended You."

---

2. *Happy who looks to the poor.* The verb *maskil*, which more commonly refers to understanding, also can mean to see or look (as "see" idiomatically in many languages can mean "to understand"). The frequent verb in rabbinic and modern Hebrew, *histakel*, "to look," is derived from the same root.

3. *maw.* More literally, the Hebrew *nefesh* refers to the gullet. In any case, the image is of being swallowed up by the enemy.

4. *You transformed his whole bed of illness.* This switch from verbs in the jussive ("May the Lord sustain him") to a perfect tense marks the transition from the generality of the prayer for the wretched to the actual subject of the psalm—thanksgiving for recovery from a grave illness. It must be said that the Hebrew here sounds awkward: literally, "All his bed You turned over in his illness."

5. *I said.* The speaker now launches on a narrative account of the time in the past when he was ill, beginning with a quotation of the prayer he uttered for healing.

6   My enemies said evil of me:
           "When will he die and his name be lost?"
7   And should one come to visit,
           his heart spoke a lie.
    He gathered up mischief,
           went out, spoke abroad.
8   One and all my foes whispered against me,
           against me plotted my harm:
9   "Some nasty thing is lodged in him.
           As he lies down, he will not rise again."
10   Even my confidant, in whom I did trust,
           who ate my bread,
                was utterly devious with me.
11   And You, O LORD, grant me grace, raise me up,
           that I may pay them back.
12   In this I shall know You desire me—
           that my enemy not trumpet his conquest of me.

---

9. *is lodged in him.* The literal sense of the Hebrew verb is "poured," a term typically used for the pouring of molten metal into a mold.

10. *was utterly devious with me.* The meaning of the Hebrew is not entirely certain. Because *ʿaqev* suggests crookedness but also means "heel" (because of the crook of the heel), the phrase might also mean "showed me his heels," "left me in the lurch."

11. *And You, O LORD, grant me grace.* This verse and the next appear to be another self-quotation of the speaker's plea to God in the time of his illness. The poem is dramatically structured around three brief speeches: the initial supplication from the bed of suffering; the harsh words of *schadenfreude*, spoken by the false friends; and a second supplication, which repeats "grant me grace" and adds to the initial prayer the desire to pay back the gloating enemies.

12. *trumpet his conquest.* The Hebrew verb *yariʿa* means to shout joyously, though in contexts such as this, vocal gloating is clearly implied. The term is also associated with the sound made by trumpets and ram's horns.

And I, in my innocence, You sustained me   13
        and made me stand before You forever.

Blessed is the Lᴏʀᴅ God of Israel   14
        forever and forever,
                amen and amen.

---

14. *Blessed is the* Lᴏʀᴅ . . . / *forever* . . . / *amen and amen.* This verse is not an integral part of the psalm but an editorial flourish to mark the end of the first of the five books (on the model of the Torah) into which the redactors retroactively divided the Book of Psalms.

42

1 To the lead player, a *maskil* for the Korahites.
2   As a deer yearns for streams of water,
                   so I yearn for You, O God.

---

1. maskil. See the comment on this term in 32:1 (page 110). If the *maskil* is generally a joyous song, the joy in this instance is relegated to the hopeful vision of being reunited with God (verses 6 and 12). This psalm is a supplication in which the speaker presents himself as a man beset by mocking enemies and also banished from God's presence in Zion to surrounding territories (verse 7).

2. *As a deer yearns for streams of water, / so I yearn for You, O God.* The poignancy of this famous line reflects the distinctive tone of this supplication, which instead of emphasizing the speaker's suffering expresses above all his passionate longing for God. He addresses his words to God but feels distant from God, at a painful remove from the temple and plagued by enemies. The "I" here is the intensive form of the first-person pronoun, *nafshi*, abundantly used in this psalm, and translated in the next verse as "my whole being" (but not in this verse, to avoid what might sound like an awkward repetition in the English). The verb rendered as "yearns" (*'arag*) appears only twice in the biblical corpus, so the exact meaning is not certain. Some think it may refer to the sound a thirsty deer makes as it drinks, others to the animal's bending its neck toward water.

My whole being thirsts for God,
    for the living God.   3
When shall I come and see
    the presence of God?
My tears became my bread day and night   4
    as they said to me all day long, "Where is your God?"
These do I recall and pour out my heart: 5
    when I would step in the procession,
when I would march to the house of God
    with the sound of glad song of the celebrant throng.
How bent, my being, how you moan for me!   6
    Hope in God, for yet will I acclaim Him
        for His rescuing presence.

---

3. *thirsts for God, / for the living God.* The verb "thirsts" of course carries forward the simile of the deer yearning for streams of water. The phrase "living God" may also continue the water imagery, because "living water" is idiomatic in biblical Hebrew for freshwater.

    and see / the presence of God. Or "and see the face of God." As elsewhere in the Bible when this phrase is used, later editorial tradition, to avoid the anthropomorphism, revocalized the verb so it reads "be seen" [in God's presence]. This psalm is the first one in the second book of Psalms, according to the canonical division, and the editors throughout this book generally use "God" (ʾelohim) instead of "LORD" (YHWH).

4. *My tears became my bread.* Eating salt tears (in the singular in the Hebrew) instead of food carries on the thirst metaphor of the previous two verses.

5. *pour out my heart.* The Hebrew again uses *nafshi,* "my life breath" or "my very self."

    the procession. The meaning of the Hebrew *sakh* is in doubt.

7   My God, my being is bent for my plight.
                Therefore do I recall You from Jordan land,
                    from the Hermons and Mount Mizar.
8   Deep unto deep calls out
                at the sound of Your channels.
                    All Your breakers and waves have surged
                    over me.
9   By day the LORD ordains His kindness
                and by night His song is with me—
                    prayer to the God of my life.

---

7. *for my plight.* The literal meaning of the Hebrew is "on me" or "about me."

from Jordan land, / from the Hermons and Mount Mizar. Though some scholars have sought to link this line with a historical exile of the Judeans, the perspective remains first person singular and the geographical sweep from Jordan in the east to Hermon in the Lebanon region scarcely suggests anything like the Babylonian exile. Anomalously, Mount Hermon appears here as a plural, perhaps because it was the most prominent in a chain of northern mountains. Mount Mizar has not been identified, though the name means Small Mountain.

8. *Deep unto deep calls out.* This could be an associative leap from the heights to the antithetical depths, from the mountains to the sea, unless one chooses to imagine that the "deeps" (or "abysses") are part of the mountainous landscape of Lebanon.

All Your breakers and waves have surged over me. The geological or cosmic "deeps" of the first verset are transformed into a metaphor for the speaker's distress. The experience of threatened drowning is a familiar image for near death in Psalms, but here it is given startling new power through the linkage with a vast creation in which abyss calls to abyss.

9. *by night His song is with me.* There is a fine ambiguity in the phrasing. This could mean that the speaker hears God's song in the nights ("song" thus directly paralleling "kindness" in the first verset). Or the sense could be that the speaker, mindful of God's kindness, responds in the night with song—such as the song of this psalm. There has been cosmic "sound" in the previous line, and perhaps the Hebrew *leqol tsinoreikha*, "at the sound of Your channels," is intended to make us think of *leqol kinoreikha*, "at the sound of Your lyres."

I would say to the God my Rock,   10
          "Why have You forgotten me?
                    Why in gloom do I go, hard pressed by the foe?
With murder in my bones, my enemies revile me   11
          when they say to me all day long, "Where is your God?"
How bent, my being, how you moan for me!   12
               Hope in God, for yet will I acclaim Him,
                         His rescuing presence and my God.

---

11. *With murder in my bones.* This shocking phrase is what the Hebrew actually appears to say. The King James Version, with no warrant, puts a sword in the bones. Others seek to relate the Hebrew noun to a root that means "crush," but in fact the verbal stem *r-ts-ḥ* everywhere means "to murder." It is best to take this as an arresting expression of the imminent threat of death. The speaker can feel the murder that others wish to perpetrate on him in his very bones at the moment his enemies revile him.

12. *How bent, my being.* This repetition of verse 6 as a concluding refrain shows two small changes: the word "my God" (*'elohai*) is climactically added at the very end, and the Masoretic text reads "my presence" (*panai*), which does not make a great deal of sense. Two manuscripts as well as a version of the Aramaic Targum read *panaw*, "His presence." This translation takes that as the probably correct reading.

43

1 Grant me justice, O God,
    take up my case against a faithless nation,
      from a man of deceit and wrong free me.

2 For You, O God, my stronghold,
    why should You neglect me?
      Why should I go in gloom, pressed by the foe?

3 Send forth Your light and Your truth.
    It is they that will guide me.
They will bring me to Your holy mountain
    And to Your dwelling-place.

---

1. *Grant me justice.* This is one of the rare psalms that begins without a super-scription. That fact, taken together with the refrain-like recurrence of whole clauses and lines from Psalm 42 (the third verset of verse 2 here is almost iden-tical with the third verset of verse 10 in Psalm 42; verse 5 here virtually repli-cates verses 6 and 12 of Psalm 42), has led most scholars to conclude that Psalms 42 and 43 were originally a single poem, broken up by editors for rea-sons not entirely clear to us. The opening line here lays out the persecution by enemies evoked in Psalm 42 in explicitly legal terms.

3. *They will bring me to Your holy mountain.* This line of poetry and the two that follow pick up the idea from Psalm 42 that the speaker has been exiled from Zion. In this supplication, which is also a kind of prospective thanksgiving, he longs for the joy of approaching the altar in Jerusalem and celebrating God with song.

And let me come to God's altar,
      to God, my keenest joy.
And let me acclaim You with the lyre,
      O God, my God.
How bent, my being, how you moan for me!
      Hope in God, for yet will I acclaim Him,
         His rescuing presence and my God.

4

5

---

4. *my keenest joy.* The Hebrew is a bracketing in the construct state of two synonyms, *simḥat gili,* "joy of my gladness," which has the idiomatic force of an
intensification or superlative.

   O God, my God. This odd-sounding collocation, *'elohim 'ehohay,* appears
with some frequency in the second book of Psalms because YHWH has been
editorially replaced by *'elohim.*

5. *How bent, my being, how you moan for me!* This repeated sentence takes on
new meaning here at the end, because the bent being stands in contrast to the
celebrant approaching the altar in the previous line, and the low murmuring
sound of complaint contrasts with the song accompanied by the lyre.

   His rescuing presence. Again, as at the end of Psalm 42, the Masoretic text
has "My presence," and, as there, two manuscripts and a version of the Targum
show "His presence."

44

1   For the lead player, for the Korahites, a *maskil*.
2   God, with our own ears we have heard,
                our fathers recounted to us
    a deed that You did in their days,
                in days of yore.
3   You, Your hand dispossessed nations—and You planted them.
                You smashed peoples and sent them away.

---

2. *with our own ears we have heard, / our fathers recounted to us*. The first-person plural at the beginning of the psalm identifies it as a collective supplication. The disaster that has occurred is to the nation, and the psalmist remembers times past when God led the people in triumph.

3. *Your hand dispossessed nations—and You planted them*. The fluidity of biblical Hebrew in pronominal reference is especially evident here. The historical event from "days of yore" referred to is the conquest of the land of Canaan in Joshua's time. Though "nations" is the object of the verb "dispossessed," the next clause is disjunctive because "them" must refer to the people of Israel planted in the land after the Canaanites were driven out (at least in this poetic fiction). "Them" in the same position at the end of the next line refers to the peoples of Canaan. In the line after that, "their" refers once more to Israel.

For not by their sword they took hold of the land,   4
        and it was not their arm that made them victorious
but Your right hand and Your arm,
        and the light of Your face when You favored them.
You are my king, O God.   5
        Ordain the victories of Jacob.
Through You we gore our foes,   6
        through Your name we trample those against us.
For not in my bow do I trust,   7
        and my sword will not make me victorious.
For You rescued us from our foes,   8
        and our enemies You put to shame.
God we praise all day long,   9
        and Your name we acclaim for all time.   selah
Yet You neglected and disgraced us   10
        and did not sally forth in our ranks.
You turned us back from the foe,   11
        and our enemies took their plunder.

---

4. *made them victorious.* The verb *hoshiʿa* (and its cognate noun *yeshuʿah*) can mean "rescue" if the object is a person or group in dire straits (the more common usage in Psalms), or, if the situation is one of straightforward military confrontation, it can mean "make victorious, grant victory." In this psalm, it occurs in both senses. In the present verse, the military sense is required. The context of verse 8 strongly suggests the connotation of "rescue."

10. *Yet You neglected . . . us.* The initial adverbial *ʾaf* here clearly is an indicator of opposition or contradiction. We praised You continually and kept faith with You, yet You allowed our enemies to triumph over us. Which enemies and what historical period are matters of conjecture. Some commentators, without warrant from the text, have wanted to situate this psalm in the second century BCE, under Greek domination; others have put it back somewhere in the first Davidic dynasty. Ancient Israel in all periods had no lack of powerful adversaries, and there is nothing in the language of the poem to enable a confident dating.

12   You made us like sheep to be eaten
               and scattered us through the nations.

13   You sold Your people for no wealth
               and set no high price upon them.

14   You made us a shame to our neighbors,
               derision and mockery to those round us.

15   You made us a byword to nations,
               an object of scorn among peoples.

16   All day long my disgrace is before me,
               and shame has covered my face,

17   from the sound of revilers and cursers,
               from the enemy and the avenger.

18   All this befell us, yet we did not forget You,
               and we did not betray Your pact.

19   Our heart has not failed,
               nor have our footsteps strayed from Your path,

---

14. *You made us a shame to our neighbors.* Repeatedly in Psalms and in the Prophets, the bitterness of defeat is thought to be compounded by a stinging sense of national humiliation, an experience vividly evoked from this verse to the end of verse 17.

15. *an object of scorn.* The literal sense of the Hebrew is "a wagging of the head"—a gesture of contempt.

16. *and shame has covered my face.* The received text reads, "and the shame of my face covered me," but a change of a single consonant in the Hebrew verb for "covered" yields a more plausible idiom, as translated here.

19. *nor have our footsteps strayed from Your path.* The Masoretic text reads, "and You made our footsteps stray from Your path," which makes little sense. An emendation of *watet* ("made stray") to *watiteh* ("strayed" [that is, our footsteps strayed]) resolves the difficulty and produces a neat parallelism with "our heart has not slipped back."

though You thrust us down to the sea monster's place   20
      and with death's darkness covered us over.
Had we forgotten the name of God   21
      and spread out our palms to an alien god,
would not God have fathomed it?   22
      For He knows the heart's secrets.
For Your sake we are killed all day long,   23
      we are counted as sheep for slaughter.
Awake, why sleep, O Master!   24
      Rouse up, neglect not forever.
Why do You hide Your face,   25
      forget our affliction, our oppression?
For our neck is bowed to the dust,   26
      our belly clings to the ground.
Rise as a help to us   27
      and redeem us for the sake of Your kindness.

---

20. *thrust us down to the sea monster's place.* This is another allusion to the Canaanite cosmogonic myth of a primordial sea monster conquered by a divine adversary, then forever imprisoned in the seabed.

23. *we are killed all day long, / we are counted as sheep for slaughter.* The insistence of images such as this in the psalm leads one to conclude that the military defeat here is no metaphor but reflects an actual historical situation in which the people of Israel suffered devastation at the hands of an armed enemy.

26. *our neck is bowed to the dust.* The context strongly suggests that the multivalent *nefesh* in this instance is used in its anatomical sense, the neck or throat, in tight parallelism with the belly crushed to the earth in the second verset. The abased figure of the nation, bowed to the earth, is an antithesis to the exhortation to God to rise and conquer.

27. *for the sake of Your kindness.* Here, and virtually everywhere else in Psalms, *ḥesed* equally implies kindness or caring as well as keeping faith, honoring covenantal obligations.

45

1　For the lead player, on *shoshanim*, for the Korahites, a *maskil*, a song
　　of love.

2　　　My heart is astir with a goodly word.
　　　　　　　I speak what I've made to the king.
　　　　　　　　　　My tongue is the pen of a rapid scribe.

3　　You are loveliest of the sons of man,
　　　　　　　grace flows from your lips.
　　　　　　　　　　Therefore has God blessed you forever.

---

1. shoshanim. This is still another unknown musical term, though the literal
meaning is "lilies."

　a song of love. This designation for a psalm occurs only here. This is a royal
psalm, as the ensuing praise of the king's beauty and his martial prowess makes
clear. But what is distinctive about this among the royal psalms is that it
appears to celebrate the king's wedding, with a foreign princess (verses 10–16).
That occasion would justify "a song of love," *shir yedidut*, making this poem a
kind of epithalamium.

2. *My heart is astir with a goodly word*. This psalm differs from all others in the
canonical collection both rhetorically and stylistically. Only here do we have a
poet who begins by celebrating his own art—a gesture that might well be
appropriate for a court poet; he announces at the outset that his tongue is like
the pen of a rapid—that is, skilled—scribe.

3. *You are loveliest*. The Hebrew verb *yafyafita*, formed from the adjective *yafeh*,
"lovely," is unique to this poem and looks like an elegant stylistic flourish suited
to the celebratory language of the psalm.

Gird your sword on your thigh, O warrior,   4
　　　your glory and your grandeur.
And in your grandeur pass onward,   5
　　　　　mount on a word of truth, humility and justice,
　　　　　　and let your right hand shoot forth terrors,
your sharpened arrows—   6
　　　　　peoples fall beneath you—
　　　　　　into the heart of the king's enemies.
Your throne of God is forevermore.   7
　　　　　A scepter of right, your kingship's scepter.
You loved justice and hated evil.   8
　　　　Therefore did God your God anoint you
　　　　　　with oil of joy over your fellows.

---

4. *Gird your sword.* From loveliness and grace, the poem quickly moves on to military might, something the kings of the ancient Near East proverbially needed to exercise in order to maintain securely the grandeur of their courts even in times of peace, such as the wedding occasion for this poem.

5. *pass onward.* The verb *tsalaḥ* can also mean "to prosper," but the juxtaposition with "mount" argues for its other use as a verb of motion.

7. *Your throne of God.* Some construe the Hebrew here to mean "Your throne, O God," but it would be anomalous to have an address to God in the middle of the poem because the entire psalm is directed to the king or to his bride. Others emend the text to keep the throne unambiguously royal.

8. *God your God.* As elsewhere, this odd phrasing is the result of an editorial substitution of *'elohim 'elohekha* for YHWH *'elohekha.*

9   Myrrh and aloes and cassia
          all your garments.
    From ivory palaces
          lutes gladdened you.

10   Princesses are your cherished ones,
          the consort stands at your right in gold of Ophir.

11   Listen, princess, and look, incline your ear,
          and forget your people, and your father's house.

12   And let the king yearn for your beauty,
          for he is your master,
             and bow down to him.

13   Daughter of Tyre, with tribute
          the people's wealthy will court your favor.

---

9. *lutes gladdened you.* The Masoretic text reads *mini* ("from"?), but *minim*, "lutes," with the support of one ancient witness, makes the otherwise enigmatic verse entirely intelligible.

10. *the consort.* The Hebrew *shegal* is probably an Akkadian loan-word. Other features of the poem's style are archaic, and some commentators, given the wedding with a Tyrian princess (see verse 13), have been tempted to see the psalm as a product of Solomon's court.

11. *princess.* The Hebrew says "daughter" (*bat*), but the context suggests that this is an ellipsis for *bat melekh*, "princess" because princesses have just been referred to in the plural as *benot melakhim*. The poet, having focused on the royal consort while still addressing the king (verse 10), now turns to the consort and addresses her directly.

12. *And let the king yearn for your beauty, / for he is your master.* This verse offers a capsule version of royal marriage in a patriarchal society. The bride provides the beauty, which rouses the king's desire, but he is her master.

All the princess's treasure is pearls,   14
       filigree of gold her raiment.
In embroidered stuff she is led to the king,   15
       maidens in train, her companions.
They are led in rejoicing and gladness,   16
       they enter the palace,
           brought to you, king.
In your fathers' stead your sons will be.   17
       You will set them as princes in all the land.
Let me make your name heard in all generations.   18
       Therefore do peoples acclaim you forevermore.

---

14. *treasure.* The Hebrew *kevudah* should be construed as a noun, "treasure," not as an adjective modifying "princess," a construction some interpreters have proposed.

All the princess's treasure is pearls. The Masoretic text reads literally "all the princess's treasure is inward," which Jewish tradition has taken as a slogan for the virtuous wife's conjugal modesty. But the immediately following word has a superfluous *mem* at the beginning. If one moves it back to the end of the previous word and inserts a second *nun* for the *mem* in the middle of the word, instead of *penimah*, "inward," the consonantal text would read *peninim*, "pearls," which makes more sense and a much better parallelism. There is also a syntactic problem here, because "princess" would have to be a vocative ("All the treasure, princess"), but because the royal bride is spoken of in the third person in the last half of the verse, the translation does not represent the vocative.

15. *maidens in train.* The Hebrew says literally "behind her."

17. *In your fathers' stead your sons will be.* As in the Renaissance epithalamium, the celebration of the beauty of bride and groom and the evocation of the pomp and circumstance of the wedding is followed by a blessing of fertility on the union about to be consummated.

18. *Let me make your name heard.* Though some interpreters understand "you" to refer to God and read this final verse as a stock psalmodic ending, it is more plausible to see it as a conclusion of the address to the king. This would be in keeping with our understanding of verse 7, "Your throne of God is forevermore," as well as with "Therefore has God blessed you forever" in verse 3.

46

1 For the lead player, for the Korahites, on the *alamoth* a song.
2   God is a shelter and strength for us,
              a help in straits, readily found.
3   Therefore we fear not when the earth breaks apart,
              when mountains collapse in the heart of the seas.

---

1. *on the* alamoth. The preposition seems to indicate that this is a musical instrument, but nothing more is known about it.

2. *God is a shelter and strength for us.* The first-person plural, with the substance of this line picked up in the refrain of verse 8 and verse 12, marks this as a national psalm, evidently a collective thanksgiving after victory over an enemy (see verses 5–8).

3. *we fear not when the earth breaks apart.* An excessive literalism has led some commentators to attach this psalm because of these lines to one of the earthquakes that hit Jerusalem during the First Temple era, mentioned elsewhere in the Bible. The hyperbolic description of mountains collapsing into the sea is hardly a realistic depiction of an earthquake. It is more likely that the images are metaphorical: Even when the whole world around us falls apart, we trust in God's help and do not fear. In fact, the seismic cataclysm may be a figurative representation of an assault by enemies because some of the same terms are used (verses 6 and 7) in the representation of a military upheaval.

Its waters roar and roil,   4
      mountains heave in its surge.   selah
A stream, its rivulets gladden God's town,   5
      the holy dwelling of Elyon.
God in its midst, it will not collapse.   6
      God helps it as morning breaks.
Nations roar and kingdoms collapse.   7
      He sends forth His voice and earth melts.

---

4. *Its waters roar and roil.* The translation seeks to approximate the strong alliterative effect of the Hebrew, *yehemu yeḥmeru meymaw*.

selah. The musical notation at the end of this verse also appears to mark the end of a unit in the poem, because "A stream" at the beginning of the next verse carries us, in a sharp antithesis, from the heaving sea to the quiet waters of Zion.

5. *A stream, its rivulets gladden God's town.* There is no actual river in Jerusalem, but there is a partly underground stream, the Shiloah, that provides a water source from the Gihon spring east of the city.

Elyon. Conventionally, the Most High, a Canaanite deity co-opted for monotheistic usage.

6. *it will not collapse.* This line picks up the vocabulary of seismic upheaval from verse 3 but turns around the meaning.

as morning breaks. After the long night of siege, ridden with terrors, God intervenes in a figurative daybreak to rescue His people.

7. *Nations roar and kingdoms collapse.* Both verbs here are drawn from the depiction of seismic cataclysm in verses 3 and 4, now applied to the realm of warfare.

He sends forth His voice. Conventionally, as in Psalm 18, God's voice would be thunder. In Canaanite mythology, as in other traditions, lightning bolts are the weapons of the sky god.

8   The Lord of armies is with us,
                a fortress for us, Jacob's God.   selah
9   Go, behold the acts of the Lord,
                Who made desolations on earth,
10   caused wars to cease to the end of the earth.
                The bow He has broken and splintered the spear,
                        and chariots burned in fire.

---

8. *The Lord of armies.* This common epithet has a special, and reassuring, application to the situation in this psalm of an embattled Zion. Untypically for this section of Psalms, God is referred to as YHWH, perhaps because of the fixed formula of the epithet. YHWH recurs in the next verse, possibly under the influence of this one.

9. *Go, behold the acts of the Lord.* These words, after the selah notation at the end of the preceding line, begin the concluding unit of the poem, in which the God Who rules over nature and men is imagined eschatologically as overmastering all the world and bringing an end to war.

   made desolations on earth. This line and the one immediately following telescope history and the glorious end-time to come. God is responsible for the vast sweeps of destruction that visit the inhabited earth, whether through natural events or military ones. But He also exercises the power to end the era of violence and bring peace to humankind.

10. *caused wars to cease to the end of the earth.* Throughout the poem, *'erets* has been used in its broader sense of "earth," not "land." Here, the large global perspective implied in that usage is made explicit.

   chariots. Though the Hebrew noun usually means "wagons," the parallelism with "bow" and "spear" suggests a more martial vehicle.

"Let go, and know that I am God.   11
        I loom among nations, I loom upon earth."
The LORD of armies is with us,   12
        a fortress for us, Jacob's God.   selah

---

11. *Let go.* This verb—etymologically, it means to relax one's grip on something—is somewhat surprising here. It might be an injunction to cease and
desist from armed struggle, to unclench the warrior's fist. At this juncture,
which is in effect the end of the poem, the eschatologically triumphant God
speaks directly, declaring His supremacy over all the world. The poem concludes by repeating the refrain, "The LORD of armies is with us, / a fortress for
us, Jacob's God."

47

1   For the lead player, for the Korahites, a psalm.
2   All peoples, clap hands,
                shout out to God with a sound of glad song.
3   For the LORD is most high and fearsome,
                a great king over all the earth.
4   He crushes peoples beneath us
                and nations beneath our feet.
5   He chooses for us our estate,
                pride of Jacob whom He loves.   selah

---

3. *For the* LORD *is most high and fearsome, / a great king over all the earth.* The
Hebrew ʿ*elyon* is adjectival here and so is translated as "most high" rather than
represented as a name for God. This is one of several psalms that take for their
subject the celebration of God's kingship. In the first half of the poem, up to
the selah that marks the end of verse 5, God's kingship is seen manifested in His
granting triumph to Israel over its enemies, a common theme in Psalms. In the
second half of the poem, ceremonial flourishes of acclaim for the divine king are
explicitly invoked, and God is imagined seated on a throne. Since Mowinckel in
the early twentieth century, many scholars have contended that this psalm is the
text of a New Year ritual (on the model of an annual Babylonian rite of coronation for the god Mardukh) in which God was crowned. It must be said that the
existence of an actual ritual of this sort is mere conjecture, and the psalm could
simply be a symbolic celebration through song of the idea that God reigns
supreme over all. This is precisely how this psalm came to be used in subsequent Jewish tradition in the New Year liturgy.

God has gone up with a trumpet-blast,   6
      the LORD with a ram's horn sound.
Hymn to God, hymn,   7
      hymn to our king, O hymn.
For king of all earth is God,   8
      hymn joyous song.
God reigns over the nations,   9
      and sits on His holy throne.
The princes of peoples have gathered,   10
      the people of Abraham's God.
For God's are the land's defenders.
      Much exalted is He.

---

6. *God has gone up.* God's loftiness or ascent is a theme that sounds through the poem from beginning to end. The psalmist may well be inviting us to imagine God ascending to take His seat on the celestial throne.

    trumpet-blast . . . ram's horn. The fanfare of these instruments marked the coronation of human kings.

8. *joyous song.* The Hebrew term here is *maskil,* the word that appears in several of the superscriptions to individual psalms. The inference that it refers in particular to joyous song is drawn from the way it is used in Amos 5:13.

10. *For God's are the land's defenders.* This sentence in all likelihood should be linked with "He crushes peoples beneath us / and nations beneath our feet." That is, God has manifested His own regal power by enabling His people to triumph over its enemies, and the warriors who have successfully defended the "estate" of the Land of Israel are victorious through God, or are in effect God's soldiers.

    Much exalted is He. The Hebrew here uses a passive verb *na'alah* (literally, "has gone up") in an adjectival sense. The verb exhibits the same root '-*l-h* detectible in the adjective '*elyon,* "most high," in verse 3.

48

1   Song, a psalm for the Korahites.
2   Great is the LORD and highly praised
              in our God's town, His holy mountain.
3   Lovely in heights, all the earth's joy,
              Mount Zion, far end of Zaphon,
                   the great King's city.
4   God in its bastions
              is famed as a fortress.

---

2. *Great is the* LORD *and highly praised, / in our God's town.* This is a psalm celebrating Zion as God's city, which He protects. Although the first half of the poem, until the division marked by selah at the end of verse 9, appears to reflect a particular military victory over an invading force from the sea, scholarly attempts to anchor the text in a specific historical event have been unavailing.

3. *all the earth's joy, / . . . far end of Zaphon.* Although Jerusalem, as some archaeologists have argued, may have actually been a small backwater capital (hence the translation here of 'ir as "town" rather than "city") among the great cities of the ancient Near East, the poet imagines it in cosmic terms. On its heights, it is a delight to all the inhabited earth, and he calls it "Zaphon" (elsewhere, a term that means "north"), the mountain that is the abode of Baal in Canaanite mythology.

    the great King's city. Given the context, it seems more likely that "King" refers to God than to the Davidic ruler.

For, look, the kings have conspired,   5
        passed onward one and all.
It is they who have seen and so been astounded,   6
        were panicked, dismayed.
Shuddering seized them there,   7
        pangs like a woman in labor.
With the east wind   8
        You smashed the ships of Tarshish.
As we heard, so we see   9
        in the town of the LORD of armies, in the town of
        our God.
                May God make it stand firm forever!   selah
We witnessed, O God, Your kindness   10
        in the midst of Your temple.

---

5. *conspired.* The Hebrew *noʿadu* puns on *nodʿa*, "is famed" (the same three consonants with the order of the *dalet* and *ʿayin* reversed) in the previous line.

6–7. *were panicked, dismayed, / Shuddering seized them.* These words are a pointed allusion to the Song of the Sea, Exodus 15:14–15, which records a different kind of victory at sea over a ruthless enemy through divine intervention.

8. *With the east wind / You smashed the ships of Tarshish.* The east wind, blowing from the desert, proverbially brings trouble. Tarshish, which has been located by different scholars at various places from Asia Minor to Iberia, is somewhere to the west on the Mediterranean, though the phrase could conceivably refer not to the port of embarkation but to the design of the ships.

10. *We witnessed, O God, Your kindness / in the midst of Your temple.* The "witnessing" (or, perhaps, "envisaging," the meaning of the Hebrew verb in this context being somewhat uncertain) is an overlap with the "seeing" of the previous verse. But this line begins a new movement in the poem, an exhortation to pilgrims ascending Mount Zion to behold the town's mighty bastions that manifest God's protecting presence.

11   Like Your name, O God, so Your praise—
        to the ends of the earth.
            With justice Your right hand is full.

12   Let Mount Zion rejoice,
        let Judea's townlets exult
            because of Your judgments.

13   Go around Zion, encircle it.
        Count its towers.

14   Set your mind to its ramparts,
        scale its bastions
            to recount to the last generation.

15   For this is God, our God, forevermore.
        He will lead us forever.

---

11. *to the ends of the earth.* This phrase picks up the global reach of "all the earth's joy" at the beginning of the psalm.

    With justice. The Hebrew *tsedeq* can also mean "victory" or "bountiful act."

12. *Judea's townlets.* The literal sense of the phrase is "Judea's daughters," but in urban contexts, "daughters" (*banot*) refers to the outlying townlets, and the city itself is sometimes called "mother."

    judgments. This Hebrew term, *mishpat*, is often paired with "justice," which appears just above in this poem.

14. *scale its bastions.* The verb occurs only here, so its meaning is disputed. This translation is based on the fact that the verb appears to reflect the same root as *pisgah*, "mountaintop," though others, relating it to a verb from this root in rabbinic Hebrew, think it may mean "pass through."

    to the last generation. Some prefer to construe this as "next generation," but the emphasis at the end on "forever" suggests that it rather means from one generation to another, to the end of time, or at least to the distant future.

15. *He will lead us forever.* The very last word of the poem, *'al-mut*, is obscure. It might mean "over death," but the preposition and the vocalization of the noun would be anomalous. Some scholars read it as *'alamot*, a musical term (see 46:1), but it would be odd to have such a term at the end of a psalm rather than at the beginning. The translation follows the suggestion of Mitchell Dahood and others that it has the same sense as *le'olam*, "forever."

49

For the lead player, for the Korahites, a psalm.
   Hear this, all peoples,
           hearken, all who dwell in the world.
   You human creatures, you sons of man,
           together the rich and the needy.
   My mouth speaks wisdom,
           my heart's utterance, understanding.
   I incline my ear to a saying,
           I take up with the lyre my theme.
   Why should I fear in evil days,
           when crime comes round me at my heels?

---

2. *Hear this, all peoples.* The address at the beginning to all inhabitants of earth is not from a triumphal national perspective, as in some other psalms, but rather reflects the universalist orientation of this text as a Wisdom psalm. Indeed, there is no other poem in the collection that has such pronounced Wisdom features.

3. *You human creatures, you sons of man.* The vocative "you" attempts to reproduce the emphatic effect of the reiterated *gam* in the Hebrew.

4. *My mouth speaks wisdom, / my heart's utterance, understanding.* This declaration that the speaker is about to pronounce words of instruction is one that often recurs in the Book of Proverbs.

5. *saying . . . theme.* These are technical terms for didactic messages cast in poetic form (*mashal* and *ḥidah*) that are frequently repeated in Proverbs (see, for example, Proverbs 1:6).

7   Who trust in their wealth
         and boast of their great riches—
8   yet they surely will redeem no man,
         will not give to God his ransom.
9   To redeem their lives is too dear,
         and one comes to an end forever.
10   Will he yet live forever?
         Will he not see the Pit?
11   For he sees the wise die,
         both the fool and the stupid man perish,
         and they abandon to others their wealth.

---

8. *yet they.* The translation, with some manuscripts, reads *'akh*, "yet," for the Masoretic *ah*, "brother."

9. *To redeem their lives is too dear, / and one comes to an end forever.* As is often the case in biblical poetry, pronoun reference is confusing, though the meaning of this verse is not in doubt. Those who trust in their wealth but are unwilling to put up money for those in need find it too expensive to redeem the lives of the needy. Before the recalcitrant rich can be prevailed on to help, the poor man in straits will perish, will be gone forever.

10. *Will he . . . live forever?* At this point, it is not entirely certain whether "he" is the poor man (and hence this verse is a direct continuation of the end of the previous verse) or whether the rich man is now being reminded that he will not live forever. The emphasis on the fate of mortality that awaits even the great of the earth (verses 11 and 12) might favor the latter interpretation.

11. *For he sees the wise die, / both the fool and the stupid man perish.* This notion of death as the grim equalizer between wise and foolish, as between rich and poor, sounds more like Ecclesiastes than Proverbs. The term for "fool," *kesil*, is a distinctive item in the lexicon of Ecclesiastes, just as the whole clause "they abandon to others their wealth" has close parallels in Ecclesiastes.

Their grave is their home forever,   12
        their dwelling for all generations,
            though their names had been called upon
            earth.
And man will not rest in splendor.   13
        He is likened to beasts that are doomed.
This way of theirs is their foolishness,   14
        and after, in words alone, they show favor.   selah

---

12. *Their grave.* The translation reads, as do several of the ancient versions, *qivram* for the Masoretic *qirbam*, "their midst." In the Hebrew, this is a simple reversal of two consonants. This reading produces an appropriately sardonic statement—that the dead, whatever their earthly acquisitions and attainments, have only the grave as their everlasting home.

    though their names had been called upon earth. The initial "though" is frankly an interpretive guess (the Hebrew says only "and"), yielding the Ecclesiastian sense that these men who were once famous on earth now have only the grave as a habitation.

13. *man will not rest in splendor.* The primary meaning of the verb *yalin* is "to spend the night." The idea would be that a man's earthly glory barely lasts a night, for, like all mere beasts, he is fated to die. But when this line is repeated as a refrain at the end of the poem, the verb used is *yavin,* "understand" or "grasp," and it is not clear which of the two readings is the authentic one, or whether the second reading is a deliberate play on the first. *Yalin,* however, makes more sense in connection with the theme of the ephemerality of human life.

14. *and after, in words alone, they show favor.* The Hebrew of this entire verset is not intelligible. Literally, it reads "and after them in their mouth they show favor." The text has almost certainly been scrambled here, but no attempt to reconstruct the original is very convincing. Even the selah at the end of the line does not mark any logical division in the poem.

15   Like sheep to Sheol they head—
        death shepherds them—
           and the upright hold sway over them in the
           morn.
    And they wear out their image in Sheol,
        a habitation for them.

16   But God will ransom my life,
        from the grip of Sheol He will take me.   selah

17   Do not fear when a man grows rich,
        when he enlarges his house's glory.

18   For in his death he will not take all,
        his glory won't go down behind him.

---

15. *and the upright hold sway over them in the morn.* This appears to express an idea, anomalous in the Bible, that the powerful will awake in the underworld to discover that the upright now rule them. A complicated emendation yields, "And straight they go down like cattle."

    their image. The translation assumes *tsuratam*, "their image," instead of the Masoretic *tsuram*, "their rock." The verb "wear out" attached to this noun is in the infinitive in the Hebrew, still another oddity in this perplexing text.

    a habitation for them. The Hebrew *mizevul lo* is another opaque moment in the text.

16. *from the grip of Sheol He will take me.* "Grip" is literally "hand." But this entire line, invoking a God Who rescues the speaker from the verge of death, seems more appropriate to a thanksgiving psalm and does not jibe well with the meditation on mortality that constitutes the poem.

For his own self he blesses when alive   19
            and acclaims You for giving him bounty.
He will come to the state of his fathers—   20
            forevermore will not see the light.
Man will not grasp things in splendor.   21
            He is likened to beasts that are doomed.

---

19. *For his own self he blesses when alive / and acclaims You for giving him bounty.*
This is another line of this psalm in which the individual words are compre-
hensible but not the way they fit together. If the received text is correct, the
meaning might be: While he was alive, this man proud of his riches congratu-
lated himself and also conceded thanks to God for his prosperity (revocalizing
the verb "acclaim" from its plural form to a singular). The speaker regards such
a man as exhibiting a highly dubious piety.

20. *the state of his fathers.* The literal sense of the Hebrew is "the generation of
his fathers." The idea is that he who reveled in his earthly possessions will
inevitably be reduced to the condition of all who came before him, enveloped
in the eternal darkness of death.

21. *Man will not grasp things in splendor.* If the shift from *yalin* to *yavin*, from
"rest" to "grasp," was actually intended by the poet, the point at the end is that
not only does man barely abide a fleeting night in worldly splendor but also that
in his attachment to such splendor, he can have no understanding of the grim
end that ineluctably awaits all men.

50

1   An Asaph psalm.
      El, the God LORD,
                He spoke and called to the earth
                        from the sun's rising-place to its setting.
2   From Zion, the zenith of beauty
                God shone forth.
3   Let our God come and not be silent.
                Before Him fire consumes,
                        and round about Him—great storming.
4   Let Him call to the heavens above
                        and to the earth to judge his people:

---

1. *An Asaph psalm.* Asaph was the ancestor of a line of Levites going back to David's time. The rest of the Asaph psalms are grouped together in the Third Book of Psalms.

El, the God LORD. The grouping of divine names is odd and may be the result of a problem in textual transmission. 'El 'elohim ("God God") is an unusual combination, and YHWH, the LORD, ordinarily goes before "God," 'elohim.

2. *God shone forth.* The shining from Zion quickly builds up to a pyrotechnic epiphany as God makes an appearance with consuming fire before Him and storm all around Him.

4. *Let Him call to the heavens above / and to the earth.* The inviting of the heavens and the earth as witnesses is a hallmark of prophetic and quasi-prophetic discourse (compare the beginning of Isaiah 1 and the beginning of the Song of Moses in Deuteronomy 32). This is clearly a prophetic psalm, with God actually quoted in direct discourse for much of the poem, as in the literary prophets.

"Gather to Me My faithful,   5
        who with sacrifice seal My pact."
And let the heavens tell His justice,   6
        for God, He is judge.   selah
"Hear, O My people, that I may speak,   7
        Israel, that I witness to you.
                God your God I am.
Not for your sacrifices shall I reprove you,   8
        your burnt-offerings always before Me.
I shall not take from your house a bull,   9
        nor goats from your pens.
For Mine are all beasts of the forest,   10
        the herds on the thousand mountains.
I know every bird of the mountains,   11
        creatures of the field are with Me.
Should I hunger, I would not say to you,   12
        for Mine is the world and its fullness.

---

5. *Gather to Me My faithful.* This verse has encouraged some interpreters to see this psalm as the liturgical text for a rite of renewal of the covenant with God by a group designated as His "faithful," but the existence of such a ritual at any time in the history of ancient Israel is pure conjecture.

6. *selah.* This notation marks the point before God launches on His long discourse.

8. *Not for your sacrifices.* The idea that God does not require animal sacrifice is a common one in prophetic literature (most memorably, in Isaiah and Micah).

10. *the herds on the thousand mountains.* This mystifying and evocative phrase has encouraged various emendations, but it may be a proverbial or even mythological reference of which we remain ignorant.

12. *Should I hunger.* The argument against sacrifice differs in emphasis from Isaiah's. The objection is not to the hypocrisy of trampling the courts of the temple with bloodstained hands but to the pagan idea that the deity actually needs the nurture provided through the animals offered up on the altar.

13 Would I eat the flesh of fat bulls,
        would I drink the blood of goats?
14 Sacrifice to God a thanksgiving,
        and pay to the High One your vows.
15 And call Me on the day of distress—
        I will free you and you shall revere me."
16 And to the wicked God said:
        "Why do you recount My statutes
            and bear My pact in your mouth,
17 when you have despised chastisement
        and flung My words behind you?
18 If you see a thief, you run with him,
        and with adulterers is your lot.
19 You let loose your mouth in evil,
        and your tongue clings fast to deceit.
20 You sit, against your brother you speak,
        your mother's son you slander.
21 These you have done and I was silent.
        You imagined I could indeed be like you.
            I reprove you, make a case before your eyes.

---

14. *Sacrifice to God a thanksgiving, / and pay to the High One your vows.* It is now made clear that God is not calling for a categorical abolition of sacrifices. If a man needs to give thanks to God, or if he has vowed an offering, the sacrifice (whether animal or grain) is an appropriate act. But no one should imagine that God somehow depends on sacrifice.

18. *run with him.* The Masoretic text has "show favor with him," the preposition after the verb being somewhat odd. This translation follows the Septuagint, the Targum, and the Syriac in vocalizing the verb differently (*watarots* instead of *watirets*). Running with the wicked and sharing their portion is a better parallelism than favoring and sharing.

Understand this, you who forget God,   22
       lest I tear you apart, with no one to save you.
He who sacrifices thanksgiving reveres Me   23
       and sets out on the proper way.
            I will show him God's rescue.

---

22. *tear you apart.* The "you" is merely implied in the Hebrew and has been added for clarity. The implied image, common in biblical poetry as a representation of fierceness, is of a lion tearing its prey to pieces.

23. *and sets out on the proper way.* Although a long tradition of interpretation understands the text here in this fashion, the two Hebrew words it renders, *wesam derekh*—literally, "and he puts the way"—are altogether cryptic.

51

1 For the lead player, a David psalm,
2 upon Nathan the prophet's coming to him when he had come to
   bed with Bathsheba.
3 Grant me grace, God, as befits Your kindness,
         with Your great mercy wipe away my crimes.
4 Thoroughly wash my transgressions away
         and cleanse me from my offense.
5 For my crimes I know,
         and my offense is before me always.

---

2. *upon Nathan the prophet's coming to him when he had come to bed with Bathsheba.* The superscription incorporates a barbed pun. The Hebrew verb used for both Nathan and David is "to come to [or "into"]," but in the former instance it refers to the prophet's entering the king's chambers, whereas the latter instance reflects its sexual sense, to have intercourse with a woman (probably intercourse for the first time). The strong character of this poem as a confessional psalm led the editors to attribute it to David when he was stricken with remorse after Nathan rebuked him for sleeping with Bathsheba and murdering her husband (2 Samuel 12). But in all likelihood, this psalm is a general penitential psalm composed centuries after David. If the reference to the rebuilding of the walls of Jerusalem in the penultimate verse is an integral part of the original psalm and not an editorial addition, the text would have to date to sometime after 586 BCE. In any case, the idea of offering God a broken spirit instead of sacrifice looks as though it may have been influenced by the later prophetic literature. The eloquent confessional mode of this psalm has made it an important liturgical vehicle for both Christians and Jews. It is one of the seven penitential psalms in Church ritual. The wrenching plea of verse 13 is used in the introduction to the penitential prayer during the Jewish Days of Awe.

You alone have I offended,
   and what is evil in Your eyes I have done.   6
So You are just when You sentence,
   You are right when You judge.
Look, in transgression was I conceived,   7
   and in offense my mother spawned me.
Look, You desired truth in what is hidden;   8
   in what is concealed make wisdom known to me.

---

7. *in transgression was I conceived, / and in offense my mother spawned me.* Christian interpreters through the ages have understood this verse as a prime expression of the doctrine of Original Sin. Some of the early rabbis register a similar notion—as they put it, David's father, Jesse, did not have relations with his wife to fulfill a higher obligation but rather out of sheer lust. Such a reading may be encouraged by the fact that the verb attached to the mother, *yaḥam*, is typically associated with animals in heat. It may, however, be unwarranted to construct a general theology of sinful human nature from this verse. The speaker of this poem certainly feels permeated with sinfulness. He may indeed trace it back to the sexual act through which he was conceived, but there is not much here to support the idea that this is the case of every human born.

8. *You desired truth in what is hidden.* This whole verse is the one line in the poem that is rather obscure. The meaning of *batuḥot,* "what's hidden," or "hidden things," is not certain. Traditional commentators generally think it refers to the inner organs. It is unclear what the line as a whole means to say—perhaps that the speaker feels he may harbor guilt for transgressions of which he is not consciously aware, and asks God to reveal these to him.

9   Purify me with a hyssop, that I be clean.
             Wash me, that I be whiter than snow.

10   Let me hear gladness and joy,
             let the bones that You crushed exult.

11   Avert Your face from my offenses,
             and all my misdeeds wipe away.

12   A pure heart create for me, God,
             and a firm spirit renew within me.

13   Do not fling me from Your presence,
             and Your holy spirit take not from me.

14   Give me back the gladness of Your rescue
             and with a noble spirit sustain me.

15   Let me teach transgressors Your ways,
             and offenders will come back to You.

---

9. *Purify me with a hyssop.* Hyssop was used in a ritual of purification. The priest dipped the hyssop branch in the blood of a sacrificial animal, then sprinkled it on the impure object or person to expunge the impurity (see Leviticus 14:4, 7). (The fine hairs on hyssop leaves may have prevented the blood from congealing.) Alternately, hyssop was used to sprinkle water (Numbers 19:18–22) to remove impurities. The claim made by some scholars that this psalm is therefore a liturgical text for a rite of purification is not altogether convincing because hyssop, familiar to the audience from such ceremonies, could easily have been invoked as a symbol of a process of purification that is spiritual, not ritual, in nature. Such a move from ritual to spiritual is strongly etched in verses 18 and 19.

Wash me, that I be whiter than snow. The same image is used in Isaiah 1:18.

13. *Do not fling me from Your presence.* As elsewhere, this Hebrew verb has a connotation of violent action for which the conventional translation of it as "cast" is too tame.

15. *Let me teach transgressors Your ways.* At the completion of the process of transformation that the confessional speaker envisages, he will be so different from his former condition as a reprobate that he will be able to teach those who err what God requires of them.

Save me from bloodshed, O God,   16
        God of my rescue.
                Let my tongue sing out Your bounty.
O Master, open my lips,   17
        that my mouth may tell Your praise.
For You desire not that I should give sacrifice,   18
        burnt-offering You greet not with pleasure.
God's sacrifices—a broken spirit.   19
        A broken, crushed heart God spurns not.
Show goodness in Your pleasure to Zion,   20
        rebuild the walls of Jerusalem.
Then shall You desire just sacrifices,   21
        burnt-offering and whole offering,
            then bulls will be offered up on Your altar.

---

19. *God's sacrifices—a broken spirit, / A broken, crushed heart God spurns not.* Although Isaiah and Micah equally stress that what God requires of man is not animal sacrifices but ethical behavior, here there is an arresting new emphasis on an inward condition of contrition. It is a person's remorse over past actions, or perhaps simply his authentic grief over his desperate plight, that God accepts instead of sacrifice.

20. *Show goodness in Your pleasure to Zion, / rebuild the walls of Jerusalem.* The poem until this moment at the end has been entirely concerned with the remorseful confession of an individual, so this prayer for the rebuilding of Jerusalem looks suspiciously like a conclusion added by an editor.

21. *Then shall You desire just sacrifices.* In the rebuilt Jerusalem—this would seem to be the specific implication of the repeated "then"—with, we may infer, a rebuilt temple, it will once again be possible to offer sacrifices. The single word "just" might by a stretch harmonize this concluding verse with 18 and 19, but it seems more likely that an editor, uneasy with the outright rejection or at least downgrading of sacrifices expressed in the psalm, added this line at the end to reaffirm the idea that God desires sacrifices, at least if they are just ones.

52

1 For the lead player, a David *maskil*,
2 when Doeg the Edomite came and told Saul and said to him,
   "David has come to the house of Achimelech."
3   Why boast of evil, O hero?
                    —God's kindness is all day long.
4   Disasters your tongue devises,
                    like a well-honed razor, doing deceit.
5   You love evil better than good,
                    a lie more than speaking justice.   selah
6   You love all destructive words,
                    the tongue of deceit.

---

2. *when Doeg the Edomite came*. Doeg is the informer who sees the fleeing David take refuge with the priest Achimelech in Nob, then denounces Achimelech to Saul (1 Samuel 21–22). Saul's response is to massacre all the priests of Nob. The lethal effect of Doeg's words may have especially encouraged the editor to create the connection with this psalm in the superscription, though the fit with the content of the psalm is far from perfect: Doeg causes harm through his report but does not in fact speak in deceit, and the sarcastic address to the man boasting of evil as "hero" is not exactly appropriate for him.

3. *God's kindness is all day long*. The likely meaning is that God in His perpetual kindness will somehow protect the victims over whom the evildoer vaunts and whom he thinks he can destroy.

God surely will smash you forever,   7
      sweep you up and tear you from the tent,
            root you out from the land of the living.   selah
And the righteous shall see and be awed   8
      and laugh over him.
Look, the man who does not make   9
      God his stronghold,
and who trusts in his great wealth,
      who would be strong in his disaster!
But I am like a verdant olive tree   10
      in the house of our God.
            I trust in God's kindness forevermore.

---

7. *sweep you up.* The root of the declined verb *yaḥtekha* is ambiguous. It might instead derive from a verbal stem meaning "reduce to rubble." Either way, the line produces an image of violent destruction of the wicked.

8. *laugh over him.* The "him" is, of course, the evil person, until now addressed in the second person. Such switches in pronoun reference are fairly common in biblical usage.

9. *would be strong in his disaster.* The verb *ya'oz* obviously plays against the noun *ma'oz*, "stronghold," that has just been used. Its employment here is evidently sardonic: Such a man imagines, foolishly, that he will remain strong in his disaster.

10. *But I am like a verdant olive tree.* A first-person singular enters the poem only now, at the conclusion. The speaker feels secure against the razor-tongued evil man destined to be uprooted, and he will flourish like an olive tree—a standard symbol for prosperity and peace—within the temple precincts.

  I trust in God's kindness forevermore. God's kindness, or keeping faith (*ḥesed*), with humankind, mentioned elliptically at the beginning of the poem, is the quality that the grateful speaker feels manifested in his own life.

11   I shall acclaim You forever, for You have acted,
                    and hope in Your name, for it is good,
                         before Your faithful.

---

11. *I shall acclaim You forever, for You have acted*. This poem, which began as a
defiant challenge to the boastful wicked, ends as a thanksgiving psalm. The act
of thanksgiving takes place within the temple, in the presence of God's community of faithful followers. The phrase "hope in Your name" is syntactically
parenthetical. It is not the hope but the acclaiming that takes place "before
Your faithful."

53

To the lead player, on the *mahalath,* a David *maskil.*   1
   The scoundrel has said in his heart,   2
         "There is no God."
They corrupt and do loathsome misdeeds.
         There is none who does good.
The Lord from the heavens looked down   3
         on the sons of humankind
   to see, is there someone discerning,
         someone seeking out God.

This psalm is a duplication of Psalm 14 (pages 40–42). In keeping with the general practice of the editor in the second book of Psalms, God, *'elohim,* is consistently substituted for YHWH, the Lord, in Psalm 14. The other changes are limited with the exception of verse 6. The divergences from Psalm 14 are noted below. For other remarks on the poem, the reader is referred to the commentary on Psalm 14.

1. *To the lead player, on the* mahalath, *a David* maskil. This is a different superscription. Psalm 14 has simply, "For the lead player, for David." The *mahalath* is presumably a musical instrument, but its nature is unknown.

2. *and do loathsome misdeeds.* Psalm 14 has ʿalilah, "acts," as against ʿawel, "misdeed[s]," here. The "and" before the verb is absent in Psalm 14.

4   All are tainted,
             one and all are befouled.
    There is none who does good.
             There is not even one.
5   Do they not know,
             the wrongdoers?
    Devourers of my people devoured them like bread.
             They did not call on God.
6   There did they sorely fear.
             —There was no fear,
    for God scattered the bones of your besieger.
             You put them to shame, for God spurned them.
7   O, may from Zion come Israel's rescue
             when God restores His people's condition.
    May Jacob exult.
             May Israel rejoice.

---

4. *All are tainted*. The Hebrew *kulo sag* differs from Psalm 14, *hakol sar*, "all turn astray."

5. *the wrongdoers*. Psalm 14 reads "all wrongdoers."

6. *There was no fear*. The least strained way to construe this clause, which does not appear in Psalm 14, is as implying "but": They—presumably, the Israelites—were afraid, but it turned out that there was no reason to fear.
    for God scattered the bones of your besieger. Psalm 14 here reads, "for God is with the righteous band." The word for "besieger" is literally "your camper" (the one encamped against you?). The defeat of besiegers has led some interpreters to see in this line a reference to the frustrated siege on Jerusalem of Sennacherib, but that is pure conjecture.
    You put them to shame, for God spurned them. Psalm 14 reads, "In your plot against the poor you are shamed, / for the LORD is his shelter." In both psalms, the grammar of the verb of shame is problematic.

54

For the lead player on stringed instruments, a David *maskil*,   1
when the Ziphites came and said to Saul, "Is not David hiding out   2
among us?"
    God, through Your name rescue me,   3
          and through Your might take up my cause.
    God, O hear my prayer,   4
          hearken to my mouth's utterances.
    For strangers have risen against me,   5
          and oppressors have sought my life.
              They did not set God before them.   selah

---

2. *when the Ziphites came.* The story alluded to is reported in 1 Samuel 23. David, in flight from Saul, is denounced by the Ziphites in whose territory he has taken refuge. In the end, he manages to elude Saul's forces. Again, the general plea for God's help, conventional in a supplication psalm, has been editorially linked with a particular incident in the life of David that it fits only in part. The complaint "strangers have risen against me" could scarcely refer to Saul, who is hostile to David but by no means a stranger to him or a foreigner (*zar*) in relation to him.

6 Look, God is about to help me,
             my Master—among those who support me.
7 Let Him pay back evil to my assailants.
             Demolish them through Your truth!
8 With a freewill offering let me sacrifice to You.
             Let me acclaim Your name, LORD, for it is good.
9 For from every strait He saved me,
             and my eyes see my enemies' defeat.

---

6. *Look, God is about to help me.* The selah at the end of the immediately preceding line clearly marks a division in this short poem. Verses 3–5 are taken up
with the supplicant's urgent plea to God to save him from his dire plight. With
the beginning of verse 6, introduced by the presentative *hineh*, "look," the
speaker sees God's help already about to happen. The participial form of the
verb used could mean either "about to help" or "is helping."

7. *Demolish them.* In a grammatical move perfectly idiomatic in biblical usage,
the line switches from a third-person reference to God in the first verset to an
imperative address in the second verset.

8. *a freewill offering . . . / Let me acclaim.* Because the deliverance has not yet
been accomplished, this gesture of sacrifice and thanksgiving at the end is a
promise, not a declaration, as at the end of a thanksgiving psalm.

9. *and my eyes see my enemies' defeat.* The Hebrew uses "eye" in the singular.
The rest of the clause says, literally, "see in [or "against"] my enemies." The
idiom *ra'ah b^e*, "see in," repeatedly occurs in Psalms in the sense of seeing one's
enemies defeated and humiliated, so the translation adds the clearly implied
"defeat."

55

For the lead player, on stringed instruments, a David *maskil*.   1

  Hearken, O God, to my prayer,   2

       and do not ignore my plea.

  Listen well to me and answer me.   3

       In my complaint I sway and moan.

From the sound of the enemy,   4

     from the crushing force of the wicked

         when they bring mischief down upon me

           and in fury harass me,

my heart quails within me   5

     and death-terrors fall upon me,

---

2. *Hearken, O God, to my prayer.* These opening words announce the poem as a psalm of supplication. As the text unfolds, however, the subject of the supplication seems to shift. In verses 4–9, the speaker appears to be set upon by armed enemies who terrify him and make him want to flee. References to battles and political treachery abound in verses 19–22. On the other hand, in verses 13–15, the speaker complains of a once dear friend who has betrayed him, and whom he addresses in the second person. One can only guess whether two poems have been spliced together or in some other fashion confusion has been introduced in the editorial process. The perplexity is compounded by the fact that there are textual difficulties in verses 19–22, especially in the first half of verse 20.

4. *From the sound of the enemy.* This riveting expression of terror by the man under attack is made all the more powerful by the fact that, in an unusual syntactic pattern, the catalog of disasters rolls on in a crescendo that is essentially one long sentence, running from the beginning of verse 4 to the end of verse 6.

6	fear and trembling enter me,
	and horror envelopes me.
7	And I say, "Would I had wings like a dove.
	I would fly off and find rest.
8	Look, I would wander far away,
	and lodge in the wilderness, selah
9	would make haste to a refuge for me
	from the streaming wind and the storm.
10	O Master, confound, split their tongue,
	for I have seen outrage and strife in the town;
11	day and night they go round it on its walls,
	and mischief and misdeeds within it,
12	disaster within it,
	guile and deceit never part from its square.
13	No enemy insults me, that I might bear it,
	no foe boasts against me, that I might hide from him.
14	But you—a man to my measure,
	my companion and my familiar,
15	with whom together we shared sweet counsel,
	in the house of our God in elation we walked.

---

9. *from the streaming wind and the storm.* The Hebrew represented as "streaming," *so'ah*, appears only here. It is presumably either a very rare word or a nonce word coined to echo the sound of *sa'ar*, "storm," a phonetic effect replicated in this translation.

10. *for I have seen outrage and strife in the town.* At this point, and for the next three verses, the subject of complaint is not an external enemy but a band of insolent scoundrels who have taken over in the town.

11. *they go round.* The antecedent is "outrage and strife."

14. *But you—a man to my measure.* Were it a known enemy showing hostility, the speaker would have found a way to bear the insult, but it is his intimate friend who has turned against him.

May death come upon them.   16
>May they go down to Sheol alive.
>>For in their homes, in their midst, are evils.

But I call to God,   17
>and the LORD rescues me.

Evening and morning and noon   18
>I complain and I moan,
>>and He hears my voice.

He has ransomed my life unharmed   19
>from my battle,
>>for many were against me—

Ishmael and Jalam and the dweller in the east,   20
>who never will change and do not fear God.

---

16. *May death come upon them.* In the context of the preceding verses, it would make no sense for the plural pronoun to refer to the treacherous friend, so the object of this curse would have to be the perpetrators of mischief and deceit mentioned above.

18. *I complain and I moan.* These two terms point back to the terms used in verse 3.

19. *unharmed.* Or "in peace."

for many were against me. The usual sense of the preposition used here, *'imadi,* is "with me," but there are some instances in which it, or its shorter form *'im,* can mean "against."

20. *Ishmael and Jalam and the dweller in the east.* The translation here adopts an emendation that has considerable scholarly support, turning this into a small list of the enemies arrayed against the speaker. The Masoretic text reads *yishmaʿ ʾel weyaʿnem weyoshev qedem,* literally, and unintelligibly, "God hears and answers them and is seated as of old." In the reconstruction, the first two words and the last two remain unchanged, but they are construed as gentilic names rather than as references to God, and *weyaʿnem* is amended to *weyaʿlam.* Jalam is mentioned in Genesis 36:5 as one of the peoples descended from Esau.

21   He reached out his hand against his allies,
                profaned his own pact.
22   His mouth was smoother than butter—
                and battle in his heart.
      His words were softer than oil,
                yet they were drawn swords.
23   Cast your lot on the LORD
                and He will support you.
                        He will never let the righteous stumble.
24   And You, O God, bring them down
                to the pit of destruction.
      Men of bloodshed and deceit
                Will not finish half their days.
                        But I shall trust in You.

---

21. *He reached out his hand.* The singular reference would be to the implacable enemies who do not fear God, with this particular kind of move from plural to singular clearly allowable in biblical usage.

22. *and battle in his heart.* The cryptic Hebrew literally says "and his heart's battle."

24. *Men of bloodshed and deceit.* These paired terms pick up at the end two different themes of the poem: "bloodshed" recalling the imagery of swords and armed attack, "deceit" harking back to the guile and deceit that never part from the town square.

56

For the lead player, on *jonath elem rehokim*, a David *michtam*, when   1
the Philistines seized him in Gath.
  Grant me grace, O God,   2
        for a man tramples me,
           all day long the assailant does press me.
  My attackers trample me all day long,   3
        for many assail me, O High One.
  When I fear, I trust in You,   4

---

1. *on* jonath elem rehokim. This is one of the most mysterious of the musical terms in Psalms. The literal sense of the three Hebrew words is haunting: the mute dove of distant places. The great medieval poet Judah Halevi responded to the evocativeness of the phrase in his poetry by turning it into a concrete image of Israel's exile.

    michtam. This is another unknown category of psalm. In later Hebrew, it comes to mean "aphorism," but that is scarcely its biblical sense.

    when the Philistines seized him in Gath. As usual, the connection is tenuous between this specific identification of an episode in David's life and the content of the psalm.

2. *Grant me grace*. The speaker now launches on a set opening formula for the psalm of supplication.

3. *O High One*. The translation here is only a guess, and perhaps a strained one. The Hebrew *marom* means "height" and is not a general designation for God. An alternative would be to read *mimarom*, "from the height," "from above."

5   in God, Whose word I praise,
                in God I trust, I shall not fear.
                      What can flesh do to me?

6   All day long they put pain in my words,
                against me all their plots for evil.

7   They scheme, they lie low,
                they keep at my heels
                    as they hope for my life.

8   For their mischief free me from them.
                In wrath bring down peoples, O God.

9   My flagrant fate You Yourself have counted out—
                put my tears in Your flask.
                    Are they not in Your counting?

---

5. *in God, Whose word I praise.* The syntax here (and in the refrain-like recurrence in verse 11) is a little crabbed. The Hebrew has no equivalent of "whose" ('*asher*), but in poetic grammar '*asher* is often elided.

6. *they put pain in my words.* The Hebrew sounds at least as odd as this. Evidence of early struggling with the text is provided by the sundry ancient versions, which variously substitute a different verb for the enigmatic one that appears in the received text.

8. *For their mischief free me from them.* The Hebrew here is obscure. Literally, it says: "For mischief free [from? for?] them." Efforts to interpret the verb *palet* as "cast out" are dubious, because it always means to free or extricate from distress.

9. *My flagrant fate.* The most likely meaning of *nod* here is pain or sorrow, though the same root can also refer to wandering. The alliterative translation, moving from "flagrant" to "flask," is a distant approximation of the Hebrew sound play, in which *nod* is played against *no'd*, "flask," at the end of the next verset.

    put my tears in Your flask. In the midst of a psalm chiefly made up of familiar formulas, we see a striking image—one that the Midrash duly elaborated—of a compassionate God gathering the tears of the sufferer in a celestial flask and counting every one.

Then shall my enemies turn back   10
      on the day I call.
            This I know, that God is for me.
In God, Whose word I praise,   11
      in the LORD Whose word I praise,
in God I trust, I shall not fear.   12
         What can man do to me?
I take upon me, O God, my vows to You.   13
         I shall pay thanksgiving offerings to You.
For You saved me from death,   14
        yes, my foot from slipping,
to walk in God's presence
        in the light of life.

---

11. *In God, Whose word I praise.* The poem now uses an extended refrain that occupies two whole verses.

13. *my vows to You.* The literal sense of the more compact Hebrew is "Your vows."

57

1 For the lead player, *al-tashchet*, a David *michtam*, when he fled from
   Saul into the cave.
2   Grant me grace, God, grant me grace,
                    for in You I have taken shelter,
              and in Your wings' shadow do I shelter
                    until disasters pass.
3   I call out to God the Most High,
                    to the god who requites me.

---

1. al-tashchet. Evidently, this is still another musical term, the meaning of
which has been lost. The medieval Hebrew commentator David Kimchi ingen-
iously links it with David's rebuke to his men when they came upon Saul sleeping in their cave: 'al-tashḥiteihu, "do him no violence." The tie-in of the
superscription with an episode in David's life seems to be an after-the-fact editorial maneuver. The poem is a general psalm of supplication, turning into a
thanksgiving psalm at the end, as many others do.

2. *in Your wings' shadow do I shelter*. The speaker thus implicitly casts himself
as a fledgling bird, protected by its parent—a recurrent biblical image.

3. *who requites me*. The translation reads, with the Septuagint, *gomel*,
"requites," instead of the Masoretic *gomer* ("finishes"?).

He will send from the heavens and rescue me   4
      —he who tramples me reviled me—   selah
        God will send his steadfast kindness.
I lie down among lions   5
      that pant for human beings.
Their fangs are spear and arrows,
      their tongue a sharpened sword.
Loom over the heavens, O God.   6
      Over all the earth Your glory.
A net they set for my steps,   7
      they pushed down my neck,
they dug before me a pit—
      they themselves fell into it.   selah

---

4. *he who tramples me reviled me.* The two Hebrew words here, *ḥeref sho'afi*, seem syntactically out of place and are obscure in meaning. The safest construction, without performing extensive surgery on the text, is to read this clause as a parenthetical remark about the speaker's desperate plight, with the "will send" of the third verset then picking up the "will send" of the first verset both semantically and syntactically.

5. *their tongue a sharpened sword.* The sword image develops, through a pun, the "panting" of the lions, because that verb, *lohatim*, is associated with "the flame [*lahat*] of the whirling sword" in Genesis 3:24.

7. *they pushed down my neck.* The verb in the received text is in the singular. Either it is a scribal error and should be in the plural, or it reflects a use of the third-person singular as an equivalent of the passive ("my neck was pushed down"). The most compelling sense of *nafshi* here is not "my life" or "me" but "my neck," because the whole context is one of physical entrapment—the net and the pit.

8 My heart is firm, O God,
          my heart is firm.
              Let me sing and hymn.
9 Awake, O lyre,
          awake, O lute and lyre.
              I would waken the dawn.
10 Let me acclaim You among the peoples, Master.
          Let me hymn You among the nations.
11 For Your kindness is great to the heavens,
          and to the skies Your steadfast truth.

----

8. *My heart is firm.* These words signal a transition, but it is by no means necessary to infer, as some scholars have, that they mark the beginning of a separate poem. The speaker, having brought the expression of his distress to a
climax, now affirms his unwavering confidence in God's saving power, a confidence so strong that he can move on from supplication to thanksgiving.

9. *Awake, O lyre.* The Masoretic text reads *kevodi* ("my glory" or, perhaps, "my
being"), but one manuscript as well as the Syriac reads *kinori*, "my lyre," which
seems more likely, yielding an incremental repetition of terms for stringed
instruments in this verse.
   I would waken the dawn. In these beautiful words the speaker imagines himself rising before daybreak with his stringed instrument to rouse the sleeping
dawn with his song. Film viewers may recall a similar notion in the classic
Brazilian film *Black Orpheus*, where the singer Orfeo explains to the two boys
whom he befriends that it is his song, played on a guitar, that makes the dawn
come up.

11. *For Your kindness is great to the heavens, / and to the skies Your steadfast truth.*
The rousing of the dawn at the eastern edge of the sky now leads the speaker-
singer to envisage God's benign presence over all the heavens. The hendiadys
ḥesed-weʾemet (as in verse 4) means something like "steadfast kindness" (literally, "kindness and truth"). Here, the two terms have been divided between the
first and second verset; "steadfast" is added in the translation to "truth" to suggest something of what they mean when joined together.

Loom over the heavens, O God.

     Over all the earth Your glory.

---

12. *Loom over the heavens.* Verse 6 is repeated here verbatim as a closing refrain. But, given the celestial focus of verse 11 and its anticipation at the end of verse 9, God's looming over the heavens takes on added meaning at the end.

58

1 For the lead player *al-tashcheth*, a David *michtam*.

2   Do you, O chieftains, indeed speak justice,
          in rightness judge humankind?

3   In your heart you work misdeeds on earth,
          weigh a case with outrage in your hands.

4   The wicked backslide from the very womb,
          the lie-mongers go astray from birth.

5   They have venom akin to the serpent's venom,
          like the deaf viper that stops up its ears,

---

2. *Do you, O chieftains, indeed speak justice.* The English reader should be warned that the Hebrew text of this psalm, from this verse to the end, with the sole exception of the ferocious verses 7 and 11, is badly mangled. As a result, a good deal of the translation is necessarily conjectural or must rely on emendation. A literal rendering of the Hebrew for this verset would be: "Indeed muteness justice you speak." The translation reads *'eylim*, "chieftains," instead of *'elem*, "muteness."

3. *weigh a case.* The translation is based on a guess that the reference is judicial, although the entire line sounds strange. Another sense of the Hebrew verb in question is "to pave a way."

4. *backslide.* The meaning of the verb *zoru* is in dispute.

5. *like the deaf viper that stops up its ears.* The peculiarity of this simile, which continues into the next verse, could conceivably derive from a piece of ancient folk zoology that we no longer possess. It is possible that the viper was thought to be deaf because it has no external ears. The wicked resemble the viper both in being venomous and in turning a deaf ear—in their case, to the pleas of their victims.

so it hears not the soothsayers' voice   6
        nor the cunning caster of spells.
God, smash their teeth in their mouth.   7
        The jaws of the lions shatter, O LORD.
Let them melt away, like water run off.   8
        Let Him pull back His arrows so they be cut down.
Like a snail that moves in its slime,   9
        a woman's stillbirth that sees not the sun,
before their thorns ripen in bramble,   10
        still alive and in wrath rushed to ruin.
The just man rejoices when vengeance he sees,   11
        his feet he will bathe in the wicked one's blood.

---

8. *Let Him pull back His arrows.* If in fact God is the subject of this verb (the Hebrew of the entire verset is rather crabbed), the image of shooting an arrow at the wicked is discontinuous with the image of their melting away like water. An alternative construction, somewhat strained in regard to the Hebrew syntax, would be "as they pull back their arrows, they are cut off."

9. *Like a snail that moves in its slime.* The crux here in the Hebrew is the otherwise unattested noun *temes*. It might derive from the root meaning "to melt" (as in the verb at the beginning of verse 8) and so could refer to the slimy secretion of the snail as an image of dissolution or transience.
    that sees not the sun. The Hebrew is opaque, especially because the verb as it stands is in the plural.

10. *before their thorns ripen in bramble.* The Hebrew seems to say, "before their thorns understand [*yavinu*] bramble." The translation assumes that two consonants have been transposed in the verb, which should read *yanivu,* "ripen."
    still alive and in wrath rushed to ruin. The translation of the cryptic Hebrew is only a guess.

12   And man will say, "Yes, there is fruit for the just.
                 Yes, there are gods judging the earth."

---

12. *And man will say.* Or "And a person will say." The two Hebrew words are
correct as to grammar, though they look odd as an idiom.

there are gods judging the earth. The psalm concludes with another oddity in
the Hebrew text. *'Elohim*, which is always treated as a singular despite its plural form when it refers to the one God, here is joined to a plural verbal form. A
traditional view that the term sometimes means "magistrates" stands on shaky
ground. Either the usage here is anomalous, with the actual meaning, "there is
a God judging the earth," or, as the translation assumes, the concluding statement is from the viewpoint of people in general ("man"), and not necessarily
monotheistic people. According to their own theological lights, all will conclude that there are just gods on earth.

59

For the lead player *al-tashcheth*, a David *michtam*, when Saul sent   1
out and they kept watch over the house to put him to death.
> Save me from my enemies, my God,   2
> > over those who rise against me make me safe.
> Save me from the wrongdoers,   3
> > and from men of bloodshed rescue me.
> For, look, they lie in wait for my life,   4
> > the powerful scheme against me
> > > —not for my wrong nor my offense, O LORD.
> For no misdeed they rush, aim their bows.   5
> > Rise toward me and see!
> And You, LORD, God of armies, God of Israel,   6
> > awake to make a reckoning with all the nations.
> > > Do not pardon all wrongdoing traitors.   selah

---

1. *when Saul sent out.* The reference is to 1 Samuel 19, when Saul sends killers to stake out David's house and murder him. In the event, with the decisive help of his wife, Michal, Saul's daughter, David manages to escape. The tenuous connection with our psalm is the speaker's sense that his life is threatened (for example, verse 4, "they lie in wait for my life"). But as the poem unfolds, it looks as though physical attack is actually a metaphor for vicious slander. David would scarcely refer to Saul's men as "all the nations."

2–3. Both these lines of poetry are cast as neat chiasms: Save me—from my enemies—those who rise against me,—make me safe; Save me—the wrong-doers—men of bloodshed—rescue me (abbá).

5. *aim their bows.* The object of the verb is merely implied in the Hebrew.

7 They come back at evening,
     they mutter like dogs.
          They prowl round the town.

8 Look, they speak out with their mouths—
     and swords in their lips—
          for who would hear?

9 And You, LORD, laugh at them,
     You mock all the nations.

10 My Strength, for You I keep watch,
     for God is my fortress.

11 My steadfast God will come to meet me,
     God will grant me sight of my foes' defeat.

---

7. *they mutter like dogs.* The muttering or growling anticipates the malicious speech of the next verse. As elsewhere, "dogs" (singular in the Hebrew) is a pejorative concept.

8. *for who would hear?* The implication seems to be that they fear no human or divine judge and so feel free to pronounce harmful slander without compunction.

10. *My Strength.* The Masoretic text reads "his strength," but several manuscripts show "my Strength."
     for You I keep watch. As an idiom for trusting in God, the Hebrew is odd. The choice of verb may be intended to play against its negative sense in the superscription.

11. *My steadfast God.* The Hebrew is *'elohey ḥasdi*. For the most part, this translation represents *ḥesed* as "kindness," but it equally means "steadfastness," "commitment to keeping covenantal obligations." The context of a plea to be rescued from enemies suggests that the latter meaning is the more salient one here. The same two Hebrew words occur again at the end of the psalm.
     grant me sight of my foes' defeat. As elsewhere, "defeat" is merely implied in the Hebrew idiom.

Do not kill them lest my people forget.   12
      Through Your force make them wander, pull them
      down,
            our shield and Master.
Through their mouth's offense, the word of their lips   13
      they will be trapped in their haughtiness,
            and through the oaths and the falsehood they
            utter.
Destroy, O destroy in wrath, that they be no more,   14
      and it will be known to the ends of the earth
            that God rules over Jacob.   selah
They come back at evening,   15
      they mutter like dogs.
            They prowl round the town.
They wander in search of food   16
      if they are not sated, till they pass the night.
But I shall sing of Your strength,   17
      and chant gladly each morning Your kindness.
For You were a fortress for me,
      a haven when I was in straits.
My Strength, to You I would hymn,   18
      for God is my fortress,
            my steadfast God.

---

12. *Do not kill them . . . / . . . make them wander.* The idea is that the frustrated enemies, in a state of exile, neediness, and humiliation, will be a living object lesson to others. But in verse 14, the speaker prays for their destruction.

15. *They come back at evening.* This verbatim repetition of verse 7 is either intended as a refrain or is an inadvertent scribal repetition. It seems ill-placed after the wish for total destruction of the enemies in the previous verse. It is conceivable that verse 14 is an interpolation, spliced in from another psalm.

16. *if they are not sated, till they pass the night.* Like the English, the Hebrew is obscure syntactically. Literally, it says "if they are not sated, and they pass the night."

60

1 For the lead player, on *shushan-eduth*, a David *michtam*, to teach,
2 when he clashed with Aram-Naharaim and Aram-Zobah, and Joab
   came back and struck down twelve thousand of Edom in the Valley
   of Salt.
3   God, You have abandoned us, breached us.
                 You were incensed—restore us to life!
4   You made the land quake, You cracked it.
                 Heal its shards, for it has toppled.

---

1. *on* shushan-eduth. This is another opaque term that refers to a musical
instrument or a musical mode.

   to teach. It is not clear whether the song is to be taught or its content
involves a moral that should be learned.

2. *when he clashed with Aram-Naharaim and Aram-Zobah.* This campaign
against these armies east of the Jordan is reported in 2 Samuel 10:15–19. The
proclamation of God's sovereignty over Moab and Edom in verse 10 may have
led to the connection claimed in the superscription, but other details do not
entirely fit the episode from the David story.

3. *restore us to life.* The Hebrew says only "restore to us," but an implied object,
nafsheinu, "our life," seems likely.

4. *You made the land quake.* Though some interpreters have taken this as a
literal reference to an earthquake, it is more probably a metaphorical image
of devastation by invaders, because the psalm as a whole is concerned with
military enemies.

You sated Your people with harsh drink,   5
      You made us drink poison wine.
You once gave to those who fear You   6
      a banner for rallying because of the truth.   selah
So that Your friends be set free,   7
      rescue with Your right hand and answer us.
God once spoke in His holiness: 8
      "Let Me exult and share out Shechem,
          and the valley of Sukkoth I shall measure.
Mine is Gilead and Mine Manasseh,   9
      and Ephraim My foremost stronghold,
          Judah My scepter.

---

5. *with harsh drink.* The Hebrew says only "with harsh," *qashah*, which may be an ellipsis (or omission) for *kos qashah*, literally, "harsh cup."

6. *You once gave.* "Once" is added for clarity. This verse flatly contradicts the previous one, but the contradiction is resolved if one assumes that the speaker is recalling an earlier time when God stood staunchly by His people.

   because of the truth. The Hebrew phrase here is doubtful. The rare term *qoshet* does mean "truth" in Aramaic. The Septuagint and the Syriac understood this to mean "because of [or "in the face of"] the bow," reading *qeshet* instead of *qoshet*, with the last consonant *taw* instead of *tet*.

8. *God once spoke.* The translation adds "once" for the same reason of clarity cited in the note to verse 6.

9. *Mine is Gilead . . . / Judah my scepter.* This bracketing of northern territories with Judah as the capital city has led some interpreters to infer that the psalm is early, before the breakup of the united kingdom after Solomon's death.

10   Moab is My washbasin,
                upon Edom I fling My sandal,
                        over Philistia I shout exultant."
11   Who will lead me to the beseiged town,
                who will guide me to Edom?
12   Have You not, O God, abandoned us?
                You do not sally forth, God, with our armies.
13   Give us help against the foe
                when rescue by man is in vain.
14   Through God we shall gather strength,
                and He will stamp out our foes.

---

10. *Moab is My washbasin, / upon Edom I fling My sandal.* These are images of contemptuous domination: Moab is a humble receptacle for bathing water, Edom a disregarded place where one casually flings a sandal. The poet intends a shocking contrast between these humble terms and the language of military strength ("stronghold," "scepter") in the previous line.

   over Philistia I shout exultant. The received text here reads, "Over Me, Philistia, shout exultant [or, perhaps, break to pieces]." But the duplicate version of this text, Psalm 108:10, has a much more plausible reading, and that is the one used for the translation here. The reference to Philistia might also argue for an early date for this psalm.

11. *Who will lead me to the beseiged town / . . . guide me to Edom.* The speaker, having quoted God's words of triumph over Edom in the past, now returns to his own plight in the present, in a desperate war with Edom and perhaps other peoples, wondering whether he can bring the siege against the enemy to a successful conclusion.

12. *Have You not, O God, abandoned us?* As the poem moves toward its conclusion, the opening phrase, in a slightly altered form, is repeated as part of an envelope structure.

   You do not sally forth, God, with our armies. This idea of the deity joining forces with its people in the battlefield is a common one in the ancient Near East. It is much in evidence in Joshua, Judges, and Samuel.

61

For the lead player, on stringed instruments, for David.   1

  Hear, God, my song,   2

             listen close to my prayer.

  From the end of the earth I call You.   3

             When my heart faints, You lead me to a rock high

             above me.

  For You have been a shelter to me,   4

             a tower of strength in the face of the foe.

  Let me dwell in Your tent for all time,   5

             let me shelter in Your wings' hiding-place.   selah

---

2. *Hear God, my song.* Though the word for "song," *rinah,* usually means "glad song," the present context is one of supplication, the speaker crying out to God as he is beset by life-threatening dangers ("When my heart faints").

3. *You lead me to a rock high above me.* The Hebrew syntax is crabbed, but given that "rock," *tsur,* regularly recurs in Psalms as a synonym for an impregnable fortress, the sense would seem to be that when the speaker's heart fails within him under the murderous assault of the foe (verse 4), God provides him a safe refuge.

5. *Let me dwell in Your tent.* As elsewhere, "tent" is a poetic epithet for the temple, also conceived as a place of refuge. The cultic context is made explicit in the reference to votary offerings ("vows") in the next line and at the end of the psalm.

6   For You, God, have heard my vows,
            You have granted the plea of those who fear Your name.

7   Days may You add to the days of the king,
            his years be like those of generations untold.

8   May he ever abide in the presence of God.
            Steadfast kindness ordain to preserve him!

9   So let me hymn Your name forever
            as I pay my vows day after day.

---

6. *granted the plea.* The Hebrew appears to say "inheritance" (*yerushat*), but it seems plausible, as many scholars have proposed, that the original reading was *'areshet*, "plea."

7. *Days may You add to the days of the king.* This petition on behalf of the king, which turns the supplication into a royal psalm, is puzzling because the speaker until this point appears to be making an entreaty about his own personal plight. Either he identifies the fate of the nation with his own fate, so that the enemies threatening the nation are imagined as menacing him personally, or these two verses have been spliced in from another psalm.

62

For the lead player, on *jeduthun*, a David psalm.   1
  Only in God is my being quiet.   2
        From Him is my rescue.
  Only He is my rock and my rescue,   3
        my stronghold—I shall not stumble.

---

1. *on* jeduthun. This is either an opaque musical term, or it might refer, as some have conjectured, to a particular group of levitical choristers. When the term appears in 39:1, the preposition attached to it is "for," and it is translated as a proper noun. Here the preposition is "on."

2. *Only in God is my being quiet.* The Hebrew says literally "toward" God. The emphatic "only" ('*akh*) begins six different lines in this poem—four of them referring to God; one, antithetically, to the relentless malevolent intentions of the speaker's enemies; and one to the ephemerality and insubstantiality of human existence. The references in the poem to enemies connects it generically with the supplication, but its leading edge is an affirmation of trust in God. This feeling is expressed with the most affecting simplicity, beginning here with the idea that in or through God the speaker's inner being (*nefesh*) finds quiet, is at peace.

3. *I shall not stumble at all.* The adverbial *rabah* in the Hebrew sounds peculiar. Because it is adjectival in form, meaning "abundant" or "much," one wonders whether there is a missing feminine noun that should precede it, such as '*et rabah*, "for long" (literally, "much time").

4   How long will you demolish a man—
        commit murder, each one of you—
   like a leaning wall,
        a shaky fence?

5   Only from his high place they schemed to shake him.
        They took pleasure in lies.
   With their mouths they blessed
        and inwardly cursed.   selah

6   Only in God be quiet, my being,
        for from Him is my hope.

7   Only He is my rock and my rescue,
        my fortress—I shall not stumble.

8   From God is my rescue and glory,
        my strength's rock and my shelter in God.

9   Trust in Him at all times, O people.
        Pour out your hearts before Him.
           God is our shelter.   selah

---

4. *like a leaning wall, / a shaky fence.* This image refers back to "demolish" (or "cause disaster to"); the intervening mention of murder specifies the nature of the demolition. Proposals to emend the verb "murder" so that it yields "smash" reflect an effort to make the text read more smoothly and more "logically" than the poet may have intended.

5. *from his high place.* The Hebrew *mise'eito* is obscure, but it might derive from a verb that means "to lift."

6. *Only in God be quiet, my being.* The poem returns in a kind of refrain to its beginning, but now it turns the quietness of the speaker's inner self into an imperative and substitutes "hope" for "rescue."

7. *I shall not stumble.* When these words from verse 3 recur here, they lack the problematic adjective *rabah*.

9. *Trust in Him at all times, O people.* Until this point, the speaker has been expressing his own profound trust in God. Now he turns, in a plural imperative, to his people and enjoins them to share this sustaining trust.

Only breath—humankind,   10
        the sons of man are a lie.
On the scales all together
        they weigh less than a breath.
Do not trust in oppression   11
        and of theft have no illusions.
Though it bear fruit of wealth,
        set your heart not upon it.
One thing God has spoken,   12
        two things have I heard:
that strength is but God's,   13
        and Yours, Master, is kindness.
For You requite a man by his deeds.

---

10. *Only breath—humankind.* The psalmist now, after the segment-marking selah, adds a new element to this meditation on the meaning of trust in God—an Ecclesiastian reflection on the flimsy, fleeting nature of human life. The term *hevel* ("breath" or "vapor," what the King James Version abstracts into "vanity") is one that Ecclesiastes uses repeatedly.

On the scales all together. The Hebrew syntax looks scrambled, but the general sense is clear. In a move of intensification, the poet, having invoked the proverbial equation of human life with mere breath, now invites us to visualize all of humanity being placed in one pan of a scales and mere breath in the other. The pan with humankind would rise higher, for even breath is more substantial.

11. *have no illusions.* The verb used is derived from the same root as *hevel*, "breath."

13. *For You requite a man by his deeds.* This line lacks any parallelism (rhythmic, syntactic, or semantic) in the Hebrew. It may be set here as a kind of prose coda to the poem. But it is a fitting conclusion to the quiet eloquence of the psalm, summing up the speaker's sense that he can trust in God because God will mete out to each man according to his deserts.

63

1 A David psalm, when he was in the wilderness of Judea.
2   God, my God, for You I search.
                    My throat thirsts for You,
    my flesh yearns for You
                  in a land waste and parched, with no water.
3   So, in the sanctum I beheld You,
                  seeing Your strength and Your glory.

---

1. *when he was in the wilderness of Judea.* The most likely moment for this allusion to the David story is when he is hiding out from Saul, precisely in this region. The superscription latches onto the evocation of a waste land in verse 2, though that evocation might in fact be only figurative.

2. *My throat thirsts for You.* The multivalent *nefesh* could conceivably mean "being" (King James Version, "soul"), but the parallelism with "flesh" suggests the anatomical sense of the term. The speaker's longing for God is so overwhelmingly intense that he feels it as a somatic experience, like the thirsty throat of a man in the desert, like yearning flesh.

3. *in the sanctum I beheld You.* Given the fluidity of verb tenses in biblical poetry, this could also be construed as a wish for future consummation, but it is at least as plausible that the speaker, achingly longing for a God from whom he feels distant, remembers a time when he stood in the temple and beheld God's glorious presence.

For Your kindness is better than life. 4
   My lips praise You.
Thus I bless You while I live, 5
   in Your name I lift up my palms.
As with ripest repast my being is sated, 6
   and with lips of glad song my mouth declares praise.
Yes, I recalled You on my couch. 7
   In the night-watches I dwelled upon You.
For You were a help to me, 8
   and in Your wings' shadow I uttered glad song.
My being clings to You, 9
   for Your right hand has sustained me.
But they for disaster have sought my life— 10
   may they plunge to the depths of the earth.
May their blood be shed by the sword, 11
   may they be served up to the foxes.

---

4. *My lips praise You.* As a thanksgiving psalm, this poem especially focuses on the lips that pronounce God's praise. Verse 6 introduces the memorable phrase *siftey renanot*, "lips of glad song."

6. *ripest repast.* The literal meaning of the Hebrew here is "suet and rich food" (King James Version, "marrow and fatness"), but that scarcely works in English as poetry.

10. *But they . . . have sought my life.* Only now does the familiar element of threatening enemies come into the psalm, but it remains background rather than foreground. And no sooner are the enemies mentioned than their wished-for defeat is imagined—because of the speaker's trust in God's protection—as a virtually accomplished fact.
 may they plunge. The literal sense of the Hebrew verb is "enter into."

11. *may they be served up to the foxes.* The literal formulation is "may they be the foxes' portion." For a corpse to lie unburied, to be consumed by scavengers, is an ultimate curse in biblical literature, as it is in Greek.

12   But the king will rejoice in God,
                all who swear by him will revel,
                        for the mouth of the liars is muzzled.

---

12. *But the king will rejoice in God.* The appearance of the king at the end of a psalm that all along has expressed the feelings of one person is surprising. Either it has been spliced in editorially as a "public" conclusion, a procedure that appears to have been used for the endings of quite a few psalms, or the speaker somehow associates the enemies threatening him with enemies of the nation.

64

For the lead player, a David psalm.
    Hear, God, my voice in my plea.
        From fear of the enemy guard my life.
Conceal me from the counsel of evil men,
        from the hubbub of the wrongdoers,
who whetted their tongue like a sword,
        pulled back their arrow—a bitter word—
to shoot in concealment the innocent,
        in a flash shot him down without fear.
They encourage themselves with evil words.
        They recount how traps should be laid.
        They say, Who will see them?

1
2

3

4

5

6

---

2. *Hear, God, my voice in my plea.* These opening words of the poem explicitly announce its status as supplication.

3. *from the hubbub.* The Hebrew *rigshah* indicates an agitated condition (it is the same root as the verb in Psalm 2:1, "Why are the nations aroused"). Given that the malice of the evil men here is expressed in slanderous speech ("who whetted their tongue like a sword"), "hubbub" seems an appropriate term for this particular agitation.

6. *encourage . . . recount.* The precise meaning of the two verbs ḥazeq and saper, common enough elsewhere, is obscure in this particular context, and there may be a textual problem.

7   "Let them search out foul deeds!
          We have hidden them from the utmost search,
   in a man's inward self,
          and deep is the heart."
8   But God will shoot an arrow at them.
          In a flash they will be struck down.
9   And their tongue will cause them to stumble,
          all who see them will nod in derision.
10   And all men will fear
          and tell of God's act,
            and His deed they will grasp.
11   May the righteous rejoice in the LORD and shelter in Him,
          and may all the upright revel.

---

7. *We have hidden.* The Masoretic text says *tamnu,* "we are finished," but several manuscripts show *tamanu* (with a *tet* rather than with a *taw*), "we have hidden."

from the utmost search. The literal sense of the Hebrew is "a searched-out search." The apparent meaning is that we have hidden our lethal intentions in the most deeply buried place—the inward heart of man.

8. *God will shoot . . . at them.* In the most explicit manner, the poem reverses the malicious intentions of the slanderers. They sought to shoot the innocent with the bow of their evil talk; instead, God will shoot them down, and their own tongue will actually cause them to stumble.

65

For the lead player, a psalm; for David, a song. ₁
    To You silence is praise, God, in Zion, ₂
                and to You a vow will be paid.
    O, Listener to prayer, ₃
                unto You all flesh shall come.
    My deeds of mischief are too much for me. ₄
                Our crimes but You atone.

---

2. *To You, silence is praise.* Despite many divergent interpretations of the Hebrew noun *dumiyah*, the most likely meaning, in view of other biblical occurrences of the verbal root it reflects, is "silence." The speaker begins this psalm of praise—in a paradoxical gesture regarding speech and silence familiar in poetry in many languages, all the way to the early modernist French poet Mallarmé—by affirming that the subject of the poem, God's greatness, is beyond what language can express, so that silence alone is due praise. The poet, however, cannot remain silent, and he goes on to celebrate God's goodness.

4. *My deeds of mischief are too much for me.* The sense of human sinfulness gets only fleeting expression in this psalm. The second verset goes on immediately to affirm the speaker's trust in God's atoning power.

5   Happy whom You choose to draw close,
            he will dwell in Your courts.
      May we be sated with Your house's bounty,
            the holiness of Your temple.

6   With awesome acts justly You answer us,
            our rescuing God,
      refuge of all the earth's ends
            and the far-flung sea,

7   Who sets mountains firm in His power,
            —He is girded in might—

8   Who quiets the roar of the seas,
            the roar of their waves and the tumult of nations.

9   And those who dwell at earth's ends will fear Your signs.
            The portals of morning and evening You gladden.

10   You pay mind to the earth and soak it.
            You greatly enrich it.
      God's stream is filled with water.
            You ready their grain, for so You ready it.

---

5. *the holiness of Your temple.* The received text says *qedosh*, which would yield "the holy one of Your temple," but several ancient versions register *qodesh*, "holiness."

6. *all the earth's ends / . . . the far-flung sea.* God's bounty to all creatures is represented in splendidly global terms. This reach across all the earth and the far-flung sea then sets the stage for the depiction of God's watering of the thirsty soil to provide crops.

8. *Who quiets the roar of the seas.* If this phrase and the one that follows draw on Canaanite mythological imagery of subduing the primordial sea monster, that background is held at a great remove. The leading edge of the line is a celebration of God's power over all nature and over humanity as well ("the tumult of nations.").

10. *You ready their grain, for so You ready it.* The repetition here seems odd, and its expressive function is not entirely clear.

Quench the thirst of its furrows, smooth out its hillocks,   11
      melt it with showers, its growth You will bless.
You crown Your bountiful year,   12
      and Your pathways drip ripeness.
The wilderness meadows do drip,   13
      and with joy the hills are girded.
The pastures are clothed with flocks   14
      and the valleys are mantled with grain.
            They shout for joy, they even sing.

---

11. *smooth out its hillocks.* The meaning at least of the verb in this clause is somewhat doubtful, but it may well derive from a root that means "to descend," or in the conjugation used here, "to bring down," hence "smooth out," *naḥet.*

13–14. *girded . . . clothed . . . mantled.* The poem concludes with a beautiful figure of attire (perhaps already prefigured in "crown") for the bucolic panorama of the flourishing hills and valleys covered with crops and livestock.

66

1 To the lead player, a song, a psalm.
    Shout out to God, all the earth.
2   Hymn His name's glory.
                     Make His praise glory.
3 Say to God, "How awesome Your deeds.
          Before Your great strength Your enemies quail."
4 All the earth bows down to You,
        and they hymn to You, hymn Your name.   selah
5 Come and see the acts of God,
        awesome in works over humankind.
6 He turned sea to dry land,
        the torrent they crossed on foot.
           There we rejoiced in Him.
7 He rules in His might forever.
        His eyes probe the nations.
           Let the wayward not rise up.   selah

---

1. *Shout out to God.* This initial imperative to acclaim God signals the beginning of a thanksgiving psalm.

6. *He turned sea to dry land, / the torrent they crossed on foot.* As in a number of other psalms, the miraculous crossing of the Sea of Reeds, telescoped with the crossing of the Jordan under Joshua, is evoked as a defining instance of God's intervention in history on behalf of His people. The association of these early water-crossings with military triumph picks up the quailing of enemies in verse 3 and anticipates God's powerful domination of nations in verse 7.

Bless, O peoples, our God,   8
       and make heard the sound of His praise,
Who has kept us in life,   9
       and not let our foot stumble.
For You tested us, God,   10
       You refined us as silver refined.
You trapped us in a net,   11
       placed heavy cords round our loins.
You let people ride over us.   12
       We came into fire and water—
       and You brought us out to great ease.

---

10. *For You tested us, God, / You refined us as silver refined.* Some interpreters have taken the imagery of testing through fire in this verse and the language of the next two verses as expressions of the ordeal of exile that began in 586 BCE There is nothing, however, in the formulations here that explicitly refers to exile, and the poet could easily have in mind any moment of impending disaster when powerful enemies threatened to overwhelm the Judean state. The speaker from verse 13 onward assumes that the temple exists. So either the whole psalm is pre-exilic or one must assume that an earlier psalm has been tacked on editorially to a later one. The switch to first-person singular beginning in verse 13 might seem to argue for this assumption, though there are many psalms that move from first-person plural to singular or the other way around, taking for granted that the fate of the individual and the fate of the nation are indivisible.

11. *heavy cords.* The Hebrew *muʿaqah* means, at least etymologically, anything heavy that presses uncomfortably.

12. *to great ease.* The Masoretic text says *lerewayah*, which would mean "abundant drink" or "satiety." But the Septuagint and two other ancient versions read *lerewaḥah* (a difference of one letter), which seems more likely.

13   I shall come to Your house with burnt-offerings
            I shall pay to You my vows
14   that my lips uttered,
            that my mouth spoke in my straits.
15   Fat burnt-offerings I shall offer up to You
            with the incense of rams,
                I shall sacrifice cattle and goats.   selah
16   Come listen and let me recount,
            all you who fear God,
                what He did for me.
17   To Him with my mouth I called out,
            exaltation upon my tongue.
18   Had I seen mischief in my heart,
            the Master would not have listened.
19   God indeed has listened,
            has hearkened to the sound of my prayer.
20   Blessed is God,
            Who has not turned away my prayer nor His kindness
            from me.

---

15. *the incense of rams.* What this telescoped phrase means is that the burning
flesh of the sacrificial lamb is a fragrant odor to God.

17. *exaltation upon my tongue.* The Hebrew literally says "exaltation under my
tongue."

20. *Blessed is God.* This concluding line, as is evident in the translation, is
unbalanced and does not scan. Because there are lines like this one at the end
of several other psalms, one suspects that it may have been an editorial practice (if not a poetic practice of the original psalmist) on occasion to add a line
of prose summary as a kind of coda to the psalm.

67

For the lead player, on stringed instruments, a psalm, a song.   1
   May God grant us grace and bless us,   2
          may He shine His face upon us.   selah
   To know on the earth Your way,   3
          among all the nations Your rescue.
   Nations acclaim You, O God,   4
          all peoples acclaim You.
   Nations rejoice in glad song,   5
          for You rule peoples rightly,
             and nations on earth You lead.   selah

---

1. *a psalm, a song.* Though this psalm begins (verse 2) with a prayer for God's favor, the emphasis quickly becomes celebratory (beginning in verse 3), and it is emphatically a thanksgiving psalm. The scholarly conjecture, first proposed in the early twentieth century, that this is the text for a harvest ritual rests on the slender evidence of the reference to crops at the beginning of verse 7, but the invocation of the nations of the earth scarcely accords with harvests. Yet the psalm does have a liturgical character in its prominent repetition of set formulas and in its symmetrical structure.

2. *shine His face upon us.* The preposition used here in the Hebrew actually means "with," but this could simply be a variation of the idiom not otherwise attested. In any case, "shine upon" seems to be the intended sense. The shining of the face is a sign of favor just as the hiding of the face is its opposite.

5. *rejoice in glad song.* Literally, "rejoice and sing gladly."

6   Nations acclaim You, O God,
              all peoples acclaim You.
7   The earth gives its yield.
              May God our God bless us.
8   May God bless us,
              and all the ends of earth fear Him.

---

6. *Nations acclaim You.* This entire verse precisely mirrors verse 4.

8. *all the ends of earth.* In this set idiom, *'erets* shows its most comprehensive sense of "earth," and the echo of the same term in the same sense from verse 3 makes a neat envelope structure. At the same time, the more limited meaning of *'erets*, "land," is probably also present in the verset on agricultural blessing, "The earth gives its yield."

68

For the lead player, for David, a psalm, a song.
  Let God arise, let His enemies scatter,
          and let His foes flee before Him.
  As smoke disperses may they disperse,
          as wax melts before fire,
               may the wicked perish before God.
  And may the righteous rejoice and exult
          before God, and be gladdened in joy.

1
2

3

4

---

2. *Let God arise, let His enemies scatter.* This entire verse is a quotation of the Song of the Ark, Numbers 10:35. The sole alteration is that the imperative verbs in Numbers become optatives here (mistakenly translated as a simple future in many modern versions, though correctly represented in the King James Version). In keeping with that change, the possessive suffix attached to "enemies" and "foes" is here third person rather than second person. But this initial quotation leaves a question about the genre of the psalm. Some have imagined that this is a liturgical text for a ceremony in which the Ark was carried into the temple. That notion, however, involves a leap of inference: The citation of the Song of the Ark could easily have been a solemn commemorative gesture in a ceremony that did not actually involve the presence of the Ark. Verses 25–30 explicitly describe a grand procession, presumably ascending the temple mount. Elsewhere, much of the poem is devoted to the evocation of a great military victory, with God commanding the battlefield. It is possible that the procession is a celebration of the victory, though there are disorienting breaks in the text (noted below). One prominent Bible scholar of the mid-twentieth century proposed that this psalm is a collage of citations from a variety of old poems, but that extreme conclusion may be a strategy of desperation. In any case, the Hebrew text is a mixture of strong and memorable lines with phrases or whole clauses that look fragmentary or scrambled.

5   Sing to God, hymn His name.
              Pave the way for the Rider of Clouds,
                    for Yah is His name, and exult before Him.
6   Father of orphans and widows' judge,
              God in His holy abode.
7   God brings the lonely back to their homes,
              sets free captives in jubilation.
                    But the wayward abide in parched land.
8   God, when You sallied forth before Your people,
              when You strode through the desert.   selah
9   The earth shook,
              the heavens, too, poured down before God,
                    Sinai itself before God, God of Israel.
10   A bountiful rain You shed, O God.
              Your estate that had languished You made firm.

---

5. *Pave the way.* Though a long line of interpreters, from the King James Version
to the present, prefers to understand the verb *solu* as meaning "praise" or
"extol," the philological evidence for that meaning is scant, and elsewhere (for
example, Isaiah 57:14, 62:10, in precisely this imperative form) the verb means
"to pave" or "prepare a highway." That would accord with the image of God as
a celestial rider mounted on clouds sweeping down over earth.

   the Rider of Clouds. The received text says ʿ*aravot*, which would appear to
mean "plains," "steppes." Either one should read ʿ*avot*, "clouds," or ʿ*aravot* here
is a variant form of ʿ*arafot*, a poetic term that means "clouds." An epithet for Baal
in Ugaritic is *rkb ʿrpt*, "rider of clouds."

7. *brings the lonely back to their homes.* The translation reads *meshiv*, "brings
back," for the Masoretic *moshiv*, "causes to dwell," though the latter would also
make sense.

   in jubilation. The translation is no more than a guess. The Hebrew *kosharot*
appears only here, and if it is really a word and not a scribal error, nobody knows
what it means.

8. *when You sallied forth before Your people.* This marks the beginning of a report of
God's awesome military triumph, accompanied by seismic upheavals and a down-
pour of rain. To "sally forth before" is a martial idiom that means "to lead an army."

Your cohorts dwelled there,   11
          You made it firm in Your goodness for the lowly, O God.
The Master gives word—   12
          the women who bear tidings are a great host:
"The kings of armies run away, run away,   13
          and the mistress of the house shares out the spoils."
If you lie down among sheepfolds . . .   14
          The wings of the dove are inlaid with silver,
               and her pinions with precious gold.

---

11. *You made it firm.* The reference is to "Your estate" in the previous verse. Because God is imagined striding through the desert in the vicinity of Mount Sinai, these lines appear to evoke the memory of victories in the Wilderness narrative—first over Egypt, then over Amalek, and later over the kingdoms of Transjordan. But as the poem continues, these early triumphs appear to blend with other victories that are more difficult for us to identify.

12. *the women who bear tidings are a great host.* Presumably, the women announce the victory, but the entire verset is obscure.

13. *the mistress of the house shares out the spoils.* This verset is a citation of another old poetic text, the Song of Deborah (Judges 5). There, it is the Canaanite women who—falsely—imagine that their men will soon return from the battle with spoils to divide among the women.

14. *If you lie down among sheepfolds.* The citation of the Song of Deborah continues here. In Judges 5, the clause refers derisively to those tribes of Israel that stayed at home and did not join in the struggle against the Canaanites. One would consequently expect these words to be followed by a negative main clause (for example, "you will be shamed in the ranks of Israel"). It looks as though something has dropped out of the text at this point.
     The wings of the dove are inlaid with silver, / and her pinions with precious gold. This exquisite line is justly famous (Henry James drew from it the title of one of his later novels), but it is unclear what it refers to. It might be an item of booty brought back by the victorious Israelite soldiers. It could even be a symbolic representation of glorious Israel.

15 When Shaddai scattered the kings there,
        it snowed on Zalmon.
16 Mountain of God, Mount Bashan,
        crooked-ridged mountain, Mount Bashan.
17 Why do you leap, O crooked-ridged mountains,
        the mountain God desired for His dwelling?
            Yes, the LORD will abide there forever!
18 The chariots of God are myriads beyond count,
        thousands of thousands.
    The Master among them
        —O, Sinai in holiness!
19 You went up to the heights,
        You took hold of your captives,
    the wayward as well—
        so that Yah God would abide.
20 Blessed be the Master day after day.
        God heaps upon us our rescue.   selah

---

15. *it snowed on Zalmon.* The meterological reference is mystifying. Snow is fairly rare in the Land of Israel, so perhaps snowfall on this mountain in the vicinity of Hebron was remembered as part of the miraculous character of the victory.

17. *Why do you leap, O crooked-ridged mountains.* The leaping of mountains accords with the seismic upheaval of verse 9. Similar imagery occurs in Psalm 114. It should be said that the meaning of the verb is in dispute.
   the mountain God desired for His dwelling. Mount Bashan is not otherwise known as a dwelling place of God.

19. *so that Yah God would abide.* This evidently means that God trampled over His enemies to establish for Himself a firm earthly abode, but, as with much of this psalm, the verset is not altogether clear.

God is to us a rescuing God.   21
    The LORD Master possesses the ways out from death.
Yes, God will smash His enemies' heads,   22
    the hairy pate of those who walk about in their guilt.
The Master said, "From Bashan I shall bring back,   23
    bring back from the depths of the sea.
That your foot may wade in blood,   24
    the tongues of your dogs lick the enemies."
They saw Your processions, O God,   25
    my God's processions, my King in holiness.
The singers came first and then the musicians   26
    in the midst of young women beating their drums.
In choruses bless God,   27
    the LORD, from the fountain of Israel.

---

21. *possesses the ways out from death.* This phrase is probably both mythological and historical. God holds sway over the realm of death, commanding the exit passages from it. In nonmythological terms, God brings back his people on the battlefield from the brink of death.

23. *bring back.* The implied object is Israel, threatened with captivity or death.

24. *That your foot may wade in blood.* This gory image would seem to be words addressed by God to collective Israel. The reference to dogs in the second verset appears to exclude the possibility that "you" is God because there is no known tradition of the God of Israel keeping dogs.
    the tongues of your dogs lick the enemies. The last word in the Hebrew here, *minehu*, is crabbed, but it might mean literally "his portion" (of food). The desecration of the corpse by canine scavengers is part of Elijah's curse of Ahab and a recurrent source of horror in the ancient world.

25. *They saw Your processions.* Without transition, the poem jumps from the victory to a ceremonial march on Mount Zion.

28   There little Benjamin holds sway over them,
           Judah's princes in their raiment,
               Zebulon's princes, Naphtali's princes.
29   Ordain, O God, Your strength,
           strength, O God, that You showed for us,
30   from Your temple, over Jerusalem.
           To You the kings bring gifts.
31   Rebuke the beast of the marsh,
               the herd of bulls among calves of the peoples—
       cringing with offerings of silver.
               He scattered peoples that delighted in battle.
32   Let notables come from Egypt,
           Cush raise its hands to God.

---

28. *Benjamin, Judah, Zebulon, Naphtali.* This brief catalog of tribes is another
link to the Song of Deborah. Benjamin, Zebulon, and Naphtali are mentioned
in Judges 5 as tribes that joined in the battle, and Judah needs to be included
here as the tribe of Judean kings. Perhaps Benjamin's "holding sway" records
a recollection, in the interests of celebrating national unity, of the first king
of Israel—Saul—who was a Benjaminite. Benjamin is "little" as the youngest
of Jacob's sons.
    raiment. The translation reads *riqmatam* for the obscure *rigmatam* in the
received text.

31. *the beast of the marsh.* Literally, "beast of the reed." Most commentators take
this as a symbolic image of Egypt.
    the herd of bulls among calves of the peoples. This designation is a negative
representation of physical strength, continuing "the beast of the marsh."
    cringing with offerings of silver. The meaning of the word translated as "offer-
ings" is uncertain. In any case, the idea is that proud Egypt is now humbled.

32. *notables.* The Hebrew term *ḥashmanim* appears only here. The translation
follows a tradition that goes back to the Hebrew commentators of the Middle
Ages. Others render it as "tribute-bearers" or as an object of tribute ("bronze
vessels").
    raise its hands. The translation reads *tarim*, "raise," for the Masoretic *tarits*,
"let run."

Kingdoms of earth, sing to God,   33
      hymn to the Master.   selah
To the Rider in the utmost heavens of yore.   34
      Look, He makes His voice ring, the voice of strength.
Acclaim strength to God,   35
      over Israel is His pride
         and His strength in the skies.
Awesome, O God, from Your sanctuaries!   36
      Israel's God—He gives strength and might to His
      people.
         Blessed is God.

---

34. *the utmost heavens.* Literally, "the heavens of the heavens"—a standard construction for indicating a superlative in biblical Hebrew.
He makes His voice ring. That would be in thunder.

69

1 For the lead player, on *shoshanim*, for David.
2   Rescue me, God,
                for the waters have come up to my neck.
3   I have sunk in the slime of the deep,
                and there is no place to stand.
    I have entered the watery depths,
                and the current has swept me away.
4   I am exhausted from my calling out.
                My throat is hoarse.
    My eyes fail
                from hoping for my God.

---

2. *Rescue me, God.* This is a common opening formula for a supplication. As in many other cases, the supplication toward the end is converted into a thanksgiving psalm (beginning with verse 31).

for the waters have come up to my neck. In this psalm, the familiar image of drowning as a metaphorical representation of near death is elaborated with arresting physiological concreteness: The rising waters come up to the neck; the speaker feels his feet slipping from under him in the water as he sinks into the mire; then the current sweeps him away.

More numerous than the hairs of my head   5
          are my unprovoked foes.
My destroyers grow strong,
          my lying foes.
What I have not stolen
          should I then give back?
God, You know my folly,   6
          and my guilt is not hidden from You.
Let not those who hope for You be shamed through me.   7
          Master, O LORD of armies.
Let those who seek You be not disgraced through me,
          God of Israel.
Because for You I have borne reproach,   8
          disgrace has covered my face.
Estranged I have been from my brothers,   9
          and an alien to my mother's sons.
For the zeal of Your house has consumed me,   10
          the reproach of Your reproachers has fallen on me.

---

5. *my lying foes.* At this point, the referent of the metaphor of drowning is spelled out: The speaker feels overwhelmed—his very life threatened—because of the calumny of his many enemies. If the end of this verse is textually sound (the Hebrew is cryptic), at least one of their false accusations is that he is guilty of theft.

10. *For the zeal of Your house has consumed me, / the reproach of Your reproachers has fallen on me.* Some interpreters have argued that this verse refers to a specific historical context—the early period of the Return to Zion after the Babylonian exile, when there were divisions within the Judean community as to whether to rebuild the temple. In this reading, the speaker would be one of the advocates of rebuilding. Some support for this interpretation may be offered by the last two verses of the psalm, which seem to address a situation in which the towns of Judea have been destroyed and its inhabitants are in the process of returning from exile.

11   And in fasting I wept for my being—
           it became a reproach for me.
12   I made sackcloth my garment
           and became for them a byword.
13   I was the talk of those who sit in the gate,
           the drunkards' taunting song.
14   But I—may my prayer to You,
           O LORD, come in a favorable hour.
     God, as befits Your great kindness,
           answer me with Your steadfast rescue.
15   Save me from the mire, that I not drown.
           Let me be saved from my foes and from the watery
           depths.
16   Let the waters' current not sweep me away
           and let not the deep swallow me,
               and let the Pit not close its mouth on me.
17   Answer me, LORD, for Your kindness is good,
           in Your great compassion turn to me.
18   And hide not Your face from Your servant,
           for I am in straits. Hurry, answer me.

---

11. *it become a reproach for me.* The speaker's grief and his acts of mourning (compare the next verse) make him an object of mockery.

14. *steadfast rescue.* As so often elsewhere, the paired terms *ḥesed* and *'emet* (literally, "kindness" and "truth" but with the idiomatic sense of "steadfast kindness," "dependability as partner in a covenant") are broken up and distributed between the two versets.

15. *Save me from the mire . . . / . . . from the watery depths.* In a da capo movement, the poem returns here and in the next verse to the imagery of drowning introduced at the beginning.

17–18. *Answer me, LORD . . . / . . . hide not Your face from Your servant.* The formulaic nature of the language of the poem is particularly pronounced here.

Come near me, redeem me.   19
> Because of my enemies, ransom me.
It is You who know my reproach,   20
> and my shame and disgrace before all my foes.
Reproach breaks my heart, I grow ill;   21
>> I hope for consolation, and there is none,
>>> and for comforters, and do not find them.
They gave for my nourishment wormwood,   22
> and for my thirst they made me drink vinegar.
May their table before them become a trap,   23
> and their allies a snare.
May their eyes grow too dark to see,   24
> make their loins perpetually shake.
Pour out upon them Your wrath,   25
> and Your blazing fury overtake them.

---

21. *Reproach breaks my heart.* The theme of humiliation and reproach was stressed from verse 7 onward. At this point, the speaker says that he has been so devastated by the revilement to which he has been subjected that it has made him physically ill.

I grow ill. The Hebrew verb here is unusual but, on philological grounds, could plausibly mean to be ill. A revocalization of the word would yield an adjective, 'anushah, "grave," referring to a feminine noun such as *makah*, "affliction," which does not actually appear in the text.

23. *their allies.* The meaning of the Hebrew *shelomim* is disputed. This translation construes it as an ellipsis for *'anshey shelomim*, "allies"; others read it, because of the proximity of "tables," as *sheleimim*, "sacrificial feasts."

26   May their encampment be laid waste,
            and in their tents may no one dwell.

27   For You—whom You struck they pursued,
            and they recounted the pain of Your victims.

28   Add guilt upon their guilt,
            and let them have no part in Your bounty.

29   Let them be wiped out from the book of life,
            and among the righteous let them not be written.

30   But I am lowly and hurting.
            Your rescue, O Lord, will protect me.

31   Let me praise God's name in song,
            and let me extol Him in thanksgiving.

32   And let it be better to the Lord than oxen,
            than a horned bull with its hooves.

33   The lowly have seen and rejoiced,
            those who seek God, let their hearts be strong.

---

27. *whom You struck they pursued.* The evident meaning of this somewhat crabbed line is that these malicious men persecuted people whom God had already singled out to punish. The idea is close to the proverbial kicking someone who is lying down.

   they recounted. The Septuagint, by altering one consonant in the Hebrew verb, reads "they added to."

30. *Your rescue, O Lord, will protect me.* These words are the turning point of the psalm. The verb is surely not an optative but a confident declaration of what God is about to do.

31. *song . . . thanksgiving.* "Thanksgiving," *todah,* in this psalm is clearly not a thanksgiving offering but the psalm itself, a tight parallel to "song."

32. *than oxen.* The point is made through a shrewd pun: The Hebrew for "song" is *shir* and for "oxen" (literally, a singular, "ox") is *shor,* so *shir* is offered as an efficacious substitute for *shor.* The idea that God will gladly accept song instead of sacrifice could reflect, as some scholars have claimed, the influence of the Prophets; but if the temple still needs to be rebuilt, in any case there would be no way to offer animal sacrifice.

For the Lord listens to the needy,   34
  and His captives He has not despised.
Let heaven and earth extol Him,   35
  the seas and all that stirs within them.
For God will rescue Zion   36
  and rebuild the towns of Judea,
    and they will dwell there and possess it.
And the seed of His servants will inherit it,   37
  and those who love His name will dwell there.

---

34. *His captives.* This term in all likelihood refers to the Judeans who were sent into Babylonian captivity. The medieval Hebrew poet Judah Halevi picks up on this term by using it to refer to all Jews in exile, whom he equally designates as "your [Zion's] captives" and "the captives of hope."

70

1 For the lead player, for David, to call to mind.
2   God, to save me,
                LORD, to my help, hasten!
3   May those who seek my life be shamed and reviled.
                May they fall back and be disgraced,
                        who desire my harm.

---

1. *to call to mind.* For a possible explanation of this unusual phrase, see the comment on Psalm 38:1 (page 134).

2. *God, to save me, / LORD, to my help, hasten!* This entire psalm is replicated, with only minor variations of wording, by Psalm 40:14–18. The indications are that this compact, powerful psalm is the original version, and that the editors of Psalm 40 decided to incorporate it into a longer psalm. The reader is referred to the commentary on Psalm 40:14–18. It is worth noting that syntactically, this opening line uses a double-duty verb at the end of the second verset (in general, double-duty verbs occur in the first verset). The result is a periodic sentence in which the crucial verb, "hasten," which completes the meaning, does not occur till the end.

Let them turn back on the heels of their shame,   4
              who say "Hurrah, hurrah!"
Let all who seek You   5
              exult and rejoice,
and may they always say "God is great!"
              —those who love Your rescue.
As for me, I am lowly and needy.   6
              God, O hasten to me!
My help, the one who frees me You are.   7
              LORD, do not delay.

---

4. *Let them turn back on the heels of their shame.* This clause illustrates why this psalm is the primary version and Psalm 40 the secondary one. The Hebrew verb here is *yashuvu*, "let them turn back." Turning back on the heels (singular in the Hebrew) is an understandable image that jibes with the falling back or retreating of the previous line. Psalm 40:16 reads *yashomu*, "let them be devastated," which does not make altogether good sense with "on the heels of their shame." One suspects that a scribe made an error in the process of copying Psalm 70. Some ancient versions correct *yashomu* in Psalm 40 to *yashuvu*, evidently with an eye to Psalm 70.

71

1   In You, O Lord, I shelter.
          Let me never be shamed.
2   Through Your bounty save me and free me.
          Incline Your ear to me and rescue me.
3   Be for me a fortress-dwelling
          to come into always.
   You ordained to rescue me,
          for You are my rock and my bastion.
4   My God, free me from the hand of the wicked,
          from the grip of the wicked and the violent.
5   For You are my hope, Master,
          O Lord, my refuge since youth.

---

1. *In You, O Lord, I shelter. Let me never be shamed.* Without superscription, this psalm begins immediately with the formulaic language of the psalms of supplication. But as early as verse 7, the speaker announces that God has been his support, so the theme of thanksgiving takes over.

5. *my refuge since youth.* A distinctive quasi-autobiographical emphasis begins at this point. The speaker, who evidently is on the brink of old age (verses 9 and 17) looks back on his life from its earliest moment, recollects how God has constantly sustained him, and thus declares that he has always been, and will continue to be, devoted to praising God.

Upon You I relied from birth.   6
      From my mother's womb You brought me out.
        To You is my praise always.
An example I was to the many,   7
      and You are my sheltering strength.
May my mouth be filled with Your praise,   8
      all day long Your glory.
Do not fling me away in old age,   9
      as my strength fails, do not forsake me.
For my enemies said of me,   10
      who stalk me counseled together,
saying, "God has forsaken him.   11
      Pursue and catch him, for no one will save him."
God, do not keep far from me.   12
      My God, hasten to my help!
May my accusers be shamed, may they perish—   13
      may they be clothed with shame and reproach,
        who seek my harm.
As for me, I shall always hope   14
      and add to all Your praise.

---

6. *From my mother's womb You brought me out.* The verb in the Masoretic text, *gozi*, is enigmatic. This translation reads *gohi*, which would make this whole clause identical with Psalm 22:10. Because there are a few verses here that closely echo verses in other psalms, it should be noted that such use of stereotypical phrases and even whole clauses is characteristic of the poetry of psalms and provides no convincing evidence, as some scholars have claimed, that this psalm is merely an assemblage of snippets from other psalms.

7. *An example.* Some interpreters construe this negatively, in the sense of "byword" or "object of mockery," but the Hebrew *mofet* (in other contexts, "portent," "sign of divine power") generally has a positive connotation, and the positive meaning is confirmed by the second verset.

14. *add to all Your praise.* The probable meaning is that the speaker has been praising God all his life and is resolved to continue doing so.

15   My mouth will recount Your bounty,
       all day long Your rescue,
          for I know not numbers.
16   I shall come in the power of the Master, the LORD.
       I shall call to mind Your bounty—You only.
17   God, You have taught me since my youth,
       and till now I have told Your wonders.
18   And even in hoary old age,
       O God, do not forsake me.
Till I tell of Your mighty arm to the next generation,
       to all those who will come, Your power,
19   and Your bounty, O God, to the heights,
       as You have done great things,
          O God, who is like You?
20   As You surfeited me with great and dire distress,
       You will once more give me life,
          and from earth's depths once more bring
          me up.

---

15. *for I know not numbers.* The Hebrew is as obscure as this English version. *Seforot,* the noun that is the object of the verb, appears to derive from the root that means to count or number, but the form of the word here is anomalous. Perhaps the sense is "I know not the numbers of Your bounty," but that is only a guess.

18. *Till I tell of Your mighty arm to the next generation.* Again and again in Psalms, it is the preeminent calling of humankind to praise God. Here the speaker pleads for strength in old age so that even then he can continue his task of praise.
    mighty arm. "Mighty" is merely implied in the Hebrew.

20. *As You surfeited me with . . . distress, / You will once more give me life.* This verse perfectly encapsulates the combination of a plea for help and thankful praise. The speaker has experienced dark hours, but, remembering God's beneficence to him from childhood on, he is confident that God will once again sustain him.

You will multiply my greatness   21
       and turn round and comfort me.
And so I shall acclaim You with the lute.   22
       —Your truth, my God.
Let me hymn You with the lyre,
       Israel's Holy One.
My lips will sing glad song when I hymn to You,   23
       and my being that You ransomed.
My tongue, too, all day long   24
       will murmur Your bounty.
For they are shamed, for they are disgraced,
       those who sought my harm.

---

24. *they are shamed.* This verse at the very end picks up, in a counterpoint envelope structure, "Let me never be shamed" from the first line of the poem.

72

1 For Solomon.
> God, grant Your judgments to the king
>> and Your righteousness to the king's son.

2 May he judge Your people righteously
> and Your lowly ones in justice.

3 May the mountains bear peace to the people,
> and the hills righteousness.

4 May he bring justice to the lowly of the people,
>> may he rescue the sons of the needy
>>> and crush the oppressor.

---

1. *For Solomon.* This is one of the most magisterial of the royal psalms. The editorial linkage with Solomon at the beginning no doubt reflects the tradition regarding the imperial grandeur of the Solomonic reign. The last line of the postscript (verse 20) appears to encourage the notion that David is the author. Thus, the medieval Hebrew exegete David Kimchi, noting the coupled terms "king" and "king's son": "This psalm was composed by David about his son Solomon." Although there is a line of interpreters who read this text as a "messianic" psalm, the poem itself offers no compelling evidence for that reading. Court poetry everywhere revels in flattering hyperbole, so the vision of the king's reigning forever to the ends of the earth and dispensing perfect justice could easily be a prayer on behalf of a flesh-and-blood monarch, without eschatological intentions.

    judgments. Solomon, one recalls, is a legendary figure of the wise judge, but the administration of justice is the mandate of every king of Israel.

May they fear you as long as the sun 5
      and as long as the moon, generations untold.
May he come down like rain on new-mown grass, 6
      like showers that moisten the earth.
May the just man flourish in his days— 7
      and abundant peace till the moon is no more.
And may he hold sway from sea to sea, 8
      from the River to the ends of the earth.
Before him may the desert-folk kneel, 9
      and his enemies lick the dust.
May kings of Tarshish and the islands 10
      bring tribute,
may kings of Sheba and Siba
      offer vassal-gifts.
And may all kings bow to him, 11
      all nations serve him.
For he saves the needy man pleading, 12
      and the lowly who has none to help him.

---

5. *May they fear you.* The second-person pronoun is anomalous. As the text stands, it makes better sense to apply "you" to the king, with "they" referring to anyone who would be tempted to be an oppressor. The Septuagint offers an attractive alternative reading: By a simple reversal of consonants in the verb (*ya'arikh* instead of *yiyra'ukha*), the Greek translators render this as "May he live long."

6. *May he come down like rain.* Kimchi plausibly understands this as a simile for the king's beneficent presence: "This king will come to the people for their good and for their rescue like rain."

8–10. *And may he hold sway from sea to sea.* The poet now begins a grand geographical sweep that touches all points of the compass. "From sea to sea" would be from the Dead Sea to the Mediterranean. The "River" is the Euphrates. The "desert-folk" would be somewhere to the east or to the south. "Tarshish and the islands" are to the west far out in the Mediterranean realm. "Sheba and Siba" are to the far south, in the region of the Red Sea. The mention of Sheba might be another reason for the editorial connection of the psalm with Solomon.

13   He pities the poor and the needy,
               and the lives of the needy he rescues,
14   from scheming and outrage redeems them,
               and their blood is dear in his sight.
15   Long may he live,
               and the gold of Sheba be given him.
      May he be prayed for always,
               all day long be blessed.
16   May there be abundance of grain in the land,
               on the mountaintops.
      May his fruit rustle like Lebanon,
               and may they sprout from the town like grass of
               the land.

---

15. *May he be prayed for . . . / . . . be blessed.* The Hebrew uses a third-person singular verb in the active voice with no subject specified ("may [one] pray for him"), which is a common equivalent of the passive in biblical usage. The same form is employed at the beginning of this verse in "the gold of Sheba be given him."

16. *abundance of grain.* The term translated as "abundance," *pisah*, appears only here, so its meaning is uncertain. This translation follows a conjecture of Abraham ibn Ezra. In any case, the logical complement to a reign of perfect justice in the ancient Near Eastern imagination was the blessings of agricultural fecundity.

on the mountaintops. Though there was terraced farming on the hillsides in the ancient period, this phrase may be hyperbolic: Grain will flourish not only in the flat fields but on the very mountaintops.

May his fruit rustle like Lebanon. The poet has in mind the lofty trees of Lebanon rustling in the wind. This is another hyperbole: The heavy ears of grain will spring high up and make as much noise in the wind as the cedars of Lebanon.

may they sprout from the town like grass of the land. What this verset refers to is unclear. Some understand "they" to be the people of the towns, who will multiply like blades of grass. It might also mean that from the cities as well as the mountaintops actual crops will come forth.

May his name be forever.   17
        As long as the sun may his name bear seed.
And may all nations be blessed through him, call him happy.

Blessed is the Lord God, Israel's God, performing wonders alone.   18
And blessed is His glory forever, and may His glory fill all the earth.   19
Amen and amen.
The prayers of David son of Jesse are ended.   20

---

17. *As long as the sun may his name bear seed.* In a concluding flourish, the eternal persistence of the sun is once more invoked. This use of the solar and lunar luminaries as images of perdurability also implies an analogy: The king in his realm is as brilliant as the sun in the heavens; he is a *roi soleil*. The verb *yinon*, "bear fruit," is unique to this psalm, but it most likely is cognate with the noun *nin*, which means "descendent."

18. *Blessed is the Lord.* The three verses that begin here are not part of the psalm but an editorial coda (compare the briefer one at the end of Psalm 41) that marks the conclusion of the second book of Psalms.

73

1 An Asaph psalm.
    Only good to Israel is God,
            to the pure of heart.
2 As for me, my feet had almost strayed,
            my steps had nearly tumbled.
3 For I envied the revelers,
            I saw the wicked's well-being:

---

1. *An Asaph psalm.* This psalm is one out of eleven among the seventeen that make up the third book of Psalms that is ascribed to the Levite Asaph. One may infer that Asaph psalms were the core of this particular collection and the others were added.

to Israel. An emendation proposed by several scholars, reading *layashar 'el* instead of the Masoretic *leyisra'el*, yields the following for the whole line: "But good is El to the upright, / God to the pure of heart." Although the received text is perfectly intelligible as it stands, the emendation has two points to recommend it: The unbalanced line (four beats, then two) becomes balanced (three beats in each verset); and the mention of "Israel," which appears to violate the individual perspective of the poem, is eliminated.

3. *For I envied the revelers.* The speaker's near straying, mentioned in the previous verse, is not through an act he committed but in his being tempted by envying the wicked, who seem to him to prosper even as they complacently disregard any prospect of retribution. The problem laid out here is essentially one that is addressed by Wisdom literature (as in Psalm 1): How is it that the wicked prosper? The answer, in keeping with the assumptions of mainline Wisdom writing, is that the worldly success of the wicked is temporary and illusory.

"For they are free of the fetters of death,   4
      and their body is healthy.
Of the torment of man they have no part,   5
      and they know not human afflictions."
Thus haughtiness is their necklace,   6
      outrage, their garment, bedecks them.
Fat bulges round their eyes,   7
      imaginings spill from their heart.
They mock and speak with malice,   8
      from on high they speak out oppression.

---

4. *For they are free of the fetters of death.* At this point, and for much of the psalm, the Hebrew becomes somewhat cloudy. The literal sense of this clause is: For there are no fetters to their death.
    their body is healthy. The meaning of the noun here, *'ul*, is doubtful.

5. *Of the torment of man they have no part.* The entire verse, like the preceding one, expresses the illusion under which the speaker labored when he envied the wicked.

6. *is their necklace.* The Hebrew uses a verb ("necklaces them").

7. *Fat bulges round their eyes.* This is one of several satiric images deployed in Psalms that represents the prospering wicked as physically swollen from the delicacies with which they have been stuffing themselves—here, the eye is imagined peeking out from its envelope of fat. (The Hebrew is somewhat crabbed, but the literal sense is: their eye protrudes from fat.)
    imaginings spill from their heart. The Hebrew is obscure, but the noun *mask-iot* elsewhere means "graven images," so the sense might be that in their arrogance they spin out all sorts of presumptuous schemes or images of their own superiority.

8. *from on high.* Despite the mention of the heavens in the next verse, this locution might refer merely to the commanding position of earthly power that the arrogant enjoy.

9   They put their mouth up to the heavens,
        and their tongue goes over the earth.

10   Thus the people turn back to them,
        and they lap up their words.

11   And they say, "How could God know,
        and is there knowledge with the Most High?"

12   Look, such are the wicked,
        the ever complacent ones pile up wealth.

13   But in vain have I kept my heart pure
        and in innocence washed my palms.

14   For I was afflicted all day long,
        and my chastisement, each new morning.

---

9. *They put their mouth up to the heavens.* Although the Hebrew preposition can also mean "against," as many interpreters claim, the parallelism with the second verset might rather indicate that the wicked distribute their arrogant speech high and low, up to the heavens and all over the earth.

10. *Thus the people turn back to them.* Any translation of this verset and the next is guesswork, because the Hebrew is not intelligible. Literally, it reads: Thus [or, therefore] his [His?] people turn back yonder. The meaning might be that because the arrogant insistently broadcast their speech, people pay attention to them.

    and they lap up their words. The literal sense of the very cryptic Hebrew is "and waters of fullness [full waters?] are wrung from them [for them?]." The text has almost certainly suffered mangling in scribal transmission here. This translation adopts an emendation proposed by Hans-Joachim Kraus: Instead of the Masoretic *umey malei' yimatsu*, he reads *umileyhem yamotsu*.

13. *But in vain have I kept my heart pure.* This is the culmination of the speaker's despair. He contemplates the triumphal complacency and success of the wicked, while he, though pure of heart, suffers untold afflictions day after day (verse 14).

If I said, Let me talk like them.   15
       Look, Your sons' band I would have betrayed.
When I thought to know these things,   16
       it was a torment in my eyes.
Till I came to the sanctuaries of God,   17
       understood what would be their end.
Yes, You set them on slippery ground,   18
       brought them down to destruction.
How they come to ruin in a moment,   19
       swept away, taken in terrors!
Like a dream upon waking, O Master,   20
       upon rising You despised their image.
When my heart was embittered,   21
       and my conscience stabbed with pain,
I was a dolt and knew nothing,   22
       like cattle I was with You.

---

15. *Let me talk like them.* The Hebrew has only "like" (*kemo* in an undeclined form), which sounds strange. The verb, moreover, usually means "tell" or "recount," though it often has the sense of "talk" in rabbinic Hebrew.

18. *You set them on slippery ground.* At this point the speaker's vindication finally unfolds, for he sees God reversing the good fortune of the wicked.

21. *my conscience.* The Hebrew says "kidneys" (King James Version, "reins"), thought to be the seat of conscience as the heart was thought to be the seat of understanding. The two terms are often joined, either in a collocation ("heart and kidneys") or, as here, in parallel versets.

22. *I was a dolt and knew nothing.* These words refer to the speaker's imagining that the wicked might have the right idea, not realizing that God was about to overturn their fate.

23   Yet I was always with You,
              You grasped my right hand.
24   You guided me with Your counsel,
              and toward glory You took me.
25   Whom else do I have in the heavens,
              and beside You whom would I want upon earth?
26   Though my flesh and my heart waste away,
              God is my heart's rock and my portion forever.
27   For, look, those far from You perish,
              You demolish all who go whoring from You.
28   But I—God's closeness is good to me,
              I make the Master the LORD my shelter,
                   to recount all Your works.

---

23. *Yet I was always with You.* This is not a contradiction but the persuasive record of inner oscillation. The speaker was on the verge of being seduced by the evident success of the wicked, but he resisted, clinging to God despite all the inducements of his observation to follow the way of the wicked.

24. *and toward glory You took me.* A long line of interpreters, especially in the Christian tradition, read this as a reference to the afterworld. (See the King James Version: "and afterward receive me in glory.") But such a belief is beyond the horizon of Psalms, and it is far more likely in terms of idiomatic usage that the Hebrew *'aḥar* is a preposition ("after" or "toward") rather than a temporal adverb ("afterward").

27. *those far from You perish.* This line summarizes the view of the fate of evil-doers that is put forth in the whole psalm. However they prosper, if they are far from God, in the end they will be destroyed.
    who go whoring from You. This metaphor of sexual betrayal is not part of the vocabulary of Wisdom literature but appears typically in cultic contexts.

28. *God's closeness is good to me.* This contrast to "those far from You" points to the emotional core of the psalm. The speaker may have suffered, but the feeling of being close to God sustains him, gives him a sense of being protected.

74

An Asaph *maskil*.

Why, O God, have You abandoned us forever?   1

    Your wrath smolders against the flock You should tend.

Remember Your cohort You took up of old,   2

    You redeemed the tribe of Your estate,

        Mount Zion where You dwelled.

Lift up Your feet to the eternal ruins,   3

    all that the enemy laid waste in the sanctuary.

---

1. *Why, O God, have You abandoned us forever?* As in a number of other psalms, the seeming logical contradiction of using "forever" in a plea to reverse the abandonment has psychological conviction: The tribulations of the nation have gone on so long that they seem eternal to the speaker. This psalm is a national supplication evoking the painful memory of the destruction of the temple. The stress on the persistence of the catastrophe may suggest a date of composition many decades after 586 BCE. Some determined commentators date the poem as late as the Hasmonean period, though the references to the profanation of the sanctuary could just as easily apply to its destruction by the Babylonians.

   the flock You should tend. A more literal rendering would be "the flock of Your tending."

3. *the eternal ruins.* As with "forever" in the first verse of the psalm, it appears to the anguished speaker as though the ruins of the temple are to go on for eternity.

4   Your foes roared out in Your meeting-place,
            they set up their signs as signs.
5   They hacked away as one brings down from above
            in a tangle of trees with axes.
6   And its carvings altogether
            with hatchet and pike they pounded.
7   They set fire to Your sanctuary,
            they profaned on the ground Your name's
            dwelling-place.
8   They said in their heart, "We shall destroy them altogether."
            They burned all God's meeting-places in the land.
9   Our own signs we did not see.
            There is no longer a prophet,
                  nor any among us who knows until when.

---

4. *they set up their signs as signs.* The translation preserves the ambiguity of the Hebrew. Some interpreters imagine these to be foreign ensigns or standards that the conquerors plant on the ruins of the temple. Others see here a reference to pagan icons. But "signs" (*'otot*) could also mean portents: They claim that their victory was ordained by portents they received. Compare the beginning of verse 9, where *'otot* appears to be used in the sense of portents.

5. *They hacked away as one brings down from above.* The Hebrew is obscure. The Masoretic text has "It became known" (*yiwada'*), but many textual critics prefer to read *yigada'* (literally, "it was hacked away"). "Brings down from above" is also odd, though the evident image is of a woodsman chopping down branches from a high tree.

8. *We shall destroy them.* The verb *ninam* is anomalous, but it may derive from the root *y-n-y*, which suggests enmity.
    all God's meeting-places. The indication of sanctuaries throughout the land is surprising because otherwise the psalm appears to assume the centralization of worship in the single temple in Jerusalem effected after 621 BCE.

9. *Our own signs we did not see.* Though "signs" is ambiguous, this verse clearly alludes to verse 4.

Until when, O God, will the foe insult,   10
     the enemy revile Your name forever?
Why do You draw back Your hand,   11
     and Your right hand hold in Your bosom?
Yet God is my king of old,   12
     worker of rescues in the midst of the earth.
You shattered the sea-god with Your strength,   13
     You smashed the monsters' heads on the waters.
You crushed the Leviathan's heads,   14
     You gave him as food to the desert-folk.

---

12. *Yet God is my king of old.* As in many psalms of supplication, whether indi-vidual or collective, a turning point occurs when the speaker, until that point a voice of desperation, affirms his faith in God's rescuing power.

13. *You shattered the sea-god.* As evidence of God's beneficent power "of old," the speaker goes back to the time of creation, invoking imagery from the Canaan-ite cosmogonic myth in which Baal subdues the chaotic force of the primordial sea monster, here referred to first as Yamm (also the ordinary Hebrew word for "sea"), then as *taninim* ("monsters"), then as Leviathan.

14. *You crushed the Leviathan's heads.* If the plural in our text is authentic, the poet would be alluding to a tradition in which Leviathan is a many-headed monster (not part of its depiction in Job). There is an a fortiori logic in this poetic use of the Canaanite myth: If God is powerful enough to have secured the order of the created world by conquering the hideous forces of aqueous chaos, he can surely confound the vile enemy who has laid waste Zion.

    You gave him as food to the desert-folk. That is, God's victory over the pri-mordial sea monster was so overwhelming that He could dissect its body and convey its flesh to the far-off dwellers of the desert for their consumption.

15   You split open a channel for spring and brook,
           You dried up the surging torrents.

16   Yours is the day, also Yours the night.
           It was You Who founded the light and the sun.

17   It was You Who laid down all the boundaries of earth,
           summer and winter, You fashioned them.

18   Remember this: the enemy insulted,
           a base people reviled Your name.

19   Do not yield to the beast the life of Your dove,
           the band of Your lowly forget not forever.

20   Look to the pact,
           for the dark places of earth fill with groans of outrage.

---

15. *You split open a channel . . . / You dried up the surging torrents.* Now God's power as master of creation is represented in natural rather than mythological terms. He creates both the vital water sources and the dry places on earth. He establishes the rhythm of day and night, summer and winter, and sets the heavenly luminaries in their place (verses 16 and 17). This whole sequence of lines beginning in verse 13 uses an emphatic second-person singular pronoun, *'atah*, at the head of almost every clause. The semantic effect is something like "It was You Who . . .", but because that formula would make most of the lines excessively long in English, it has been used in the translation only in lines 16B and 17A.

19. *Do not yield to the beast the life of Your dove.* The translation assumes that the noun *ḥayat* (ordinarily, "beast of") is a poetic form of *ḥayah* ("beast" not in the construct state—that is, not attached to the noun that follows it). The question about the text is compounded by the fact that in the second verset *ḥayat* appears to be a homonym, meaning "band" or "military contingent."

20. *with groans of outrage.* The Masoretic text seems to say, "with habitations of outrage," which sounds odd coming after "dark places of earth." The Septuagint reads—instead of *ne'ot*, "habitations"—*'enkot*, "groans," and that reading is adopted here.

Let not the poor man turn back disgraced.   21
       Let the lowly and needy praise Your name.
Arise, God, O plead Your cause.   22
       Remember the insult to You by the base all day long.
Forget not the voice of Your foes,   23
       the din of those against You perpetually rising.

---

23. *the din of those against You perpetually rising.* "Perpetually" at the end picks up "forever" at the beginning. As a concluding gesture, the image is powerfully expressive. The speaker's ears are outraged by the insulting, triumphant clamor of Judea's enemies rising up day after day, seemingly without end, and he implores God to arise and finally put a stop to it.

75

1 For the lead player, *al-tashcheth*, an Asaph psalm, a song.
2   We acclaim You, O God, we acclaim You,
                and Your name is near.
                        They recount Your wonders.
3   "When I seize the appointed time,
                I Myself shall judge rightly.
4   Earth and its dwellers would melt,
                had I not set fast its pillars.   selah
5   I said to the revelers, Do not revel,
                and to the wicked, Lift not your horn.

---

2. *We acclaim You.* The introduction of the verb *hodah* (the common cognate noun is *todah*, "thanksgiving") announces this as a thanksgiving psalm. But it is distinctive in representing God as speaker in the body of the poem as He proclaims the meting out of divine justice, which is the reason for human thanksgiving.

Your name is near. This usage reflects a tendency in the later biblical period to interpose the divine name as an intermediary or buffer between humankind and the actual presence of God.

They recount Your wonders. The switch from first-person plural to third-person plural may be slightly confusing, though it is within the limits of biblical idiomatic usage. "They" has the implied meaning of "people."

5. *Lift not Your horn.* This commonplace of biblical poetry, probably drawn from the image of the large curving horns that the ram uses to gore its natural enemies, is a symbol of assertive power. This poem takes up the raising of the horn as its central metaphor, repeating it in the next verse and coming back to it in the concluding line of the psalm.

Lift not your horn on high.   6
       You would speak arrogance against the Rock.
For not from the east and not from the west   7
       and not from the desert is one lifted up.
But God is the judge,   8
       it is He Who brings down and lifts up.
For there is a cup in the hand of the LORD,   9
       with foaming wine full for decanting.
He will pour from it,
       yes, its dregs they will drain,
         all the earth's wicked will drink."

---

6. *Lift not your horn on high.* Now the conventional horn image becomes a vivid representation of the arrogant displaying their power presumptuously. Though some interpreters see in "on high" a reference to God or to the heavens, the image stands effectively enough as a spatial indication of loftiness, of pretension to superiority.

    against the Rock. The Masoretic text has *betsaw'ar,* "with throat," which seems otiose and not altogether idiomatic (literally, "speak arrogance with throat"). This translation follows the reading of the Septuagint, which shows *batsur,* "against the Rock."

7. *not from the desert is one lifted up.* The last two Hebrew words are *mimidbar harim.* In the Masoretic vocalization, the last syllable of *mimidbar* shows a *patah* as the vowel, which would join it to *harim* as the construct state, yielding "from the desert of mountains." Many manuscripts, however, vocalize this syllable with a *qamats,* which would introduce a pause after *mimidbar* and thus make *harim* a verb in the infinitive, "to lift up." This small change gives the sentence an otherwise absent predicate and accords with this poet's fondness for pointed repetition of terms.

10   As for me, I shall tell it forever,
            let me hymn to the God of Jacob.
11   "And all the horns of the wicked I shall hack off.
            The horns of the just will be lifted!"

---

10. *As for me.* At this point, just before the end, the speaker breaks into God's speech to proclaim his resolution to sing hymns to God, as is conventional in the conclusion of a thanksgiving psalm. But the next verse appears to switch back to God's speech, for it is clearly God, not the psalmist, who brings low the wicked.

11. *the horns of the wicked I shall hack off.* The violence of this punishing act is an answer to the arrogance of the wicked who have raised their horns on high.

The horns of the just will be lifted! In antithetical symmetry, and with the repetition of the key verb "lift," the just will be triumphant. This closing verse pointedly opposes two judicial terms: "the wicked" being applicable to those with a wrongful case in court, and "just" to the man judicially vindicated.

76

For the lead player with stringed instruments, an Asaph psalm,   1
a song.
    God becomes known in Judah,   2
        in Israel His name is great.
    And in Salem was set His pavilion,   3
        His dwelling in Zion.
    There did He shatter the bow's fiery shafts,   4
        the shield and the sword and the battle.   selah
    Refulgent You were,   5
        mightier than the mountains of prey.

---

2. *God becomes known in Judah.* This psalm is a celebration of God's power in history. Perhaps it was composed to mark a particular victory over enemies who assailed Jerusalem, but the text does not provide sufficient evidence for any specific historical identification. As in the exodus story and elsewhere, God "becomes known" by exerting His triumphant power.

3. *Salem.* This is a variant, perhaps archaic, form of the name Jerusalem, something made clear by the parallelism with "Zion" in the second verset.

5. *mightier than the mountains of prey.* This phrase is strange, powerful, and haunting, and it does not call for emendation, as many scholars have claimed. "The mountains of prey" are the wild mountains where lions and other predatory beasts roam. God is seen here as even more awesome than that scary realm.

6   The stout-hearted were despoiled,
         they fell into a trance,
             and all the men of valor could not lift a hand.
7   By Your roar, O God of Jacob,
         chariot and horse were stunned.
8   You, O fearsome are You,
         and who can stand before You, in the strength of Your
         wrath?
9   From the heavens You made judgment heard,
         the earth was afraid and fell silent,
10 when God rose up for judgment
         to rescue all the lowly of earth.   selah
11 Even human fury acclaims You
         when You gird on all furies' remains.

---

6. *could not lift a hand.* The Hebrew says literally, "could not find their hands." The idiomatic English equivalent, which fits nicely with the idea of the warriors' being stunned, is borrowed from the New Jewish Publication Society translation.

7. *chariot and horse.* The use of this phrase would seem to be a direct allusion to the Song of the Sea (Exodus 15), the paradigmatic poem celebrating God's triumph over the enemies of Israel.

8. *in the strength of Your wrath.* The Masoretic text shows "since Your wrath," which is problematic, because one would expect a verb to follow. This translation reads—instead of the Masoretic *me'az*, "since"— *me'oz*, "in [or "from"] the strength of."

11. *Even human fury acclaims You / when You gird on all furies' remains.* The Hebrew, here represented more or less literally, is obscure. Without performing extensive reconstructive surgery on the text, one may tentatively propose the following sense: Even human beings in the momentum of their fury are compelled to acknowledge God when they see Him exercising the mere residue of all the furies at His disposal (or, alternately, exercising all possible furies to their last remains).

Make vows and fulfill them to the LORD your God.   12
      All round Him bring tribute to the Fearsome One.
He plucks the life-breath of princes.   13
      He is fearsome to the kings of the earth.

---

12. *the Fearsome One.* The received text reads *mora'*, which would mean fear, but several ancient versions reflect *nora'*, "fearsome," a term used in verse 8 and again in the concluding line of the poem. That epithet is apt for a triumphant LORD of armies.

13. *plucks.* The Hebrew verb here, *batsar*, is normally used for the act of harvesting grapes. Perhaps it may by extension mean to sever, to break off or cut off, as the King James translators inferred.

77

1 For the lead player on *jeduthun*, an Asaph psalm.

2 My voice to God—let me cry out.

          My voice to God—and hearken to me.

3 In the day of my straits I sought the Master.

          My eye flows at night, it will not stop.

          I refused to be consoled.

4 I call God to mind and I moan.

          I speak and my spirit faints.   selah

5 You held open my eyelids.

          I throbbed and could not speak.

---

2. *let me cry out. / . . . hearken to me.* The psalm begins with the formulaic language of an individual supplication, though in the second half of the poem, beginning in verse 12, when the speaker recalls God's "wonders of old," he reverts to national memory.

3. *My eye flows at night, it will not stop.* The Masoretic text reads, incomprehensibly, "my hand (*yadi*) flows." The emendation adopted here from "hand" to "eye" (*'eyni*) is based not only on the verb used but also on a similar formulation in Lamentations 3:49: "My eye flowed and was not silent, without stop."

4. *I call God to mind.* This verb (root *z-k-r*) is used four times in the poem: first the speaker recalls his recent nocturnal experiences, then the great story of the national past evidence of God's beneficence.

5. *You held open my eyelids.* This arresting image for insomnia sets the stage for the evocation of long nights of agitation in the next few lines.

I ponder the days of yore,	6
the years long gone.	
I call to mind my song in the night.	7
To my own heart I speak, and my spirit inquires.	
Will the Master forever abandon me,	8
and never again look with favor?	
Is His kindness gone for all time,	9
His word done for time without end?	
Has God forgotten to show grace,	10
has He closed off in wrath His compassion?	
And I said, it is my failing,	11
that the High One's right hand has changed.	

---

6. *I ponder the days of yore.* This nocturnal reflection on the past prepares us for the poetry of national memory that will be introduced from verse 12 onward.

7. *I call to mind my song in the night.* Though the speaker may be remembering some earlier point in his life when, in contrast to his present condition, he sang joyously in the night, it is also possible that "song" (*neginah*, unlike its synonym *rinah*, which is almost always joyous) refers to a heartfelt chanted prayer and so is linked with his present fate of restless nights of anguish.

8. *abandon me.* The object of the verb is merely implied in the Hebrew.

10. *closed off.* The Hebrew verb used is the one for clenching the hand into a fist and hence for withholding.

11. *it is my failing, / that the High One's right hand has changed.* There is an evident problem in the Hebrew text here, which is obscure. Both the grammar and the meaning of the verbal noun (if it is that) *haloti*, "it is my failing," are ambiguous; and though "right hand" is the idiomatic token of efficacious power, it is far from certain that *shenot* means "has changed" (it could also mean "repeated," or could be a noun, "years of"—neither of which possibilities is helpful).

12   I call to mind the acts of Yah
               when I recall Your wonders of old.

13   I recite all your works,
               Your acts I rehearse.

14   God, Your way is in holiness.
               Who is a great god like God?

15   You are the god working wonders.
               You made known among peoples Your strength.

16   You redeemed with Your arm Your people,
               the children of Jacob and Joseph.   selah

17   The waters saw You, O God,
               the waters saw You, they trembled,
                    the depths themselves shuddered.

---

12. *Yah.* This is another name for the God of Israel. Most scholars regard it as a shortened form of Yahweh, though that is not entirely certain. It occurs frequently as a theophoric suffix to names for men (in English transcription, *-iah*). It is left untranslated here and elsewhere to convey something of the high poetic or perhaps archaic coloration it seems to have in the Hebrew.

14. *Who is a great god like God?* In the first instance, "god" is *'el*, the common noun for a deity. In the second instance, "God" is *'elohim*, generally used as a proper name for God. In the next verse, *'el* is again the term employed in "the god working wonders."

16. *You redeemed with Your arm.* The translation adds "Your" for clarity. As the subsequent verses make clear, the reference is to the redemption from Egyptian slavery and the victory at the Sea of Reeds.

17. *The waters saw You, O God.* Because this sequence of lines concludes with Moses and Aaron leading the people, the waters in question would be the waters of the Sea of Reeds, first pushed back miraculously to allow the Israelites to cross over, then surging forward to drown the Egyptian army. But the imagery has such a strong cosmic character that the mythological image of God triumphing over the primordial powers of the sea is superimposed on the image of the exodus story.

The clouds streamed water.   18
          The skies sounded with thunder.
                    Your bolts, too, flew about.
Your thunder's sound under the wheel—   19
          lightning lit up the world.
                    The earth shuddered and shook.
In the sea was Your way,   20
          and Your path in the mighty waters,
                    and Your footsteps left no traces.
You led Your people like a flock   21
          by the hand of Moses and Aaron.

---

18. *The skies sounded with thunder.* The literal sense of the Hebrew is, "The skies gave out a sound," but *qol*, "sound," when linked to the sky, also means "thunder."

Your bolts. The celestial bolts are lightning, the weapon of the sky god in many mythologies.

19. *Your thunder's sound under the wheel.* Here the poet uses both *qol*, "sound," and *ra'am*, "thunder." Many interpreters take this as a metaphoric comparison between the sound of thunder and the clattering of wheels, but because the sky god in Canaanite mythology sometimes rides a celestial chariot, this could plausibly be a mythic image of God riding across the skies in His awesome chariot, which rumbles with thunder as it goes.

20. *In the sea was Your way.* This entire passage amounts to a poetic reinterpretation of the story told in Exodus 14. There, no mention was made of God's actually entering the sea; here, He descends from the skies after an artillery barrage of thunder and lightning and strides into the sea, making it shake—and, by implication, pull back.

and Your footsteps left no traces. Literally, "And Your footsteps were not known." In an amusing shift of contexts, this phrase is often applied in modern Hebrew to a fugitive who disappears without trace.

78

1   An Asaph *maskil*.
    Hearken, my people, to my teaching.
        Lend your ear to the sayings of my mouth.
2   Let me open my mouth in a rhapsody,
        let me voice the verses of old,
3   that we have heard and we have known,
        and that our fathers recounted to us.

---

1. *Hearken, my people, to my teaching. / Lend your ear to the sayings of my mouth.* This sort of formal and formulaic beginning to the poem is reminiscent of didactic poetic texts such as *Shirat Ha'azinu*, the Song of Moses (Deuteronomy 32). In fact, some of the phrases used (for example, verse 8, "a wayward, rebellious generation") are similar to formulations in Deuteronomy 32. This is a historical psalm, which recapitulates in poetry the Plagues Narrative and the victory at the Sea of Reeds from Exodus as well as certain later events. The narrative purpose is the reason for the lengthiness of the psalm. For once, the scholarly conjecture about a ritual purpose for the psalm seems plausible: It distinctly looks as though it originally served a function of commemoration of national history, cast in the mnemonic form of verse, which might have also lent itself to public chanting, perhaps in a temple ceremony. The strong didactic bent of the commemoration is reflected in the fact that the hortatory preamble runs to the end of verse 8, much of it in a long, run-on sentence. It must also be said that a good deal of the poetry of this psalm is no more than perfunctory—a recasting in parallelistic verse of the narrative in Exodus, borrowing some terms from the prose story and substituting many synonyms.

2. *the verses of old.* The story goes back to the earliest national traditions, and the poet makes a point of stressing at the beginning the purported antiquity of his poem.

We shall not conceal from their sons,   4
            to the last generation recounting
the praise of the LORD and His might
            and His wonders that He did.
He established a precept in Jacob   5
            and His teaching put forth in Israel,
this He charged to our fathers
            to make them known to their sons,
so that the last generation might know,   6
            sons yet to be born
                        might arise and recount to their sons,
and place their trust in God   7
            and forget not the acts of God,
                        and observe His commands.
That they be not like their fathers,   8
            a wayward, rebellious generation,
a generation that was not firm of heart,
            and its spirit not faithful to God.
The Ephraimites, deft wielders of bows,   9
            turned tail on the day of battle,
and did not keep God's pact,   10
            and His teaching refused to follow.

---

5. *precept . . . teaching.* The language here (*'edut, torah*) may have a Deuteron-omistic coloration.

8. *a generation that was not firm of heart.* In the first instance, this is the Ephraimites, but this rebellious generation will then merge with that of the Israelites in the Wilderness.

9. *The Ephraimites, deft wielders of bows.* The literal sense of the Hebrew is "armed with and shooters of bows," but the conjunction of near synonyms in all likelihood indicates an intensification of the term—hence "deft wielders" in the translation. The specific historical incident has not been identified, though it is clearly one in which the Ephraimites showed cowardice on the battlefield.

11 And they forgot His acts
  and His wonders that He showed them.
12 Before their fathers He did wonders,
  in the land of Egypt, in Zoan's field.
13 He split open the sea and let them pass through,
  He made water stand up like a heap.
14 And He led them with the cloud by day
  and all night long with the light of fire.
15 He split apart rocks in the wilderness
  and gave drink as from the great deep.
16 He brought forth streams from stone,
  and poured down water like rivers.
17 And still they offended him more,
  to rebel against the High One in parched land.
18 And they tried God in their heart
  to ask food for their gullet.
19 And they spoke against God.
  They said: "Can God set a table in the wilderness?
20 Look, He struck the rock and water flowed
  and currents streamed.
  Can He also give bread?
  Will He ready flesh for His people?"
21 Then the LORD heard and was angered,
  and a fire was lit against Jacob
  and wrath, too, went up against Israel.

---

13. *made water stand up like a heap.* This is a direct quotation from the Song of the Sea, Exodus 15:8.

16. *He brought forth streams from stone.* The line alludes to the incident reported in Exodus 17.

18. *to ask food for their gullet.* The stress on gluttony suggests that *nefesh* here has its anatomical sense. The incident referred to occurs in Exodus 16.

For they had no faith in God   22
          and did not trust in His rescue.
And He charged the skies above,   23
          and the doors of the heavens He opened,
and rained on them manna to eat   24
          and the grain of the heavens He gave to them.
Princely bread a man did eat,   25
          provisions He sent them to sate them.
He moved the east wind across the heavens   26
          and drove the south wind with His might,
and rained flesh upon them like dust   27
          and like sand of the seas wingèd fowl,
brought it down in the midst of His camp,   28
          round about His dwelling-place.
And they ate and were fully sated,   29
          what they craved He brought to them.
They were not revolted by their craving,   30
          their food was still in their mouths,
when God's wrath went up against them,   31
          and He killed their stoutest fellows.
                    Israel's young men He brought to their knees.
Even so, they offended still   32
          and had no faith in His wonders.
And they wasted their days in mere vapor   33
          and their years in dismay.

---

24. *and rained on them manna to eat.* The gift of manna is part of the story in Exodus 16.

30. *They were not revolted by their craving, / their food was still in their mouths.* The language here is based on Numbers 11:20 and 11:33.

33. *vapor . . . dismay.* The Hebrew uses a neat bit of sound play: "vapor," *hevel*, is followed by *behalah*, the same three consonants (*h-b-l*) with the order of the first two switched.

34 When He killed them, they sought Him out,
            and came back and looked for God.
35 And they recalled that God was their rock
            and the Most High God their redeemer.
36 Yet they beguiled Him with their lips,
            and with their tongue they lied to Him
37 and their heart was not firm with Him,
            and they were not faithful to His pact.
38 Yet He is compassionate, He atones for crime and does not destroy,
            and abundantly takes back His wrath
                    and does not arouse all His fury.
39 And He recalls that they are flesh,
            a spirit that goes off and does not come back.
40 How much they rebelled against Him in the wilderness,
            caused Him pain in the waste land!
41 And again did they try God,
            and Israel's Holy One they provoked.
42 They did not recall His great hand,
            the day He ransomed them from the foe,

---

38. *Yet He is compassionate.* This declaration of God's attributes is too long to scan as a line of poetry. One suspects it may have been a doxological formula inserted into the middle of the poem.

39. *a spirit that goes off.* The simple verb "to go" is sometimes used in the Bible as a euphemism for dying.

41. *And again did they try God.* This reiteration in the poem of the pattern of rebellion picks up the stubborn repetition of acts of rebellion in the Wilderness stories.
    provoked. The Hebrew verb *hitwu* ordinarily means "to place a mark on." Its use here, if the text is correct, is puzzling, and the translation is based on context.

42. *great hand.* The Hebrew says only "hand," but the idiomatic force is "exertion of great power."

when He set out His signs in Egypt   43
      and His portents in Zoan's field,
and He turned their rivers to blood,   44
      their currents they could not drink.
He sent against them the horde to consume them   45
      and the frogs to destroy them.
And He gave to the cicada their produce   46
      and their labor to the locust.
He blighted their vines with the hail,   47
      and their sycamores with the frost.
He gave over to the pestilence their beasts,   48
      and their cattle to the murrain.
He sent against them His smoldering fury,   49
      anger, indignation, and distress,
            a cohort of evil messengers.
He blazed a path for his fury,   50
      He did not keep them from death,
            and to the pestilence He gave their life.
And He struck down each firstborn in Egypt,   51
      first fruit of manhood in the tents of Ham.

---

44. *He turned their rivers to blood.* The term for rivers is taken from the Egyptian word for Nile (Hebrew, *ye'or*), but here it is used poetically in the plural. This verse begins the narration of the plagues in Egypt, which continues to the end of verse 51. There are only seven plagues mentioned in the psalm, and they are not entirely in the same order as the ones reported in Exodus, though, as in Exodus, turning the Nile into blood is at the beginning, and the killing of the firstborn is at the end. The scholarly inference that these lines reflect a different "tradition" from the one registered in Exodus is by no means necessary. That is, a poetic recapitulation of the familiar Plagues Narrative from Exodus would not have been obliged to repeat all the material from Exodus, or to follow the identical order.

47. *frost.* The Hebrew *ḥanamal* occurs only here, and the somewhat conjectural translation is based only on the context.

52 And He led His people forward like sheep,
    drove them like sheep in the wilderness.
53 And He guided them safely—they feared not,
    and their enemies the sea covered.
54 And He brought them to His holy realm,
    the mount His right hand had acquired.
55 And He drove out nations before them
    and set them down in a plot of estate,
      and made Israel's tribes dwell in their tents.
56 Yet they tried God the Most High and rebelled,
    and His precepts they did not keep.
57 They fell back and betrayed like their fathers,
    whipped around like an untrusty bow.
58 They vexed Him with their high places,
    incensed Him with their idols.
59 God heard and was angry,
    wholly rejected Israel.

---

52. *And He led His people forward like sheep.* The poetic narrative now proceeds from the last of the Ten Plagues to the actual exodus from Egypt.

53. *and their enemies the sea covered.* This verset picks up the story of the miracle at the Sea of Reeds, already evoked in greater detail in verse 13.

54. *He brought them to His holy realm, / the mount His right hand had acquired.* The language of this verse is meant to recall the Song of the Sea, Exodus 15:13 and 15:17.

55. *He drove out nations before them.* The poetic narrative, having alluded to incidents of "murmuring" from the Wilderness stories, now skips directly from the crossing of the Sea of Reeds to the conquest of the land.

57. *whipped around like an untrusty bow.* The image seems to be of a bow that flips out of the hands of the archer, shooting the arrow in the wrong direction, or not shooting it at all.

He abandoned the sanctuary of Shiloh, 60
  the tent where He dwelled among men.
And He let His might become captive, 61
  gave His splendor to the hand of the foe.
He gave over his people to the sword, 62
  against His estate He was enraged.
His young men the fire consumed 63
  and His virgins no wedding song knew.
His priests fell to the sword, 64
  and His widows did not keen.
And the Master awoke as one sleeping, 65
  like a warrior shaking off wine.
And He beat back His foes, 66
  everlasting disgrace He gave them.
Yet He rejected the tent of Joseph, 67
  and the tribe of Ephraim He did not choose.

---

60. *He abandoned the sanctuary of Shiloh.* The Shiloh sanctuary had been an important one in the period of the Judges. It is here that Elkanah and Hannah come each year to offer sacrifice (1 Samuel 1). Archaeological evidence suggests it was destroyed, probably by the Philistines, in the eleventh century BCE. The poet, following what appears to be a Deuteronomistic line of thinking, takes the destruction of the sanctuary as a sign of God's displeasure with Israel.

64. *His priests fell to the sword.* This could be a continuation of the story of the destruction of Shiloh, in which case the priests in question would be Hofni and Phineas, the sons of Eli. Alternately, the sequence from verse 62 to this verse could refer to some other devastating defeat, perhaps later than the destruction of Shiloh.

68   And He chose the tribe of Judah,
                Mount Zion that He loves.

69   And He built on the heights His sanctuary,
                like the earth He had founded forever.

70   And He chose David His servant
                and took him from the sheepfolds.

71   From the nursing ewes He brought him
                to shepherd Jacob His people
                    and Israel His estate.

72   And with his heart's innocence he shepherded them,
                with skilled hands he guided them.

---

68. *And He chose the tribe of Judah.* The rejection of Ephraim and the selection of Judah is an endorsement of the Davidic dynasty, sprung from the tribe of Judah, and of the centralization of the cult in Jerusalem ("He built on the heights His sanctuary"). The stigmatization of "the high places" (local rural altars on hilltops) in verse 58 is a distinctly Deuteronomistic notion that reinforces the idea of one exclusive temple in Jerusalem.

69. *on the heights.* The received text, *kemo-ramim,* appears to say "like the high ones." This translation reads here *bemeromim,* "on the heights."
    like the earth He had founded forever. This comparison suggests a cosmic conception of the sanctuary in Jerusalem. Just as God eternally founds the earth, the solid foundation of His dwelling place in Zion is to stand forever.

71. *to shepherd Jacob His people.* This is an instance, at the end of the poem, in which the poet in an act of interpretation makes explicit an idea merely implicit in the traditional prose narrative. David's beginnings as a shepherd point to his fitness to be the leader of his people (the figure of shepherd for king is a commonplace in the ancient Near East). That link is made clear here by the twice-used verb "shepherd" for "rule."

79

An Asaph psalm.
   God, nations have come into Your estate,
         they have defiled Your holy temple.
             They have turned Jerusalem to ruins.
   They have given Your servants' corpses
         as food to the fowl of the heavens,
             the flesh of Your faithful to the beasts of the
             earth.
   They have spilled their blood like water
         all around Jerusalem,
             and there is none to bury them.
   We have become a disgrace to our neighbors,
         scorn and contempt to all round us.

---

1. *God, nations have come into Your estate.* This entire psalm, a cry of anguish over the destruction of Jerusalem and the defilement of the temple, vividly testifies to the use of the psalm form as a poetic vehicle not only for set liturgical occasions but also for a strong response to historical events. Though some interpreters have sought to locate this psalm in the Hasmonean period, the reference to reducing Jerusalem to ruins accords far better with the catastrophe of the Babylonian conquest in 586 BCE.

3. *and there is none to bury them.* The object of the verb is merely implied in the Hebrew.

5   How long, O Lord, will You rage forever,
                Your fury burn like fire?
6   Pour out Your wrath on the nations
                that did not know You
     and on the kingdoms
                that did not call on Your name.
7   For they have devoured Jacob
                and his habitation laid waste.
8   Do not call to mind against us our forebears' crimes.
                Quickly, may Your mercies overtake us,
                        For we have sunk very low.
9   Help us, our rescuing God
                for Your name's glory,
     and save us and atone for our sins
                for the sake of Your name.

---

5. *How long, O Lord.* Here the psalmist borrows a set formula from the psalms of supplication for his historical purpose.

6. *Pour out Your wrath.* This verse, memorably recited at the Passover seder service as the door of the house is ceremonially opened, picks up the verb *shafakh*, which is used for the spilling or shedding of blood earlier (verse 3) and later (verse 10).

7. *devoured Jacob /. . . his habitation laid waste.* The poetic parallelism pointedly identifies the two principal disasters of the conquest—the massacre of the population and the razing of the city.

8. *Do not call to mind against us our forebears' crimes.* The speaker palpably feels the weight of the accumulated transgressions of past generations for which the nation has now been punished, and he pleads with God not to hold the devastated survivors accountable for the sins of the past.

Why should the nations say, "Where is their god?"   10
> Let it be known among the nations before our eyes—
>> the vengeance for Your servants' spilled blood.
Let the captive's groan come before You,   11
> by Your arm's greatness unbind those marked for death.
And give back to our neighbors sevenfold to their bosom   12
> their insults that they heaped on You, Master.
But we are Your people and the flock that You tend.   13
> We acclaim You forever.
>> From generation to generation we recount
>> Your praise.

---

10. *before our eyes*. The idiomatic force of this phrase is "here and now."

11. *captive's . . . / . . . those marked for death*. In addition to the killings, those who have survived are being marched off into captivity, to an uncertain fate that could well mean death. This verse tempts one to infer that the psalm may have actually been composed by one of the Judeans taken off to exile in Babylonia.

13. *the flock that You tend*. Literally, "the flock of Your tending."
We acclaim You forever. The conclusion of this psalm gives us a glimpse of the sustaining belief that enabled the exiled Judeans to persist as a distinctive group. The nation has undergone the most catastrophic defeat, but its God has suffered no diminution. Even in exile, the people acclaims God and is unswerving in its belief in His rescuing power.

80

1 For the lead player, on the *shoshanim*, an *eduth*, an Asaph psalm.
2 Shepherd of Israel, hearken,
       He Who drives Joseph like sheep,
          enthroned on the cherubim, shine forth.
3 Before Ephraim and Benjamin and Manasseh
      rouse Your might
         and come to the rescue for us.
4 O God, bring us back,
      and light up Your face that we may be rescued.
5 Lᴏʀᴅ, God of armies,
      how long will You smolder against Your people's prayer?

---

1. eduth. The general meaning of this Hebrew term is "precept," "pact," or "treaty obligation." Here it would appear to have a musical or perhaps a literary meaning ("testimony"?), but we have no way of knowing precisely what it indicates.

2–3. *He Who drives Joseph like sheep, / . . . rouse Your might.* "Joseph," in contrast to "Judah" or "Jacob," is a reference to the northern kingdom. The Septuagint includes in its superscription for this psalm, "concerning the Assyrians." It may well have been composed at a moment when the northern kingdom of Israel was threatened but, on the basis of the content of the poem, not yet destroyed by Assyria.

3. *Before Ephraim and Benjamin and Manasseh.* The tribe of Benjamin and the two half tribes of Ephraim and Manasseh were all part of the northern kingdom.

You fed them bread of tears   6
     and made them drink triple measure of tears.
You have put us in strife with our neighbors,   7
     and our enemies mock us.
God of armies, bring us back,   8
     and light up Your face that we may be rescued.
You carried a vine out of Egypt,   9
     You drove away nations and planted it.
You cleared space before it   10
     and struck its roots down,
          and it filled the land.
The mountains were covered by its shade,   11
     and by its branches the mighty cedars.

---

6. *triple measure.* The Hebrew says "a third"—evidently, a third of some very large unit of measure. Because in English the use of the fraction would suggest smallness rather than large quantity, this translation turns the number three into a multiplier.

7. *mock us.* The received text says "mock them," but two manuscripts and three ancient translations show "mock us."

9. *You carried a vine out of Egypt.* The vine as a symbol of the nation would have been a familiar idea to the ancient audience (it is variously deployed in Isaiah, Hosea, and Jeremiah). As the image is elaborated through the next few verses, it develops a logic that the Israelite agriculturalists would have readily grasped: Why would anyone go to the trouble of transplanting a vine from one region to another—clearing the ground all around it, cultivating it so that it grows to splendid proportions—if in the end one breaches its protective wall and allows noxious wild beasts to destroy it?

11. *the mighty cedars.* The phrase *'arzey 'el* has sometimes been misconstrued as "the cedars of God," but *'el* here and in a good many other places is a suffix of intensification, not a reference to the deity.

12   You sent forth its boughs to the sea
                 and to the River its shoots.
13   Why did You break through its walls
                 so all passers-by could pluck it?
14   The boar from the forest has gnawed it,
                 and the swarm of the field fed upon it.
15   God of armies, pray, come back,
                 look down from the heavens and see,
                       and take note of this vine,
16   and the stock that Your right hand planted,
                 and the son You took to Yourself—
17   burnt in fire, chopped to bits,
                 from the blast of Your presence they perish.
18   May Your hand be over the man on Your right,
                 over the son of man You took to Yourself.
19   And we will not fall back from You.
                 Restore us to life and we shall call on Your name.

---

12. *to the River.* The probable hyperbolic reference is to the Euphrates, though it could conceivably be, less grandiosely, the Jordan.

14. *the swarm.* The Hebrew *ziz* suggests "moving thing," in all likelihood a reference to insects and other crawling things. In the quasi-allegorical vehicle of the violated vine, the Assyrian army is imagined as other than human—a wild boar, a ravenous swarm of pestilential crawling creatures.

16. *the son You took to Yourself.* If the received text shows an authentic reading here, there is a slightly disconcerting shift from the vehicle of the metaphor (the vine) to its tenor (the people of Israel as God's son). Some interpreters have understood *ben* as a poetic term for "branch" or as a scribal error for some other word that means "branch," but the verb attached to it—*'imatsta*, which suggests adoption of a child—is appropriate for a son, not a plant.

LORD God of armies, bring us back.   20
          Light up Your face, that we may be rescued.

---

20. LORD *God of armies, bring us back.* This refrain of supplication, which was
introduced near the beginning and then in the middle of the poem, now
becomes its apt conclusion.

81

1 For the lead player, on the *gittith,* for Asaph.
2 Sing gladly to God our strength,
   shout out to the God of Jacob.
3 Lift your voices in song and beat the drum,
   the lyre is sweet with the lute.
4 Blast the ram's horn on the new moon,
   when the moon starts to wax, for our festival day.
5 For it is an ordinance in Israel,
   a rule of the God of Jacob.

---

3. *Lift your voices in song.* The Hebrew says, perhaps elliptically, "Lift song."

4. *Blast the ram's horn on the new moon.* The subject—which will prove to be only an ostensible subject—of the psalm is now made explicit: The glad song and the sounding instruments are part of the ritual celebration of the new moon, which was a major feast day in biblical times. A whole orchestral ensemble is specified here: singing, stringed instruments, a percussion instrument, and a horn section.
   when the moon starts to wax. The Hebrew *keseh* derives from the verb that means "to cover." Though many interpreters understand it as a reference to the full moon, it is something of a stretch to imagine that the festive celebration of the new moon invoked in the first verset somehow goes on to a point in time fourteen days later in the second verset. In any case, "cover" accords far better with the time of month when the moon is only a thin sliver than with the time when it is bright and full.

5. *For it is an ordinance in Israel.* The ordinance referred to is the celebration of the new moon in all its ritual propriety.

A decree He declared it for Israel   6
      when He sallied forth against Egypt's land—
          a language I knew not, I heard.
"I delivered his shoulder from the burden   7
      his palms were loosed from the hod.
From the straits you called and I set you free.   8
      I answered You from thunder's hiding-place.
          I tested you at the waters of Meribah.   selah
Hear, O my people, that I may adjure you.   9
      Israel, if You would but hear Me.
There shall be among you no foreign god   10
      and you shall not bow to an alien god.
I am the LORD your God   11
      Who brings you up from the land of Egypt.
          Open your mouth wide, that I may fill it.

---

6. *A decree He declared . . . / when He sallied forth.* In an associative slide, the antiquity of the regulations governing the new moon carries us back to the beginnings of Israelite history in the exodus story.

    a language I knew not, I heard. These words are a kind of interjection on the part of a speaker who is a representative Israelite, recalling "his" time of enslavement in Egypt when his taskmasters spoke an alien tongue.

7. *I delivered his shoulder from the burden.* The celebratory psalm now segues into a prophetic psalm, with God addressing the people.

    the hod. The Hebrew *dud* refers to the basket-like receptacle in which the laborers carried bricks or material for the manufacture of bricks.

8. *I answered You from thunder's hiding-place.* In all likelihood, this fine if somewhat mystifying phrase refers to God's wielding thunder (or lightning) as a weapon, following the precedent of the Canaanite sky god.

10–11. *There shall be among you no foreign god . . . / I am the* LORD *your God / Who brings you up from the land of Egypt.* The entirety of these two verses is a free paraphrase of the beginning of the Ten Commandments.

12   But My people did not heed My voice
                and Israel wanted nothing of Me.
13   And I let them follow their heart's willfulness,
                they went by their own counsels.
14   If My people would but heed Me,
                if Israel would go in My ways,
15   in a moment I would humble their enemies,
                and against their foes I would turn My hand.
16   Those who hate the LORD would cringe before Him,
                and their time of doom would be everlasting.
17   And I would feed him the finest wheat,
                and from the rock I would sate him with honey."

---

12. *But My people did not heed My voice.* This sequence is a thumbnail summary of the Wilderness narrative—and, by implication, of subsequent Israelite history: God generously provides for the urgent needs of the people ("Open your mouth wide, that I may fill it"), but the people repeatedly rebels.

16. *Those who hate the LORD.* These are Israel's enemies. God is still speaking, but, in a grammatical move fairly common in biblical Hebrew, He refers to Himself in the third person.
    their time of doom. The Hebrew says only "their time." The translation follows the inference of most interpreters, which, one must concede, is chiefly based on the need to make sense of the term in context. An emendation yields "their terror."

17. *I would feed him the finest wheat.* The "him" must refer to Israel. Such switches without signaling transition in pronominal reference occur frequently in biblical usage. The Masoretic text also shows a third-person verb ("and He would feed him"), but many scholars emend this to the first person, as does this translation.
    I would sate him. The poem concludes with still another grammatical anomaly because the received text reads "I would sate you." It is at least conceivable that the poet wanted to revert at the very end from the historical third-person reference to a direct address to Israel, as in verses 8–11. In English this would be confusing, and one manuscript version as well as the Septuagint and the Syriac reads "him."

82

An Asaph psalm.   1
   God takes His stand in the divine assembly,
         in the midst of the gods He renders judgment.
   "How long will you judge dishonestly,   2
         and show favor to the wicked?   selah
   Do justice to the poor and the orphan.   3
         Vindicate the lowly and the wretched.
   Free the poor and the needy,   4
         from the hand of the wicked save them.

---

1. *God takes His stand in the divine assembly.* Like the psalms of supplication, this poem is concerned with the infuriating preponderance of injustice in the world. It differs from them, however, not only because God is the principal speaker (from verse 2 through verse 7) but also because the psalm is frankly mythological in character. Alternatively, one could describe it as a poem about the transition from mythology to a monotheistic frame of reference because in the end the gods are rudely demoted from their divine status.

   in the midst of the gods. The efforts of traditional commentators to understand '*elohim* here as "judges" are unconvincing. God speaks out in the assembly of lesser gods and rebukes them for doing a wretched job in the administration of justice on earth.

2. *How long will you judge dishonestly.* The plot of the poem that begins to unfold is a mythological account of the existential problem that would vex the Job poet: Why is it that the just often seem to suffer, whereas the wicked prosper? The answer given here is that the gods, administrators of the old polytheistic order, impose a crooked scheme of justice on humanity, showing favoritism to the wicked and ignoring the pleas of the helpless.

5 They do not know and do not grasp,
            in darkness they walk about.
                        All the earth's foundations totter.
6 As for Me, I had thought: you were gods,
            and the sons of the Most High were you all.
7 Yet indeed like humans you shall die,
            and like one of the princes, fall."

---

5. *in darkness they walk about.* Ibn Ezra, the pastmaster among exegetes in seeing intra-biblical connections, brilliantly links this image of judges stumbling through darkness with Exodus 23:8—"No bribe shall you take, for a bribe blinds the sighted and perverts the words of the innocent."

All the earth's foundations totter. This is not, as may first appear, a non sequitur. The order of creation itself, in the view of biblical monotheism, is founded on justice. When the lesser gods allow injustice to become rampant, the very foundations of earth are shaken—the perversion of justice is the first step toward the apocalypse.

6. *As for Me, I had thought.* God confesses to have been taken in by the polytheistic illusion. He imagined that these sundry gods entrusted with the administration of justice on earth would prove or justify their divine status by doing the job properly. In the event, He was sadly disappointed.

7. *like humans you shall die, / and like one of the princes, fall.* Because the gods have failed in their crucial role as executors of justice, they are henceforth compelled to relinquish their supposedly divine status and suffer the same fate of mortality as human beings. The parallel term to 'adam ("humans," or "man," though the Hebrew does not imply gender), "one of the princes," reflects a kind of hierarchical logic. One does not readily imagine the ex-gods turning into peasants, but all people know that even the most elevated of human beings—princes and potentates—are fated to die.

Arise, O God, judge the earth,   8
       for You hold in estate all the nations.

---

8. *Arise, O God, judge the earth.* The psalm concludes, after God's address to the unjust gods, with a speaker who exhorts the one authentic divine being to impose upon earth the reign of true justice to which He alone is committed.

for You hold in estate all the nations. Why does the speaker need to say this at the very end? In the ancient world, the multiplicity of nations is associated with a multiplicity of gods: Each nation has its patron god (see, for example, Jephthah's words to the Amorite king about YHWH and the Amorite deity Cemosh in Judges 11:24) as well as a variety of gods and goddesses presiding over the various realms of nature. But that order has now proven to be judicially and morally bankrupt, and it is the God of Israel alone Who holds in estate (the verb could also be construed as a future, "will hold in estate") all the nations of earth.

83

1   A song, an Asaph psalm.
2   O God, no silence for You!
            Do not be mute and do not be quiet, God.
3   For, look, Your enemies rage,
            and those who hate You lift their heads.
4   Against Your people they devise cunning counsel
            and conspire against Your protected ones.
5   They have said: "Come, let us obliterate them as a nation,
            and the name of Israel will no longer be recalled."
6   For they conspired with a single heart,
            against You they sealed a pact—

---

3. *For, look, Your enemies rage.* The situation of an alliance of surrounding nations plotting an all-out assault on Judea identifies this as a militant national supplication. Many interpreters have inferred that it was actually composed in a time of national emergency to be recited in public worship in an entreaty to God to intervene on behalf of His people. When that might have been remains a matter of scholarly debate, although the list of hostile peoples in verses 7 and 8 as well as the invocation of the Song of Deborah in verse 10 argues for an early date, close to or even within the period of the Judges (before 1000 BCE). The mention of Assyria, on the other hand, could be an indication of a late eighth-century date, unless, as has been proposed, "Assyria" in this text is not the great empire—after all, why would it ally itself with these small, mainly Transjordanian kingdoms?—but rather a modest-size eastern nation antecedent to the empire.

the tents of Edom and the Ishmaelites,   7
    Moab and the Hagrites,
Gebal and Ammon and Amalek,   8
    Philistia with the dwellers of Tyre.
Assyria, too, has joined them,   9
    has become an arm for the sons of Lot.   selah
Do unto them as to Midian, as to Sisera,   10
    as to Jabin at the brook of Kishon.
They were destroyed at En-Dor,   11
    they turned into dung for the soil.
Deal with their nobles as with Oreb   12
    and as with Zeeb and Zebah and Zulmunna, all their
    princes,
who said, "We shall take hold for ourselves   13
    of all the meadows of God."
O God, make them like the thistledown,   14
    like straw before the wind.
As fire burns down forests   15
    and as flame ignites the mountains,

---

7. *the tents of Edom.* Because these are semi-nomadic peoples, "tents" is an appropriate synecdoche for their concentrations of population.

8. *Philistia.* It is worth noting that the Philistines ceased to be a serious threat to the Israelites not long after the establishment of the Davidic dynasty at the beginning of the first millennium BCE.

10. *as to Sisera, / as to Jabin.* Jabin was the Canaanite king whose army, under the command of Sisera, was defeated by Barak, with Deborah behind him, as recorded in Judges 4–5.

12. *Oreb . . . Zeeb . . . Zebah . . . Zalmunna.* These were the Midianite chieftains defeated by Gideon, as reported in Judges 8.

16   so shall You pursue them with Your storm
            and with Your tempest dismay them.
17   Fill their faces with infamy
            that they may seek Your name, O LORD.
18   May they be shamed and dismayed forever,
            may they be disgraced and may they perish.
19   And may they know that You, Your name is the LORD.
            You alone are most high over all the earth.

---

16. *pursue them with Your storm.* As in Canaanite mythology, the storm is the weapon of the sky god—in particular, the bolts of lightning, clearly implied in the fire imagery of the previous verse.

19. *You alone are most high over all the earth.* YHWH, the God of Israel, is not just a powerful national god but the deity that rules all the earth. This cosmic supremacy of the God of Israel, in the gesture of prayer that concludes the psalm, is a fact that the hostile nations will come to recognize through their own disastrous defeat, just before they perish.

84

For the lead player on the *gittith,* for the Korahites, a psalm.   ¹
   How lovely Your dwellings,   ²
          O Lord of armies!
   My being longed, even languished,   ³
          for the courts of the Lord.
   My heart and my flesh
          sing gladness to the living God.
   Even the bird has found a home,   ⁴
          and the swallow a nest for itself,

---

2. *How lovely Your dwellings.* The term translated as "lovely," *yedidot,* is associated with *dod,* "lover," and *dodim,* "lovemaking," and conveys a virtually erotic intensity in the speaker's longing for the temple on Mount Zion. (The King James Version, entirely missing the register, translates *yedidot* as "amiable.") This text, then, is one of the pilgrim psalms, expressing the speaker's powerful longing to enjoy the aura of God's presence in the temple. The repeated epithet "Lord of armies" (YHWH *tsev'aot*) does not appear to tap the military connotations of that designation in the present context.

4. *Even the bird has found a home.* This image provides the most poignant focus for the speaker's longing. Small birds such as swallows may well have nested in the little crevices of the roughly dressed stones that constituted the temple facade. The speaker, yearning for the sacred zone of the temple, is envious of these small creatures happy in the temple precincts, whereas he, like an unrequited lover, only dreams of this place of intimacy with the divine. "Sing gladness" in the previous line may have been the associative trigger for thinking about the birds.

that puts its fledglings by Your altars,
> LORD of armies, my king and my God.

5   Happy are those who dwell in Your house,
> they will ever praise You.   selah

6   Happy the folk whose strength is in You,
> the highways in their heart,

7   who pass through the Valley of Baca,
> they make it into a spring—
>> yes, the early rain cloaks it with blessings.

8   They go from rampart to rampart,
> they appear before God in Zion.

---

6. *Happy the folk.* The Hebrew *'adam* means "person," "human being," or "man" (as it is translated at the end of the poem). The translation choice here of "folk" is to facilitate the transition, otherwise odd in English, from the singular in this verset to the plural in the second verset ("their heart").

the highways in their heart. If the received text is correct, this would most likely mean, "their every thought is on the pilgrim highways leading to Jerusalem."

7. *they make it into a spring.* It seems that a miraculous manifestation of divine grace is vouchsafed to the pilgrims. As they come through the Valley of Baca on their way up to Mount Zion, springs gush.

the early rain cloaks it with blessings. The descent of the early rain complements the bursting forth of springs. Alternately, as ibn Ezra proposes, *moreh* could be a place name in parallel with the Valley of Baca. That would yield the following: Moreh is cloaked in blessings.

8. *from rampart to rampart.* "Rampart" is one of several meanings of the Hebrew *ḥayil* and makes good sense in this context of pilgrims making their way up to Jerusalem. However, *ḥayil* also means strength, and "to go from strength to strength" has become proverbial in Hebrew as in English.

they appear before God in Zion. The vocalization could be, as elsewhere, a euphemistic substitution for "they see God," though the usual object of the verb, "the face of," is absent, and the preposition *'el* ("to" or "before") is unusually introduced. All this might be the result of tampering by pious scribes.

Lord, God of armies, hear my prayer.   9
     Hearken, O God of Jacob.   selah

Our shield, O God, see,   10
     and regard Your anointed one's face

For better one day in Your courts   11
     than a thousand I have chosen,
standing on the threshold in the house of my God,
     than living in the tents of wickedness.

For a sun and shield is the Lord,   12
     God is grace and glory.
The Lord grants, He does not withhold
     bounty to those who go blameless.

O Lord of armies,   13
     happy the man who trusts in You.

---

10. *Our shield.* The reference, as the second verset makes clear, is to the king. The pilgrim longing for Zion, which is also the capital of the kingdom, asks God to show favor to the anointed king. But in verse 12, it is God who is invoked as shield.

11. *than a thousand I have chosen.* "I have chosen," *baḥarti*, looks redundant in relation to "better than." Some scholars emend it to *beḥadri*, "in my chamber."
     than living in the tents of wickedness. The imperfect parallelism with the first verset might be an argument for the proposed emendation, "in my chamber." A private chamber empty of God's presence is a sorry thing, only a step away from the tents of wickedness.

85

1 For the lead player, for the Korahites, a psalm.
2   You favored, O Lord, Your land,
           You restored the condition of Jacob.
3   You forgave Your people's crime,
           You covered all their offense.   selah
4   You laid aside all Your wrath,
           You turned back from Your blazing fury.

---

2. *You favored, O Lord, Your land.* There is scarcely a more striking example in the Bible of the temporal ambiguity or fluidity of Hebrew verbs. The verbs used through to the end of verse 4 are in the perfective or "suffix" form, which, lacking an initial *waw* that would convert them into a future, appear to indicate actions completed in the past. But what is reported here as completed action is precisely what the speaker prays for beginning in verse 5. Either he is remembering a time in the past when God forgave His people and favored the land as a precedent for the present plight, or he is imagining what he is about to pray for as though it were already an accomplished fact.

You restored the condition of Jacob. The Hebrew *shevut* (or in the variant used here, *shevit*), when it is coupled with the cognate verb *shuv*, means "previous condition." (It is precisely the idiom used at the end of Job, 42:10, to indicate God's restoration of all Job's losses.) The appearance of the expression in this verse, joined with the idea of God's favoring His land after it had fallen out of favor, suggests that the psalm may have been composed after the Babylonian exile in 586 BCE, though references to exile are not entirely explicit. "Turning back" becomes a key phrase of the poem. It is used five times, including verse 7, where the idiomatic sense in context leads this translation to render it adverbially as "again."

Turn back, pray, God of our rescue   5
     and undo Your anger against us.
Will You forever be incensed with us,   6
     will You draw out Your fury through all generations?
Why, You—will again give us life,   7
     and Your people will rejoice in You.
Show us, O LORD, Your kindness,   8
     and Your rescue grant to us.
Let me hear what the LORD God would speak   9
     when He speaks peace to His people and to His
     faithful,
          that they turn not back to folly.
Yes, His rescue is near for those who fear Him,   10
     that His glory dwell in our land.
Kindness and truth have met,   11
     justice and peace have kissed.

---

5. *Turn back.* The Hebrew text says "Turn us back," which doesn't make much sense in this verse (and the verb in the *qal* conjugation does not take personal objects). The translation reads *shuv na'*, "turn back, pray," instead of the Masoretic *shuveinu*.

9. *that they turn not back to folly.* The key verb expresses a kind of quid pro quo: God is implored to turn back from His wrath, and the people will accordingly not turn back to folly.

10. *that His glory dwell in our land.* This rather generalized clause could well refer to the restoration of Judea after exile. Because God's rescue is near at hand, His glory will again be manifest in the land.

11. *Kindness and truth.* The two terms of the familiar hendiadys *hesed we'emet* ("steadfast loyalty") are separated and turned into figures, along with another pair, justice and peace, in a kind of allegory of the ideal moment when God's favor is restored to the land.
    justice and peace have kissed. This bold metaphor focuses the sense of an era of perfect loving harmony. Rashi imagines a landscape in which all Israelites will kiss one another.

12   Truth from the earth will spring up,
           as justice from the heavens looks down.

13   The LORD indeed will grant bounty
           and our land will grant its yield.

14   Justice before Him goes,
           that He set His footsteps on the way.

---

14. *that He set His footsteps on the way.* Although some scholars have sought to emend this final clause, a vivid image is suggested by the text as we have it. Justice leads the way, and God, preparing to walk about the earth after having withdrawn from it in His wrath, follows the path marked out by justice.

86

A David prayer. 1
  Incline Your ear, LORD, answer me,
      for lowly and needy am I.
  Guard my life, for I am faithful. 2
      Rescue Your servant who trusts in You
        —You, my God.
  Grant grace to me, Master, 3
      for to You I call all day long.
  Gladden Your servant, 4
      for to You, O Master, I lift up my being.
  For You, O Master, are good and forgiving, 5
      abounding in kindness to all who call to You.
  Hearken, O LORD, to my prayer, 6
      and listen well to the sound of my pleas.

---

1. *Incline Your ear, LORD, answer me.* The poem begins with a formula of the psalms of supplication, and this psalm is highly formulaic from beginning to end. A reader who has been going through the Book of Psalms in sequence by this point will have encountered almost every line of this poem, with minor variations, elsewhere.

4. *for to You . . . I lift up my being.* The idiom, which occurs elsewhere in Psalms, means to pray, to implore, to long desperately. "My being," *nafshi,* also has the sense of "my very self," "my life breath."

5. *abounding in kindness to all who call to You.* The epithets for God are borrowed from Exodus 34:6. Verse 15 provides a fuller quotation of God's benevolent attributes spelled out in the same passage in Exodus

7   When I am in straits I call You,
           for You will answer me.

8   There is none like You among the gods, O Master
           and nothing like Your acts.

9   All the nations You made
           will come and bow before You, Master
              and will honor Your name.

10   For You are great and work wonders.
           You alone are God.

11   Teach me, O LORD, Your way.
           I would walk in Your truth.
              Make my heart one to fear Your name.

12   Let me acclaim You, O Master, my God, with all my heart,
           and let me honor Your name forever.

13   For Your kindness to me is great,
           and You saved me from nethermost Sheol.

14   O God, the arrogant rose against me,
           and a band of the violent sought my life
              and did not set You before them.

15   But You, Master, are a merciful, gracious God,
           slow to anger and abounding in steadfast kindness.

---

7. *When I am in straits.* Literally, "in the day of my strait."

8. *There is none like You among the gods, O Master.* This line quotes the Song of the Sea, Exodus 15:11. The move from this quotation to verses 9 and 10 traces the trajectory from henotheism to proper monotheism. In the old poem in Exodus, other gods are imagined as existing but are feeble in power compared to YHWH, God of Israel; here the poet goes on to affirm that "You alone are God."

13. *nethermost Sheol.* The addition of the adjective *taḥtiyah*, "nethermost" or "down below," suggest something of the terror of death in this culture oriented toward life in the here and now. Sheol, the underworld, rather like the Homeric Hades, is imagined as a deep pit far below the busy surface where human creatures for a brief time look on the bright sunlight.

Turn to me and grant me grace.   16
      Give Your strength to Your servant
         and rescue Your handmaiden's son.
Show me a sign for good,   17
      that those who hate me may see and be shamed.
         For You, LORD, have helped me and consoled
      me.

---

16. *Your handmaiden's son.* This is a poetic invention often introduced because of the necessity of having an equivalent term in the poetic parallelism for "servant." *'Eved*, the word for servant, can also mean, depending on context, "slave," just as *'amah*, "handmaiden," often means "slavegirl."

87

1 For the Korahites, a psalm, a song.
     His foundation on the holy mountains—
2   The LORD loves the gates of Zion
             more than all the dwellings of Jacob.
3   Splendid things are spoken of you,
         O town of God.   selah

---

1. *His foundation on the holy mountains.* Despite the inclusion of this verset by the medieval editors in the superscription in verse 1, it clearly is the initial element of a triadic line of poetry continuing through verse 2, in semantic parallelism with "the gates of Zion." The third verset, as often happens in triadic lines, is not a semantic parallel but, in this case, a modifier of the predicate "loves." This poem is explicitly a psalm of Zion. Its general sense of exalted celebration of Zion is clear, though some of the particular formulations, as will be noted, are obscure.

Let me recall Rahab and Babel to my familiars.   4
         Look, Philistia and Tyre together with Cush,
               —this one was born there.
And of Zion it shall be said: 5
         every man is born in it,
            and He, the Most High, makes it firm-founded.
The Lord inscribes in the record of peoples: 6
         this one was born there.   selah
And singers and dancers alike: 7
         "All my wellsprings are in you."

---

4. *Let me recall Rahab and Babel to my familiars.* Rahab, the sea monster, is sometimes used as a poetic epithet for Egypt, and the appearance of that name in a list of surrounding nations makes it likely that this is its meaning here. If, as some claim, the speaker is God, then "my familiars" (*yodʿai*) would have to be rendered as "those who know Me." It seems more plausible that the speaker is a Judahite celebrating Zion's greatness.

    Cush. Traditionally identified with Ethiopia, or perhaps Nubia.

4–5. *this one was born there / . . . every man is born in it.* The wording is certainly cryptic, but it might convey a universalist message about Jerusalem. Though as a biographical fact every person is born in his or her native place in the surrounding region, all who come up to Zion to acclaim God's kingship there are considered to be reborn in Zion.

5. *the Most High.* This word, *ʿelyon*, occurs at the end of the sentence in the Hebrew, but it is difficult to construe it as an adjectival object of the verb because it would then have to refer to Zion, which is feminine, whereas *ʿelyon* is masculine.

7. *And singers and dancers alike.* The simplest way to understand this phrase, without tampering with the text, is that there is an elided "say."

    All my wellsprings are in you. The "you" refers to Zion. Beginning with some of the ancient translations, sundry readers have variously emended this clause, but it makes a certain degree of sense as it stands. In a semi-arid climate, "wellsprings" (*maʿayanim*) is an understandable idiom for sources of life.

88

1　A song, a psalm for the Korahites, for the lead player, on the
　　mahalath, to sing out, a *maskil* for Heyman the Ezrahite.
2　　　Lᴏʀᴅ, God of my rescue,
　　　　　　　　by day I cried out,
　　　　　　　　　　by night, in Your presence.
3　　　May my prayer come before You.
　　　　　　　　Incline Your ear to my song.
4　　　For I am sated with evils
　　　　　　　　and my life reached the brink of Sheol.
5　　　I was counted among those who go down to the Pit.
　　　　　　　　I became like a man without strength,

---

1. *Heyman the Ezrahite.* Scarcely anything is known about the identity of this
figure—a choral leader? a psalmist?—or about Ethan the Ezrahite, who
appears in the superscription of the next psalm. Both are mentioned in 1
Chronicles 2:6 as sons of Zerah from the tribe of Judah. "The Ezrahite" may be
a familial designation derived from "Zerah."

2. *by day I cried out.* The formulas of this verse and the next signal the genre of
supplication. What distinguishes this particular supplication is its special con-
centration on the terrifying darkness of the realm of death that has almost
engulfed the supplicant. In consonance with this focus, the psalm deploys an
unusual abundance of synonyms for the underworld: Sheol, the Pit, the grave,
the depths, perdition, the land of oblivion.

among the dead cast away,   6
      like the slain, those who lie in the grave,
whom You no more recall,
      and they are cut off by Your hand.
You put me in the nethermost Pit,   7
      in darkness, in the depths.
Your wrath lay hard upon me,   8
      and all Your breakers You inflicted.
You distanced my friends from me,   9
      you made me disgusting to them;
         imprisoned, I cannot get out.
My eyes ache from affliction.   10
      I called on You, Lord, every day.
         I stretched out to You my palms.
Will You do wonders for the dead?   11
      Will the shades arise and acclaim you?   selah
Will Your kindness be told in the grave,   12
      Your faithfulness in perdition?

---

6. *among the dead cast away.* The predominant meaning of the adjective *ḥofshi* is "free," but a negative sense is surely required here, and in 2 Kings 15:5, *beyt haḥofshit* means the place of quarantine in which lepers are segregated. The Ugaritic cognate, moreover, appears to be a designation for the underworld; in fact, in verse 9 the speaker talks of imprisonment.

8. *all Your breakers You inflicted.* As in other psalms, the descent into the Pit of death is imagistically equated with drowning beneath the waves of the sea. Compare the apposition at the end of verse 7, "in darkness, in the depths."

11. *Will You do wonders for the dead?* This is a recurrent idea in Psalms: The dead will not rise, will never again be able to fulfill the ultimate human vocation of praising the Creator.

12. *perdition.* The Hebrew noun *'avadon*, transparently derived from the verb that means to perish or to be lost, is probably a mythological proper name for the underworld, like Sheol.

13   Will Your wonder be known in the darkness,
            Your bounty in the land of oblivion?
14   As for me—to You, LORD, I shouted,
            and in the morn my prayer would greet You.
15   Why, LORD, do You abandon my life,
            do You hide Your face from me?
16   Lowly am I and near death from my youth
            I have borne Your terrors, I am fearful.
17   Over me Your rage has passed,
            Your horrors destroy me.
18   They surround me like water all day long,
            they encircle me completely.
19   You distanced lover and neighbor from me.
            My friends—utter darkness.

---

14. *in the morn*. The Hebrew phrase is rendered literally, but its idiomatic sense is "every morning"; therefore, the verb "greet" is translated here as an iterative.

16. *I am fearful*. The Hebrew verb *'afunah* is anomalous and its meaning is uncertain. The translation follows a proposal by ibn Ezra.

18. *They surround me like water*. The water simile conveys the sense of total engulfment and carries forward the idea of death as drowning.

19. *You distanced lover and neighbor from me*. This clause picks up the idea of verse 9, using the same verb: The speaker, perhaps because he has been suffering from a repulsive illness or simply because his fortunes have met with disaster (like Job), has become an object of disgust to his friends.
   My friends—utter darkness. "Utter" is added in the translation for the sake of intelligibility. This abrupt statement, just two words in the Hebrew, closes the poem on the theme of darkness that has dominated it throughout. The sense is either that the speaker's friends, because they have rejected him and withdrawn their presence from him, are nothing but darkness to him, or that now the only "friend" he has left is darkness.

89

A *maskil* for Ethan the Ezrahite.

Let me sing the LORD's kindnesses forever.

For all generations I shall make known with my mouth Your faithfulness.

1
2

---

1. *Ethan the Ezrahite.* According to the list in 1 Chronicles 2:6, he would be the brother of Heyman the Ezrahite mentioned in the superscription to Psalm 88.

2. *Your faithfulness.* The Hebrew word *'emunah*, "faithfulness," "trustworthiness," "dependability in fulfilling obligations," is the key word of this psalm, repeated eight times in the poem, with an additional two occurrences in adjectival form. The reiteration of this term also suggests why those scholars who claim that this psalm is an amalgam of three different genres are unconvincing. This is a psalm about God's pact with the House of David; if one prefers, it is a royal psalm. But it is clearly composed at a moment when the fortunes of the Davidic king have taken a disastrous turn in the face of victorious enemies. (Exactly when that might have been is difficult to determine, though many scholars set this text in the period of the First Commonwealth.) The psalmist insists on his belief in God's faithfulness to His covenantal commitments in the face of present catastrophes. There is, then, a logical progression in the poem: first, a celebration of God's cosmic power, by virtue of which He could easily rout all the enemies of the Davidic throne if He chose to do so; then the choice of David and his seed by this all-powerful and trustworthy cosmic deity; then the conditional nature of the covenant, which is contingent on the people's adherence to God's laws, and the consequent disaster that has befallen them; and, finally, a plea to God to remember how ephemeral man is and to relent from His seemingly endless wrath against His people and against His anointed king.

3   For I said: forever will kindness stand strong,
            in the heavens You set Your faithfulness firm.
4   "I have sealed a pact with my chosen one,
            I have sworn to David My servant.
5   Forevermore I shall make your seed stand firm,
            and make your throne stand strong for all
            generations."   selah
6   And the heavens will acclaim Your wonder, O LORD,
            Your faithfulness, too, in the assembly of the holy.
7   For who in the skies can compare to the LORD,
            who can be like the LORD among the sons of the gods?
8   A God held in awe in the council of the holy,
            mighty and fearsome above all His surroundings.
9   LORD, God of armies, who is like You,
            powerful Yah, with Your faithfulness round You?
10 You rule over the tide of the sea.
            When its waves lift up, it is You who subdue them.

---

3. *stand strong.* The literal sense of the Hebrew is "be built."

in the heavens You set Your faithfulness firm. The syntax and the Hebrew of this verset are ambiguous. The literal word sequence is "Heavens You set firm Your faithfulness in them." Various emendations, none entirely convincing, have been proposed.

5. *stand strong.* Again, the Hebrew says, "build."

8. *A God held in awe in the council of the holy.* The council envisaged is a council of the gods—still another instance in Psalms of the survival, at least in poetic imagery, of a pre-monotheistic mythology in which YHWH is not alone but reigns supreme over lesser gods. The same idea is reflected in the previous verse.

It is You Who crushed Rahab like a corpse—   11
        with the arm of Your might You scattered Your enemies.
Yours are the heavens, Yours, too, the earth.   12
        The world and its fullness, You founded them.
The north and the south, You created them.   13
        Tabor and Hermon sing glad song in Your name.
Yours is the arm with the might.   14
        Your hand is strong, Your right hand raised.
Justice and law are the base of Your throne.   15
        Steadfast kindness and truth go before Your presence.
Happy the people who know the horn's blast.   16
        O Lord, they walk in the light of Your presence.
In Your name they exult all day long,   17
        and through Your bounty they loom high.
For You are their strength's grandeur,   18
        and through Your pleasure our horn is lifted.
For the Lord's is our shield,   19
        and to Israel's Holy One, our king.
Then did You speak in a vision   20
        to Your faithful and did say:
"I set a crown upon the warrior,
        I raised up one chosen from the people.

---

11. *It is You Who crushed Rahab.* Rahab is one of several names for the primordial sea beast of Canaanite mythology. Thus, this line is continuous with the more naturalistic image of God's ruling over the tide and subduing the waves of the sea in the previous verse.

19. *For the Lord's is our shield.* "Our shield" refers to the monarch, as the second verset makes clear.

20. *I set a crown.* The Masoretic text says "help" (*'ezer*), which does not sound idiomatic coupled with the verb used here. Many scholars read instead *nezer*, "crown," as does this translation.

21 I found David my servant,
> with My holy oil anointed him,

22 that My hand hold firm with him,
> My arm, too, take him in.

23 No enemy shall cause him grief
> and no vile person afflict him.

24 And I will grind down his foes before him
> and defeat those who hate him.

25 My faithfulness and My kindness are with him,
> and in My name his horn will be lifted.

26 And I shall put his hand to the sea
> and his right hand to the rivers.

27 He will call me: 'My father You are,
> my God and the rock of my rescue.'

28 I, too, shall make him My firstborn,
> most high among kings of the earth.

29 Forever I shall keep My kindness for him
> and My pact will be faithful to him.

30 And I shall make his seed for all time
> and his throne as the days of the heavens.

31 If his sons forsake My teaching
> and do not go in my law,

32 if they profane My statutes
> and do not keep My commands,

33 I will requite their crime with the rod,
> and with plagues, their wrongdoing.

34 Yet My steadfast kindness I will not revoke for him,
> and I will not betray My faithfulness.

---

26. *his hand to the sea / . . . his right hand to the rivers.* This is an image of imperial dominion.

31. *If his sons forsake My teaching.* Here begins the emphatic set of conditions upon which the keeping of the covenant by God is contingent.

I will not profane My pact   35
    and My mouth's utterance I will not alter.
One thing I have sworn by My holiness—   36
    that David I will not deceive.
His seed shall be forever,   37
    and his throne like the sun before Me,
like the moon, firm-founded forever—   38
    and the witness in the skies is faithful."   selah
And You, You abandoned and spurned,   39
    You were furious with Your anointed.
You canceled the pact of Your servant,   40
    You profaned his crown on the ground.
You broke through all his walls,   41
    You turned his forts into rubble.
All passers-by plundered him,   42
    he became a disgrace to his neighbors.
You raised the right hand of his foes,   43
    You made all his enemies glad.
You also turned back his sword's flint   44
    and did not make him stand up in the battle.
You put an end to his splendor,   45
    and his throne You hurled to the ground.

---

38. *the witness in the skies is faithful.* The idea, at least according to the formulation of the received text, is that the moon above will be eternal witness to the abiding pact between God and the House of David. An emendation yields "and as long as the skies, faithful."

44. *his sword's flint.* Some scholars emend *tsur harbo* to *mitsar harbo*, yielding "his sword from the foe." But it is perfectly plausible that "flint" is an archaic linguistic survival from the period when knives and swords were actually made of flint and hence became a poetic designation for the blade of the sword.

45. *his splendor.* The anomalous form *mithar* transparently derives from *tohar*, "purity," but in a few texts *tohar* is associated with brilliance, as pure substances shine brightly.

46   You cut short the days of his prime.
               You enveloped him with shame.   selah
47   How long, LORD, will You hide forever,
               will Your wrath burn like fire?
48   Recall how fleeting I am,
               how futile You made all humankind.
49   What man alive will never see death,
               will save his life from the grip of Sheol?   selah
50   Where are Your former kindnesses, Master,
               that you vowed to David in Your faithfulness?
51   Recall, O Master, Your servants' disgrace,
               that I bore in my bosom from all the many peoples,
52   as Your enemies reviled, O LORD,
               as Your enemies reviled Your anointed one's steps.

53   Blessed be the LORD forever, amen and amen.

---

48. *Recall how fleeting I am.* The grounds for the plea for mercy resemble those that Job repeatedly invokes: If human life lasts but a moment, why should the eternal God persist in making man's life so miserable?

how futile You made all humankind. Most translations follow the lead of the King James Version in understanding this as a question: "Wherefore hast thou made all men in vain?" But the structure of the line both semantically and syntactically is parallel (the first verset uses *meh*, "how," the second, *'al-mah*, also "how"): Man's life is ephemeral (first verset); it is without substance, empty, futile (second verset).

49. *What man alive.* The literal structure of the Hebrew is, what man will live and not see death.

51. *from all the many peoples.* Kol-rabim 'amim in the Hebrew is intelligible but ungrammatical, and there is in all likelihood a textual problem here.

53. This verse is not part of the poem but rather a prose formula of conclusion that marks the end of the third book of the five into which Psalms is divided.

90

A prayer of Moses, man of God.   1
    O Master, You have been our abode
            in every generation.
   Before mountains were born,   2
         before You spawned earth and world,
                from forever to forever You are God.

---

1. *A prayer of Moses, man of God.* This psalm is unique in attributing the text to Moses. Some interpreters have seen linguistic connections with the Song of Moses (Deuteronomy 32), but these are tenuous and, if they really exist, are very few. Given the focus of the psalm on the limitations of the human condition, the editor may have been thinking of the reiterated zero-degree epithet for the lawgiver, "the man Moses": Moses is the great founding leader and yet but a man, granted the great life span of 120 years that would become proverbial, yet circumscribed by mortality, never to enter the Promised Land. Of the eight times that the name of Moses is mentioned in Psalms, seven occur in the fourth book of Psalms, which begins here, so this may have been a signature device on the part of the editor.

2. *from forever to forever You are God.* This evocation of God's eternality introduces the topic of the two temporal scales, God's and man's, which is the awesome subject of the psalm.

3   You bring man back to the dust
          and say, "Turn back, humankind."

4   For a thousand years in Your eyes
          are like yesterday gone,
               like a watch in the night.

5   You engulf them with sleep.
          In the morn they are like grass that passes.

6   In the morning it sprouts and passes,
          by evening it withers and dies.

---

3. *You bring man back to the dust*. The word represented as "dust," *daka'*, is associated with a root that indicates lowness, or crushing down, but is reasonably understood here as a poetic substitute for "dust" (ordinarily, *'afar*). God's abasement of man, followed in the next verset by His exhortation to humankind to turn back, or repent, suggests that this psalm is a collective penitential supplication, perhaps recited at a moment when the community has been overtaken by disaster ("bring man back to the dust"). But the nature of the disaster is not specified, and there is no mention either of Israel or the temple. Thus the supplication becomes the vehicle for a Wisdom-style meditation on the transience of human life, cast in the universal terms characteristic of Wisdom literature. There is, in fact, a certain kinship between this poem and passages in both Job and Ecclesiastes.

4. *For a thousand years in Your eyes*. In the eloquent triadic structure of this line, the poet moves from a thousand years to a passing day to a watch in the night (a mere third of the night). Thus, he concretizes a vision of time seen from God's end of the telescope.

5. *You engulf them with sleep*. Both the verb and the syntax in the Hebrew sound odd, and there may be a textual problem here, but the sundry efforts to emend it chiefly exhibit the logic of scholars, not of biblical poets.
    In the morn they are like grass that passes. The verb translated as "passes" could also mean "changes." The poem here enters the sphere of human temporality, which is only from morning to evening. Terms marking units of time—days, years—continue to be invoked in the poem.

For we are consumed in Your wrath,   7
          and in Your fury we are dismayed.
You have set our transgressions before You,   8
          our hidden faults in the light of Your face.
For all our days slip away in Your anger.   9
          We consume our years like a sigh.
The days of our years are but seventy years,   10
          and if in great strength, eighty years.
And their pride is trouble and grief,
          for swiftly cut down, we fly off.
Who can know the strength of Your wrath?   11
          As the fear of You is Your anger.
To count our days rightly, instruct,   12
          that we may get a heart of wisdom.
Come back, O Lord! How long?—   13
          and have pity on Your servants.

---

7. *For we are consumed in Your wrath.* Because the words for both "wrath" and "fury" in the Hebrew suggest hotly burning breath, the language carries forward the image of grass withering and dying.

9. *like a sigh.* The Hebrew *hegeh* also means "murmur."

10. *cut down.* Though the meaning of this word in the Hebrew is clear, the grammar is problematic because the verb is masculine singular and so does not readily attach to the first-person plural subject that follows.
   As the fear of You is Your anger. That is, with good reason are people afraid of You because the manifestations of Your anger are indeed awesome.

12. *To count our days rightly, instruct.* In effect, this is precisely what the poem as a whole—with its powerful images for representing the limitations of human existence over against God's eternal being—has achieved for its audience.

13. *have pity.* The verb used means literally, "change your mind."

14   Sate us in the morn with Your kindness,
             let us sing and rejoice all our days.
15   Give us joy as the days You afflicted us,
             the years we saw evil.
16   Let Your acts be seen by Your servants
             and Your glory by their children.
17   And may the sweetness of the Master our God be upon us
             and the work of our hands firmly found for us,
                    and the work of our hands firmly found!

---

14. *Sate us in the morn with Your kindness.* Such an act would enable a different kind of flourishing from the grass that sprouts in the morn and then withers. God's kindness has the power to move human joy beyond the fleeting
framework of a few hours to "all our days."

15. *as the days . . . / the years.* God's kindness to humanity makes possible a different order of human temporality, in which the days add up to the years in a
round of joyful fulfillment, even within the limited span of seventy or eighty
years of a human life.

17. *and the work of our hands firmly found.* The poet uses a triadic line, the third
verset a virtual repetition of the second verset, as a concluding flourish. The
verb *konen,* "firmly found," is strategically important. It is the word used for
keeping dynasties or buildings unshaken. Against the dismaying ephemerality
of human existence, in which a life sprouts and withers like grass, God can give
fleeting human experience solid substantiality.

91

He who dwells in the Most High's shelter,   1
    in the shadow of Shaddai lies at night—
I say of the LORD, "My refuge and bastion,   2
    my God in whom I trust."
For He will save you from the fowler's snare,   3
    from the disastrous plague.

---

1. *He who dwells in the Most High's shelter.* This psalm is one of a number that
have no superscription (though the Septuagint shows—or adds—"a David
psalm"). It also does not belong to any obvious cultic genre of psalms. The
Israeli scholar Yair Hoffman, noting its eloquent expression of God's unflagging
providential protection, has interestingly characterized the poem as an "amulet
psalm," with the idea that its recitation might help a person attain or perhaps
simply feel God's guarding power.

2. *I say of the* LORD. Although the Septuagint corrects this to "He says of the
LORD," evidently in the interests of consistency, such unmarked transitions
from one speaker to another (it is now the man who shelters in God who
speaks) are not uncommon in biblical literature. In fact, there are three speakers in the poem: the poet (verse 1, verses 3–13), the man who trusts in God
(verse 2), and God (verses 14–16).

4   With His pinion He shelters you,
            and beneath His wings you take refuge,
                a shield and a buckler, His truth.
5   You shall not fear from the terror of night
            nor from the arrow that flies by day,
6   from the plague that stalks in darkness
            nor from the scourge that rages at noon.
7   Though a thousand fall at your side
            and ten thousand at your right hand,
                you it will not reach.
8   You but look with your eyes,
            and the wicked's requital you see.
9   For you—the Lord is your refuge,
            the Most High you have made your abode.

---

4. *His pinion . . . His wings.* It may be misguided to conclude that God is imagined as a large mother bird. The sheltering care of the bird for her fledglings is
a recurrent biblical image for solicitous protection; thus, the metaphor appears
to refer to the function, not to the imagined appearance of the deity. But such
metaphorical usages may have had something to do with the later representation of the Shekhina (the feminine manifestation of the deity) by Jews and the
Holy Spirit by Christians as a dove.

7. *Though a thousand fall at your side.* In all likelihood, the setting evoked is a
raging epidemic in which vast numbers of people all around are fatally stricken.
The image of martial danger, however, introduced by the flying arrow of verse
5 and the shield and buckler of verse 4, is superimposed on the image of danger from the plague, life imagined as a battlefield fraught with dangers.
    you it will not reach. In this triadic line, after the formulaic semantic paral-
lelism of "a thousand" and "ten thousand," the third member of the line is not
semantically parallel but instead marks a strong contrast—you who will remain
untouched over against all those who fall.

8. *the wicked's requital.* This phrase suggests that there is a blending in the
poem of danger from the plague and danger from hostile people.

9. *your refuge.* The received text reads, confusingly, "my refuge."

No harm will befall you,   10
       nor affliction draw near to your tent.
For His messengers He charges for you   11
       to guard you on all your ways.
On their palms they lift you up   12
       lest your foot be bruised by a stone.
On lion and viper you tread,   13
       you trample young lion and serpent.
"For Me he desired and I freed him.   14
       I raised him high, for he has known My name.
He calls Me and I answer him,   15
       I am with him in his straits.
                I deliver him and grant him honor.

---

10. *draw near to your tent.* This archaic reference to nomadic existence occurs elsewhere in Psalms and is in keeping with the somewhat archaic coloration of biblical poetic diction. It seems worth preserving in English.

12. *lest your foot be bruised by a stone.* The literal sense of the verb is "bump against." In the rocky landscape of the Judean hills, in which there were no paved roads until the Romans introduced them, this image of a person lifted up on the palms of divine messengers to protect him from all painful stumbling has particular force. It is also a concrete focusing of "guard you on all your ways," at the end of the previous line.

13. *lion . . . viper . . . young lion . . . serpent.* These noxious creatures of the wild would have been actual dangers to the wayfarer passing over the rocky roads of Judea. "Young lion" (following the King James Version) is a translator's strategy of desperation: There are four different terms in biblical Hebrew for "lion," and it is safe to assume that they designated different kinds or categories of lion, in an era when this animal was much more common in the countryside of Judea. But we have no way of recovering the distinctions, and, in any case, there are no synonyms for "lion" in English.

16   With length of days I shall sate him,
           and show him my rescue."

---

16. *show him.* Some scholars propose emending the Masoretic *we'areihu* to *we'arweihu,* "slake his thirst," to make a neat parallelism with "sate him" in the first verset. It is a question, however, whether the biblical poets were always committed to such neatness in deploying parallel versets, and "show him" makes perfect sense.

92

A psalm, a song for the Sabbath day. 1
  It is good to acclaim the LORD 2
      and to hymn to Your name, Most High,
  to tell in the morning Your kindness, 3
      Your faithfulness in the nights,
  on ten-stringed instrument and on the lute, 4
      on the lyre with chanted sound.
  For You made me rejoice, LORD, through Your acts, 5
      of the work of Your hands I sing in gladness.

---

1. *a song for the Sabbath day.* It is a reasonable inference that this psalm was actually sung as part of the temple rite for the Sabbath. In post-biblical Judaism, it was included in the Sabbath liturgy, and six other psalms were chosen for recitation on each of the six other days of the week.

2. *It is good to acclaim the LORD.* Although the language of acclaim or thanksgiving (*hodot*) and hymning (*zamer*) immediately aligns this text with the psalms of thanksgiving, it also has a strong Wisdom coloration as an attempt to explain why the wicked seem to flourish and what is the true order of justice in the world.

5. This line of poetry takes the form of a neat chiasm (abb́a) as do verse 6 and verse 12. The translation mirrors this formal pattern.

6 How great Your works, O LORD,
      Your designs are very deep.
7 The brutish man does not know,
      nor does the fool understand this:
8 the wicked spring up like grass,
      and all the wrongdoers flourish—
         to be destroyed for all time.
9 And You are on high forever, O LORD!
10 For, look, Your enemies, O LORD,
      for, look, Your enemies perish,
         all the wrongdoers are scattered.
11 And You raise up my horn like the wild ox.
      I am soaked in fresh oil.

---

6. *Your designs are very deep.* This clause lays the ground for the rest of the poem, and for the next two verses in particular. God's designs are deep. Superficial observation might lead to the conclusion that crime pays, but, despite appearances to the contrary, God prepares due punishment for the wicked. It is this unapparent system of justice that the brutish man is incapable of understanding.

8. *to be destroyed for all time.* The likely force of the metaphor is that grass grows high only the more readily to be mowed.

9. *And You are on high forever, O LORD!* This verse lacks any parallelism and does not scan in the Hebrew. It would seem to be an interjection in prose inserted at the midpoint of the poem: Man is ephemeral; God reigns on high forever.

10. *For look, Your enemies, O LORD, / for, look, Your enemies perish.* The use of incremental repetition in these two versets harks back to the earliest stratum of biblical poetry (as, for example, in the Song of Deborah). In fact, a line occurs in one of the Ugaritic poems that is very close in language and structure to this one, though with "Baal" as the deity addressed rather than YHWH.

And my eyes behold my foes' defeat, 12
        those hostile toward me, my ears hear their fall.
The righteous man springs up like the palm tree, 13
        like the Lebanon cedar he towers.
Planted in the house of the LORD, 14
        in the courts of our God they flourish.
They bear fruit still in old age, 15
        fresh and full of sap they are,
to tell that the LORD is upright, 16
        my rock, there is no wrong in Him.

---

12. *my foes' defeat.* As elsewhere, "defeat" is merely implied by the idiom "to see ["in" or "against"] my foes." This line is unusual in adding to the seeing a symmetrical element of hearing in the second verset. Again the noun "fall" has been added to make the meaning clear.

13. *like the palm tree, / like the Lebanon cedar.* These proverbially stately trees with their deep roots are an obvious antithesis to the metaphor of ephemeral grass used to represent the wicked. The contrast is akin to the one in the first psalm between the righteous as a tree planted by waters and the wicked as chaff blown by the wind.

15. *fresh and full of sap.* This entire line carries forward the image of the righteous as a flourishing tree. "Fresh"— *ra'anan*, which has a semantic range from vibrant to luxuriant to fresh—is the very term the speaker used in verse 11 to characterize the oil with which he was pleasurably anointed. (The translation reverses the order of the two Hebrew adjectives for the sake of rhythm.) *Ra'anan* is also a term often linked with trees.

16. *to tell that the LORD is upright.* At the very end, the psalm picks up "to tell" from the beginning, thus marking an envelope structure. The poem begins and concludes by affirming what a good and fitting thing it is to tell God's greatness.

93

1   The LORD reigns, in triumph clothed,
        clothed is the LORD, in strength He is girded.
              Yes, the world stands firm, not to be shaken.
2   Your throne stands firm from of old,
        from forever You are.

---

1. *The LORD reigns.* This brief, powerful psalm begins without superscription. It is clearly one of a group of psalms that celebrate God's kingship. The once popular notion, put forth by Sigmund Mowinckel in the early twentieth century, that it is the liturgy for an annual festival in which YHWH was enthroned, has come more and more to seem like a scholarly exercise in historical fiction because there is no evidence for the existence of such a rite in ancient Israel. God's grandeur as king of all the world would have been a perfectly appropriate theme for a Hebrew poet without a cultic apparatus.

    triumph. The Hebrew *gei'ut* covers a range from splendor, grandeur, and greatness to the image of surging high (as it is used in the Song of the Sea, playing against the sense of the term as "tide," as is evidently the case in this poem as well).

The streams lifted up, O Lord,   3
>   the streams lifted up their voice,
>   the streams lift up their roaring.
More than the sound of many waters,   4
>   the sea's majestic breakers,
>   majestic on high is the Lord.

---

3. *The streams lifted up.* The rising waters of the sea—it is not until the end of
the second verset that the verb receives an object, "their voice" (or "their
sound"), which turns it into an idiom used for human speech—are an antithesis to the firmly founded world and divine throne of the two previous verses.
Although this poem may glance back, as many scholars have proposed, to
Canaanite cosmogonic myths of the conquest of a primordial sea monster, the
mythology is no more than a distant memory here. Indeed, the idea that God is
"forever," before all national entities, is an implicit argument against a primordial battle of the gods. This notion of creation as assuring the safety and firm-
ness of the land against the sea is one that makes special sense for a culture
flourishing along the edge of the Mediterranean (in biblical idiom, "the Great
Sea"). The waves pounding against the shore are a reminder of the precarious
existence of the land dwellers, but God's majestic power, far greater even than
the power of the sea, is a reassuring guarantee of the stability of civilized life.
The forceful use of incremental repetition in this line—"the streams lifted up
. . . / the streams lifted up their voice, / the streams lift up their roaring," may be
deliberately deployed to suggest a wavelike movement in the formal pattern of
the verse.

4. *More than the sound of many waters / . . . majestic on high is the Lord.* The
middle verset in this triadic line ("the sea's majestic breakers") stands in apposition to the first verset. The entire line is a wonderful use of a periodic sentence: At first we are not sure what or who is "more" than the sound of the
majestic breakers, and at the end—YHWH is the last word of the line—we
learn that it is God. The qualifier "on high" is strategic: The breakers of the sea
may rise up terrifically high, inspiring awe or even fear in the observer, but
YHWH is high above them.

5   Your statutes are very faithful.
            Holiness suits Your house.
                The Lord is for all time.

---

5. *Your statutes.* The mention of law at the end of the poem is something of a surprise, but perhaps not for the Israelite believer. God's supreme power over nature is followed by His giving to Israel a set of laws that can endow their lives with stable order and moral coherence. He also grants them a temple ("Your house"), standing firm like God's celestial throne, where Israel can repeatedly affirm a bond with Him.

for all time. The Hebrew *le'orekh yamim* means literally "for length of days." (It is the same idiom as the one used at the end of Psalm 23.) Though the temporal frame of reference of the phrase is more human than divine, it may be employed here as a synonymous variation of "forever," which has already been used twice in the poem (verse 3) with two different locutions.

94

God of vengeance, O Lord,   1
     God of vengeance, shine forth!
Rise up, O judge of the earth,   2
     bring down on the proud requital.
How long the wicked, O Lord,   3
     how long will the wicked exult?
They utter arrogance, speak it,   4
     all the wrongdoers bandy boasts.

---

1. *God of vengeance.* This boldly aggressive characterization of God, *'el neqamot,* which occurs only here, is fudged by the modern translations that render it in mitigating language as "God of retribution." As in many psalms of supplication, to which this poem is roughly allied, the speaker is filled with rage at the dominance of injustice in the world and exhorts God to manifest a spectacular appearance ("shine forth") in order to exact grim vengeance against the perpetrators of evil.

3. *how long will the wicked exult?* In the typical psalm of supplication, this is the kind of question that a beleaguered speaker asks personally, on his own behalf. Here, however, though the speaker does stress the first-person singular toward the end of the poem (verses 16–22), most of the psalm expresses a generalized concern about the prevalence of injustice.

5   Your people, O Lord, they crush,
            and Your estate they abuse.
6   Widow and sojourner they kill,
            and orphans they murder.
7   And they say, "Yah will not see,
            and the God of Jacob will not heed."
8   Take heed, you brutes in the people,
            and you fools, when will you be wise?
9   Who plants the ear, will He not hear?
            Who fashions the eye, will He not look?
10 The chastiser of nations, will He not punish,
            Who teaches humankind knowledge?
11 The Lord knows human designs,
            that they are mere breath.
12 Happy the man whom Yah chastises,
            and whom from His teaching He instructs,
13 to make him quiet in evil days
            until a pit is dug for the wicked.

---

5. *Your people, O Lord, they crush.* Although some interpreters have taken this as a reference to a national disaster, such as conquest by an enemy, the subsequent reference to the murder of the disadvantaged—proverbially, in biblical usage, the sojourner, the widow, and the orphan—suggests that what the speaker has in view is a practice of criminal, social, and economic oppression within the nation. This reading is reinforced by the use of the phrase "You brutes in [or "among"] the people."

12. *Happy the man whom Yah chastises, / and whom from His teaching He instructs.* This is the turning point in the poem, the moment when a rationale is offered for the present suffering of the innocent. The man who is engulfed in suffering—that is, who is "chastised" by God—can take comfort in the lesson of God's teaching, which is that punishment (the "pit" that is dug) awaits the evildoer. This certain knowledge has the power to give inner calm to the just man in the midst of his afflictions. This same idea is rephrased in verse 19: "With my many cares within me, / Your consolations delighted me."

For the LORD will not abandon His people,   14
      and His estate He will not forsake.
For justice will join with judgment,   15
      and all the upright will follow it.
Who will rise for me against evildoers,   16
      who will take a stand for me against the wrongdoers?
Were not the LORD a help to me,   17
      I would have almost dwelled in the silent realm.
When I thought my foot had stumbled,   18
      Your kindness, LORD, sustained me.
With my many cares within me,   19
      Your consolations delighted me.
Will the throne of disaster consort with You,   20
      that fashions trouble against the law?

---

14. *not abandon His people, / . . . His estate . . . not forsake.* This is the one moment in the poem when individual oppression appears to be displaced by (or merge with) the oppression of the nation, especially because "estate," *naḥalah*, is a common poetic epithet for the people or the land.

15. *For justice will join with judgment.* The Hebrew at this point sounds a little crabbed. A very literal rendering: "For unto justice will judgment come back."

16. *Who will rise for me against evildoers.* Now we hear a voice in the first-person singular. The immediate answer to these rhetorical questions is that no one will come to the aid of the embattled speaker except God.

17. *in the silent realm.* The Hebrew *dumah* simply means "silence," implying death. The Vulgate actually renders this as *in inferno*.

20. *that fashions trouble against the law?* Although the meaning of each word and of the clause as a whole is quite transparent, the verset sounds a little strange because one would expect the verb "fashions" (*yotser*, as in the second Creation story) to be attached to a conscious agent, not to a throne. Perhaps the poet is simply thinking of "throne" metonymically as an epithet for the king of evil who sits on it.

21   They band together against the just man's life,
                and innocent blood condemn.
22   But the LORD became my fortress,
                and my God, my sheltering rock.
23   He will turn back against them their wickedness,
                through their evil He will destroy them,
                        the LORD our God will destroy them.

---

21. *and innocent blood condemn.* The paradigmatic crime of the wicked is the perversion of the judicial system, which again leads to the inference that what the speaker complains of is injustice within his own society, not a military assault on it by external powers.

23. *He will turn back against them their wickedness.* The idea is both that the wicked will finally be tripped up by their own vicious scheming and that they will be paid back measure for measure.

   the LORD our God will destroy them. As often happens in biblical poetry, a triadic line—here, with incremental repetition of the second verset—is used to mark closure at the end of the poem.

95

Come, let us sing gladly to the LORD,   1
      let us shout out to the Rock of our rescue.
Let us greet Him in acclaim,   2
      in songs let us shout out to Him.

---

1. *Come, let us sing*. Without superscription, like the rest of the sequence of psalms from Psalm 93 to Psalm 99 (with the marginal exception of Psalm 98), the first-person plural exhortation to sing suggests that this is a public celebration of God.

2. *acclaim*. The Hebrew *todah*, as elsewhere in Psalms, straddles "acclaim" and "thanksgiving." Some interpreters think it refers here to the thanksgiving sacrifice because the idiom used for "greet," *qadem 'et peney*, is sometimes linked with sacrifice. However, the strong poetic parallelism with "songs," woven in a tight chiastic pattern (greet [a]—in acclaim [b]—in songs [b̕]—shout out [á]), argues against this understanding.

3   For a great god is the LORD
            and great king over all the gods.
4   In Whose hand are the depths of the earth,
            and the peaks of the mountains are His.
5   His is the sea and He made it,
            and the dry land His hands did fashion.
6   Come, let us bow and kneel,
                bend the knee before the LORD our maker.

---

3. *For a great god is the* LORD, / *and great king over all the gods.* The language
here harks back to a period when YHWH was thought of not as the one exclusive deity but as the most powerful of the gods, though it is unclear whether
the formulation in this psalm reflects active belief or merely a linguistic survival. In any case, the next two verses proceed to proclaim that YHWH alone
is the master of depths and heights, the maker of sea and earth, an idea that
would seem to preclude the notion of sundry gods having jurisdiction over the
various realms of nature. Scholars attached to the hypothesis of an annual ritual of the coronation of YHWH of course have seized on this psalm as a liturgical text for the rite, but its existence remains conjectural. Later Jewish
tradition made this the first in a sequence of psalms chanted as a prelude to
the Friday-evening prayer for welcoming the Sabbath, evidently because the
Sabbath was seen as a celebration of creation.

4. *the depths of the earth.* The Hebrew for "depths" is not the ordinary *tehomot*
but the more unusual *meḥqerey,* which by etymology means "the utmost
reaches that can be searched out."

For He is our God   7
        and we are the people He tends
        and the flock of His hand.
If you would only heed His voice!
    "Do not harden your heart as at Meribah,   8
        as on the day at Massah in the wilderness,
when your forefathers tested Me,   9
    tried Me, though they had seen My acts.
Forty years I loathed a generation,   10
    and I said, 'They are a people of wayward heart.
        And they did not know My ways.'
Against them I swore in My wrath,   11
    'They shall not come to My resting-place.'"

---

7. *the flock of His hand.* This unusual phrase may be employed here to pick up
the references to God's hand in verses 4 and 5.

If you would only heed His voice! Although this sentence appears at the end
of the verse according to the conventional verse breaks, it is actually the initial
verset of a new triadic line that continues in verse 8. It marks an abrupt pivot
in the poem, as the psalm of acclaim turns into a psalm of prophetic rebuke.

8. *Meribah . . . Massah.* These place names, meaning Dispute and Testing, appear
in Exodus 17 in the story of the Israelites' resentful plea for water in the wilderness. One of the earliest of the episodes of "murmuring," it is invoked here typologically as an image of Israel's wayward, rebellious behavior through all the
generations. Perhaps the implicit connection with the acclaiming of God's kingship in the first part of the poem is that Israel can authentically recognize God
as king only by obedience to His commands.

10. *Forty years I loathed a generation.* The obvious reference is to God's decree,
after the incident of the ten faint-hearted spies (Numbers 14), that the people
would have to wander in the wilderness forty years, until the whole refractory
generation had died out.

11. *They shall not come to My resting-place.* The "resting-place" is the Promised
Land. The psalm thus ends on a rather stern note of admonition, one that its
listeners are expected to take to heart.

96

1   Sing to the Lord a new song!
          Sing to the Lord, all the earth.
2   Sing to the Lord, bless His name,
          Bring tidings every day of His rescue.
3   Recount among the nations His glory,
          among all the peoples His wonders.
4   For great is the Lord and most praised,
          awesome is He over all the gods.

---

1. *Sing to the Lord a new song!* In this celebration of God's majesty, it is of course in the interests of the psalm poet to proclaim that this is a fresh and original composition. In point of fact, it is a weaving together of phrases and whole lines that appear elsewhere. Yair Hoffman actually characterizes it as a "mosaic" of lines drawn from familiar psalms. The very familiarity, of course, might have enhanced its accessibility to the Israelite worshipper.

3. *the nations . . . / . . . all the peoples.* The perspective of this poem is decidedly global rather than national. All the inhabitants of earth are enjoined to celebrate God's kingship.

For all gods of the peoples are ungods,
        but the LORD has made the heavens.   5
Greatness and grandeur before Him,
        strength and splendor in His sanctuary.   6
Grant to the LORD, O families of peoples,
        grant to the LORD glory and strength.   7
Grant to the LORD His name's glory,
        bear tribute and come to His courts.   8
Bow to the LORD in sacred grandeur;
        quake before Him, all the earth.   9
Say among the nations: The LORD reigns.
        Yes, the world stands firm, will not shake.   10
        He metes out justice to peoples righteously.

---

5. *For all gods of the peoples are ungods.* The previous line, "awesome is He over all the gods," which also has a close parallel in Psalm 95:3, looks as though it is a line inherited from an early stratum of Hebrew poetry. In this case, the psalmist immediately attaches a kind of monotheistic rejoinder to it by asserting that all the other gods have no real existence: "ungods," *'elilim*, is a polemic coinage that appears frequently elsewhere, punningly formed on *'al*, ("no," "not") and *'el* ("god"), to which a diminutive or pejorative suffix is appended. The standard meaning of the term in all subsequent Hebrew is "idols."

6. *Greatness and grandeur.* The alliteration approximates the effect of the Hebrew *hod wehadar.*

8. *bear tribute.* The Hebrew *minḥah* also has the cultic sense of "offering," and a pun is surely intended here, but the emphasis on celebrating God as king of all the earth invites seeing "tribute" as the leading edge of the pun.

10. *righteously.* The Hebrew *meysharim*, which has a Mesopotamian cognate, is an abstract noun derived from *yashar*, "straight" or "upright," and has the sense of fairly, even generously, administered justice.

1   Let the heavens rejoice and the earth exult,
                 let the sea and its fullness thunder.
2   Let the field be glad and all that is in it,
                 then shall all the trees of the forest joyfully sing
13   before the LORD, for He comes,
                 He comes to judge the earth.
4   He judges the world in justice
                 and peoples in His faithfulness.

---

11. *Let the heavens rejoice.* Given that the poet has already proclaimed God's all-embracing reign over the sundry realms of creation, it is an apt conclusion that, at the end, sky and sea and the fields of earth are all urged to rejoice in God's kingship.

97

The LORD reigns—let earth exult,   1
      let the many islands rejoice.
Cloud and dense fog around Him,   2
      justice and judgment the base of His throne.
Fire goes before Him   3
      and all round burns His foes.
His lightnings lit up the world;   4
      the earth saw and quaked.
Mountains melted like wax before the LORD,   5
      before the Master of all the earth.

---

1. *The LORD reigns.* These initial words signal another psalm in this series celebrating God's kingship. All these poems are variations on a theme, using an abundance of set formulas. One difference between this psalm and the preceding ones is that there is no reference to God's conquest of the primordial sea. Instead, deploying a different imagery that goes back to Canaanite mythology, the poet represents God surrounded by fire and hurling lightning bolts down on the world.

the many islands. The Hebrew *'iyim* always refers to remote regions.

2. *Cloud and dense fog.* These two overlapping elements, *'anan* and *'arafel*, traditionally surround God. Compare the occurrence of the same paired terms in Deuteronomy 4:11.

6   The heavens told His justice,
      and all peoples saw His glory.
7   All idol-worshippers are shamed,
      who boast of the ungods.
          All gods bow down to Him.
8   Zion heard and rejoiced,
      and Judea's villages exulted
          because of Your judgments, Lord.
9   For You, Lord, are most high over all the earth;
      You are greatly exalted over all the gods.
10 You who love the Lord, hate evil!
      He guards the lives of His faithful.
          From the hand of the wicked He saves them.

---

6. *The heavens told His justice.* This particular celebration of God's kingship puts special emphasis not merely on God's overwhelming power but on His bringing a reign of justice to humankind.

7. *All gods bow down to Him.* For the somewhat ambiguous background of formulations of this sort in this sequence of psalms, see the comments on 95:3 and 96:5. At least on the surface, this clause appears to be a flat contradiction of the two preceding versets, which speak of "idol-worshippers" and "ungods." (For an explanation of the Hebrew background to this latter term, see the note on 96:5). One must allow the possibility that the psalmist thought idol worship absurd, not because the idols were mere sticks and stones, as Deutero-Isaiah imagined them, but rather because they were images of deities who had no real power, who were totally subservient to the one supreme God, and therefore were not worthy of worship. In that case, *'elilim,* "ungods," would mean something like "paltry pseudo-gods."

8. *Judea's villages.* The Hebrew *banot* has the literal sense of "daughters." It could actually refer to exulting young women, but, given the poetic parallelism with "Zion"—that is, Jerusalem—it is more likely that the term here is used in its other sense of the outlying villages outside a city.

Light is sown for the just,   11
      and for the upright of heart there is joy.
Rejoice, O you just, in the LORD,   12
      and acclaim His holy name.

---

11. *Light is sown for the just, / and for the upright of heart there is joy.* In a resonant envelope structure, the poem that began in rejoicing ends in rejoicing.
The delicate agricultural image of light sown—presumably, to bear refulgent
fruit—is an elegant counterpoint to the fierce fire that burns up God's enemies
and to the lightning that makes the earth quake.

98

1 A psalm.
    Sing to the Lord a new song,
        For wonders He has done.
    His right hand gave Him victory,
        and His holy arm.
2   The Lord made known His victory,
        before the nations' eyes He revealed His bounty.

---

1. *A psalm.* This is a zero-degree superscription. The Septuagint adds "David."
   Sing to the Lord a new song. The comment on this same clause at the beginning of Psalm 96 is also relevant to this poem.
   gave Him victory. Although the verbal root *y-sh-ʿ* generally means "rescue," in military contexts the meaning shades into "victory," and the invocation of God's right hand clearly suggests the role of divine warrior. The poem does not specify the enemy, but, given its cosmic sweep and the background of similar psalms, the most likely candidate would be the primordial forces of chaos.

2. *bounty.* Though in a good many contexts *tsedaqah* means "righteousness," it also often has the sense in poetry of "bounty" or "beneficent act," and the interlinear parallelism with verse 3 indicates that meaning here.

He recalled His kindness and His faithfulness 3
    to the house of Israel.
All the ends of the earth have seen
    the victory of our God.
Shout out to the LORD, all the earth. 4
    Burst forth in glad song and hymn.
Hymn to the LORD on the lyre, 5
    on the lyre with the sound of hymning.
With trumpets and the sound of ram's horn, 6
    sound loud before the king, the LORD.
Let the sea and its fullness thunder, 7
    the world and those dwelling in it.
Let the rivers clap hands, 8
    let the mountains together sing gladly
before the LORD, for He comes 9
    to judge the earth.
He judges the world in justice 10
    and peoples righteously.

---

3. *All the ends of the earth have seen.* As in the other psalms celebrating God's kingship, the perspective is global, for His reign extends over all the earth. But here, in contradistinction to Psalm 97, the poet also invokes God's relationship with his covenanted people ("His kindness and His faithfulness / to the house of Israel").

7. *Let the sea and its fullness thunder.* There is a concordance between the human orchestra—in all likelihood, an actual orchestra accompanying the singing of this psalm—with its lutes and rams' horns, and the orchestra of nature, both groups providing a grand fanfare for God the king. The thundering of the sea is a percussion section, joined by the clapping hands of the rivers, then the chorus of the mountains. This simple, compact poem, drawing extensively on the formulas of the kingship psalms, is resonantly expressive: the Israelites chanting the poem's words of exaltation, to the accompaniment of musical instruments, are invited to imagine their musical rite as part of a cosmic performance.

99

1　The Lord reigns—peoples tremble,
　　　　　enthroned upon cherubim—the earth shakes.
2　The Lord is great in Zion
　　　　　and exalted over all the peoples.
3　They acclaim Your name:
　　　　　"Great and fearful,
　　　　　　　　He is holy.

---

1. *The Lord reigns—peoples tremble.* The awesome power of God as king of all
the earth makes both the inhabitants of the earth and the earth itself tremble
in fear. But from verse 6 to the end of the psalm, the global perspective
switches to a national one, introducing national historical memory and the cult
on Mount Zion.

　　cherubim. Readers should be reminded that these are not the dimpled dar-
lings of Christian iconography but fierce mythological beasts—with the body
of a lion, large wings, and a human face—that were imagined as God's celestial steeds and also as the throne on which God sat (cherubim were carved on
the top of the Ark of the Covenant).

3. *Great and fearful.* The translation infers that these are the words with which
the peoples acclaim God's name. That would provide a ready motivation for the
switch from second to third person in the references to God. Such switches,
however, often occur in biblical usage, so the assumption that these are the
words pronounced by the peoples is not certain.

And with a king's strength He loves justice."   4
    You firmly founded righteousness,
        judgment and justice in Jacob You made.
Exalt the LORD our God   5
    and bow down to His footstool.
        He is holy.
Moses and Aaron among His priests   6
    and Samuel among those who call on His name
        called to the LORD and He answered them.
In a pillar of cloud did He speak to them.   7
    They kept His precepts and the statute He gave them.
LORD our God, it was You Who answered them,   8
    a forbearing God You were to them,
        yet an avenger of their misdeeds.
Exalt the LORD our God   9
    and bow to His holy mountain,
        for the LORD our God is holy.

---

4. *And with a king's strength.* There appears to be a small glitch in the Hebrew text at this point. The Hebrew *'oz melekh* merely says "a king's strength." And "with" in the translation—perhaps there was a deleted particle b^e in the original text—is added to make sense of the whole clause.

5. *footstool.* A king sitting on a high throne could well have used a footstool on which to rest his feet; in fact, kings are depicted doing this in Egyptian paintings.

6. *Moses and Aaron . . . and Samuel.* This little catalog gives us the prototypes of prophet and priest (Samuel was both, and Moses was from a priestly clan). The historical memory invoked provides a rationale and reassurance for the act of cultic celebration carried out through the psalm. Just as Moses and Aaron in the wilderness, and Samuel after them, were answered when they called out to God, the throng of celebrants—led by the priests of their own day, and enjoined here to exalt God on Mount Zion—will also be answered.

100

1 A thanksgiving psalm.
> Shout out to the Lord, all the earth,
2   worship the Lord in rejoicing,
                      come before Him in glad song.
3 Know that the Lord is God.
           He has made us, and we are His,
              His people and the flock He tends.

---

1. *A thanksgiving psalm.* There is a strong cultic emphasis in this psalm, and "thanksgiving," *todah*, probably refers both to the act of giving thanks to or acclaiming God in song and to a thanksgiving offering. The two would have been imagined as part of the same gesture of gratefulness to God.

2. *come before Him.* The Hebrew preposition also has the sense of "His presence." The spatial reference is to the temple, where God's presence is conceived to dwell, an idea that will be developed in verse 4.

3. *and we are His.* The translation follows the marginal correcting note of the *qeri*, which the traditional editors use to indicate variant readings. The received consonantal text reads "and not we," which is logically possible but sounds unnatural in the Hebrew. The difference in the Hebrew is between *lo* and *l'o* (the latter having an *aleph*).

Come into His gates in thanksgiving,   4
       His courts in praise.
Acclaim Him,
        Bless His name.
For the LORD is good,   5
         forever His kindness,
            and for all generations His faithfulness.

---

4. *Come into His gates . . . / His courts.* The gates are the threshold, the point where the pilgrim crosses from the zone of the profane into the sacred precincts of the temple. It is understandable that they appear in various psalms as a beckoning image, the place where the lover enters the realm of his desires. The two versets of this line also neatly illustrate the frequent phenomenon of narrative development from the first verset to the second. First, the pilgrims are enjoined to enter the gates; then they are standing within, in the courts of the temple.

101

1   A David psalm.
      Kindness and justice I would sing.
            To You, O Lord, I would hymn.
2   I would study the way of the blameless:
            when will it come to me?
      I shall go about in my heart's innocence
            within my house.

---

2. *I would study the way of the blameless.* The verb *haskil* means both to observe or gaze upon and to get wisdom. This is preeminently a Wisdom psalm, proclaiming in terms reminiscent of the Book of Proverbs the speaker's firm resolution to keep himself from all who do evil and to follow the ways of the just. Many scholars since Hermann Gunkel have claimed that it is a royal psalm, but any language that might be attached to a king is quite oblique—mainly, in the suggestion that the speaker has the power to destroy the wicked and that just men will serve him. It is possible that these are references to the situation of a king, but the inference is not entirely compelling.

   when will it come to me? The antecedent would be "the way of the blameless." But it is also possible to construe this clause as "When will You come to me?"

I shall not set before my eyes
        any base thing.
I hate committing transgressions.
        It will not cling to me.
May a twisted heart turn far from me.
        May I not know evil.
Who defames in secret his fellow,
        him shall I destroy.
The haughty of eyes and the proud of heart,
        him shall I not suffer.
My eyes are on the land's faithful,
        that they dwell with me.
Who walks in the way of the blameless,
        it is he who will serve me.

3
4
5
6

---

3. *I shall not set before my eyes / any base thing.* It is worth noting that there is no semantic parallelism between the two halves of this line, and the same is true of several other lines in the poem. Perhaps this abandonment of parallelism is driven by the plainly expository nature of this Wisdom psalm. In any case, as often happens in biblical poetry, the poet compensates for the lack of parallelism between versets by introducing interlinear parallelism (compare verses 6, 7, and 8).

    transgressions. The Hebrew *setim* is obscure but might possibly derive from the verbal stem *s-t-h*, which means "to go astray."

5. *the proud of heart.* The literal sense is "the broad of heart."

6. *My eyes are on the land's faithful.* The use of "eyes" here picks up "haughty of eyes" from the previous line and turns around the meaning. My own eyes, the speaker says, are directed toward the land's faithful. In the same fashion, he speaks of studying "the ways of the blameless."

    it is he who will serve me. This formulation does presuppose that the speaker is someone who enjoys a position of eminence and resolves to staff his house with decent people. It is possible, though far from certain, that it is the royal house that he speaks of.

7   Within my house there shall not dwell
                one who practices deceit.
     A speaker of lies shall not stand firm
                before my eyes.
8   Each morning I shall destroy
                all the wicked of the land,
     to cut off from the town of the LORD
                all the wrongdoers.

102

A prayer for the lowly when he grows faint 1
and pours out his plea before the LORD.
  LORD, O hear my prayer, 2
              and let my outcry come before You.
  Hide not Your face from me 3
            on the day when I am in straits.
  Incline Your ear to me.
            On the day I call, quickly answer me.
  For my days are consumed in smoke, 4
           and my bones are scorched like a hearth.
  My heart is stricken and withers like grass, 5
          so I forget to eat my bread.

---

1. *A prayer for the lowly.* This is unusual as a superscription because it scans nicely as a line of poetry. Consequently, one could infer that it was composed by the poet as the first line of the poem rather than added by an editor.

4. *For my days are consumed in smoke, / and my bones are scorched like a hearth.* This haunting image focuses two ideas, ephemerality and suffering. The supplicant's days burn away to mere smoke, like any rapidly combustible substance set on fire, and the result of the blaze of torment within him is bones charred like a hearth after the fire has burned out. This poem is distinctive among the psalms of supplication in its powerful emphasis on the transience and insubstantiality of human life, an emphasis at certain points reminiscent of Job.

6   From my loud sighing,
                  my bones cleave to my flesh.
7   I resemble the wilderness jackdaw,
                  I become like the owl of the ruins.
8   I lie awake and become
                  like a lonely bird on a roof.
9   All day long my enemies revile me,
                  my taunters invoke me in curse.
10   For ashes I have eaten as bread,
                  and my drink I have mingled with tears—
11   because of Your wrath and Your fury,
                  for You raised me up and flung me down.
12   My days inclined like a shadow,
                  and I—like grass I withered.
13   And You Lord, forever enthroned,
                  and Your name—for all generations.

---

6. *my loud sighing.* The literal sense of the Hebrew is "the voice of my sighing."
   my bones cleave to my flesh. The image is one of emaciation, the person reduced to skin and bones.

7. *the wilderness jackdaw.* As with many biblical terms for fauna, the exact identity of this sad nocturnal bird is uncertain.

8. *like a lonely bird on a roof.* There is something uncanny about the specificity of this location, immediately after the mention of the two wilderness birds. Underneath, on his bed, the insomniac tosses and turns, feeling somehow similar to the lonely bird he imagines on the roof above.

12. *My days inclined like a shadow, / and I—like grass.* The similes again are selected with beautiful aptness. The life span races toward its inevitable end like lengthening shadows toward evening (one should remember that sundials were used in ancient Israel). Then the speaker himself, feeling his waning strength, withers like grass, in an appropriately organic image.

You, may You rise, have mercy on Zion,   14
> for it is the hour to pity her, for the fixed time has
> come.

For Your servants cherish her stones   15
> and on her dust they take pity.

And the nations will fear the name of the LORD,   16
> and all kings of the earth, Your glory.

For the LORD has rebuilt Zion,   17
> He is seen in His glory.

He has turned to the prayer of the desolate   18
> and has not despised their prayer.

Let this be inscribed for a generation to come,   19
> that a people yet unborn may praise Yah.

---

14. *have mercy on Zion.* The sudden introduction of the theme of Zion destroyed by its enemies is surprising because until this point the speaker's complaint has concentrated entirely on his own devastated condition as an afflicted mortal. It is possible, as some interpreters have proposed, that this prayer for the restoration of Zion was grafted onto an earlier psalm of individual supplication—perhaps because the desperate voice of the supplicant was felt to be appropriate for the sense of national desperation after the destruction of Jerusalem and the loss of national sovereignty. It is well to keep in mind that diachronic collage was an accepted technique of composition in biblical literature.

15. *take pity.* The pity of the Judeans for the ruined stones of Zion is meant to be a signpost for the pity God should show.

16. *And the nations will fear the name of the LORD.* This notion that in the return to Zion all nations will recognize the uncontested sovereignty of the God of Israel has numerous analogues in the prophecies of Deutero-Isaiah.

18. *desolate.* The rare Hebrew term ʿarʿar might be related to ʿariri, "desolate," or might designate a humble desert bush, used here metaphorically to indicate desolation.

19. *yet unborn.* The literal meaning of the Hebrew is "being created."

20   For the LORD has gazed down from His holy heights,
                from heaven to earth He has looked
21   to hear the groans of the captive,
                to set loose those doomed to die,
22   that the name of the LORD be recounted in Zion
                and His praise in Jerusalem
23   when peoples gather together
                and kingdoms, to serve the LORD.
24   He humbled my strength on the highway,
                he cut short my days.
25   I say, "O my God.
                Do not take me away in the midst of my days!
                    Your years are for all generations.
26   Of old You founded the earth,
                and the heavens—Your handiwork.

---

20. *For the* LORD *has gazed down.* These words launch a long complex sentence, unusual in biblical poetry, that runs all the way to the end of verse 23. The syntax follows the long vertical line of the divine gaze from heaven to earth, then takes in the panorama of God's suffering servants and moves on to the prospect and the purpose of His act of liberation.

24. *He humbled my strength.* The antecedent of the masculine pronoun (in the Hebrew indicated merely by the conjugated form of the verb) is the enemy, not God.

25. *Do not take me away in the midst of my days!* With these words, the psalm appears to revert to the prayer of an individual supplicant who fears he is on the brink of death and feels all too keenly the brevity of his life.

They will perish and You will yet stand.   27
    They will all wear away like a garment.
Like clothing You change them, and they pass away.
    But You—Your years never end.   28
The sons of Your servants dwell safe,   29
    their seed in Your presence, unshaken."

---

27. *You will yet stand.* The "yet" is added to clarify the meaning. God's eternal existence, which makes even the heavens seem ephemeral, provides the stark contrast to the fleeting moment of life vouchsafed the supplicant.

Like clothing You change them, and they pass away. The clothing image is worked two ways. First, it is a garment worn thin or to shreds through long use, then a garment removed to be replaced by another, as God is free to do with the seemingly eternal heaven and earth. At the same time, the verb *ḥ-l-f,* "to change," is used in two different senses—first, to change a garment, then to pass away, to vanish.

29. *The sons of Your servants . . . / their seed.* The poem aptly concludes with the mention of offspring. An individual life lasts only a moment, but a kind of perpetuity may be granted to humanity through its continuing progeny. Thus, the last word of the psalm, the verb *yikon* ("unshaken"), is a word attached in general biblical usage to dynasties, to grand public buildings, and to heaven and earth.

103

1   For David.
    Bless, O my being, the LORD,
                and everything in me, His holy name.
2   Bless, O my being, the LORD,
                and do not forget all His generous acts.
3   Who forgives all your wrongs,
                heals all your illnesses,
4   redeems your life from the Pit,
                crowns you with kindness, compassion,
5   sates you with good while you live—
                you renew your youth like the eagle.

---

1. *Bless, O my being, the* LORD. The speaker's exhortation to his inner self or essential being (*nefesh*) to bless the LORD is an unusual rhetorical move in Psalms, repeated in the next psalm as well. (The Hebrew for "bless" also has something of the force of "praise," but the core meaning of blessing is worth retaining to distinguish it from three other common verbs that emphatically mean "praise.") This exhortation imparts a sense of exaltation to this psalm of thanksgiving, the occasion for which may be the recovery from a grave illness, as verses 3 and 4 suggest.

5. *sates you with good while you live.* The received text here looks dubious. Literally, it seems to say "sates with good your ornament." This translation adopts the text evidently used by the Septuagint, which instead of 'edyekh, "your ornament," reads 'odekhi, "while you live."
    like the eagle. This image alludes to the eagle's shedding its feathers and growing new ones.

The LORD performs righteous acts   6
  and justice for all the oppressed.
He makes known His ways to Moses,   7
  to the Israelites, His feats.
Compassionate and gracious, the LORD,   8
  slow to anger and abounding in kindness.
He will not dispute forever   9
  nor nurse His anger for all time.
Not according to our offenses has He done to us   10
  nor according to our crimes requited us.
For as the heavens loom high over earth,   11
  His kindness is great over those who fear Him.
As the east is far from the west,   12
  He has distanced from us our transgressions.
As a father has compassion for his children,   13
  the LORD has compassion for those who fear Him.

---

8. *Compassionate and gracious, the* LORD, / *slow to anger and abounding in kindness.* This entire line is a direct quotation of the revelation of the divine attributes to Moses in Exodus 34:6. It is introduced in the previous line by "He makes known His ways to Moses." What is left out from the passage in Exodus is God's "reckoning the crimes of fathers with sons and sons of sons." Here, on the contrary, the exclusive emphasis is on divine compassion and forgiveness.

10. *Not according to our offenses has He done to us.* The theology of forgiveness that pervades this psalm is based on the idea that as long as Israel is God-fearing, committed to upholding its pact with God, whatever trespasses, however egregious, it may have committed will not be held against it by God.

11. *For as the heavens loom high over earth.* This vertical simile of vast distance is neatly complemented in the next verse by a horizontal simile of distance, from east to west. Appropriately, the vertical image is for the overtowering kindness of God on high to humankind below, whereas the horizontal image, pertaining to the terrestrial realm, is for the distance between the human transgressors and their own misdeeds.

14   For He knows our devisings,
              recalls that we are dust.
15   Man's days are like grass,
              like the bloom of the field, thus he blooms—
16   when the wind passes by him, he is gone,
              and his place will no longer know him.
17   But the Lord's kindness is forever and ever
              over those who fear Him
                      and His bounty to the sons of sons,
18   for the keepers of His pact
              and those who recall His precepts to do them.
19   The Lord set His throne firm in the heavens
              and His kingdom rules over all.
20   Bless the Lord, O His messengers,
              valiant in power, performing His word,
                      to heed the sound of His word.

---

14. *For He knows our devisings.* The pointed noun, *yester*, is the same one used
in Genesis 8:21—"For the devisings of the human heart are evil from youth."

19. *The Lord set His throne firm in the heavens.* The throne is implicitly the
throne of justice, the quality by which God rules the world. At the same time,
the switch of focus to the celestial realm sets the stage for the grand conclusion of the psalm, in which the heavenly powers are exhorted, just as the
speaker exhorted himself at the beginning of the poem, to praise God.

20. *His messengers.* This term, traditionally rendered as "angels," designates the
celestial beings who form God's royal entourage and carry out his commands.
As the next verset makes clear, these figures are imagined as divine warriors, an
idea that Milton would pick up in *Paradise Lost*.

Bless the LORD, all His armies,   21
     His servants performing His pleasure.
Bless the LORD, O all His works,   22
     in all places of His dominion.
         Bless, O my being, the LORD!

---

21. *all His armies.* This term carries forward the "valiant in power" of the previous line and alludes to God's identity as "LORD of armies," YHWH *tsev'aot*.

performing His pleasure. In this instance, the King James Version, which also represents the Hebrew *ratson* as "pleasure," is quite accurate, whereas the sundry modern translations that render it as "will" confuse the sense of the term in rabbinic and later Hebrew with its biblical meaning. The idea is that God, as a great monarch, has armies of messengers or courtiers to perform every act that will please Him.

22. *all His works / in all places of His dominion / . . . O my being.* In a grand concluding flourish, all creation is pulled together in the exhortation to praise God. "All His works" includes all sentient beings, from the celestial armies to humankind. God's dominion extends to all imagined places. And in this vast cosmic setting, the speaker repeats the words of his initial injunction to his own being to bless God, now making himself part of the great chorus of all creation.

104

1   Bless, O my being, the LORD!
                LORD, my God, You are very great.
                Grandeur and glory You don.
2   Wrapped in light like a cloak,
                stretching out heavens like a tent-cloth.

---

1. *Bless, O my being, the* LORD! This psalm shares the formula of self-exhortation used at the beginning of Psalm 103, but that formula seems even more appropriate for this poem, which is not a meditation on God's providential justice but rather an ecstatic celebration of God's dominion over the vast panorama of creation.

Grandeur and glory You don. The first two nouns in the translation emulate the strong alliteration of the Hebrew *hod wehadar*. These terms refer to the trappings of majesty, but it will immediately become clear in the next line that God's royal robes and chariot are not the stuff of earthly majesty but the elements of the natural world.

2. *Wrapped in light.* The Hebrew actually uses an active participle ("wrapping"), and this inaugurates an unusual formal pattern in which God is represented in a whole chain of present participles without pronouns. The poet imagines the presence of divinity in the world as a dynamic series of actions—wrapping, stretching out, setting, making, walking, and so forth. This translation seeks to reproduce some of that participial activity, though the necessities of readable English have led to the introduction of at least a few pronouns and actual verbs (for example, in verse 3C, "He goes on the wings of the wind" instead of the literal "going on the wings of the wind").

Setting beams for His lofts in the waters,   3
     making His chariot the clouds,
          He goes on the wings of the wind.
He makes His messengers the winds,   4
     His ministers, glowing fire.
He founded earth on its solid base,   5
     not to be shaken forevermore.
With the deep You covered it like a garment—   6
     over mountains the waters stood.
From Your blast they fled,   7
     from the sound of Your thunder they scattered.
They went up the mountains, went down the valleys,   8
     to the place that You founded for them.
A border You fixed so they could not cross,   9
     so they could not come back to cover the earth.

---

3. *Setting beams for His lofts in the waters.* The modern reader may be puzzled as to why the divine builder should set beams in water, but the cosmological image would have been transparent to the ancient audience. Above the vault (*raqi'a*) of the heavens are the upper waters (see Genesis 1), where God builds His "lofts" or "upper chambers."
    making His chariot the clouds. One of God's epithets is "rider on the clouds." The image is borrowed from Canaanite mythology.

6. *With the deep You covered it like a garment.* This evocation of the waters of the primordial abyss (*tehom*) covering all of the dry land refers in all likelihood not to the Flood story (though that remains a possibility or perhaps rather a superimposed image) but to creation itself. One can see that in this particular psalm the idea drawn from Canaanite mythology of a cosmogonic conquest of the sea god or sea monster has been domesticated in monotheistic terms. A primordial engulfing of the land by the sea is envisaged, but without personi- fication or mythic imagery. God is the agent controlling the waters, and His "blast" (or "rebuke") drives the waters back into their appointed bed. Indeed, Leviathan, the sea monster, appears in this poem as nothing more than a tame aquatic pet (verse 26) among the other manifold creatures of the sea.

10   You let loose the springs in freshets,
            among the mountains they go.

11   They water all beasts of the field,
            the wild asses slake their thirst.

12   Above them the fowl of the heavens dwell,
            from among the foliage they send forth their voice.

13   He waters mountains from His lofts,
            from the fruit of Your works the earth is sated.

14   He makes the hay sprout for cattle,
            grass for the labor of humankind
               to bring forth bread from the earth,

---

10. *You let loose the springs in freshets.* Against the potentially destructive waters of the sea, now driven back to their appointed place beyond the shore, God releases on land powerful streams of fresh water to sustain the life of all creatures.

11. *the wild asses slake their thirst.* As in the Voice from the Whirlwind in Job, the wild ass, resistant to all domestication, is an image of unfettered freedom. God's sustenance of His creatures extends to the wild and the tame, to beast and man (again, as in Job).

12. *Above them the fowl of the heavens dwell.* That is, up above all the beasts of the field. The fowl are said to "dwell" because their realm is the sky, though perhaps one might infer that the force of the verb in context could be something like "glide."
    their voice. The Masoretic text has merely "voice" (*qol*), but one manuscript and some ancient versions read "their voice" (*qolam*).

13. *He waters mountains from His lofts.* The reference of course is to rain, coming down from the celestial chambers above the vault of the heavens. The rain is the complement to the freshets bubbling up from the earth.
    from the fruit of Your works. This is odd as a designation for rain, but the various proposed emendations are contorted, without warrant in the manuscripts or ancient versions.

and wine that gladdens the heart of man   15
        to make faces shine brighter than oil,
               and bread that sustains the heart of man.
The trees of the Lord drink their fill,   16
        the Lebanon cedars He planted,
where the birds make their nest,   17
        the stork whose home is the cypresses,
the high mountains for the gazelles,   18
        the crags a shelter for badgers.
He made the moon for the fixed seasons;   19
        the sun—He appointed its setting.
You bring down darkness and it turns to night   20
        in which all beasts of the forest stir.

---

15. *to make faces shine brighter than oil.* Most translators understand the letter *mem* that is prefixed to *shemen*, "oil," as a causative, somehow inferring that oil makes the face brighten. It may be more plausible to construe the *mem* as a *mem* of comparison ("than")—the faces shine brighter than olive oil seen in sunlight.

17–18. *stork . . . gazelles . . . badgers.* The sprawling zoological panorama, all of it under God's providential care, again has analogies in the Voice from the Whirlwind in Job.

19. *the sun—He appointed its setting.* The Masoretic text seems to say, "The sun knew its setting," a less forceful formulation that requires a new subject for the verb in this second verset. By simply revocalizing *yada'*, "knew," as *yida'*, "appointed," a reading warranted by one version of the Septuagint, the line makes better sense theologically and poetically.

20. *You bring down darkness and it turns to night.* Darkness here is not a mythological realm of terrors but part of the diurnal cycle controlled by God.

21   The lions roar for prey,
                seeking from God their food.
22   When the sun comes up, they head home,
                and in their dens they lie down.
23   Man goes out to his work
                and to his labor until evening.
24   How many Your deeds, O LORD,
                all of them You do in wisdom.
                        All the earth is filled with Your riches.

---

21. *The lions roar for prey.* The idea that God provides for even the fiercest of predatory beasts is again one that is prominent in the Voice from the Whirlwind. But, as scholarship has abundantly documented, this line, like several others in the psalm, sounds quite close to a line from the fourteenth-century BCE hymn to the sun associated with the Pharaoh Akhenaton that was found at Amarna. Because poetry in all eras works through allusion, it is hardly necessary to understand this poem as an "adaptation" of Akhenaton's hymn. The Hebrew poet may well have borrowed phrases from it, or from a Canaanite intermediary, but in the psalm there is no sun god. On the contrary, the sun and the moon and the stars and the winds of the heavens are all God's instruments.

23. *Man goes out.* This is a beautifully imagined diurnal cycle of seeking sustenance. The hunting lion returns to its lair at daybreak, and man then goes out to labor till evening.

24. *How many Your deeds.* With these words, the poet launches on a grand summation of the great hymn to God as master of all creation that he has produced.
    riches. This translation follows the King James Version. The Hebrew *qinyanim* might mean "creations" because the verb that is cognate to it occasionally means "to create." That sense sounds awkward here, and the word also means "acquisitions"—hence "riches."

This sea great and wide,   25
        where creatures beyond number stir,
                the little beasts and the large.
There the ships go,   26
        this Leviathan You fashioned to play with.
All of them look to You   27
        to give them their food in its season.
When You give them, they gather it in,   28
        when You open Your hand, they are sated with good.
When You hide Your face, they panic,   29
        You withdraw their breath and they perish,
                and to the dust they return.
When You send forth Your breath, they are created,   30
        and You renew the face of the earth.
May the LORD's glory be forever,   31
        may the LORD rejoice in His works,

---

25. *This sea great and wide.* As above, this is a post-mythological sea, very much part of the map of creation.

    where creatures beyond number stir. Literally, "where there are stirring creatures beyond number." The term *remes* is part of the vocabulary of the Priestly creation story. This poem reads distinctly like a poetic free improvisation on themes from the creation story at the beginning of Genesis, rendered from the perspective of a human observer rather than through the magisterial omniscience of the narrator in Genesis.

26. *There the ships go.* The sea teems with creatures but also with the works of human civilization. Thus Leviathan can be reduced to a plaything.

29. *their breath.* The Hebrew term equally means "spirit," but the background of Genesis argues for the sense of "breath" because it is God's breath there that brings life into being. The Septuagint reads "Your breath." Either reading makes sense.

31. *May the LORD's glory be forever.* The psalm now concludes with a kind of doxology. This is the explicit meaning of "blessing" the LORD.

32 Who but looks down to earth, and it trembles,
            but touches the mountains—they smoke.
33 Let me sing to the LORD while I live,
            let me hymn to my God while I breathe.
34 Let my speech be sweet unto Him.
            As for me, I rejoice in the LORD.
35 Let offenders vanish from earth
            and the wicked be no more.
      Bless, O my being, the LORD,
            Hallelujah!

---

33. *while I breathe*. The literal sense of the Hebrew is "as long as I [am]."

35. *Let offenders vanish*. This reference to evildoers introduces an issue of transgression and justice nowhere in evidence in the body of the poem. It may be, as is the case with the concluding lines of quite a few psalms, an editorially added gesture of piety.

105

Acclaim the LORD, call out His name,　　　　　　　　　　1
　　　make His deeds known among the peoples.
Sing to Him, hymn to Him,　　　　　　　　　　　　　　2
　　　speak of all His wonders.
Revel in His holy name.　　　　　　　　　　　　　　　3
　　　Let the heart of the LORD's seekers rejoice.
Inquire of the LORD and His strength,　　　　　　　　　4
　　　seek His presence always.

---

1. *Acclaim the LORD . . . / make His deeds known.* The initial formulas of this psalm reflect a kinship with the psalms of thanksgiving, but the "deeds" (or "feats") referred to are God's wondrous acts in history on behalf of Israel, as the next few lines make clear. This is, then, a historical psalm, reviewing in versified summary (perhaps as part of a temple ritual) the following sequence of events familiar from Genesis and Exodus: the covenantal promise to the Patriarchs (verses 6–15); Joseph's descent into Egypt and his eventually triumphant career there (verses 16–23); the enslavement of the Hebrews, the mission of Moses and Aaron, and the Plagues (verses 24–36); the exodus and God's providence to Israel in the wilderness (verses 37–43); and the inheritance of the Promised Land (verses 44 and 45). The length of the psalm is dictated by the necessity to cover all this narrative material. Even more than in the analogous Psalm 78, the poetry does not go much beyond a simple versification of known events.

5   Recall the wonders that He did,
                His portents and the judgments He issued,
6   O seed of Abraham His servant,
                sons of Jacob, His chosen ones.
7   He is the LORD our God—
                through all the earth, His judgments.
8   He recalls His pact forever—
                the word He ordained for a thousand generations—
9   which He sealed with Abraham,
                and His vow to Isaac,
10   and He set it for Jacob as a statute,
                for Israel an eternal pact,
11   saying,
                "To you will I give the land of Canaan
                    as the plot of your estate,"
12   when they were a handful of men,
                but a few, and sojourners there.
13   And they went about from nation to nation,
                from one kingdom to another people.

---

5. *the wonders that He did.* The literal sense of the Hebrew is "His wonders that He did."

the judgments He issued. Literally, "the judgments of His mouth."

6. *O seed of Abraham His servant.* This is almost certainly a vocative, as it is translated here. The whole national community of Israel is exhorted to contemplate and celebrate God's great deeds on behalf of the nation.

11. *saying.* This formulaic term for the introduction of direct speech is used here as a preface to the quotation of God's words that convey the essence of His pact with the Patriarchs—the promise of the Land.

12. *when they were a handful of men.* The unusual phrase used here, *metey mispar*, is a direct quotation of Jacob's words to his sons in Genesis 34:30 about the vulnerable smallness of his clan as sojourners in the land of Canaan.

He allowed no man to oppress them   14
    and warned kings on their account:
"Touch not My anointed ones,   15
    and to My prophets do no harm."
And He called forth famine over the land,   16
    every staff of bread He broke.
He sent a man before them—   17
    as a slave was Joseph sold.
They tortured his legs with shackles,   18
    his neck was put in iron,
until the time of his word had come,   19
    the LORD's utterance that purged him.
The king sent and loosed his shackles,   20
    the ruler of peoples set him free,

---

14. *He allowed no man to oppress them / and warned kings on their account.* The most likely reference is to the three sister-wife stories (Genesis 12, 20, and 26). The mention of "nation to nation" and "from one kingdom to another people" would refer to Egypt and Gerar, where Abraham and then Isaac went in a time of famine. "Anointed ones" in the next verse then conflates the terminology of the later monarchy with the idea of the Patriarchs as God's elected ones.

16. *every staff of bread.* Some scholars think this refers to a pole on which the round, flat loaves of bread were spooled.

18. *his neck was put in iron.* Literally, "his neck came into iron." The Hebrew *nefesh* refers here to the neck (a complementary parallel to the shackled feet) and certainly does not mean "soul."

19. *the time of his word.* The formulation is somewhat crabbed, but this has to mean the prophecy (through the dream vision) of Joseph's future greatness.
    the LORD's utterance that purged him. The translation follows the received text, though the verb used in it is cryptic. The idea seems to be that God's word or promise now exonerates Joseph of the crime of which he had been accused.

20. *shackles.* This is merely implied in the Hebrew.

21 made him master of his house
and ruler of all his possessions,
22 to admonish his princes as he desired
and to teach wisdom to his elders.
23 And Israel came to Egypt,
Jacob sojourned in the land of Ham.
24 And He made His people very fruitful,
made them more numerous than their foes.
25 He changed their heart to hate His people,
to lay plots against His servants.
26 He sent Moses his servant,
Aaron, whom He had chosen.
27 They set among them the words of His signs,
His portents in the land of Ham.
28 He sent darkness, and it grew dark,
yet they did not keep His word.

---

22. *to admonish.* The translation reads, with the Septuagint, *leyaser* instead of the Masoretic *le'esor*, "to bind." The sense of "bind" is possible (as a counterpoint to Joseph's having been loosed from his shackles), but "admonish" is a much more plausible parallel to "teach wisdom."

24. *very fruitful . . . more numerous.* This is a direct citation of Exodus 1:7.

27. *the words of His signs.* This is a literal representation of the Hebrew, the idea being that the signs are not just spectacles but bear a message. "Signs and portents" are key terms in the narrative of the mission of Moses and Aaron in Egypt.

28. *darkness.* The recapitulation of the Plagues narrative does not entirely follow the order of the story in Exodus. It begins here with the ninth plague, then goes back to the first, second, fourth, and third, the seventh, the eighth, and the tenth. The blight of the cattle and the epidemic of burning rash are not mentioned in this version.

He turned their waters to blood   29
    and made their fish die.
Their land swarmed with frogs,   30
    into the chambers of their kings.
He spoke, and the swarm did come,   31
    lice in all their region.
He turned their rains into hail,   32
    tongues of fire in their land.
And He struck their vines and their fig trees   33
    and shattered the trees of their region.
He spoke, and the locust came,   34
    grasshoppers without number.
And they ate all the grass in their land   35
    they ate up the fruit of their soil.
And He struck down each firstborn in their land,   36
    the first yield of all their manhood.
And He brought them out with silver and gold,   37
    and none in His tribes did falter.
Egypt rejoiced when they went out,   38
    for their fear had fallen upon them.
He spread a cloud as a curtain   39
    and fire to light up the night.
They asked, and He brought the quail,   40
    and with bread from the heavens He sated them.
He opened the rock, and water flowed,   41
    it went forth in parched land as a stream.
For He recalled His holy word   42
    with Abraham His servant.

---

40. *They asked.* The received text here has "he asked," but the letter *waw* at the
end of the verb, which would make it a plural, in all likelihood was inadvertently dropped in scribal copying because the next word in the text also begins
with a *waw*.

43   And He brought out His people in joy,
                in glad song His chosen ones.
44   And He gave them the lands of nations,
                they took hold of the wealth of peoples,
45   so that they should keep His statutes,
                and His teachings they should observe.
                        Hallelujah!

---

43. *in joy, / in glad song.* This could refer to the triumphant Song of the Sea (Exodus 15), even though the stories of the quail and the water from the rock follow it in Exodus. Its position here might be because it is a grand summary of the story of the exodus.

44. *He gave them the lands of nations.* The verse narrative now leaps forward to the conquest of the Land, skipping the Sinai epiphany, for reasons that remain unclear.
    the wealth of peoples. The literal sense of the Hebrew 'amal is "toil," wealth being the product of the toil.

45. *so that they should keep His statutes.* The psalm concludes on a didactic, perhaps Deuteronomistic, note. The people's inheritance of the Land, the fulfillment of the promise first made to Abraham, is not simply to possess political sovereignty over territory but to observe God's statutes, which is Israel's part in the covenantal agreement.

106

Hallelujah!
 Acclaim the LORD, for He is good,1
   for His kindness is forever.
 Who can utter the LORD's mighty acts,2
   can make heard all His praise?

---

2. *Who can utter the* LORD's *mighty acts.* This invocation of God's "mighty acts" (*gevurot*) in the second line of the poem signals its status as a historical psalm. Once again, the large historical picture leads to a relatively lengthy psalm; and once again, the rehearsal in poetry of familiar events recorded in the Torah produces a rather perfunctory order of poetry. It requires little commentary here, beyond identification of the episodes from the Torah alluded to and observations on a couple of places where the text looks doubtful. Some scholars have characterized this psalm as a companion piece to Psalm 105, perhaps even publicly chanted together with it. Although that remains a possibility, these two historical psalms may simply have been set in sequence in the collection by the editors because of the generic connection between them. In any case, they present antithetical views of the nation's history. Psalm 105 is a celebration of God's providential care of Israel, with no mention of the people's transgressions. Psalm 106, beginning with verse 6, is an unrelenting account of Israel's rebellious behavior, from the exodus itself through the wilderness to its later collective life in its national territory. The notion of Israel's betrayal of the covenant unleashing divine retribution may well be colored by Deuteronomy, and there are indications in the psalm of an exilic setting (see, for example, verse 46. "And He granted them mercy / in the eyes of all their captors").

3   Happy those who keep justice,
           who do righteousness at all times.

4   Recall me, O Lord, when You favor Your people,
           mark me for Your rescue,

5   to see the good of Your chosen ones,
           to rejoice in the joy of Your nation,
               to revel with Your estate.

6   We offended like our fathers,
           we wronged, we did evil.

7   Our fathers in Egypt
           did not grasp Your wonders.
    They did not call to mind Your many kindnesses
           and rebelled by the sea, at the Sea of Reeds.

8   Yet He rescued them for His name's sake,
           to make known His might.

---

3. *Happy those who keep justice.* This platitude of the Wisdom psalms proves to have, as the psalm unfolds, a particular historical context. It will become clear that the nation as a whole has failed to keep justice and has suffered the consequences.

4. *Recall me, O Lord, when You favor Your people.* It will emerge that the psalmist in exile is specifically awaiting the moment when God will again favor His people and bring them back to their land. That consummation is in all likelihood what is implied in the general language of verse 5.

7. *rebelled by the sea.* In Exodus 14:11, the fearful people at the shore of the Sea of Reeds complain to Moses, "Was it for lack of graves in Egypt that you took us to die in the wilderness?"

8. *Yet He rescued them.* As elsewhere, the oscillation between second person and third person is common in biblical usage.

He blasted the Sea of Reeds, and it dried up,   9
      and He led them through the deep as through
      wilderness.
And He rescued them from the hand of the hostile   10
      and redeemed them from the hand of the enemy.
And the waters covered their foes,   11
      not one of them remained.
And they trusted His words,   12
      they sang His praise.
Quickly they forgot His deeds,   13
      they did not await His counsel.
And they felt a sharp craving in the wilderness,   14
      they put God to the test in the waste land.
And He gave them what they had asked,   15
      sent food down their throats.

---

9. *He blasted the Sea of Reeds.* This image may be poetic license: In the account in Exodus, the sea parts when Moses raises his staff.

11. *not one of them remained.* This clause is a direct quotation of Exodus 14:28.

12. *they sang His praise.* The poet obviously has in mind the Song of the Sea, Exodus 15.

14. *felt a sharp craving.* The literal sense is "craved a craving." The line refers to the story told in Numbers 11, where this same phrase is used.

15. *sent food down their throats.* The Masoretic text reads *razon*, "thinness" (or "famine"), which can be justified only by exegetical contortion. This translation follows the Septuagint and the Syriac, which read instead *mazon*, "food." The reference is to the quail sent to the Hebrews by God, which Moses says they will eat "till it comes out of your noses and becomes a loathsome thing to you" (Numbers 11:20).

16   And they were jealous of Moses in the camp,
                of Aaron, the Lord's holy one.
17   The earth opened and swallowed Dothan
                and covered Abiram's band.
18   And fire burned through their band,
                flame consumed the wicked.
19   They made a calf at Horeb
                and bowed to a molten image.
20   And they exchanged their glory
                for the image of a grass-eating bull.
21   They forgot the God their rescuer,
                Who did great things in Egypt,
22   wonders in the land of Ham,
                awesome deeds at the Sea of Reeds.

---

16. *And they were jealous of Moses*. The incident in view is the double rebellion against Moses reported in Numbers 16.

19. *They made a calf at Horeb*. The poet clearly does not feel obliged to follow the order of events as they occur in the text of the Torah. He now backtracks to the episode of the Golden Calf, Exodus 32.

20. *their glory*. This term in context refers to God.
    for the image of a grass-eating bull. This mocking characterization of the idol worshipped by Israel is much in the spirit of the polemic against idolatry in Deutero-Isaiah. The term translated as "bull," *shor*, can equally mean "ox," but the cultic context argues for the sense of bull because images of bulls were objects of worship.

21–22. *did great things in Egypt, / wonders in the land of Ham, / awesome deeds at the Sea of Reeds*. The perfunctory character of the poetry is especially evident in the stringing together of formulaic phrases here.

And He would have wiped them out   23
        were it not for Moses His chosen one—
he stood in the breach before Him
        to turn back His wrath from destruction.
And they despised the land of desires,   24
        they did not trust His word.
And they muttered in their tents,   25
        they did not heed the voice of the LORD.
And He raised His hand against them,   26
        to make them fall in the wilderness,
to disperse their seed among the nations,   27
        to scatter them among the lands.
And they clung to Baal Peor   28
        and ate sacrifices to the dead.
And they provoked Him through their acts,   29
        and the scourge broke out among them.

---

23. *he stood in the breach.* Moses's intercession on behalf of Israel is reported in Exodus 32:11–14.

24. *the land of desires.* The Hebrew has "desire" in the singular, but in English that might have an erotic connotation. The despising of the Promised Land refers to the incident of the ten faint-hearted spies sent to scout out the land in Numbers 13.

26. *to make them fall in the wilderness.* This phrase quotes Numbers 14:29.

27. *to disperse their seed among the nations.* The Masoretic text reads, "to make their seed fall" (*lehapil*), which looks suspiciously like an inadvertent scribal repetition of *lehapil* near the end of the previous verse. This translation reads, with the Septuagint, *lehafits*, "to disperse," a difference of just one consonant.

28. *Baal Peor.* This episode of orgiastic idolatry is recounted in Numbers 25, where the zealous priest Phineas (verse 30) slaughters the cultic traitors, an act not mentioned here.

30   And Phineas stood and prayed,
                and the scourge was held back
31   and it was counted for him as merit,
                generation to generation forever.
32   And they caused fury over the waters of Meribah,
                and it went badly for Moses because of them,
33   for they rebelled against him,
                and he pronounced rash things with his lips.
34   They did not destroy the peoples
                as the LORD had said to them.
35   And they mingled with the nations
                and learned their deeds.
36   And they worshipped their idols,
                which became a snare to them.

---

32. *the waters of Meribah.* This incident of rebellion moves back to Exodus 17, with a matching episode in Numbers 20.

and it went badly for Moses because of them. It was because of Moses's actions in the second episode of bringing water from the rock that he was condemned never to enter the Land.

33. *and he pronounced rash things with his lips.* The Hebrew merely says, "he pronounced with his lips," but the most reasonable way to make sense of this cryptic clause is to assume that a rash utterance is implied. This line may reflect an interpretive inference from what is succinctly stated in the story in Numbers 20: The rash things would be Moses's words to the people. "Shall we bring forth water for you from this rock?" (Numbers 20:10), implying that it is Moses and Aaron rather than God who will make the water flow from the rock.

34. *They did not destroy the peoples.* This idea has a strong Deuteronomistic tinge: Israel was enjoined to wipe out the idolatrous peoples of the land; instead, it mingled with them and adopted their idolatrous practices.

And they sacrificed their sons   37
      and their daughters to the demons.
And they shed innocent blood,   38
      the blood of their sons and their daughters
when they sacrificed to Canaan's idols,
      and the land was polluted with blood-guilt.
And they were defiled through their deeds   39
      and went whoring through their actions.
And the LORD's wrath blazed against His people,   40
      and He abhorred His estate,
and gave them into the hand of nations,   41
      their haters ruled over them.
And their enemies oppressed them,   42
      and they were subject to their power.
Many times did He save them,   43
      and they rebelled against His counsel
            and were brought low through their misdeeds.
And He saw when they were in straits,   44
      when He heard their song of prayer.
And He recalled for them His pact,   45
      relented through his many kindnesses.

---

37. *they sacrificed their sons.* Child sacrifice is strategically invoked as the paradigmatic abomination of the Canaanite idolators.

40. *His estate.* This is an epithet not for the land but for God's people. Compare
verse 5.

44. *He saw when they were in straits, / when He heard their song of prayer.* The
scenario of the poem is rebellion and betrayal of the covenant followed by
defeat and exile, which then lead to contrition and a sincere turning to God,
Who is then moved to relent.

46   And He granted them mercy
              in the eyes of all their captors.
47   Rescue us, LORD our God
              and gather us from the nations
       to acclaim Your holy name
              and to glory in Your praise.

48   Blessed is the LORD God of Israel forever and ever. And all the
       people say: Amen, hallelujah!

---

46. *granted them mercy / in the eyes of all their captors.* "In the eyes of" is literally "before." This could be a reference to the Persian emperor Cyrus, who
authorized the return of the Babylonian exiles to Zion, though that identification is not entirely certain.

47. *Rescue us . . . / . . . gather us from the nations.* The language used here clearly
has in view a return from exile. The purpose of the return, as the next line of
verse indicates, is again to be able to celebrate God's greatness (a glance at the
opening lines of the poem) in the place He has chosen.

48. *Blessed is the LORD.* This verse is not part of the psalm proper but is rather
a doxology that marks the conclusion of the fourth book of Psalms.

107

Acclaim the Lord, for He is good,
   for His kindness is forever.   1
Let the Lord's redeemed ones say,
   whom he redeemed from the hand of the foe, 2
and gathered them from the lands,
   from east and west, from north and south. 3
They wandered in wilderness, waste land,
   found no road to a settled town,   4
hungry, thirsty, too,
   their life-breath failed within them.   5

---

1. *Acclaim.* The first word of this psalm, which has no superscription, is *hodu,* "acclaim" or "give thanks," announcing this as a thanksgiving psalm. In this instance, as the poem unfolds, it is clear that the thanksgiving is collective.

2. *redeemed ones.* The term is not theological but political: These are people who have been redeemed from captivity or from dangerous enemies, "from the hand of the foe."

3. *and gathered them from the lands.* The language suggests some sort of return from exile, and this psalm could conceivably have been recited at a public ceremony of thanksgiving during the return to Zion in the sixth century BCE. Some scholars, however, date the text earlier.
 south. The received text says *umiyam,* "and from the sea," which would be a second occurrence of west as a direction here. It is preferable to read *umiyamin* (adding just one consonant), "and from the south."

6   And they cried to the Lord from their straits,
        from their distress He saved them.

7   And He led them on a straight road
        to go to a settled town.

8   Let them acclaim to the Lord His kindness
        and His wonders to humankind.

9   For He sated the thirsting throat
        and the hungry throat He filled with good—

10   dwellers in dark and death's shadow,
        prisoners of tormenting iron.

11   For they rebelled against God's sayings,
        the Most High's counsel they despised.

12   And He brought their heart low in troubles.
        They stumbled with none to help.

13   And they cried to the Lord from their straits,
        from their distress He rescued them.

14   He brought them out from the dark and death's shadow
        and their bonds He sundered.

---

6. *And they cried to the Lord from their straits.* This is the first of two recurring refrains in the poem, a device appropriate for a liturgical text chanted in a public celebration.

8. *Let them acclaim to the Lord His kindness.* This is the second refrain, which is repeated verbatim further on and also picks up phrases from the first line of the psalm.

10. *dwellers in dark and death's shadow.* The second verset of this line speaks of prisoners, so it is plausible, as several interpreters have suggested, that the concrete image is a dark, windowless, dungeon-like place of captivity.
   tormenting iron. The literal sense of the Hebrew is "torment and iron," but this translation assumes it is a hendyadis and thus renders the first of the two nouns as a participle.

14. *He brought them out from the dark.* This line is a phrase-by-phrase answer to the condition of distress represented in verse 10.

Let them acclaim to the LORD His kindness   15
        and His wonders to humankind.
For He shattered the doors of bronze   16
        and the iron bars He hacked off.
Fools because of their sinful way,   17
        because of their misdeeds they were afflicted.
All food their throat rejected,   18
        they came to the gates of death.
And they cried to the LORD from their straits,   19
        from their distress He rescued them.
He sent forth His word and healed them,   20
        and delivered them from their pit.
Let them acclaim to the LORD His kindness,   21
        and His wonders to humankind,
and offer thanksgiving sacrifices   22
        and recount His deeds in glad song.

---

16. *the doors of bronze / . . . the iron bars.* These heavy bolted doors are what lock up the prisoners in their dark dungeon.

17. *Fools because of their sinful way.* The translation follows the wording of the received text, but the Hebrew looks problematic, with the word for "fools," *'ewilim*, especially doubtful.

18. *All food their throat rejected.* In their desperate plight, perhaps as prisoners, these miserable people lose all appetite and retch at the thought of food, so that they are on the verge of dying.

20. *from their pit.* The form of the Hebrew noun is plural and also odd. Some scholars emend the word as it stands, *mishehitotam* to *mishahat hayatam,* "from the Pit their life," which reads more smoothly. In any case, the reference to near death is not in doubt.

22. *offer thanksgiving sacrifices / . . . recount . . . in glad song.* This verse provides an explicit reference to the temple ritual that this psalm would have accompanied.

23 Those who go down to the sea in ships,
    who do tasks in the mighty waters,
24 it is they who have seen the deeds of the Lord,
    and His wonders in the deep.
25 He speaks and raises the stormwind
    and it makes the waves loom high.
26 They go up to the heavens, come down to the depths,
    their life-breath in hardship grows faint.
27 They reel and sway like a drunkard,
    all their wisdom is swallowed up.
28 And they cry to the Lord from their straits
    from their distress He brings them out.
29 He turns the storm into silence,
    and its waves are stilled,

---

23. *Those who go down to the sea in ships.* These famous lines (Melville recalls them in *Moby-Dick*) about the dangers besetting mariners are only loosely connected with the imagery of captives in foreign lands that has been the center of the poem till this point. Perhaps the sailors belong here as a different but related category of people who have been at death's door but are saved by God. It should be noted that in the Hebrew text, verses 21–26 are marked in the right margin with an inverted letter *nun*, a device that seems to have been used by the ancient scribes to indicate some questioning of the text or even a virtual erasure of it. Although the unit about sea travel continues through verse 30, this scribal indication makes one wonder whether the whole section might have been regarded as a different poem that was somehow inserted into our psalm.

27. *They reel and sway like a drunkard, / all their wisdom is swallowed up.* This line and some of the phrases before and after are put to remarkable use by the twelfth-century Hebrew poet Judah Halevi in his brilliant sea poems, a kind of poetic chronicle of his voyage from Spain toward the Land of Israel. The biblical word for "wisdom" also means something close to "craft"; thus, the idea here is that all the technical expertise of the sailors is baffled or made futile by the fury of the storm.

and they rejoice that these have grown quiet,   30
        and He leads them to their bourn.
Let them acclaim to the LORD His kindness   31
        and His wonders to humankind.
Let them exalt Him in the people's assembly   32
        and in the session of elders praise Him.
He turns rivers into wilderness   33
        and springs of water into thirsty ground,
fruitful land into salt flats,   34
        because of the evil of those who dwell there.
He turns wilderness to pools of water,   35
        and parched land to springs of water,
and settles there the hungry,   36
        firmly founds a settled town.
And they sow fields and they plant vineyards,   37
        which produce a fruitful yield.
And He blesses them and they multiply greatly,   38
        and their beasts He does not let dwindle.

---

30. *their bourn.* This rather antiquated English term reflects a high-poetic locution for "destination" in the Hebrew, which is literally "the realm of their desire."

33. *He turns rivers into wilderness.* God's awesome powers of transformation work in both directions: He can turn desolation into lush fecundity (verses 35–37), and he can also turn fruitful places into arid desert.

40   He pours contempt upon the princes,
             and makes them wander in trackless waste.
39   And they dwindle and are bowed down,
             from harsh oppression and sorrow.
41   And He raises the needy from affliction,
             and increases his clans like flocks.
42   Let the upright see and rejoice,
             and all wickedness shut its mouth.
43   He who is wise will watch these
             and take to heart the LORD's kindnesses.

---

40. *He pours contempt upon the princes.* This verse also shows an inverted *nun* at its right margin, and in this instance that device clearly indicates a glitch in the text. Verse 39 ("And they dwindle and are bowed down") makes no sense immediately after verse 38, which is taken up with the blessings of those redeemed by God. The inverted nun is a recognition that this verse is out of place in the received text. If we place it before verse 39 rather than after it, the whole sequence here becomes perfectly coherent. It is worth noting that this whole clause also appears verbatim in Job 12:21A.

39. *they dwindle.* This indication is in pointed contrast to the condition of those favored by God, whose very cattle are not allowed to dwindle.

41. *increases his clans like flocks.* The image of the dwindling of the wicked is sandwiched on both sides with images of the increase of the righteous.

108

A song, a David psalm.	1
My heart is firm, O God.	2

       Let me sing and hymn
           with my inward being, too.

Awake, O lute and lyre.   3
       I would waken the dawn.

Let me acclaim You among the peoples, LORD.   4
       Let me hymn You among the nations.

---

2. *My heart is firm, O God.* From these initial words of the poem proper to the very end, this text is a stitching together of two previous psalms in the collection. Verses 2–6 here are virtually identical, with only minor variations, to Psalm 57:8–12. Verses 7–14 similarly reproduce Psalm 60:6–14. Psalm 57 is an individual supplication, and Psalm 60 is a national supplication. It remains unclear why sections of both poems should have been spliced together to make the present psalm. Some scholars have speculated, without much evidence, that the composite psalm was intended to serve a new ritual purpose. It is also distinctly possible that the joining of texts was the result of an inadvertency or confusion in the ancient editorial process. Readers are referred to the comments on the relevant verses in Psalm 57 and Psalm 60 for elucidation of the language and imagery. Some brief notes on points of divergence from the duplicated text follow here.

    with my inward being. The Masoretic text has *kevodi*, "my glory," instead of which this translation reads *keveidi*, literally, "my liver." Psalm 57 also has *kevodi*, but because the placement of the term is different there, it seemed preferable to read it, following one ancient manuscript, as *kinori*, "my lyre."

5   For Your kindness is great over the heavens,
              and Your steadfast truth to the skies.
6   Loom over the heavens, O God.
         Over all the earth Your glory,
7   that Your beloved ones be saved,
              rescue with Your right hand, answer me.
8   God once spoke in His holiness:
         "Let Me exult and share out Shechem,
              and the valley of Sukkoth I shall measure.
9   Mine is Gilead, Mine Manasseh,
              and Ephraim My foremost stronghold,
                   Judah My scepter.
10   Moab is My washbasin,
              upon Edom I fling My sandal,
                   over Philistia I shout exultant."
11   Who will lead me to the fortified town,
              who will guide me to Edom?
12   Have You not, O God, abandoned us?
              You do not sally forth, God, with our armies.
13   Give us help against the foe
              when rescue by man is in vain.
14   Through God we shall gather strength,
              and He will stamp out our foes.

---

5. *great over the heavens.* Psalm 57 has a different preposition, "to the heavens" (*'ad* instead of *me'al*, as here).

10. *I shout exultant.* Psalm 60 at this point has a feminine imperative form of the verb rather than the first-person singular. In fact, the imperative does not make sense in context, and the translation of Psalm 60 corrected the verb to read as it does here.

109

For the lead player, a David psalm.   1
        God of my praise, do not be silent.
For the wicked's mouth, the mouth of deceit,   2
        has opened against me,
                they spoke to me with lying tongue.
And words of hatred swarmed round me—   3
        they battle me for no cause.
In return for my love they accuse me,   4
        though my prayer is for them.

---

1. *God of my praise, do not be silent.* This opening formula aligns this text with the psalms of supplication. What is unusual about this particular supplication is that the long central section of the psalm, verses 6–19, is, in the most persuasive reading, an extensive quotation of the venomous words of accusation and imprecation that the speaker's accusers pronounce against him.

2. *the wicked's mouth, the mouth of deceit.* The attention here at the beginning to malicious speech prepares us for the words of calumny that follow. Some scholars, in the interest of neatly parallel statement, prefer to revocalize *rasha'*, "wicked," as *resha'*, "wickedness."

4. *though my prayer is for them.* The literal sense of the received text is "and I am prayer." The consensus of Hebrew tradition has understood this to mean something like "and I am all prayer." The ancient Syriac version may have worked from a Hebrew text that read *tefilati lahem*, "my prayer is for them." That reading would be more cogent as a parallel to "in return for my love" in the first verset.

5   And they offer me evil in return for good
          and hatred in return for my love:
6   "Appoint a wicked man over him,
          let an accuser stand at his right.
7   When he is judged, let him come out guilty,
          and his prayer be an offense.
8   Let his days be few,
          may another man take his post.
9   May his children become orphans
          and his wife a widow.
10   May his children wander and beg,
          driven out from the ruins of their homes.
11   May the lender snare all that he has
          and may strangers plunder his wealth.

---

6. *Appoint a wicked man over him.* These words inaugurate the hostile speech of the accusers. A clue to the fact that the speaker is the object of the curse is that the reviled man is referred to throughout in the singular, whereas the plural is used for his accusers. Their speech includes both scathing curses against the man and his family and specific indications that they want to frame a case against him in a court of law. The term "accuser," *satan*, which is used as a verb in verse 4 and recurs in the plural at the end of this speech in verse 20 and again in verse 29, has a juridical connotation, as it does in the frame story of Job, where it designates Job's accuser or adversary in the celestial assembly.

7. *and his prayer be an offense.* This is no doubt a malicious antithesis to the mention of benevolent prayer in verse 4.

8. *may another man take his post.* One may infer from these words that the speaker is some sort of official whom his enemies seek to disgrace and unseat through judicial proceedings.

10. *driven out from the ruins of their homes.* The Masoretic text says, "they seek [bread?] from the ruins of their homes," which is a possible reading, though it sounds cryptic. The translation follows others in emending *wedarshu*, "they seek," to *wegorshu*, "are driven out," a reading shown in the Septuagint.

May no one extend to him kindness   12
      and no one pity his orphans.

May his offspring be cut off,   13
      in the next generation his name wiped out.

May the wrong of his fathers be recalled by the LORD   14
      and his mother's offense not be wiped out.

Let these be ever before the LORD,   15
      that He cut off from the earth their name.

Because he did not remember to do kindness   16
      and pursued the poor and the needy,
          the heartsore, to put him to death.

He loved a curse, may it come upon him,   17
      he desired not blessing—may it stay far from him.

He donned curse as his garb—   18
      may it enter his innards like water
        and like oil in his bones.

May it be like a garment he wraps round him   19
      and like a belt he girds at all times."

---

13. *his name.* The Masoretic text reads "their name," but many Hebrew manuscripts as well as the Septuagint have the more likely singular possessive suffix.

14. *fathers . . . mother's.* The biblical imagination tends to conceive human destiny in terms of the familial line. The accusers want the man's posterity to be cut off and presume that his forebears before him have accumulated a large account of transgressions that now deserves sweeping retribution.

15. *their name.* The plural is used here because of the reference to fathers and mother.

18. *enter his innards like water / and like oil in his bones.* It is obvious enough that when you drink water, it quickly goes down into the stomach. Oil in the bones may reflect a notion that oil consumed in food entered into the bone marrow.

20 This be the plight of my accusers from the Lord,
          and those who speak against my life.
21 And You, O Lord, Master,
               act on my behalf for the sake of Your name,
                    for Your kindness is good. O save me!
22 For poor and needy am I,
          and my heart is pierced within me.
23 Like a lengthening shadow I go off,
          I am shaken away like the locust.
24 My knees falter from fasting
          and my flesh is stripped of fat.
25 As for me, I become a reproach to them.
          They see me, they shake their heads.
26 Help me, O Lord, my God
          Rescue me as befits Your kindness,
27 that they may know that Your hand it is,
          it is You, O Lord, Who did it.
28 Let them curse, and You, You will bless.
          They will rise and be shamed, and Your servant will
          rejoice.

---

20. *This be the plight of my accusers from the* Lord. The most plausible construction of these words is that they mark the end of the quoted speech of the accusers. The speaker now prays that all their vicious curses directed at him be turned against them. The phrase "from the Lord" refers to "plight" (or, more literally, "action"). It is God Who will carry out all these dire curses against the malicious men who pronounced them.

28. *Let them curse, and You, You will bless.* This reversal from negative intention to positive outcome complements the wish the speaker expresses in verse 20 that the curse be turned against the cursers. That wish is picked up again in the second verset of this line.

Let my accusers don disgrace,   29
      and let them wrap round like a robe their shame.
I highly acclaim the LORD with my mouth,   30
      and in the midst of the many I praise Him,
for He stands at the needy's right hand   31
      to rescue him from his condemners.

---

29. *Let my accusers don disgrace, / . . . wrap round like a robe their shame.* The image of dressing or enveloping oneself in shame answers the garment imagery of verses 18 and 19.

30. *acclaim the LORD . . . / . . . in the midst of the many.* The verb "acclaim" (or "give thanks," *'odeh*) signals the conversion of the supplication at the end into a psalm of thanksgiving, as happens frequently elsewhere. The speaker in his trust in God is persuaded that his prayer is already accomplished, for he understands it as a fixed attribute of God that "He stands at the needy's right hand / to rescue him from his condemners." The phrase "in the midst of the many" is one of several used by the psalmists to refer to the throng in the temple where the thanksgiving celebrant is to praise God's works.

110

1 A David psalm.
    The Lord's utterance to my master:
      "Sit at My right hand
             till I make your enemies
                   a stool for your feet."
2   Your mighty scepter
            may the Lord send forth from Zion.
               Hold sway over your enemies.

---

1. *to my master.* Though many translations render this as "my Lord," with a capital *L*, the Hebrew clearly shows *'adoni*, with a first-person-singular suffix, whereas the noun at the beginning of verse 5 reads *'adonai*, showing the plural suffix invariably used when the noun *'adon* is a designation for God. This is a royal psalm, and the speaker, by referring to the king as his master, would appear to be a court poet.

    till I make your enemies / a stool for your feet. God's protection of the king against the nation's enemies is a prominent theme in most of the royal psalms. Some Egyptian murals actually depict an enthroned pharaoh with feet resting on the heads of kneeling captives.

Your people rally to battle   3
     on the day your force assembles
on the holy mountains, from the womb of dawn,
     yours is the dew of your youth.
The Lord has sworn, He will not change heart.   4
     "You are priest forever.
          By my solemn word, my righteous king."

---

3. *Your people rally to battle.* It is at this point that the language of this psalm begins to be cryptic, a problem that will persist to the end of the poem. The literal sense of the Hebrew here (just two words) is "your-people acts-of-volunteering." But the noun *'am,* "people," and the verbal root *n-d-b,* "to volunteer," "to act nobly," in conjunction are associated with volunteering to do battle, as in the Song of Deborah, Judges 5:9. So this translation assumes an ellipsis with that general sense here.

    on the day your force assembles. The Hebrew says only "on the day of your force." Again, an ellipsis is assumed.

    holy mountains. The Masoretic text reads "holy majesties," *hadrey qodesh,* which sounds very odd in the Hebrew. But many manuscripts show *harerey qodesh,* "holy mountains," and the similar-looking letters *dalet* and *resh* are often switched in scribal transcription.

    from the womb of dawn. The second of the two nouns here in the Masoretic text, *mishḥar,* is doubtful in meaning. The translation follows the Septuagint in reading *mireḥem shaḥar,* "from the womb of dawn." A scribe may have inadvertently repeated the *mem* at the end of *reḥem* and at the beginning of *shaḥar* as well (an instance of dittography). The image is evidently of an army sallying forth at daybreak.

    yours is the dew of your youth. This somewhat mystifying phrase might refer to the fresh energy of a young king. Many manuscripts read "I gave you birth" instead of "your youth" (a difference only of vocalization), but this scarcely improves matters because the idea of giving birth to the king like (?) dew is puzzling.

4. *You are priest forever.* At least in the David story, there is some indication of combining the functions of king and priest, though later they would be clearly separated. Some interpreters imagine that this psalm actually refers to David.

    my righteous king. This could be a proper noun, Malchizedek, or a punning reference to that name. Malchizedek is the king priest of Jerusalem who participates in Abraham's victory over the alliance of eastern kings in Genesis 14:18.

5   The Master is at your right hand.
            On the day of His wrath He smashes kings.
6   He exacts judgment from the nations,
                fills the valleys with corpses,
                        smashes heads across the great earth.
7   From a brook on the way He drinks.
                Therefore He lifts up His head.

---

5. *On the day of His wrath He smashes kings.* In this celebration of the imagined military victory of the king, God appears as a warrior at the king's right hand, crushing the enemy.

6. *fills the valleys with corpses.* The cryptic Hebrew of the received text merely reads "filled with corpses" (*malei' gewiyot*). Something is clearly wrong with the text. The translation, following a suggestion of two ancient Greek versions, reads *milei' gei'ayot gewiyot*, "fills the valleys with corpses." The similarity of the Hebrew words for "valleys" and "corpses" may have led a scribe to skip the former in copying the text.

7. *From a brook on the way He drinks.* This is evidently an image of God as warrior pausing to drink during or after hot pursuit of the enemy.

III

Hallelujah.

א   I acclaim the LORD with full heart
ב   in the council of the upright and the assembly.
ג   Great are the deeds of the LORD,   2
ד   discovered by all who desire them.

---

1. *Hallelujah.* Although scholars often classify this as a psalm of thanksgiving, it is more accurate to call it a psalm of praise because it is a list of God's provident attributes rather than an expression of gratitude over a particular act of benevolence, such as being saved from a grave illness. In keeping with this recitation of divine attributes, the psalm is framed as an alphabetic acrostic (one of eight in the Psalter)—in all likelihood as an aid to memory, though it is possible that the twenty-two letters of the Hebrew alphabet were also thought of as a manifestation of comprehensiveness. This and the next psalm in sequence are Short Acrostics: Instead of one line of poetry for each letter, each half line, or verset, begins with a different letter of the alphabet in sequence. (By way of contrast, Psalm 119 is a Long Acrostic, with eight lines of poetry for each letter of the alphabet.) Most of the lines begin with either a noun or an adjective exhibiting the appropriate alphabetical character in its initial letter, and this translation mirrors that syntactic "fronting." For example, in the Hebrew we have *Gedolim maʿsey* YHWH (*gimel,* "Great are the deeds of the LORD"); *Derushim lekhol heftseyhem* (*dalet,* "discovered by all who desire them"); *Hod wehadar poʿolo* (*heh,* "Glory and grandeur His acts").

the council of the upright and the assembly. The first term suggests an elite group, the second a larger convocation.

2. *who desire them.* The Masoretic text reads "their desires." The translation revocalizes the word as *ḥafeitseyhem,* "those who desire them."

3	Glory and grandeur His acts	ה
	and His bounty stands for all time.	ו
4	A remembrance He made of His wonders,	ז
	gracious and merciful the LORD.	ח
5	Sustenance He gives to those who fear Him,	ט
	He recalls forever His pact.	י
6	The power of His deeds He told His people,	כ
	to give them the nations' estate.	ל
7	His handiwork, truth and justice,	מ
	trustworthy all His precepts,	נ
8	Staunch for all time, forever,	ס
	fashioned in truth and right.	ע
9	Redemption He sent to His people,	פ
	forever commanded His pact.	צ
	Holy and awesome His name.	ק
10	The beginning of wisdom—the fear of the LORD,	ר
	good knowledge to all who perform it.	ש
	His praise stands for all time.	ת

---

3. *His acts.* The Hebrew uses a singular.

6. *The power of His deeds He told His people.* The second verset of this line suggests that the "telling" consists of God's giving land to His people.

8. *right.* This word in the Hebrew, *yashar*, is vocalized as though it meant
"upright," an adjectival form, but some manuscripts read, more plausibly,
yosher, the noun "right."

10. *The beginning of wisdom—the fear of the LORD.* This biblical commonplace
is a fitting end for this poem, which as a kind of doxology is little more than a
versification of standard formulas about God's greatness and His kindness to
His people.

112

Hallelujah.

א   Happy the man who fears the LORD.

ב   His commands he keenly desires.

ג   A great figure in the land his seed shall be,   2

ד   the generation of the upright shall be blessed.

ה   Abundance and wealth in his home,   3

ו   and his righteousness stands forever.

ז   Light dawns in darkness for the upright,   4

ח   gracious and merciful and just.

ט   Good is the man who shows grace and lends,   5

י   he sustains his words with justice.

כ   For he shall never stumble,   6

ל   an eternal remembrance the just man shall be.

---

1. *Happy the man.* Like the previous psalm, this is a Short Acrostic, one letter of the Hebrew alphabet in sequence beginning each verset, or two to a line. As in Psalm 111, the last two lines, corresponding to verses 9 and 10, are triadic, thus incorporating three letters of the alphabet instead of two. As a result, in both psalms, we have ten lines of poetry, ten verses, for the twenty-two letters of the Hebrew alphabet. The initial formula, "Happy the man," announces this as a Wisdom psalm (compare Psalm 1). If Psalm 111 is a catalog of God's attributes of beneficence, this psalm is a catalog of the exemplary attributes of the virtuous person and the reward they will bring him. Given the subject, it is hardly surprising that the language is stereotypical.

2. *A great figure.* The Hebrew *gibor* usually means "warrior" or "hero," but in Ruth 2:1 it is used to designate Boaz as a prosperous landowner, and prosperity is immediately invoked at the beginning of the next line.

7   From evil rumor he shall not fear.   מ
      His heart is firm, he trusts in the LORD.   נ
8   His heart is staunch, he shall not fear,   ס
      till he sees the defeat of his foes.   ע
9   He disperses, he gives to the needy,   פ
      his righteousness stands forever.   צ
          His horn shall be raised in glory.   ק
10   The wicked man sees and is vexed,   ר
      he gnashes his teeth and he quails.   ש
          The desire of the wicked shall perish.   ת

---

7. *From evil rumor.* This is the counterpoint of the eternal remembrance in the previous line. The name of the good person is always mentioned for the good deeds he has done, even after he is dead. So it goes without saying that in his lifetime he has no reason to fear evil rumor.

8. *the defeat.* As elsewhere, this word is added in the translation to indicate what the elliptical Hebrew idiom implies.

10. *The wicked man sees and is vexed.* As in many Wisdom texts—again, compare Psalm 1—the wicked man is introduced as a neat foil in acts and fate to the prospering just man.
    quails. The literal sense of the Hebrew verb is "to melt" or "to dissolve."

113

Hallelujah.   1
  Praise, O servants of the LORD,
            praise the LORD's name.
  May the LORD's name be blessed   2
            now and forevermore.
  From the place the sun rises to where it sets,   3
            praised be the name of the LORD.
  High over all nations, the LORD,   4
            over the heavens His glory.
  Who is like the LORD our God,   5
            Who sits high above,

---

1. *Hallelujah.* This Hebrew imperative, which has become an English word, of course means "praise God." It is immediately picked up in the next Hebrew word of the psalm, *hallelu,* "Praise." This is the first of six psalms of praise collectively known as the *hallel* that are recited in synagogues during the festival service.

servants of the LORD. Many scholars imagine that this term designates a particular group of priests taking part in the temple service, although that identification is not certain. The phrase could be a general one for the faithful Israelites assembled to celebrate the cult.

3. *From the place the sun rises to where it sets.* This spatial indication, from east to west, follows the temporal indication of the preceding verset, "now and forevermore." Both in time and space, God's praise extends between all conceivable limits. The next line then complements the horizontal extension of God's greatness with a vertical extension, "High over all nations."

6   Who sees down below
                in the heavens and on the earth?

7   He raises the poor from the dust,
                from the dungheap lifts the needy,

8   to seat him among princes,
                among the princes of his people.

9   He seats the barren woman in her home
                a happy mother of sons.
                Hallelujah.

---

6. *in the heavens and on the earth.* The evident image is that God is above the visible heavens ("over the heavens His glory"), looking down on them and on the earth far below them. His "sitting" high above suggests being seated on a throne, a meaning of the verb that is also activated in verse 8.

7. *the dust, / . . . the dungheap.* This is a neat illustration of the operation of intensification in poetic parallelism. The poor dwell not only in a lowly state, in the dust, but in a place where refuse is piled up, yet even from there God will raise them up.

9. *He seats the barren woman in her home.* The literal sense of the Hebrew is "He seats the barren woman of the house." There is a further play here on the causative verb "to seat," *hoshiv.* Just as God seats, or enthrones, the needy among princes. He seats, or ensconces, the barren woman in her home as a happy mother of sons. Given the gender divisions of biblical society, it is not surprising that the woman is accorded her triumphant fulfillment within the house, as childbearer, whereas the man is elevated to a position of political pre-eminence in the public realm, among princes.

114

When Israel came out of Egypt,
>> the house of Jacob from a barbarous-tongued folk,   1
Judah became His sanctuary,   2
>> Israel His dominion.

---

1. *When Israel came out of Egypt.* It is unusual for a biblical poem to begin in
this way with a subordinate clause (doubled, with the verb elided, in the second verset), given the strong predominance of parallel independent clauses
(parataxis) in this body of literature. It is a strategy for sweeping us up from the
beginning of the poem in a narrative momentum that invokes but also goes
beyond the story of the exodus. In a famous letter to Can Grande once attributed to Dante, this psalm is used to illustrate the fourfold levels of interpreting
a sacred text (literal, allegorical, moral, and anagogical or mystic). James Joyce
picked up, in a vein of serious parody, the purportedly Dantean view of this
psalm, quoting Psalm 114 in Latin in *Ulysses*. The original intention of the
psalmist, however, seems clearly literal—which is to say, historical—a celebration of God's spectacular intervention in history on behalf of the people of
Israel.

a barbarous-tongued folk. The Hebrew *lo'ez* corresponds exactly to the Greek
term from which "barbarous" and "barbaric" are derived. Both indicate the
utterance of unintelligible sounds instead of the articulate speech of a civilized
people. This notion that the anguish of oppression is sharpened by the fact that
the oppressor speaks an unintelligible language appears in a number of biblical
texts, from Deuteronomy to the Prophets.

2. *Judah became His sanctuary.* The Hebrew term represented as "sanctuary,"
qodesh, also has the more general meaning of "holiness." When Judah becomes
God's covenanted people, it is henceforth the vehicle or the place of abode of
God's holiness.

3 The sea saw and fled,
    Jordan turned back.
4 The mountains danced like rams,
    hills like lambs of the flock.
5 What is wrong with you, sea, that you flee,
    Jordan, that you turn back,
6 mountains, that you dance like rams,
    hills like lambs of the flock?
7 Before the Master, whirl, O earth,
    before the God of Jacob,

---

3. *The sea saw and fled, / Jordan turned back.* This compact line is a powerful telescoping of two different events linked typologically in biblical narrative but separated by forty years. The first is the parting of the Sea of Reeds, in this poetic version a consequence of the sea's terror before the awesome presence of God and not as a result of Moses's stretching out his staff over the sea. The second event is the dividing of the Jordan, recounted in Joshua, so that the Israelites could cross over. If there is some recollection here of the mythic conquest of the primordial sea monster (also called *yam,* "sea"), it is no more than a distant allusion in this historical context.

5. *What is wrong with you.* The poetic strategy here is unusual—a verbatim repetition of the two previous lines, merely recast as rhetorical questions that register the extraordinary disruption of the order of nature in God's miraculous intervention.

7. *Before the Master, whirl, O earth.* One proposed emendation eliminates the verb and reads "before the Master of all the earth." The emendation, motivated by the formulaic smoothness of the "corrected" version, seems unnecessary. The imperative verb here picks up the imagery of dancing and fleeing from the previous lines. The Hebrew verb *ḥul* could mean "tremble" or "dance," and the choice of "whirl" in the translation is an attempt to convey both these senses.

Who turns the rock to a pond of water,
      flint to a spring of water.

8

---

8. *rock to a pond of water, / flint to a spring of water.* The obvious reference is to Moses's drawing water from the rock in Exodus 17. In keeping with a common pattern of biblical poetry, we move from the general term "rock" in the first verset to a heightened equivalent, the extreme hardness of "flint," in the second verset. The concluding line focuses an underlying development in this psalm: First water fled, then the hills and mountains danced, and now hard rock, through the metamorphic power of God's overwhelming presence, turns into water. At least two contemporary interpreters have detected—in the Hebrew of the last line—sound play on the beginning of the poem: from *mitsrayim,* "Egypt," to *tsur / mayim,* "rock / water."

115

1   Not to us, O Lord, not to us
        but to Your name give glory
                for Your kindness and Your steadfast truth.
2   Why should the nations say,
            "Where is their god?"
3   when our God is in the heavens—
            all that He desired He has done.
4   Their idols are silver and gold,
            the handiwork of man.
5   A mouth they have but they do not speak,
                eyes they have but they do not see.

2–3. *Why should the nations say, / "Where is their god?" / when our God is in the heavens.* These lines lay the grounds for the polemic against idolatry in verses 4–8. The nations, accustomed to the idea that every deity is represented by carved images, mockingly question the existence of the imageless God of Israel, to which the psalmist rejoins that the true God is not visible because He resides in the heavens, a vantage point from which He exerts absolute power ("all that He desired He has done"). The idea that this psalm goes on to develop of idols as mere impotent chunks of matter has a marked kinship with the polemic against idolatry of Deutero-Isaiah, the prophet of the Babylonian exile. Most scholars in fact place the composition of this text in the Second Temple period.

5. *A mouth they have.* The syntactic positioning of all these body parts at the beginning of a sequence of versets sharpens the polemic edge of these lines. The shape of the idols is anthropomorphic, but the idols, sheer inert stuff, have none of the capacities of sentient life, making those who worship them ridiculous.

Ears they have but they do not hear,   6
     a nose they have but they do not smell.
Their hands—but they do not feel;   7
     their feet—but they do not walk;
          they make no sound with their throat.
Like them may be those who make them,   8
     all who trust in them.
O Israel, trust in the LORD,   9
     their help and their shield is He.
House of Aaron, O trust in the LORD,   10
     their help and their shield is He.
You who fear the LORD, trust in the LORD,   11
     their help and their shield is He.
The LORD recalls us, may He bless,   12
     may He bless the house of Israel,
          may He bless the house of Aaron.
May He bless those who fear the LORD,   13
     the lesser with the great.

---

8. *Like them may be those who make them.* This statement takes the form of a curse: May the idol worshippers turn to lifeless wood and stone like the objects they have fashioned.

9. *O Israel.* Beginning at this point, the psalm provides a series of indications of its liturgical nature. Different groups of celebrants in the temple rite are enjoined to trust in the LORD: the general community ("Israel"), the priests and Levites ("the house of Aaron"), and what may be a distinct third group ("those who fear the LORD")—the early rabbis identified these as proselytes, a possibility not to be excluded in the Second Temple period.

12. *may He bless.* As is appropriate for this sort of liturgical text, the concluding section of the psalm is devoted to the invocation of blessings on the community of worshippers.

14 May the LORD grant you increase,
          both you and your children.
15 Blessed are you by the LORD,
          maker of heaven and earth.
16 The heavens are heavens for the LORD,
          and the earth He has given to humankind.
17 The dead do not praise the LORD
          nor all who go down into silence.
18 But we will bless Yah
          now and forevermore,
                    hallelujah.

---

16. *The heavens are heavens for the* LORD, / *and the earth He has given to humankind.* This line picks up the idea put forth in verse 3: God is enthroned above in the heavens but has bestowed the realm of earth to humankind for its enjoyment and fulfillment.

17. *The dead do not praise the* LORD. The view of this late poem remains faithful to the outlook of earlier biblical literature: There is only one life, here and now, and it should be used to celebrate God's greatness. This ending completes a vertical cosmological picture: God above in the heavens; humankind on earth; and still farther below, the realm of death, which is a place of eternal silence, where none can sing or praise.

116

I love the LORD, for He has heard
        my voice, my supplications.
For He has inclined His ear to me
        when in my days I called.
The cords of death encircled me—
        and the straits of Sheol found me—
          distress and sorrow did I find.
And in the name of the LORD I called.
        "LORD, pray, save my life."
Gracious the LORD and just,
        and our God shows mercy.
The LORD protects the simple.
        I plunged down, but me He did rescue.

1   2   3   4   5   6

---

1. *I love the* LORD. The Hebrew syntax is a little odd because "the LORD," YHWH, comes at the end of the verset. This word order makes possible a different construction, "I love when the LORD hears," but that is not a characteristic sentiment of Psalms. In any case, the LORD's hearing a plea announces this as a thanksgiving psalm.

2. *when in my days I called.* An emendation, warranted by one ancient translation, yields "on the day I called," which sounds more idiomatic.

3. *The cords of death encircled me.* This line may be an indication that the speaker has recovered from a near fatal illness. But in Psalm 18:5, a similar formulation refers to danger in battle.

7   Return, my being, to your calm,
          for the LORD has requited you.

8   For You freed me from death,
          my eyes from tears,
              my foot from slipping.

9   I shall walk before the LORD
          in the lands of the living.

10   I trusted, though I did speak—
          Oh, I was sorely afflicted—

11   I in my rashness said,
          "All humankind is false."

12   What can I give back to the LORD
          for all He requited to me?

13   The cup of rescue I lift
          and in the name of the LORD I call.

---

7. *Return, my being, to your calm.* The speaker seems to be exhorting himself to return to a condition of tranquility after the agitation of the terrible dangers from which he has escaped.

9. *I shall walk before the LORD.* This idiom has a double meaning: to walk about and to perform service. The speaker, restored to life, will do both.

10. *I trusted.* The implied object of the verb is in all likelihood God. The seeming contradiction of the utterance is not difficult to follow: The speaker, in his moment of desperation, rashly declared that all men were false, but even then, he never entirely abandoned his trust in God's goodness.

12. *What can I give back to the LORD.* There is no adequate return that he can offer God, but at least he can participate in the ritual of thanksgiving, which is spelled out in the next two verses.

13. *The cup of rescue.* Given the cultic setting, this in all likelihood refers to the cup from which libation is poured on the altar. It is a "cup of rescue" because the libation expresses the celebrant's thanks for having been rescued by God.

My vows to the LORD I shall pay 14
     in the sight of all His people.
Precious in the eyes of the LORD 15
     is the death of His faithful ones.
I beseech You, LORD, 16
     for I am Your servant.
I am Your servant, Your handmaiden's son.
     You have loosed my bonds.
To You I shall offer a thanksgiving sacrifice 17
     and in the name of the LORD I shall call.
My vows to the LORD I shall pay 18
     in the sight of all His people,
in the courts of the house of the LORD, 19
     in the midst of Jerusalem.
       Hallelujah.

---

14. *My vows to the LORD I shall pay.* These are vows to offer the thanksgiving sacrifice, as verse 17 makes clear.

19. *in the courts of the house of the LORD.* The reference, of course, is to the courts of the temple that the worshipper enters to offer the thanksgiving sacrifice before the assembled people.

    in the midst of. The suffix of the preposition could be either a poetic form of the construct state, indicating "of," or a second-person singular feminine ending ("in your midst, O Jerusalem"). An apostrophe to the city does not seem characteristic of the rhetorical stance of this poem, or of Psalms in general, so the construct state is more likely.

117

1   Praise the LORD, all nations;
            extol Him, all peoples.
2   For His kindness overwhelms us,
            and the LORD's steadfast truth is forever.
                    Hallelujah.

---

1. *Praise the LORD.* This succinct poem amounts to a kind of zero-degree psalm of thanksgiving. Just two verses long, it is not only the shortest psalm in the collection but also the shortest chapter in the Bible. No specific details of God's beneficence are offered, only the great measure of His kindness and steadfast truth.

all nations . . . all peoples. The one element of difference in this thanksgiving psalm is that not Israel but all nations are enjoined to praise the God of Israel. The occasion for gratitude, then, is collective rather than individual: God has overwhelmed Israel by keeping faith with His commitment to His people. One could easily imagine that such a concise psalm of thanksgiving might have been composed to celebrate the restoration of the cult in the rebuilt temple, but the evidence is far too scanty to make any confident identification of this sort.

118

Acclaim the LORD, for He is good,
          forever is His kindness.
Let Israel now say:
          forever is His kindness.
Let the house of Aaron now say:
          forever is His kindness.
Let those who fear the LORD now say:
          forever is His kindness.
From the straits I called to Yah.
          Yah answered me in a wide-open place.
The LORD is for me, I shall not fear.
          What can humankind do to me?

1
2
3
4
5
6

---

1. *Acclaim the* LORD. The initial word, "acclaim" (or "give thanks to") marks the generic identity of the poem as a thanksgiving psalm. Some of its segments seem disjunct with others, and there are medieval manuscripts that divide this text into as many as five different psalms.

2. *Let Israel now say.* As in Psalm 115, this repeated formula reflects a liturgical script involving three different groups—Israel, the house of Aaron, and those who fear the LORD—that are here formally called upon (perhaps by a chorus leader) to recite the refrain "forever is His kindness."

5. *From the straits I called to Yah.* This particular formula is the language of a personal thanksgiving psalm that sounds rather different from the liturgical invocation of verses 1–4. "Yah" is, according to the consensus of biblical scholars, a shortened variant of Yahweh, though it could conceivably be a separate, perhaps archaic name for the deity assimilated with Yahweh by folk etymology.

7   The LORD is for me among my helpers,
         and I shall see the defeat of my foes.
8   Better to shelter in the LORD
         than to trust in humankind.
9   Better to shelter in the LORD
         than to trust in princes.
10 All the nations surrounded me.
         With the LORD's name I cut them down.
11 They swarmed round me, oh they surrounded me.
         With the LORD's name I cut them down.
12 They swarmed round me like bees,
         burned out like a fire among thorns.
              With the LORD's name I cut them down.
13 You pushed me hard to knock me down,
         but the LORD helped me.
14 My strength and my might is Yah,
         and He has become my rescue.

---

7. *the defeat.* As elsewhere, this object of the verb is merely implied in the Hebrew.

8. *Better to shelter in the LORD.* This and the next line are cast in a formulation typical of biblical proverbs ("better *x* than *y*").

10. *All the nations surrounded me.* Now the plight from which the speaker has been rescued is expressed in military terms. The "I" thus might be the king, though it is also possible that the image of battling armies is a metaphor for some other kind of distress.

I cut them down. The exact meaning of the Hebrew verb *'amilam* is uncertain. This translation follows a widely adopted guess that it is derived from the root *mol*, which in a different conjugation means "to circumcise."

13. *to knock me down.* The literal sense is simply "to fall."

A voice of glad song and rescue   15
        in the tents of the just:
                The Lord's right hand does valiantly.
The Lord's right hand is raised,   16
        the Lord's right hand does valiantly.
I shall not die but live   17
        and recount the deeds of Yah.
Yah harshly chastised me   18
        but to death did not deliver me.
Open for me the gates of justice—   19
        I would enter them, I would acclaim Yah.
This is the gate of the Lord—   20
        the just will enter it.
I acclaim You for You have answered me,   21
        and You have become my rescue.
The stone that the builders rejected   22
        has become the chief cornerstone.

---

15. *A voice of glad song.* It is also possible to construe the initial Hebrew word *qol* not as a noun but as an interjection meaning "Hark!"

the just. Throughout this section, *tsadiq*, "just," and *tsedeq*, "justice," could also mean, respectively, "victorious" and "victory." The military context might argue for that meaning, but because in the theology of Psalms God vindicates the just and makes them triumph, the other meaning of the root makes at least as good sense. It is perhaps more likely that the temple gates were thought of as the gates of justice than as the gates of victory, but one cannot be certain about this.

17. *I shall not die but live / and recount the deeds of Yah.* This line picks up in a positive affirmation the recurrent idea in Psalms that only the living can praise God, and that such praise is the true vocation of living men and women.

22. *The stone that the builders rejected.* This metaphor has a metonymic trigger: The speaker, having entered the temple gates and now standing within the courts of the resplendent building, compares himself in his former abject state to a stone at first considered unfit by the builders but then made the chief cornerstone of a grand edifice.

23 From the LORD did this come about—
                    it is wondrous in our eyes.
24 This is the day the LORD has wrought.
                    Let us exult and rejoice in it.
25 We beseech You, LORD, pray, rescue.
                    We beseech You, LORD, make us prosper.
26 Blessed who comes in the name of the LORD.
                    We bless you from the house of the LORD.
27 The LORD is God and He shines upon us.
                    Bind the festive offering with ropes
                            all the way to the horns of the altar.
28 You are my God, and I acclaim You,
                    my God, and I exalt You.
29 Acclaim the LORD, for He is good,
                    forever is His kindness.

---

25. *We beseech You, LORD.* These words of prayer for divine favor, expressed from a communal point of view, mark still another distinct segment of this psalm.
    make us prosper. "Us" is merely implied in the Hebrew.

26. *Blessed who comes in the name of the LORD.* These words, too, sound as though they may have served a formal ceremonial purpose in the temple ritual. A group—perhaps of Levitical choristers—standing within the temple, "the house of the LORD," intones a blessing to the celebrants who are approaching the altar.

27. *He shines upon us.* This is probably an ellipsis for "shines His face upon us."
    Bind the festive offering with ropes. The offering is, of course, an animal that is about to be slaughtered on the altar.
    the horns of the altar. Israelite and Canaanite altars were fashioned with carved horns—perhaps symbols of strength—at their four corners.

28. *You are my God, and I acclaim You, / my God, and I exalt You.* The Hebrew uses two different designations for God—first *'el*, then *'elohim*.

29. *Acclaim the LORD.* It is in keeping with the liturgical nature of this psalm as a hymn of celebration that it uses the identical line at the beginning and at the end as a refrain.

119

א   Happy whose way is blameless,   1
              who walk in the LORD's teaching.

---

1. *Happy whose way is blameless.* The first Hebrew word, *'ashrey*, with an initial *aleph* marks the beginning of what we may call the Long Acrostic—an alphabetic acrostic in which each of the twenty-two letters of the Hebrew alphabet begins eight lines of poetry. The result is the longest psalm in the collection and the longest chapter in the Hebrew Bible, 176 verses or lines of poetry. Perhaps this extravagant mnemonic was deemed appropriate because of the manifestly didactic nature of the poem. The edifying truth of unflagging loyalty to God's word was intended to be inculcated in those who recited the text, inscribed in their memory.

way . . . teaching. Both these terms—the "way" as an image of the right ordering of life (and the psalm uses three synonyms for it) and "teaching," *torah*—are characteristic of Wisdom literature. It is not entirely certain whether *torah* refers to an actual book or simply to God's instruction to man, though there is some likelihood that the former sense may be used here. This stress on *torah* suggests that the psalm was composed after the promulgation of Deuteronomy in 621 BCE, and many scholars date this text to the post-exilic period. Given both the eightfold acrostic and the didactic purpose, it is understandable that the psalm should swarm with synonyms—*torah*, *ʿedut* ("precept"), *piqudim* ("decrees"), *'imrah* ("utterance"), *davar* ("word"), *ḥoq* ("statute"), *mishpat* ("law"). In this poetic context, the terms appear to overlap and not to express technical distinctions. One must concede that the poetic language is highly formulaic and rather routine, though occasionally a striking line appears (for example, verse 54, "Songs were Your statutes to me, / in the house of my sojourning," or the unusual simile for suffering of a leather water skin cured over a smoking fire in verse 83, "I was like a skin-flask in smoke"). It also should be said that some of the acrostic composition is mechanical. The most egregious instance is the letter *waw*,

2   Happy who keep His precepts,
           with a whole heart they seek Him.

3   Yes, they did no wrong,
           in His ways they have walked.

4   You ordained Your decrees
           to be strictly observed.

5   Would that my ways be firm
           to observe Your statutes.

6   Then I would not be shamed
           when I look upon all Your commands.

7   I shall acclaim You with an honest heart
           as I learn Your righteous laws.

8   Your statutes I shall observe.
           Do not utterly forsake me.

9   How shall a lad make his path worthy   ב
           to observe as befits Your word.

10   With all my heart I sought You.
           Make me not stray from Your commands.

11   In my heart I kept Your utterance
           so that I would not offend against You.

---

which is also the Hebrew particle that means "and." There are very few other Hebrew words that begin with this letter (in the biblical corpus, no more than three), so the poet simply begins each of the eight lines of the *waw* stanza with "and." Because of the repetitiousness and the use of stereotypical language, the brief comments that follow do not engage in poetic analysis and mainly are limited to explaining difficulties in the text. The lines are rhythmically compact, usually having three accented syllables in the first verset and two in the second. The translation tries wherever possible to replicate this rhythm, though often there is one extra accent in the English.

9. *a lad.* This somewhat surprising term probably reflects the Wisdom character of the psalm. At a number of points in Proverbs, a "lad" or an innocent young man needing instruction in the ways of the world is introduced.

Blessed are You, O Lord.   12
    Teach me Your statutes.
With my lips I recounted   13
    all the laws You pronounced.
I rejoiced in the way of Your precepts   14
    as over all kinds of wealth.
Let me dwell on Your decrees   15
    and let me look upon Your paths.
In Your statutes I delight,   16
    I shall not forget Your word.

ג Requite Your servant—I shall live,   17
    and let me observe Your word.
Unveil my eyes that I may look   18
    upon the wonders of Your teaching.
A sojourner am I in the land.   19
    Do not hide from me Your commands.
I pine away desiring   20
    Your laws in every hour.
You blast the cursed arrogant   21
    who stray from Your commands.
Take away from me scorn and disgrace   22
    for Your precepts I have kept.

---

18. *Unveil my eyes that I may look / upon the wonders of Your teaching.* Throughout the psalm, the speaker not only affirms his adherence to God's teaching but prays for the capacity to understand it. This desire for insight may suggest that what is at issue is a text to be read and interpreted.

19. *A sojourner am I in the land.* This could also be rendered as "A sojourner am I on earth." In any case, the idea is that the speaker's existence is transient and vulnerable, and therefore he needs the guide of God's commands to show him how to make his way through his fleeting life.

20. *I pine away.* The verb *garas* occurs only here in the biblical corpus; hence the meaning is conjectural, though backed by scholarly consensus.

23 Even when princes sat to scheme against me,
        Your servant dwelled on Your statutes.
24 Yes, Your precepts are my delight,
        my constant counselors.

25 My being cleaves to the dust.   ד
        Give me life as befits Your word.
26 My ways I recounted and You answered me.
        Teach me Your statutes.
27 The way of Your decrees let me grasp,
        that I may dwell on Your wonders.
28 My being dissolves in anguish.
        Sustain me as befits Your word.
29 The way of lies remove from me,
        and in Your teaching grant me grace.
30 The way of trust I have chosen.
        Your laws I have set before me.
31 I have clung to Your precepts.
        O Lord, do not shame me.
32 On the way of Your commands I run,
        for You make my heart capacious.

---

24. *my constant counselors.* The literal sense of the Hebrew is "the men of my counsel."

32. *You make my heart capacious.* The poet clearly refers here to the biblical notion of the heart as the seat of understanding.

ה   Instruct me, LORD, in the way of Your statutes,   33
        that I may keep it without fail.
     Give me insight that I may keep Your teaching   34
        and observe it with a whole heart.
     Guide me on the track of Your commands,   35
        for in it I delight.
     Incline my heart to Your precepts   36
        and not to gain.
     Avert my eyes from seeing falsehood.   37
        Through Your ways give me life.
     Fulfill for Your servant Your utterance,   38
        which is for those who fear You.
     Avert my disgrace that I feared,   39
        for Your laws are good.
     Look, I have desired Your decrees.   40
        In Your bounty give me life.

ו   And let Your favors befall me, LORD,   41
        Your rescue as befits Your utterance,
     that I may give answer to those who taunt me,   42
        for I have trusted in Your word.
     And do not take the least word of truth from my mouth,   43
        for I have hoped for Your laws.
     And let me observe Your teaching always,   44
        forevermore.

---

33. *without fail.* The Hebrew word ʿeqev has puzzled interpreters. As a noun it means "heel." As a subordinate conjunction, it means "because" or "in consequence" (probably because the heel is an image of following after something). The word appears to serve here as an adverb, so it might have the sense of acting consequentially or without fail.

43. *the least word of truth.* The Hebrew says literally, "a word of truth very much."

45 And let me walk about in an open space,
      for Your decrees I have sought.
46 And let me speak of Your precepts
      before kings without being shamed.
47 And let me delight in Your commands
      that I have loved.
48 And let me lift up my palms to Your commands
      that I have loved, and dwell on Your statutes.

49 Recall the word to Your servant   ז
      for which You made me hope.
50 This is my consolation in my affliction,
      that Your utterance gave me life.
51 The arrogant mocked me terribly—
      from Your teaching I did not turn.
52 I recalled Your laws forever,
      O LORD, and I was consoled.
53 Rage from the wicked seized me,
      from those who forsake Your teaching.
54 Songs were Your statutes to me,
      in the house of my sojourning.
55 I recalled in the night Your name, O LORD,
      and I observed Your teaching.
56 This did I possess,
      for Your decrees I kept.

57 The LORD is my portion, I said,   ח
      to observe Your words.
58 I entreated You with a whole heart,
      grant me grace as befits Your utterance.

---

45. *in an open space*. This is the antithesis of the recurrent "straits," as in verse 143.

48. *lift up my palms*. As elsewhere, this is a gesture of prayer.

I have reckoned my ways,   59
    and turned back my feet to Your precepts.
I hastened, and did not linger,   60
    to observe Your commands.
The cords of the wicked ensnared me—   61
    Your teaching I did not forget.
At midnight I rose to acclaim You   62
    for Your righteous laws.
A friend am I to all who fear You,   63
    and to those who observe Your decrees.
With Your kindness, Lord, the earth is filled.   64
    Teach me Your statutes.

ט Good You have done for Your servant,   65
    O Lord, as befits Your word.
Good insight and knowledge teach me,   66
    for in Your commands I trust.
Before I was afflicted, I went astray,   67
    but now Your utterance I observe.
You are good and do good.   68
    Teach me Your statutes.
The arrogant plaster me with lies—   69
    I with whole heart keep Your decrees.
Their heart grows dull like fat—   70
    as for me, in Your teaching I delight.
It was good for me that I was afflicted,   71
    so that I might learn Your statutes.
Better for me Your mouth's teaching   72
    than thousands of pieces of silver and gold.

---

71. *It was good for me that I was afflicted.* This is, suffering impels reflection, which in turn leads the sufferer to embrace God's teaching as the guide to turning his life around.

73   Your hands made me and set me firm.   ʾ
                Give me insight, that I may learn Your commands.
74   Those who fear You see me and rejoice,
                for I hope for Your word.
75   I know, LORD, that Your laws are just,
                and in faithfulness You did afflict me.
76   May Your kindness, pray, console me,
                as befits Your utterance to Your servant.
77   May Your mercies befall me, that I may live,
                for Your teaching is my delight.
78   May the arrogant be shamed, for with lies they distorted my name.
                As for me, I shall dwell on Your decrees.
79   May those who fear You turn back to me,
                and those who know Your precepts.
80   May my heart be blameless in Your statutes,
                so that I be not shamed.

81   My being longs for Your rescue,   כ
                for Your word I hope.
82   My eyes pine for Your utterance,
                saying, "When will You console me?"
83   Though I was like a skin-flask in smoke,
                Your statutes I did not forget.
84   How many are the days of Your servant?
                When will You exact justice from my pursuers?
85   The arrogant have dug pitfalls for me,
                which are not according to Your teaching.

---

78. *distorted my name.* The Hebrew merely says "distorted me," which does not
work as an English idiom.

84. *How many are the days of Your servant?* The logic is similar to that repeatedly
invoked by Job: If my life is so brief, why does not God grant me justice before
it is over?

All Your commands are trustworthy,   86
      For no reason they pursued me—help me!
They nearly put an end to me on earth,   87
      yet I forsook not Your decrees.
As befits Your kindness give me life,   88
      that I may observe Your mouth's precept.

ל   Forever, O LORD,   89
      Your word stands high in the heavens.
For all generations Your faithfulness.   90
      You made the earth firm and it stood.
By Your laws they stand this day,   91
      for all are Your servants.
Had not Your teaching been my delight,   92
      I would have perished in my affliction.
Never shall I forget Your decrees,   93
      for through them You gave me life.
I am Yours, O rescue me,   94
      for Your decrees I have sought.
Me did the wicked hope to destroy.   95
      I gained insight from Your precepts.
For each finite thing I saw an end—   96
      but Your command is exceedingly broad.

מ   How I loved Your teaching.   97
      All day long it was my theme.

---

91. *By Your laws they stand.* The switch to the plural is slightly disorienting, but the implied antecedent is probably "all created things" or "heaven and earth."

98   Your command makes me wiser than my enemies,
        for it is mine forever.

99   I have understood more than all my teachers
        for Your precepts became my theme.

100   I gained insight more than the elders
        for Your decrees I kept.

101   From all evil paths I held back my feet,
        so that I might observe Your word.

102   From Your laws I did not swerve,
        for You Yourself instructed me.

103   How sweet to my palate Your utterance,
        more than honey to my mouth.

104   From Your decrees I gained insight,
        therefore I hated all paths of lies.

105   A lamp to my feet is Your word
        and a light to my path.

106   I swore and I will fulfill it—
        to observe Your just laws.

107   I have been sorely afflicted.
        O Lord, give me life, as befits Your word.

108   Accept my mouth's free offerings, Lord,
        and teach me Your laws.

109   My life is at risk at all times,
        yet Your teaching I do not forget.

110   The wicked set a trap for me,
        yet from Your decrees I did not stray.

111   I inherit Your precepts forever,
        for they are my heart's joy.

---

108. *my mouth's free offerings.* The reference is not to the voluntary pledge of a sacrifice but to the words of prayer, which serve instead of sacrifice.

109. *My life is at risk.* The literal sense of the Hebrew idiom is "my life is in my palm."

I inclined my heart to do Your statutes 112
    forever without fail.

ס   The perverted I hated 113
    and Your teaching I loved.
My shelter and shield are You. 114
    For Your word I have hoped.
Turn away from me, evildoers, 115
    that I may keep the commands of my God.
Support me as befits Your utterance, that I may live, 116
    and do not shame me in my expectation.
Uphold me that I may be rescued 117
    to regard Your statutes at all times.
You spurned all who stray from Your statutes, 118
    for their deception is but a lie.
Like dross You destroy all the earth's wicked; 119
    therefore I love Your precepts.
My flesh shudders from the fear of You, 120
    and of Your laws I am in awe.

ע   I have done justice and righteousness; 121
    do not yield me to my oppressors.
Vouch for Your servant for good. 122
    Let not the arrogant oppress me.
My eyes pined for Your rescue 123
    and for Your righteous utterance.
Do for Your servant as befits Your kindness 124
    and teach me Your statutes.

---

112. *without fail.* See the comment on this expression in verse 33.

119. *Like dross You destroy.* The Hebrew says simply "dross You destroy." Some scholars emend *hishbata*, "You destroyed," to *hashavta*, "You considered."

125   Your servant I am, grant me insight,
          that I may know Your precepts.

126   It is time to act for the LORD—
          they have violated Your teaching.

127   Therefore I love Your commands
          more than gold, and more than fine gold.

128   Therefore by all Your ordinances I walked a straight line.
          All paths of lies I have hated.

129   Wondrous Your precepts,
          therefore did I keep them.   פ

130   The portal of Your words sends forth light,
          makes the simple understand.

131   I opened my mouth wide and panted,
          for Your commands I craved.

132   Turn to me, grant me grace,
          as is fit for those who love Your name.

133   Make firm my footsteps through Your utterance,
          and let no wrongdoing rule over me.

134   Ransom me from human oppression,
          that I may observe Your statutes.

135   Shine Your face upon Your servant
          and teach me Your statutes.

---

126. *It is time to act for the* LORD— / *they have violated Your teaching.* The first clause might also be construed as, "It is time for the LORD to act." This entire verse became proverbial in Hebrew, though understandings of what it meant varied. One common if quite unlikely construction: In a time of emergency when one must act for the LORD, it is permissible to abrogate the Torah.

128. *I walked a straight line.* The Hebrew text, which may be doubtful at this point, says literally, "Therefore Your ordinances of all I made straight."

130. *The portal of Your words sends forth light.* Could Kafka have been remembering this verse when, in "Before the Law," he imagined the closed gate in the parable opening to reveal a brilliant light shining from within?

Streams of water my eyes have shed   136
    because men did not observe Your teaching.

א   Just are You, O LORD,   137
    and upright are Your laws.
You ordained Your just precepts,   138
    and they are most trustworthy.
My zeal devastated me,   139
    for my foes forgot Your words.
Your utterance is most pure,   140
    and Your servant has loved it.
Puny am I and despised,   141
    yet Your decrees I have not forgotten.
Your righteousness forever is right,   142
    and Your teaching is truth.
Straits and distress have found me—   143
    Your commands are my delight.
Right are Your precepts forever.   144
    Grant me insight that I may live.

ק   I called out with a whole heart.   145
    Answer me, LORD. Your statutes I would keep.
I called to You—rescue me,   146
    that I may observe Your precepts.
I greeted the dawn and cried out,   147
    for Your word did I hope.

---

136. *men did not observe.* The Hebrew says only "they," but "men" is introduced here to avoid the possibility that the plural pronoun might refer to "eyes" or even to "streams of water."

147. *greeted.* The Hebrew verb here, *qidem*, and also in verse 148, can equally mean "to anticipate," "to go before." Hence the King James Version renders it as "prevent," using that English verb with precisely this meaning, which is now obsolete.

148   My eyes greeted the night-watches
                 to dwell on Your utterance.
149   Hear my voice as befits Your kindness.
                 O Lord, as befits Your law, give me life.
150   The pursuers of the loathsome draw near,
                 from Your teaching they have gone far away.
151   You are near, O Lord,
                 and all Your commands are truth.
152   Of old I have known of Your precepts,
                 because You have fixed them forever.

153   See my affliction and free me,   ר
                 for Your teaching I have not forgotten.
154   Argue my cause and redeem me,
                 through Your utterance give me life.
155   Far from the wicked is rescue,
                 for Your statutes they have not sought.
156   Your mercies are great, O Lord,
                 as befits Your laws give me life.
157   Many are my pursuers and my foes,
                 yet from Your decrees I have not swerved.

---

148. *night-watches.* This verse and the preceding one present us, in reverse chronological order, the picture of a supplicant who spends the whole night in a prayer vigil that lasts till daybreak.

150. *The pursuers of the loathsome.* This phrase, given the different uses of the construct state in Hebrew, could mean either "those who pursue loathsome things" or "loathsome pursuers."

152. *Of old I have known of Your precepts.* The implicit idea is that God's precepts are built into the very order of creation ("because You have fixed them forever"). Rabbinic Judaism would develop out of such hints the concept of an eternal Torah that pre-existed creation.

I have seen traitors and quarreled with them,   158
        who did not observe Your utterance.
See that I love Your decrees.   159
        O Lord, as befits Your kindness give me life.
The chief of Your words is truth,   160
        and forever all Your righteous laws.

ש   Princes pursued me without cause,   161
        yet my heart has feared Your word.
I rejoice over Your utterance   162
        as one who finds great spoils.
Lies I have hated, despised.   163
        Your teaching I have loved.
Seven times daily I praised You   164
        because of Your righteous laws.
Great well-being to the lovers of Your teaching,   165
        and no stumbling-block for them.
I yearned for Your rescue, O Lord,   166
        and Your commands I performed.
I observed Your precepts   167
        and loved them very much.
I observed Your decrees and Your precepts,   168
        for all my ways are before You.

ת   Let my song of prayer come before You, Lord.   169
        As befits Your word, give me insight.

---

160. *The chief of Your words is truth.* Some understand this to mean "the first of Your words is truth."

169. *Let my song of prayer come before You.* These words, which initiate the last group of eight lines, each beginning with the letter *taw*, mark the concluding segment as a formal coda in which the speaker asks, in each of the eight lines, that God accept the prayer he has uttered in this psalm.

170   Let my supplication come before You,
                as befits Your utterance, save me.

171   Let my lips utter praise,
                for You taught me Your statutes.

172   Let my tongue speak out Your utterance,
                for all Your commands are just.

173   May Your hand become my help,
                for Your decrees I have chosen.

174   I desired Your rescue, O Lord,
                and Your teaching is my delight.

175   Let my being live on and praise You,
                and may Your laws help me.

176   I have wandered like a lost sheep.
                Seek Your servant, for Your commands I did not forget.

120

A song of ascents.   1

  To the LORD when I was in straits
          I called out and He answered me.

  LORD, save my life from lying lips,   2
          from a tongue of deceit.

  What can it give you, what can it add,   3
          a tongue of deceit?

---

1. *A song of ascents.* This is the first in a sequence of fifteen psalms that bear this heading. Most scholars assume that "ascents" refers to pilgrimages to Jerusalem. (The verb "ascend" or "go up" is the technical term used for pilgrimage.) But among other meanings that have been proposed, it could be a musical term, perhaps referring to an ascent in pitch or a crescendo in the song, or it could refer to the pattern of incremental repetition that is common to many of these poems. There are some linguistic indications that these psalms were composed in the Second Temple period, and one of them, Psalm 126, explicitly invokes the return to Zion.

   I called out and He answered me. These words are a formula for the thanksgiving psalm. Because the rest of the poem expresses the anguished plea of a beleaguered person, one must construe what follows as a full quotation of the speaker's "calling out" to God in his time of distress.

2. *lying lips, / . . . tongue of deceit.* This emphatic parallelism clearly indicates that the source of distress is that the speaker has been the target of malicious slander.

4   A warrior's honed arrows
            with broom-wood coals.

5   Woe to me for I have sojourned in Meshech,
            dwelt among the tents of Kedar.

6   Long has my whole being dwelt
            among those who hate peace.

7   I am for peace, but when I speak,
            they are for war.

---

4. *A warrior's honed arrows / with broom-wood coals*. At first glance, this line may seem to be a leap without transition, but in Psalms malicious speech is characteristically represented as a sharp arrow or sword. Broom wood was known to burn hot for a long time, even when the surface of the coals had turned to ash, so the image of intense burning complements the image of piercing arrows.

5. *Meshech . . . Kedar*. These are two far-flung locations. Meshech is to the extreme northwest in Asia Minor, between the Black Sea and the Caspian Sea (it is mentioned in the Table of Nations in Genesis 10:2). Kedar is to the southeast in the Arabian Peninsula. One might wonder about the history of peregrinations of the speaker, but because it seems unlikely that a single person would have sojourned in both these places, it may be plausible to understand them as metaphors for living among people who behave like strangers, even if those people were within a stone's throw of Jerusalem (as someone today might say, I felt as though I were living in Siberia or Timbuktu).

6. *those who hate peace*. The Masoretic text shows a singular noun here, but other Hebrew manuscripts, the Septuagint, and the Syriac have the more likely plural.

7. *I am for peace*. The Hebrew appears to say "I am peace," but, without emending the text, the most plausible way to understand these two words, *'ani shalom*, is that they function as though there were an elided "for" (in the Hebrew not a word but the particle *l^e*). This antithesis between peace and war at the end neatly picks up the idea that slander is a harmful weapon—piercing arrows and burning coals.

121

A song of ascents.   1
   I lift up my eyes to the mountains:
          from where will my help come?
   My help is from the Lord,   2
          maker of heaven and earth.
   He does not let your foot stumble.   3
          Your guard does not slumber.

---

1. *I lift up my eyes to the mountains: / from where will my help come?* Those scholars who think that the "songs of ascents" are psalms framed for pilgrims to
Jerusalem see here a specific reference to the mountains around Jerusalem and
imagine that the going and coming of the last line refer to the pilgrim's depar-
ture from Jerusalem after coming to the temple, to travel through the potentially dangerous Judean hill country. All this may be excessively specific. We
cannot be sure that these are actually pilgrimage psalms, and the resonant language of the poem is quite general: The speaker, fearful of unspecified dangers—of the sort that any person might encounter in life—looks up at the
mountains around him and wonders who or what will help him.

3. *He does not let your foot stumble.* From here to the end of the psalm, we have
what looks like a response to the question and affirmation of the speaker at the
beginning. The form of the psalm, then, untypically, would be a dialogue.
Adherents of the pilgrimage theory claim that the second speaker is a priest.

4   Look, He does not slumber nor does He sleep,
             Israel's guard.

5   The Lord is your guard,
             the Lord is your shade at your right hand.

6   By day the sun does not strike you,
             nor the moon by night.

7   The Lord guards you from all harm,
             He guards your life.

8   The Lord guards your going and your coming,
             now and forevermore.

---

4. *He does not slumber nor does He sleep.* The beautiful simplicity of the language of the psalm turns on cadenced repetition. The key word of assurance, "guard" (*shomer*), occurs six times in the eight lines of the poem. There is virtually no figurative language here, the sole exception being the lexicalized metaphor (hence a barely visible one) for protection, "shade," to which perhaps the stumbling of the foot might be added as a synecdoche for falling into danger. Without poetic ornamentation, the psalm becomes a moving expression of trust in God, using traditional language and patterned repetition.

6. *By day the sun does not strike you.* The dead metaphor of "shade" is resuscitated in this notion of protection from sunstroke, a real danger in the semi-desert climate of the Land of Israel.

    nor the moon by night. In all likelihood these words refer to the danger of being moonstruck, evidently thought to be a cause of madness in ancient Israel, as it has been imagined in many cultures.

7. *The Lord guards.* In a climactic pattern of asserted trust, three of the six repetitions of "guard" occur in the last two lines of the poem.

8. *now and forevermore.* This concluding reference to the eternality of God's protection completes an arc begun with the reference to creation at the beginning of the poem in the designation of God as "maker of heaven and earth."

122

A song of ascents for David. 1
  I rejoiced in those who said to me:
        "Let us go to the house of the Lord."
  Our feet were standing 2
        in your gates, Jerusalem.
  Jerusalem built like a town 3
        that is joined fast together,
  where the tribes go up, 4
        the tribes of Yah.

---

1. *Let us go to the house of the Lord.* These words are a clear indication that this is a psalm of Zion founded in the pilgrimage experience. But because many of the other "songs of ascents" do not refer to pilgrimage, whereas a good many other psalms do, this text provides no conclusive evidence that "ascents" means "pilgrimage."

2. *Our feet were standing / in your gates, Jerusalem.* As in other psalms of Zion, the liminal experience of crossing into the walled city, or into the temple precincts, is strongly marked.

3. *joined fast together.* The most probable reference is to the fortifications of Jerusalem or, specifically, to the protective wall that encloses it.

4. *where the tribes go up, / the tribes of Yah.* "Go up" is the technical verb for pilgrimage. Jerusalem as the locus of the central cult is envisaged here as the focus of national unity. All this makes it highly likely that this psalm was composed sometime after the centralization of the cult in Jerusalem by King Josiah around 621 BCE.

An ordinance it is for Israel
        to acclaim the name of the LORD.
5   For there the thrones of judgment stand,
        the thrones of the house of David.
6   Pray for Jerusalem's weal.
        May your lovers rest tranquil!
7   May there be well-being within your ramparts,
        tranquility in your palaces.
8   For the sake of my brothers and my companions,
        let me speak, pray, of your weal.
9   For the sake of the house of the LORD our God,
        let me seek your good.

---

5. *For there the thrones of judgment stand.* The Hebrew says, "For there the thrones of judgment sit," with the use of that verb perhaps encouraged by the fact that one sits on a throne. It is noteworthy that cultic centrality is here joined with the centralization of judicial authority—and, implicitly, of political authority as well—in the Davidic dynasty's capital. This is very much in line with Josiah's program.

6. *May your lovers rest tranquil!* The "your" is feminine singular in the Hebrew, clearly addressing Jerusalem, after the plural imperative of the first verset directed to the people. Such switches in pronominal reference are common in biblical Hebrew. The verb translated as "rest tranquil," *yishlayu*, richly alliterates with *yerushalayim*, "Jerusalem," and with *shalom*, "weal," "well-being," or "peace." The poet's repeated insistence in the concluding lines of the psalm on *shalom* is probably an etymological play on the name of the city.

7. *ramparts . . . palaces.* As in many lines of biblical poetry, there is a narrative progression from the first verset to the second—first the ramparts, then the palaces within them, following the path of the pilgrim coming up to the city.

123

A song of ascents.
  To You I lift up my eyes,
        O dweller in the heavens.
  Look, like the eyes of slaves to their masters,
        like the eyes of a slavegirl to her mistress,
  so are our eyes to the Lord our God
        until He grants us grace.
  Grant us grace, Lord, grant us grace.
        for we are sorely sated with scorn.

1

2

3

---

1. *To you I lift up my eyes.* This initial gesture of prayer of the psalm of supplication is cast in the first-person singular, but, as sometimes happens elsewhere, the psalm glides easily in the next verse from singular to plural, from individual to collective.

2. *like the eyes of slaves to their masters.* In the affecting simplicity of this compact psalm, virtually the only metaphor (one may exclude the weak metaphoric force of "sated" in verses 3 and 4) is this comparison with the abject dependency of the slave on his master.

  like the eyes of a slavegirl to her mistress. It is formulaic in the parallelism of biblical poetry that if *'eved* ("slave" or "servant") appears in the first verset, *shifḥah* or *'amah* ("slavegirl" or "handmaiden") appears in the second verset. Here, however, the extension to the other gender conveys a sense of inclusiveness: Everyone in this community, man and woman, looks urgently to God for a sign of grace.

4   Sorely has our being been sated
                with the contempt of the smug,
                      the scorn of the haughty.

---

4. *the contempt of the smug, / the scorn of the haughty.* Unlike other supplications, where the cause of the complaint is specified (slander, illegitimate lawsuits, schemes against the life of the speaker), all we are told here, at the end of the psalm, is that the collective supplicants have been treated with contempt by persons identified only as "the smug," "the haughty." A triadic line is used at the end as a marker of closure.

124

A song of ascents for David.   1
   Were it not the Lord Who was for us
         —let Israel now say—
   were it not the Lord Who was for us   2
         when people rose against us,
  then they would have swallowed us alive   3
         when their wrath flared hot against us.

---

1. *Were it not the Lord Who was for us / —let Israel now say.* The second of these two versets is a formal exhortation, probably on the part of a choral leader, to the community of worshippers to chant the words of the liturgical text that begins in the first verset and continues in verse 2 through to the end of the psalm. This is a collective thanksgiving psalm, though some of the language is drawn from the traditional formulations of individual thanksgiving psalms. The Hebrew, with its abundant use of incremental repetition, has a strong rhythmic character that would have lent itself to singing or chanting.

2. *when people rose against us.* The reference to "people" (or "humankind," *'adam*) is very general, though, given the collective viewpoint, the psalmist is surely thinking of national enemies. He could be alluding specifically to the Babylonian conquest of Judea and the exile of part of its population, though that is not certain.

4   Then the waters would have swept us up,
            the torrent come up past our necks.
5   Then it would have come up past our necks—
            the raging waters.
6   Blessed is the LORD,
            Who did not make us prey for their teeth.
7   Our life is like a bird escaped
            from the snare of the fowlers.
     The snare was broken
            and we escaped.
8   Our help is in the name of the LORD,
            maker of heaven and earth.

4–5. These two lines are an especially effective use of the emphatic structure of incremental repetition. Verse 4 displays semantic parallelism without verbal repetition in its two halves ("waters" / "torrent," "swept us up," / "come up past our necks." Then 5A repeats "come up past our necks" and 5B repeats "the waters" from 4A, adding the adjectival increment "raging" and so producing a climactic effect. Being engulfed by a raging torrent is a metaphor for near death picked up from the psalms of individual supplication and thanksgiving.

6. *prey for their teeth.* This switch from the metaphor of drowning to the metaphor of being consumed by a wild beast follows "they would have swallowed us alive" from verse 3.

7. *The snare was broken / and we escaped.* Although this line looks rather like a gloss on the simile of the previous line of verse, it is perfectly plausible that for a liturgical text to be chanted by the community, the poet wanted to spell things out.

8. *Our help is in the name of the* LORD, */ maker of heaven and earth.* This concluding line is quite close to Psalm 121:2, and in general some exchange of language is noticeable among the various songs of ascents. The imposition of "the name of the LORD" between God and Israel as a kind of mediation is a development that becomes progressively pronounced in the Second Temple period.

125

A song of ascents.
    Those who trust in the LORD
        are like Mount Zion never shaken,
          settled forever.
    Jerusalem, mountains around it,
        and the LORD is around His people
          now and forevermore.

---

1. *like Mount Zion never shaken, / settled forever.* This psalm, which, like the other songs of ascents, appears to have been composed in the exilic or immediately post-exilic period, expresses a national sense of trust in God despite the domination of an oppressive foreign power ("the rod of wickedness"). The Israelite community as a whole is represented as "the righteous." Jerusalem and the temple may have been laid waste by the Babylonian invaders, but the solid persistence of the mountain on which the city was built is a token of the perdurability of the people that made its capital on this mountain. Most translations render "settled" here as "endure," "stand," or "abide." Although, by a small stretch, the Hebrew verb *y-sh-b* could have that meaning, it is repeatedly used in the *qal* conjugation as here to mean "be settled" (see, among other examples, Joel 4:20, "and Judea will be settled [*teshev*, exactly as here] forever"). The point is that Mount Zion will not only stand solid forever but will continue to be a place of habitation, despite the exile of some of its population. The reference of this verb to those who trust in God is that they will dwell, be securely settled, forever.

2. *Jerusalem, mountains around it.* The encircling mountains convey a sense of protection as a kind of natural defensive perimeter.

3   For the rod of wickedness will not rest
               on the portion of the righteous,
    so that the righteous not set their hands
               to wrongdoing.

4   Do good, O Lord, to the good
               and to the upright in their hearts.

5   And those who bend to crookedness,
               may the Lord take them off with the wrongdoers.
               Peace upon Israel!

---

3. *the rod of wickedness.* The Hebrew noun *shevet* equally means "scepter," but the sense of punishing force may be the more relevant one here.

the portion of the righteous. The word for "portion," *goral*, is repeatedly used in Joshua and occasionally in Numbers for the division of the land according to the tribes. The portion of the territory of Judea may have been usurped by invaders, but this is not a condition that will persist.

so that the righteous not set their hands / to wrongdoing. The evident idea of this somewhat cryptic clause is that the righteous, deprived of the land that belongs to them, might be tempted to acts of lawlessness in their desperation, whether brigandism or some sort of imitation of the violent aliens who have oppressed them. It is notable that this psalm co-opts the language of the Wisdom psalms (the opposition of the righteous and the wicked) for national purposes.

126

A song of ascents.   1
  When the LORD restores Zion's fortunes,
        we should be like dreamers.
  Then will our mouth fill with laughter   2
        and our tongue with glad song.
  Then will they say in the nations:
        "Great things has the LORD done with these."
  Great things has the LORD done with us.   3
        We shall rejoice.

---

1. *Zion's fortunes.* The Hebrew *shivat* (ostensibly, "return," though in the King James Version and other translations rendered as "captivity") is a mistake for either *shevut* or *shevit* (as in verse 4), both attested to in various Hebrew manuscripts. The term means "previous condition." Precisely this idiom for the restoration of a previous condition is used at the end of Job (42:10). The English rendering of the term as "fortunes" is adopted from the New Jewish Publication Society translation.

2. *Then will our mouth fill with laughter.* Given the fluidity of verb tenses in biblical poetry, there is disagreement as to whether the verbs here and in what follows are to be understood as past or future. The prayer for the restoration of national fortunes in verse 4 is a strong argument that the fulfillment indicated here has yet to take place. (The interpretation proposed, among others, by Hans-Joachim Kraus—that the exiles have already returned from Babylonia but are now praying for the full restoration of the national home—seems strained.) The anticipated gladness, then, is imagined to be so intense that it would be like a dream—the realization, we might say, of a wish-fulfillment dream.

4   Restore, O Lord, our fortunes
                like freshets in the Negeb.

5   They who sow in tears
                in glad song will reap.

6   He walks along and weeps,
                the bearer of the seed-bag.
    He will surely come in with glad song
                bearing his sheaves.

---

4. *like freshets in the Negeb.* This is a familiar detail of topography and climate invoked elsewhere in biblical poetry. The reference is to wadis, or dry water gulches, that with the onset of the rainy season are filled with streams of water. It is an apt image for restoring the previous condition of a desolate Zion, and the idea of rushing water after aridity prepares the ground for the image of sowing and reaping in the last two verses of the psalm.

5. *They who sow in tears / in glad song will reap.* The long cycle of the agricultural year, beginning in the labor of planting and concluding with the fulfillment of the harvest, is an eloquent metaphor for a structure of historical time that moves from a difficult present to a happy future. That idea of reversal through time is neatly reinforced by the tight antithetical chiasm of the line: a ("sow"), b ("in tears"), b́ ("in glad song"), á ("reap"). The term *rinah,* "glad song," is the thematic thread that ties the psalm together, appearing in verse 2, here, and again in verse 6. It is as though this psalm, a prayer for national restoration that is presumably sung or chanted, were striving to turn into glad song.

6. *He walks along . . . / He will surely come in.* The effectiveness of these two concluding lines of the poem, with their neat interlinear antithetical parallelism, is in the unadorned directness of the parallel syntactic-semantic structure, and it seems a mistake to convert the lines into explanatory subordinate syntax (for example, by placing a "though" at the beginning of verse 6, as several modern translations do). Rather, we are invited to envisage two coordinate images, separated in time and precisely antithetical in meaning: "He walks along" (*halokh yelekh*), then "He will surely come in" (*bo' yavo',* the same emphatic structure of infinitive followed by imperfective verb). "Come in" refers to coming in from the fields after binding the sheaves of grain.

127

A song of ascents for Solomon.   1
  If the Lord does not build a house,
            in vain do its builders labor on it.
  If the Lord does not watch over a town,
            in vain does the watchman look out.
  In vain you who rise early, sit late,   2
            eaters of misery's bread.
                  So much He gives to His loved ones in sleep.

---

1. *for Solomon.* The ascription to Solomon probably is triggered by the reference to the building of a house at the beginning of the poem, "house" in Hebrew also being the term for the temple.

    build a house. The Hebrew *bayit* equally means "house" and "home." The emphasis in the second half of the psalm on progeny suggests that both senses of the word are in play here.

2. *sit late.* That is, sit to eat (an activity mentioned in the next verset) after a long day of labor. The idea of labor is picked up from verse 1.

    eaters of misery's bread. This Hebrew phrase, *leḥem ha'atsabim*, looks like an allusion to Genesis 3:17, "with pangs (*be'itsavon*) shall you eat of it [of the soil] all the days of your life."

    So much He gives to His loved ones in sleep. This whole verset is rather crabbed in the Hebrew. In the Masoretic text one finds a singular "loved one," though two manuscripts and the Septuagint and Syriac show a plural. The spelling of "sleep," *shena'*, with an *aleph* instead of a *heh* at the end, is odd, and the word lacks the prepositional prefix ("in") that one might expect. The somewhat conjectural meaning, which many interpreters propose, is that while people labor long and hard to earn their bread, God gives just as much to those He favors even while they sleep.

3   Look, the estate of the LORD is sons,
        reward is the fruit of the womb.
4   Like arrows in the warrior's hand,
        thus are the sons born in youth.
5   Happy the man
        who fills his quiver with them.
    They shall not be shamed
        when they speak with their enemies at the gate.

---

3. *sons.* The Hebrew *banim* can also mean "children" (as in the King James Version), but the martial imagery of the rest of the poem argues for the masculine sense of the term.

4. *Like arrows in the warrior's hand, / thus are the sons born in youth.* This line appears to reflect an idea that sons begotten when a man is young are especially vigorous—hence the simile of swiftly flying missiles—because their begetter is vigorous. (In Lamentations 3:13, "sons of his quiver" is a kenning for "arrows," and this verse may well be a play on that poetic formula.) The man who begets many sons in his youth creates the equivalent of a little army on which he can depend. In the social structure of ancient Israel, this may not have been an entirely fanciful notion. One might recall that David's original power base was in part a kind of family militia, led by his three nephews.

5. *They shall not be shamed / when they speak with their enemies at the gate.* Some scholars correct the plural verbs of the Masoretic text to the singular to make them refer to the man who has begotten all these sons. But because the gate was a place where one confronted attacking enemies, and because "to be shamed" is often linked in Psalms with military defeat, the more likely reference is to the brave sons parleying with the enemy and preparing, if necessary, to do battle.

128

A song of ascents.
   Happy all who fear the LORD,
        who walk in His ways.
When you eat of the toil of your hands,
        happy are you, and it is good for you.

1

2

---

1. *Happy all who fear the* LORD. As elsewhere, this initial formula signals the affiliation of this psalm with Wisdom literature (Psalm 1 once more is a useful point of reference). The rewards of the good life are spelled out here in an idyll of domesticity. The language is simple and direct; the only two metaphors, the vine and the young olive trees, link the family (evidently an urban family living in Jerusalem) with the world of productive horticulture. The Hebrew uses a singular subject from the beginning ("Happy everyone who fears . . ."), but the plural has been adopted in the translation for the sake of rhythm.

2. *When you eat of the toil of your hands.* This line stands in contrast to sundry biblical curses, such as those in Deuteronomy 28, that the people will toil and others will eat the fruit of their labor. It should be observed that the good life is not imagined in terms of wealth but of sufficiency—a man's enjoying the fruit of his own labor.

3   Your wife is like a fruitful vine
                    in the recesses of your house,
     your children like young olive trees
                    around your table.
4   Look, for it is thus
                    that the man is blessed who fears the LORD.
5   May the LORD bless you from Zion,
                    and may you see Jerusalem's good
                            all the days of your life.
6   And may you see children of your children.
                    Peace upon Israel!

---

3. *Your wife is like a fruitful vine / in the recesses of your house.* The vocation of the wife is to produce children, as this line and the next make clear. She is removed from the public sphere, in the "recesses" (*yarketayim,* a term for a secluded corner of the house not adequately represented by the conventional translation "within").

   olive trees. Like the vine, these are cultural symbols of fruitfulness, and the olive played a significant role in Israelite economy.

6. *may you see children of your children.* In a culture that did not envisage the persistence of a soul after death, perpetuity was imagined through offspring and was thought of as the greatest blessing. It is implied, of course, that the God-fearing man who is privileged to enjoy grandchildren as well as children will be granted the gift of longevity.

129

A song of ascents.

  Much they beset me from my youth
         —let Israel now say—
  much they beset me from my youth,
         yet they did not prevail over me.

2

  My back the harrowers harrowed,
         they drew a long furrow.

3

  The Lord is just.
         He has slashed the bonds of the wicked.

4

  May they be shamed and fall back,
         all the haters of Zion.

5

---

1. *Much they beset me from my youth.* The first-person language makes this initially sound like an individual complaint, but as the reference to "the haters of Zion" in verse 5 indicates, the first person is speaking on behalf of the nation, and the enemies referred to are probably the foreign oppressors who have conquered Judea.

    let Israel now say. As in Psalm 124:1, this interjection would be words of direction called out by the choral leader.

3. *harrowers . . . furrow.* This agricultural image for laceration and torment, vivid enough in itself, leads (moving chronologically from plowing to reaping) to the agricultural simile of the curse in verses 6–8.

6   May they be like the grass on rooftops
                 that the east wind withers,
7   with which no reaper fills his hand,
                 no binder of sheaves his bosom,
8   and no passers-by say, "The LORD's blessing upon you!
                 We bless you in the name of the LORD."

---

6. *like the grass on rooftops.* Grass uprooted to serve as thatch of course quickly withers.

that the east wind withers. The Masoretic text, *sheqadmat shalaf yavesh*, is opaque. One might translate it as "before it is pulled up it dries out," but the (Aramaic?) form of the first word is peculiar, and the grammar of the second word (it shows the form of an active transitive verb) is wrong. This translation follows an emendation first proposed by Hermann Gunkel, *sheqadim tishdof*.

7. *no reaper fills his hand, / no binder of sheaves his bosom.* The withered, wind-blasted grass on the rooftops produces an anti-harvest—nothing to grasp, nothing to bind and gather in. This image for the fate of the wicked is related to the one used in Psalm 1:4, "like chaff that the wind drives away."

8. *"The LORD's blessing upon you!"* These words are fairly close to the exchange of greetings between Boaz and the harvesters in Ruth 2:4, so one may assume that such formulas of mutual blessing were customarily exchanged between reapers and passers-by during the harvest, itself a season of blessing through the produce of the fields. For this reason, it makes better sense to construe "We bless you in the name of the LORD" as part of this harvest dialogue and not as a liturgical benediction at the end of the psalm. In Ruth, it should be observed, both Boaz and the harvesters pronounce blessings.

130

A song of ascents.   1
From the depths I called You, LORD.
   Master, hear my voice.   2
          May Your ears listen close to the voice of my plea.
   Were You, O Yah, to watch for wrongs,   3
          Master, who could endure?
   For forgiveness is Yours,   4
          so that You may be feared.

---

1. *From the depths I called You.* Repeatedly in Psalms, "the depths" are an epithet for the depths of the sea, which in turn is an image of the realm of death. Generations of readers, Christian and Jewish, have responded to the archetypal starkness of this phrase: The speaker, from the darkness of profound despair, on the verge of death, calls out to God. This psalm, of course, is a penitential psalm, focusing not on the evil of Israel's enemies, as does Psalm 129, but on the wrongs Israel has done. It resembles Psalm 129 in beginning with a first-person singular that turns into the expression of a collective plea, as the last two verses make clear.

3. *watch for wrongs.* The verb *sh-m-r* in this context has the particular sense of "keep track of," but the translation "watch for" preserves the play in the Hebrew with the double occurrence of the same verbal stem in "more than dawn-watchers watch for the dawn."

4. *so that You may be feared.* That is, the fear of or reverence for God is not sheer terror but a response of awe to a deity who is both all-powerful and compassionately forgiving. (The Hebrew verb *y-r-ʾ* covers a semantic range from "fear" to "awe" to "reverence.")

5   I hoped for the LORD, my being hoped,
                and for His word I waited.
6   My being for the Master—
                more than the dawn-watchers watch for the dawn.
7   Wait, O Israel, for the LORD,
                for with the LORD is steadfast kindness,
                        and great redemption is with Him.
8   And He will redeem Israel
                from all its wrongs.

---

5. *and for His word I waited.* Two manuscripts read "for Your word." This would turn the first clause into a vocative ("I hoped, O LORD"), which is a tempting construction because the verb "hoped" in the first verset is not followed in the Hebrew by a preposition ("for" being assumed in the translation as an ellipsis). The awaited word from God is presumably a word of forgiveness.

6. *My being for the Master— / more than the dawn-watchers watch for the dawn.* Previous translators have all supplied a predicate here ("is eager," "is turned to," or the King James Version's "waiteth," duly italicized to show that it is merely implied in the Hebrew). But the power of the line in the original is precisely that the anticipated verb ("wait" having appeared twice in the preceding line) is choked off: my inner being, my utmost self—for God more than watchmen watch for the dawn. (The Hebrew noun *boqer* also has the more general sense of "morning," but in this context of watchmen through the night awaiting the first light, "dawn" is strongly indicated.) Previous translators render the four Hebrew words *mishomrim laboqer shomrim laboqer* as a simple repetition (for example, the New Jewish Publication Society, "than watchmen for the morning, watchmen for the morning." But *shomrim* can be either a verbal noun ("watchmen") or a plural verb ("watch"). The line becomes more vivid and energetic if the second occurrence is understood as a verb: more than the watchmen watch for the dawn, I watch—elliptically implied—for the LORD. The force of the image is evident: The watchmen sitting through the last of the three watches of the night, peering into the darkness for the first sign of dawn, cannot equal my intense expectancy for God's redeeming word to come to me in my dark night of the soul.

131

A song of ascents for David.
   Lord, my heart has not been haughty,
        nor have my eyes looked too high,
   nor have I striven for great things,
        nor for things too wondrous for me.

---

1. *Lord, my heart has not been haughty.* This simple, concise, and affecting expression of humility shows no signs of cultic or public function, and is a good illustration of how the psalm as a poetic form of spiritual expression often stands outside the generic categories that scholars have constructed.

   striven for great things. The literal sense of the Hebrew is "gone about in [or "among"] great things."

2 But I have calmed and contented myself
    like a weaned babe on its mother–
      like a weaned babe I am with myself.
3 Wait, O Israel, for the Lord,
    now and forevermore.

---

2. *I have calmed and contented myself / like a weaned babe on its mother.* There is some margin of doubt about the precise meaning of the two Hebrew verbs. The first sometimes has the sense of "to level" or "to make even," which may be applicable here. The second probably means "to quiet." The evident image is of a newly weaned baby embraced and comforted (the force of the preposition "on") by its mother and therefore calm, even though deprived of the breast.

 like a weaned babe I am with myself. The Hebrew says literally "like a weaned babe I am on myself." The wording is cryptic, though the idea that emerges is quite touching: the person content with his lot, who does not aspire to grand things, is able to give himself the kind of reassuring calm that a loving mother gives the weaned child whom she comforts. After the rejection of images of reaching beyond—the eyes looking high, the striving for or going about among great things—the speaker evokes a sense of beautiful self-containment, an embracing of one's self like a child.

3. *Wait, O Israel, for the Lord.* Either this conclusion on a collective note is an editorial addition, or the condition of quiet contentment of the speaker is being proposed as a model for how a trusting Israel should wait for the Lord.

132

A song of ascents.
   Recall, O Lord, for David
         all his torment
  when he swore to the Lord,
         vowed to Jacob's Champion:
"I will not come into the tent of my home,
         I will not mount my couch,
I will not give sleep to my eyes
         nor slumber to my lids
until I find a place for the Lord,
         a dwelling for Jacob's Champion."

                             1
                             2
                             3
                             4
                             5

1. *Recall, O Lord, for David / all his torment.* The suffering referred to would be the tribulations David underwent as a warrior king until his conquest of Jerusalem and to his self-sacrificing dedication to finding a "resting-place" for the Ark of the Covenant. This psalm is related to the royal psalms, but it places a distinctive emphasis on the story about bringing up the Ark to Jerusalem, which is told in 2 Samuel 6–7.

3. *I will not come into the tent of my home, / I will not mount my couch.* The psalmist uses poetic-archaic terms for both "house" ("the tent of my home") and "bed" ("couch," *'eres yetsu'ai*).

4. *I will not give sleep to my eyes.* No such vow involving renunciation of sleep is reported in the narrative in 2 Samuel, but this appears to be a widespread literary motif. Several Mesopotamian texts have a monarch vowing not to sleep until he restores the image of his god to its temple.

6   Look, we heard of it in Ephratha,
               we found it in the fields of Jaar.

7   Let us come to His dwelling,
               let us bow to His footstool.

8   Rise, O Lord, to Your resting-place,
               You and the Ark of Your strength.

9   Let Your priests don victory,
               and let Your faithful sing gladly.

---

6. *we heard of it.* The "it" is the Ark. Although the poem reconstructs the moment when the Ark is brought forth from its temporary resting place and carried up to Jerusalem, it is very unlikely that the psalm is actually contemporaneous with David. In fact, verse 10 seems to designate "David," then "Your anointed" as two separate figures: David is the faithful founder of the dynasty for whose sake God is implored to stand by the current incumbent of the throne, the anointed one. Scholars bent on recovering cultic settings for the various psalms have proposed an annual ritual commemorating the introduction of the Ark to Jerusalem, but, as with the theory of an enthronement festival (which has also been applied to this psalm), there is no real evidence for the conjecture.

    the fields of Jaar. This place name ("fields" is in the singular in the Hebrew) seems to be an alternate designation for Kiriath-Jearim, mentioned in 1 Samuel 7 as the place where the Ark was kept for two decades. "Jaar" (*ya'ar*) means "forest."

7. *His dwelling . . . His footstool.* Both terms seem to refer to the Ark itself rather than to Jerusalem, because the move to Jerusalem is introduced only in the next verse.

9. *don victory.* The noun *tsedeq*, which elsewhere in Psalms often means "justice" or "righteousness," here probably has its other sense of "victory" because of the analogous line in verse 16, "And its priests I will clothe with victory" as well as the antithetical line at the end of the psalm, "His enemies I will clothe with shame." ("Shame" often is used to indicate military defeat, and *tsedeq*, "victory," and *yesha'*, "rescue," are paired terms for triumph in battle.) Perhaps the victory in question is David's original conquest of Jerusalem.

For the sake of David Your servant,   10
       do not turn away Your anointed.
The Lord swore to David   11
       a true oath from which He will not turn back:
"From the fruit of Your loins
       I will set up a throne for you.
If your sons keep My pact   12
       and My precept that I shall teach them,
their sons, too, evermore
       shall sit on the throne that is yours."
For the Lord has chosen Zion,   13
       He desired it as His seat.
"This is My resting-place evermore,   14
       Here will I dwell, for I desired it.
I will surely bless its provisions,   15
       its needy I will sate with bread.
And its priests I will clothe with triumph,   16
       and its faithful will surely sing gladly.
There will I make a horn grow for David,   17
       I have readied a lamp for my anointed.
His enemies I will clothe with shame,   18
       but on him—his crown will gleam."

---

15. *provisions . . . bread.* "Bread," as elsewhere, is a synecdoche for "food." Providing sustenance for the city is linked with the theme of victory because a walled town under siege, as many biblical texts remind us, would be reduced to starvation.

17. *make a horn grow.* As elsewhere, the horn is a symbol of strength.

18. *his crown will gleam.* Most scholars construe the verb *yatsits* in this fashion, though its more common meaning is "to blossom." The cognate noun *tsits* means "diadem" (perhaps because the crown was imagined as a glorious efflorescence or was wrought with floral motifs), so perhaps the verb here might mean something like "will be a splendid diadem."

133

1   A song of ascents for David.
    Look, how good and how pleasant
            is the dwelling of brothers together.
2   Like goodly oil on the head
            coming down over the beard,
    Aaron's beard that comes down
            over the opening of his robe.

---

1. *Look, how good and how pleasant / is the dwelling of brothers together.* This poem is a kind of idyll celebrating harmonious life together in a fruitful land. A sense of quiet rapture is conveyed at the outset through three words of emphasis—"look" (*hineh*), and then twice "how" (*mah*).

2. *Like goodly oil on the head.* In the Israelite world, as in ancient Greece, rubbing the hair and body with aromatic olive oil was one of the palpable physical pleasures of the good life.
    Aaron's beard that comes down / over the opening of his robe. This initially puzzling line makes good associative sense. The "coming down" of the oil from head to beard is picked up in the "coming down" of the beard itself—a beard of evidently proverbial amplitude, that of the first high priest—over the opening of the robe. The full beard is presumably an image of vigor and abundance.

Like Hermon's dew that comes down
  on the parched mountains.   3
For there the LORD ordained the blessing—   4
  life forevermore.

---

3. *Like Hermon's dew that comes down.* Now we have a third "coming down"—
the dew on this northern mountain. The dew is understood to be an agency of
fruitfulness, especially important in the long dry season when no rain falls.

on the parched mountains. The Masoretic text reads "on the mountains of
Zion," which does not make much sense because Mount Hermon is geograph-
ically removed from the Judean mountains around Jerusalem, and dew certainly does not travel in this fashion. The translation adopts a small
emendation, reading *tsiyah,* "parched land," for *tsiyon,* "Zion."

134

1 A song of ascents.
> Look, bless the Lord,
>> all you servants of the Lord,
>>> who stand in the Lord's house through the
>>> nights.

2   Lift up your hands toward the holy place
>> and bless the Lord.

3   May the Lord bless you from Zion,
>> He Who makes heaven and earth.

---

1. *bless the Lord, / all you servants of the Lord*. This extremely succinct psalm, the last of the fifteen songs of ascents, has a pronounced liturgical character. The worshippers are enjoined to bless—that is, to praise—the Lord, and God in turn is asked to bless—that is, to provide bounty to—the individual worshipper. The effect of summarizing liturgical intonation was perhaps deemed appropriate as a conclusion to the cycle of fifteen psalms.

who stand in the Lord's house through the nights. The acts of the sacrificial cult were completed by sundown, but the reference here could be either to the tending of the fires and the temple lamps through the night or to those who stayed to pray, or perhaps to partake of the sacrificial feast, through the hours of the night.

2. *holy place*. The Hebrew *qodesh* ("holiness") is often a designation of the sanctuary, although it might also be an epithet for the heavens, as the poetic parallelism of Psalm 150:1 suggests: "Praise God in His holy place [*qodsho*], / praise Him in the vault of His power."

135

Hallelujah.   1
   Praise the name of the Lord,
       O praise, you servants of the Lord,
   who stand in the house of the Lord,   2
       in the courts of the house of our God.
   Praise Yah, for the Lord is good,   3
       hymn His name, for it is sweet.
   For Yah has chosen for Himself Jacob,   4
       Israel as His treasure.
   For I know that the Lord is great,   5
       and our Master more than all the gods.

---

1. *Hallelujah. / Praise the name of the* Lord. Formally, this is a psalm of praise or thanksgiving, but it also incorporates historical elements (verses 8–12), and verse 14 may suggest that the nation has fallen on hard times and awaits, or prays for, God's intervention on its behalf.

2. *who stand in the house of the* Lord, / *in the courts of the house of our God.* This clause concretely evokes the temple setting in which this liturgical exhortation to praise God is enacted.

3. *hymn His name, for it is sweet.* The conjunction of the root z-m-r ("hymn," "sing," "make music") and the root n-ʿ-m ("sweet" or "pleasant") is idiomatic in biblical Hebrew. Thus, David is called "the sweet singer of Israel" (*neʿim zemirot yisraʾel*), 2 Samuel 23:1.

6   All that the LORD desired He did
             in the heavens and on the earth,
                  in the seas and all the depths.
7   He brings up the clouds from the ends of the earth;
             lightning for the rain He made;
                  He brings forth the wind from His stores.
8   Who struck down the firstborn of Egypt
             from humankind to beast.
9   Sent forth signs and portents in the midst of Egypt
             against Pharaoh and against all his servants.
10   Who struck down many nations
             and killed mighty kings—
11   Sihon, the Amorite king
             and Og, king of the Bashan,
                  and all the kingdoms of Canaan.
12   And gave their land as an estate,
             an estate to Israel, His people.
13   LORD, Your name is forever,
             LORD, Your fame for all generations.

---

6. *in the heavens and on the earth, / in the seas and all the depths.* The poet, having just proclaimed that the God of Israel is greater than all other gods, now invokes a post-mythological cosmic arena in which YHWH reigns everywhere, without antagonists such as the primordial sea god.

8. *the firstborn of Egypt.* In this rapid poetic summary of God's triumphant acts in history, the psalmist leaps from the victory over Pharaoh in the exodus story to the victory over the Transjordanian kings (verses 10 and 11) reported in Numbers 21.

11. *Og, king of the Bashan.* In Deuteronomy 3:11, Og is described as a giant.

13. LORD, *Your name is forever.* The historical summary concludes with this line of praise for God's enduring greatness, which in turn serves as a transition to the implied prayer, or declaration of trust, of the next verse.

For the Lord champions His people,   14
　　and for His servants He shows change of heart.
The nations' idols are silver and gold,   15
　　the work of human hands.
A mouth they have and they do not speak,   16
　　eyes they have and they do not see.
Ears they have and they do not hear,   17
　　nor is there breath in their mouth.
Like them may their makers be,   18
　　all who trust in them.
House of Israel, bless the Lord,   19
　　House of Aaron, bless the Lord.

---

14. *For the* Lord *champions His people, / and for His servants He shows change of heart.* This entire line is identical with Deuteronomy 32:36 and should probably be thought of as a deliberate quotation. There are some linguistic indications that this psalm is relatively late (for example, the use of the Aramaic-influenced accusative *lamed* before the three nouns in verse 11), though it is not altogether certain that the national disaster after which the psalmist awaits vindication is the Babylonian exile.

15. *The nations' idols are silver and gold.* This and the next three verses repeat, with minor changes, Psalm 115:4–8. The closeness to the anti-idolatry polemic of the anonymous prophet of the exile referred to as Deutero-Isaiah is striking. The thematic connection with what precedes is that God, controller of all realms of creation and of history, will surely now vindicate His people that has been humiliated by worshippers of sticks and stones.

17. *they do not hear.* Unlike the parallel verse in Psalm 115, the verb used here is not *shamaʿ* but *heʾezin*, built from the same root as *ʾozen*, "ear."

18. *Like them may their makers be.* In the implicitly historical context of this psalm, the curse that the idolators be reduced to the nullity of their idols has special force.

20   House of Levi, bless the LORD.
         Those who fear the LORD, bless the LORD.
21   Blessed is the LORD from Zion,
         Who dwells in Jerusalem.
               Hallelujah!

---

20. *House of Levi.* That is, the Levites in distinction to the priests proper ("house of Aaron").

136

Acclaim the LORD, for He is good, 1
       for His kindness is forever.
Acclaim the greatest God, 2
       for His kindness is forever.
Acclaim the greatest Master, 3
       for His kindness is forever.
Who alone performs great wonders, 4
       for His kindness is forever.

---

1. *Acclaim the* LORD. With the initial verb of "acclaim" or "thanks," this text announces itself as a thanksgiving psalm. It takes the form of acclaiming God as creator of heaven and earth, then moving rapidly through God's intervention in history in the exodus story and in the conquest of Canaan. Because of the emphasis on the exodus, some scholars have proposed that this was used in a temple rite on Passover, but that link is not certain because in any case the liberation from Egyptian bondage was thought of as the central instance of God's benevolence in history to Israel.

for His kindness is forever. This repeated refrain clearly must have been an antiphonal response in the liturgy, perhaps by the whole community of worshippers, to the lines of the chorus. As elsewhere, "kindness" also implies steadfast faithfulness.

2. *the greatest God.* The literal Hebrew formulation, "the God of Gods," might mean that the God of Israel is more powerful than all the other supposed gods. But the idiomatic pattern, "*x* of *x*s" (as in "Song of Songs") is also a form of superlative, so it probably means "the greatest God." The same is true of the greatest "Master" in the next verse.

5   Who makes the heavens in wisdom,
              for His kindness is forever.
6   Who stamps firm the earth on the waters,
              for His kindness is forever.
7   Who makes the great lights,
              for His kindness is forever.
8   The sun for dominion of day,
              for His kindness is forever.
9   The moon and stars for dominion of night,
              for His kindness is forever.
10   Who strikes Egypt in its firstborn,
              for His kindness is forever.
11   And brings out Israel from their midst,
              for His kindness is forever.
12   With a strong hand and an outstretched arm,
              for His kindness is forever.
13   Who split the Reed Sea into parts,
              for His kindness is forever.

---

6. *stamps firm the earth.* The verb *raqaʿ* means to "pound" or "stamp flat," and is cognate with *raqiʿa*, the term used for the vault of the heavens in Genesis 1. There is, then, a solid slab or "firmament" that is the sky, and another one below that is the earth. Beneath the earth is the great deep—hence the earth is "on the waters." As is evident in the Flood story, there are waters above the heavens and waters below the earth (see Genesis 7:11).

7. *makes the great lights.* This verse and the next are a virtual citation of Genesis 1:16, though a variant form of the word for "lights" (*ʾorim* instead of *meʾorot*) is used here.

12. *a strong hand and an outstretched arm.* The phrase is quoted from Deuteronomy 4:34, 5:15, and 26:8.

13. *split.* A different verb is used here from the one in Exodus 14, but the meaning is essentially the same.

And made Israel pass through its midst,   14
    for His kindness is forever.
And shook Pharaoh and his force into the Reed Sea,   15
    for His kindness is forever.
Who led His people in the wilderness,   16
    for His kindness is forever.
Who struck down great kings,   17
    for His kindness is forever.
And killed mighty kings,   18
    for His kindness is forever.
Sihon, king of the Amorites,   19
    for His kindness is forever.
And Og, king of the Bashan,   20
    for His kindness is forever.
And gave their land as an estate,   21
    for His kindness is forever.
An estate for Israel His servant,   22
    for His kindness is forever.
Who recalled us when we were low,   23
    for His kindness is forever.
And delivered us from our foes,   24
    for His kindness is forever.

---

15. *shook.* This unusual and vivid verb also appears in Exodus 14.

23. *recalled us when we were low.* The reference is vague but must allude to some point in Israelite history after the conquest of the Land, when the nation was at the mercy of its enemies. (See the next verse, "And delivered us from our foes.") Because this psalm is probably post-exilic, it could refer to the Babylonian captivity. But in keeping with the overall aim of thanksgiving, national tribulations are no more than glanced at here.

25   Who gives bread to all flesh,
          for His kindness is forever.
26   Acclaim the God of the heavens,
          for His kindness is forever.

---

25. *Who gives bread to all flesh.* As elsewhere, "bread" indicates all kinds of food. In an apt gesture of closure, the celebration of God's enduring kindness, having begun with His acts as creator, concludes by moving beyond the national perspective to God's providence to all living creatures.

137

By Babylon's streams,   1

        there we sat, oh we wept,

                when we recalled Zion.

On the poplars there   2

        we hung up our lyres.

---

1. *By Babylon's streams, / there we sat, oh we wept.* This psalm was almost certainly composed shortly after the deportation of the Judeans by the Babylonians in 586 BCE—the experience of exile is fresh and acutely painful. Scholars committed to seeing a ritual setting for virtually every psalm have proposed a rite of lamentation among the exiles, but there is no persuasive evidence for that in the text, and such a view underestimates the use of the psalm form as a vehicle for the expression of spontaneous emotion—in this case, collective emotion. The first Hebrew noun, *neharot*, generally means "rivers," but because the more probable reference is to the network of canals that connected the Tigris and the Euphrates, "streams" is a preferable translation here. It should be noted that, in keeping with the evolution of Hebrew poetry in the later biblical period, semantic parallelism within the lines in this poem is weak, an absence occasionally compensated for by interlinear parallelism.

2. *On the poplars there.* The literal sense of the Hebrew behind "there" is, as the King James Version has it, "in the midst thereof." But that is confusing because it is not clear what the "thereof" refers to (presumably the land of Babylon). In any case, *sham*, "there," is twice repeated, expressing the alienation of the collective speakers from the place they find themselves, which, logically, should be "here" rather than "there."
    we hung up our lyres. This would seem to be a gesture of renunciation of their use, though some commentators have imagined that the exiles are hiding their lyres in the foliage.

3   For there our captors had asked of us
                words of song,
    and our plunderers—rejoicing:
                "Sing us from Zion's songs."

4   How can we sing a song of the LORD
                on foreign soil?

5   Should I forget you, Jerusalem,
                may my right hand wither.

6   May my tongue cleave to my palate
                if I do not recall you,

---

3. *our plunderers.* The Hebrew *tolaleinu* is anomalous but is probably a variant form of the familiar term for plunderers, *sholaleinu*, perhaps encouraged—as the Israeli scholar Meir Gruber has proposed—by the opportunity for sound play with *talinu*, "we hung up," at the end of the preceding line.

Sing us from Zion's songs. The assumption is that the singers of the Jerusalem temple were known for the beauty of their music, and their captors want to be entertained by them. A bas-relief from the palace of Sennacherib in Nineveh actually shows three prisoners carrying lyres marching under the surveillance of an Assyrian soldier. "Zion's songs" would be any of the songs sung in the temple and not necessarily the special category of psalm we now call "psalms of Zion," which celebrate the city.

4. *a song of the* LORD. This should not be thought of as a technical category of "Yahweh songs" (H.-J. Kraus), for almost all the psalms are in one way or another directed to the God of Israel and invoke Him. Meir Gruber aptly observes that from the Babylonian perspective, what their captives sing are national songs, "Zion's songs," whereas the Judeans themselves view them as sacred music, "a song of the LORD."

5. *may my right hand wither.* The Masoretic text reads "may my right hand forget [*tishkah*]." This is problematic because there is no evidence elsewhere for an intransitive use of the verb "to forget"—hence the strategy of desperation of the King James Version in adding, in italics, an object to the verb, "its cunning." But a simple reversal of consonants yields *tikhhash*, "wither." The loss of capacity of hand and tongue is linked with the refusal of song, for the right hand is needed to pluck the lyre and the tongue to sing the song.

if I do not set Jerusalem
>> above my chief joy.
Recall, O Lord, the Edomites,   7
>> on the day of Jerusalem, saying:
"Raze it, raze it,
>> to its foundation!"
Daughter of Babylon the despoiler,   8
>> happy who pays you back in kind,
>> > for what you did to us.
Happy who seizes and smashes   9
>> your infants against the rock.

---

7. *Recall, O Lord, the Edomites.* After the solemn vow never to forget the longed-for Jerusalem, the poem moves into a second angry phase that follows the sorrow of the first: a flashback to the terrible moment when Jerusalem was destroyed by the Babylonians with the gleeful encouragement of their Edomite allies. Obadiah 1:8–15 provides a vivid picture of the appalling actions of the Edomites at this historical moment.

on the day of Jerusalem. This phrase means the day of the destruction or conquest of Jerusalem, but the painful noun of destruction is suppressed, as though it stuck in the throat of the poet.

8. *Babylon the despoiler.* The Masoretic text shows *hashedudah*, "the despoiled," a reading that can be saved only by an exegetical contortion in which the passive form of the verb is understood to mean "about to become despoiled." A simple reversal of consonants with an adjustment of vocalization yields *hashodeidah*, "the despoiler."

9. *Happy who seizes and smashes / your infants against the rock.* No moral justification can be offered for this notorious concluding line. All one can do is to recall the background of outraged feeling that triggers the conclusion: The Babylonians have laid waste to Jerusalem, exiled much of its population, looted and massacred; the powerless captives, ordered—perhaps mockingly—to sing their Zion songs, respond instead with a lament that is not really a song and ends with this bloodcurdling curse pronounced on their captors, who, fortunately, do not understand the Hebrew in which it is pronounced.

138

1 For David.
   I acclaim You with all my heart,
           before gods I hymn to You.
2 I bow toward Your holy temple,
           and I acclaim Your name
   for Your kindness and Your steadfast truth,
           for You have made Your word great across all Your
           heavens.

---

1. *I acclaim You.* As repeatedly elsewhere, the initial verb for acclaim or thanks signals a thanksgiving psalm. The individual who is offering thanks here appears to have been rescued from enemies who sought his undoing (verse 7), though it is unclear whether these are actual martial enemies or hostile people who wanted to harm him in some other way (perhaps judicially).

before gods. This implicitly polytheistic phrase has troubled interpreters through the ages. The Aramaic Targum rendered it, not very convincingly, as "judges." Following this line, Rashi and other medieval exegetes understood it as a reference to the Sanhedrin (!). It is most plausible to see here either a linguistic fossil from polytheism or even an anti-polytheistic polemic gesture: I hymn to You in defiant presence before all those deities that people imagine to be real gods.

2. *for You have made Your word great across all Your heavens.* The Hebrew is problematic. The literal sense of the received text is "for You have made Your word greater than all Your name." This translation adopts a frequently proposed emendation, reading instead of *shimkha,* "Your name," *shameykha,* "Your heavens."

On the day I called You answered me,   3
            You made strength well up within me.
All kings of the earth will acclaim You, LORD,   4
            for they have heard the words of Your mouth.
And they will sing of the ways of the LORD,   5
            for great is the LORD's glory.
For high is the LORD yet the lowly He sees,   6
            and the lofty, from a distance, He knows.
Though I walk in the midst of straits,   7
            You give me life in spite of my enemies' wrath.
You stretch out Your hand,
            and Your right hand rescues me.

---

3. *You made strength well up within me.* The verb *hirhiv* is surprising because it would generally mean something like "to make proud." It could have an extended meaning here, or it could be a mistake for *hirhiv* (literally, "to broaden") or *hirbah* ("to increase"), as several of the ancient versions show.

4. *All kings of the earth . . . / . . . have heard the words of Your mouth.* The background of this line is not self-evident. The idea that the rulers of all the nations will acclaim the God of Israel is in keeping with a reiterated theme of Deutero-Isaiah, as many scholars have noted. But, at least on the face of it, the saving act of YHWH in this psalm is in the life of one individual, so the kings of the earth would scarcely be aware of it. Perhaps hearing God's words—realizing the truths He has revealed to humankind—is an action entirely independent of the plight from which the thankful speaker of the poem has been rescued. God has shown His kindness to the speaker, and this same attribute, for different reasons, is recognized across the earth.

6. *the lofty, from a distance, He knows.* The Hebrew syntax also allows a different construction, "the Lofty [One] from a distance knows," but that adjective (*gavoah*) is not generally used as an epithet for God, and the pairing of antithetical objects to the verb in each half of the line is much more in keeping with biblical poetic practice.

8   The LORD will requite me.
              O LORD, Your kindness is forever.
                    Do not let go of Your handiwork.

---

8. *requite me.* The Hebrew verb *gamar* might also mean "finish" or "complete"
(its fixed meaning in later Hebrew), but the context suggests that here it is the
equivalent of the verb *gamal*, "requite."

   Do not let go of Your handiwork. The Hebrew verb has a concreteness diluted
by the conventional translation as "forsake." The verb *hirpah* means to relax the
muscles of the hand so that what it holds is dropped or released. The speaker,
as a human creature, reminds God that he is God's own handiwork. The use of
the "hand" component in all likelihood encouraged the poet to choose this particular verb. God is thus implicitly figured as a potter (as in Genesis 2) who is
implored not to loose his hand and allow what he has made to fall and shatter.

139

For the lead player, a David psalm.   1
LORD, You searched me and You know,
   It is You Who know when I sit and I rise,   2
          You fathom my thoughts from afar.
   My path and my lair You winnow,   3
          and with all my ways are familiar.
   For there is no word on my tongue   4
          but that You, O LORD, wholly know it.

---

1. LORD, *You searched me and You know.* These words inaugurate one of the most remarkably introspective psalms in the canonical collection. Although the invocation of bloody-minded enemies in verses 19 and 20 indicates a connection with the psalms of supplication, this poem is essentially a meditation on God's searching knowledge of man's innermost thoughts, on the limitations of human knowledge, and on God's inescapable presence throughout the created world. The reflection on the wonder of man's creatureliness in verses 13–16 is reminiscent of Job 10, and certain linguistic features of the Hebrew recall if not Job directly then the late period in which Job was composed.

3. *My path and my lair You winnow.* The word represented as "lair," *rov'a*, is unusual; interchangeable with the root *r-b-ts*, it generally indicates the place where an animal lies down. The verb here, from the root *z-r-h*, reflects an extension of its agricultural meaning, an extended sense also in usage in English ("winnow" in the sense of "to analyze and critically assess").

5   From behind and in front You shaped me,
            and You set Your palm upon me.
6   Knowledge is too wondrous for me,
            high above—I cannot attain it.
7   Where can I go from Your spirit,
            and where from before You flee?
8   If I soar to the heavens, You are there,
            if I bed down in Sheol—there You are.
9   If I take wing with the dawn,
            if I dwell at the ends of the sea,
10   there, too, Your hand leads me,
            and Your right hand seizes me.
11   Should I say, "Yes, darkness will swathe me,
            and the night will be light for me,

---

5. *From behind and in front You shaped me.* The verb could also mean something like "besiege," "bring into straits," but the sense of shaping or fashioning like a potter seems more likely here, especially as the poem moves ahead to the imagining of the forming of the embryo in the womb. In this understanding, "You set Your palm upon me" is not a menacing act but rather the gesture of the potter.

9. *If I take wing with the dawn, / if I dwell at the ends of the sea.* Some interpreters have understood this as a simple indication of east and west (a different Hebrew term for "dawn" means "east," and "sea" can sometimes mean "west"). The image of the line, however, is more vividly mythological than that. The speaker imagines taking wing with the dawn as it appears in the east, then soaring with the sun on its westward path to the limits of the imagined world, "the ends [singular in the Hebrew] of the sea."

11. *darkness will swathe me.* This fantasy of being enveloped in darkness picks up the idea of bedding down in Sheol, the underworld.
    and the night will be light for me. That is, I will immerse myself in darkness, acting as though the pitch-black of night could be my light, could serve instead of the illumination of daylight existence.

Darkness itself will not darken for You,   12
        and the night will light up like the day,
                the dark and the light will be one.
For You created my innermost parts,   13
        wove me in my mother's womb.
I acclaim You, for awesomely I am set apart,   14
        wondrous are Your acts,
                and my being deeply knows it.
My frame was not hidden from You,   15
        when I was made in a secret place,
                knitted in the utmost depths.

---

13. *innermost parts.* The literal meaning of the Hebrew is "kidneys." Though the kidneys are generally thought of as the seat of conscience in the Bible, the context here (see the parallel verset, "wove me in my mother's womb") suggests that in this case the term is a synecdoche for all the intricate inner organs of the human creature. The location in the womb is associatively triggered by the idea of being enveloped in darkness expressed in verses 11 and 12.

14. *for awesomely I am set apart.* The Hebrew *ki nora'ot nifleiyti* is not clear. Most interpreters understand *nifleiyti* as a variant spelling of *niflei'ta*, a verb whose root means "wonder" and render it here as "wondrously made." But there is scant evidence that this verb can mean "wondrously made" rather than simply "was wondrous." Spelled as it is with a *heh* and not an *aleph*, the verb means "to be set apart" or "to be distinct." That meaning might be appropriate for the speaker's reflection on how he evolved in the womb from an unformed embryo to a particular human being with the consciousness of his own individuality.

15. *knitted in the utmost depths.* The literal sense of the Hebrew phrase is "in the depths of the earth." With the movement from the enveloping darkness of a cosmic netherworld to the womb earlier in the poem, at this point there is an archetypal association between womb and the chthonic depths. (The Aramaic Targum renders this phrase flatly as *kereisa de'ima*, "mother's womb.") This translation chooses an English phrase that might suggest both womb and netherworld.

16   My unformed shape Your eyes did see,
                and in Your book all was written down.
      The days were fashioned,
                not one of them did lack.
17   As for me, how weighty are Your thoughts, O God,
                how numerous their sum.
18   Should I count them, they would be more than the sand.
                I awake, and am still with You.
19   Would You but slay the wicked, God—
                O men of blood, turn away from me!—

---

16. *and in Your book all was written down.* The Hebrew is obscure—an obscurity compounded by the introduction of a plural (literally, "they all are written down").

The days were fashioned. The textual difficulties continue. If the received text is correct, it might mean "the future days of the child to be born were already given shape in the womb."

not one of them did lack. The enigmatic Hebrew text says literally, "and not one in them." The verb "did lack"—in Hebrew, this would be *yeḥsar*—is added as an interpretive guess.

17. *weighty.* The Hebrew root *y-q-r* more often means "precious," but the sense of "weighty" registers an Aramaic influence, reflecting the late composition of this psalm.

18. *I awake.* The effort of many modern interpreters to link the verb with *qets*, "end," is dubious, because *heqitsoti* elsewhere always means "I awake." What the poet may be imagining is that after the long futile effort of attempting to count God's infinite thoughts, he drifts off in exhaustion, then awakes to discover that God's eternal presence, with all those endless divine thoughts, is still with him.

19. *God.* The name used here is *'eloah*, which occurs only in poetry and is especially common in Job.

Who say Your name to scheme,   20
        Your enemies falsely swear.
Why, those who hate You, LORD, I hate,   21
        and those against You I despise.
With utter hatred I do hate them,   22
        they become my enemies.
Search me, God, and know my heart,   23
        probe me and know my mind.
And see if a vexing way be in me,   24
        and lead me on the eternal way.

---

20. *say Your name.* The Hebrew says only "say You," but "name," as the parallelism with swearing falsely (the same idiom as in the Decalogue) indicates, is implied.

21. *those against you.* Some scholars, with an eye to the symmetry of expression, prefer to read—instead of the Masoretic *tequmemekha*—a noun cognate with the verb, *mitqotetekha*, "those who despise You."

23. *Search me, God, and know my heart.* The echo of verse 1 marks a closure through envelope structure.
    my mind. The Hebrew says "my thoughts," but because a different word is used from the one that occurs in verses 2 and 17, the translation opts for "mind."

24. *vexing.* Others understand this as "idolatrous," but the word for "idol" is *ʿetsev*, whereas the form appearing here, *ʿotsev*, would usually mean "pain," "sorrow," "vexation." Wayward thoughts are imagined to vex God.
    lead me. The very verb that in verse 10 had an ambiguous sense, perhaps of entrapment, here at the end is wholly positive.

140

1 For the lead player, a David psalm.
2   Free me, LORD, from evil folk,
                    from a violent man preserve me.
3   Who plot evil in their heart,
                    each day stir up battles.
4   They sharpen their tongue like a serpent,
                    venom of spiders beneath their lip.   selah
5   Guard me, LORD, from the wicked man's hands,
                    from a violent man preserve me,
                        who plots to trip up my steps.
6   The haughty laid down a trap for me,
                    and with cords they spread out a net.
                        Alongside the path they set snares for
                        me.   selah
7   I said to the LORD, "My God are You.
                    Hearken, O LORD, to the sound of my pleas."

---

2. *Free me, LORD, from evil folk.* The poem immediately launches on a series of formulas of the psalm of supplication that continue to the end.

3. *stir up battles.* The Masoretic text appears to say "fear [*yaguru*] battles." A minor emendation of the verb to *yegaru*, which is the reading reflected in three ancient translations, yields the more likely "stir up."

LORD, Master, my rescuing strength,   8
       You sheltered my head on the day of the fray.
Do not grant, O LORD, the desires of the wicked,   9
       do not fulfill his devising.
              They would rise.   selah
May the mischief of their own lips   10
       cover the heads of those who come round me.
May He rain coals of fire upon them,   11
       make them fall into ravines, never to rise.

---

8. *on the day of the fray.* The literal sense of the Hebrew is "on the day of weapons."

9. *They would rise.* At this point, continuing to the end of verse 12, the text shows numerous signs of mangling in scribal transmission. Attempts to reconstruct it have not been notably successful, though one might adopt the proposal of adding the negative *'al,* yielding "Let them not rise." "They would rise" (a single word in the Hebrew) does not make evident sense in context, and the doubts about its textual authenticity are compounded by the fact that as one word with one accented syllable it does not scan and could not constitute a verset.

10. *May the mischief of their own lips.* The translation of the entire verse is no more than a plausible guess. The syntax looks odd, and "mischief" for *'amal* (elsewhere, either "toil" or "trouble") is something of a stretch in order to make sense of these words.

11. *May He rain.* The Masoretic text has a plural verb, *yimotu,* which means "will slip down" and is not the word that would be used for the coming down from the sky of a shower of fiery coals. This translation follows one version of the Syriac in reading *yamteir,* "May He rain," the same verb used in Genesis to describe the destruction of Sodom.

    ravines. The Hebrew *mahamurot* appears only here. It seems to mean a deep pit or a natural crevice, as this translation guesses.

12   May no slanderer stand firm in the land,
            may the violent evil man be trapped in pitfalls.
13   I know that the LORD will take up
            the cause of the lowly, the case of the needy.
14   Yes, the righteous will acclaim Your name,
            the upright will dwell in Your presence.

---

12. *slanderer.* The literal meaning of the Hebrew is "man of the tongue."

may the violent evil man be trapped in pitfalls. The Hebrew here, like the translation, is ungainly and seems too long to constitute a verset. The verb "may be trapped" is literally "may he trap him," though sometimes in biblical Hebrew the third-person singular is used as an equivalent of the passive form of the verb. "Pitfalls," *madheifot,* occurs only here but shows a verbal stem that means "to push over."

13–14. The plea to be rescued from the hands of evildoers concludes with an affirmation of trust that God will intervene on behalf of the oppressed and that the righteous will enjoy God's presence, giving thanks to Him as is due.

141

A David psalm.
O Lord, I call You. Hasten to me.
Hearken to my voice when I call You.
May my prayer stand as incense before You,
my uplifted hands as the evening offering.
Place, O Lord, a watch on my mouth,
a guard at the door of my lips.
Incline not my heart to an evil word
to plot wicked acts
with wrongdoing men,
and let me not feast on their delicacies.

---

1. *O Lord, I call You.* This is another highly formulaic psalm of supplication.

3. *a watch on my mouth, / a guard at the door of my lips.* As in many of the supplications, the malicious intention of the speaker's enemies seems to manifest itself in vicious speech. The special emphasis here is on the speaker's prayer that he not answer them in kind, that he keep his own speech from slander and invective.

4. *an evil word.* Though *davar* can also mean "thing," the focus on acts of speaking suggests that its other sense, of "word," is more salient here. A revocalization proposed by Rabbi Israel Stein, *ledaber* instead of *ledavar*, yields "to speak evil."

5   Let the righteous man strike me,
            the faithful rebuke me.
    Let no wicked man's oil adorn my head,
            for still my prayer is against their evils.
6   Let their leaders slip on a rock,
            and let them hear my words which are sweet.

---

5. *the faithful rebuke me.* It is at this point that the coherence of the Hebrew text breaks down, and grave textual problems persist till the end of verse 7. The Masoretic text appears to say literally, "May the righteous man strike me kindness." Attempts to rescue this by interpreting *ḥesed* as "with kind intention" or "in loyalty" are strained. The translation reads instead of *ḥesed* the noun *ḥasid*, meaning "the faithful person" and making it the subject of "rebuke me," dropping the *waw* ("and") before that verb.

Let no wicked man's oil adorn my head. This whole clause is problematic in the Hebrew, which seems to say "Let not oil of the head negate [?] my head." The translation assumes that the first *ro'sh* ("head") has been inadvertently duplicated from the second, and originally read *rasha'*, "wicked man." The verb *yani* here is anomalous, lacking the aleph at the end that would make it mean "negate" and not corresponding to any recognizable Hebrew verb formation. The translation guesses it may derive from the root *n-'-h* ("to be beautiful," yielding *noy*, "beauty" in post-biblical Hebrew). Oil on the head was regarded as a pleasure and an enhancement. Whatever the obscurity, the line means to contrast the preferability of being rebuked by the righteous to the pleasures of the wicked.

6. *Let their leaders slip on a rock.* Everything in this segment of text is doubtful. The noun *shoftim* usually means "judges," but in the Book of Judges it designates an ad hoc military leader, and the judicial sense may be unlikely here. The phrase "slip on a rock" is peculiar, especially because the Hebrew says, quite unidiomatically, "in the hands of a rock," and the form of the verb used here does not ordinarily indicate a jussive. Perhaps "rock" belongs somewhere in the splitting of the earth of the next verse.

As when the earth is parted and split,
>   our bones are scattered in the mouth of Sheol.   7
For to You, O Lord, my eyes turn.
>   In You I take refuge. Expose not my life.   8
Guard me from the trap they laid for me
>   and the snares of the wrongdoers.   9
May the wicked fall in their nets.
>   I alone shall go on.   10

---

7. *As when the earth is parted and split.* Here it is the grammar that is baffling because both Hebrew verbs are active and transitive, with no grammatical subject in sight. Rashi proposes an elided "tree" as the subject of the parting and splitting, though the imagery looks more like an earthquake.

our bones are scattered in the mouth of Sheol. As the text stands, this would be an expression of the dire plight of the speaker and his friends (the latter rather suddenly introduced, it must be said) beset by evil people. One version of the Septuagint and the Syriac reads instead "their bones," making this a continuation of the catastrophe that overtakes the wicked in the previous verse.

8. *my eyes turn.* "Turn" is merely implied in the Hebrew.

142

1 A David *maskil*, when he was in the cave, a prayer.
2 With my voice I shout to the LORD,
  with my voice I plead to the LORD.
3 I pour out my speech before Him,
  my distress before Him I tell,
4 when my spirit faints within me,
  You, You know my path.
  On the path on which I walk
  they have laid a trap for me.
5 Look on the right and see—
  there is no one who knows me.
  Escape is gone for me,
  no one inquires for me.

---

1. *A David* maskil, *when he was in the cave.* Because of the urgency of this compact supplication, the editors link it in the superscription with David's moment of distress when he was hiding from Saul (1 Samuel 22).

4. *when my spirit faints within me.* The literal sense of the Hebrew is "when my spirit faints upon me."
   You, You know my path. The addition of the usually elided pronoun 'atah makes this emphatic.

5. *Look on the right.* In Psalms, help is repeatedly on the right hand, so it is dismaying when there is no one there who knows the speaker.

I shouted to You, O LORD.   6
    I said, You are my shelter,
        my lot in the land of the living.
Listen close to my song of prayer,   7
    for I have sunk very low.
Save me from my pursuers,
    for they are too strong for me.
Bring me out from the prison   8
    to acclaim Your name.
For the righteous will draw round me
    when You requite me.

---

8. *Bring me out from the prison*. Some scholars have understood this literally, making this psalm a prisoner's supplication. The speaker has been entrapped (verse 4); he is incarcerated with no one around to help him (verse 5); and he pleads to be freed. But all this may be fanciful because prison, like "straits," is a ready metaphor for a condition of acute distress, and the binary opposition between restrictive enclosure and wide-open space is common in the figurative language of Psalms.

    the righteous will draw round me. The meaning of the verb *yakhtiru* is in dispute. Normally, it would mean "to crown," but the verbal stem suggests "to go around" (a crown going around the head). Either the Masoretic *yakhtiru* has the sense here of *yekhatru* (the same root in another conjugation), "to surround," or should be revocalized as *yekhatru* (in the consonantal text, it lacks the *yod*, as the form *yekhatru* does). This is the reading of the Septuagint.

143

1   A David psalm.
> LORD, hear my prayer,
>> hearken to my pleas.
>>> In Your faithfulness answer me, in Your bounty.

2   Do not come into judgment with Your servant,
>> for no living thing is acquitted before You.

3   For the enemy pursued me,
>> thrust my life to the ground,
>>> made me dwell in darkness like those long
>>> dead.

4   And my spirit fainted within me,
>> in my breast my heart was stunned.

5   I recalled the days of old,
>> I recited all Your deeds,
>>> of Your handiwork I did speak.

---

1. LORD, *hear my prayer.* From these opening words, the psalm abounds in the stereotypical language of the psalm of supplication.

2. *for no living thing is acquitted before You.* The idea here is in accord with a theme in Job—that no creature (not even the angels, according to Job) can hope to be blameless before God's inexorable judgment. The Hebrew phrase *kol ḥay* is not restricted to humankind, as many translations suggest, but embraces all living creatures.

3. *like those long dead.* The sense of this phrase might also be "like the forever dead."

I stretched out my hands to You—
    my being like thirsty land to You.   selah 6
Quick, answer me, O Lord,
    my spirit pines away. 7
Do not hide Your face from me,
    lest I be like those gone down to the Pit.
Let me hear Your kindness in the morning,
    for in You I trust. 8
Let me know the way I should go,
    for to You I lift up my being.
Save me from my enemies, Lord;
    with You is my vindication. 9
Teach me to do what will please You,
    for You are my God. 10
Let Your goodly spirit guide me
    on level ground.
For the sake of Your name, Lord, give me life,
    in Your bounty bring me out from the straits. 11

---

6. *my being like thirsty land to You.* Rain in this climate and therefore in this body of literature is characteristically thought of as a desperately needed blessing. Hence God's responsive presence is metaphorically represented as the rain that the parched land awaits to quicken it with growth.

8. *in the morning.* What is implied is waiting through a long, dark night—perhaps, like a city under siege—to discover rescue as day breaks.
  for to You I lift up my being. This is a gesture of prayer or entreaty, an idiomatic extension of lifting up the hands in prayer.

9. *with You is my vindication.* This is the one textual crux in the psalm. The Hebrew seems to say "to You I covered" (*'elekha kisiti*). This translation revocalizes the second of these two words to read *kesuti*, a term that in Genesis 20:16 has the sense of "vindication." Some scholars, anticipated by at least one medieval Hebrew exegete, prefer to read *hasiti*, "I sheltered."

12   And in Your kindness devastate my enemies
                and destroy all my bitter foes,
                      for I am Your servant.

---

12. *devastate my enemies* / . . . *destroy all my bitter foes*. The psalm gives no real indication of the identity of these enemies or of the concrete nature—judicial? military?—of their assault on the speaker. Some interpreters have seized on the reference to dwelling in darkness at the beginning as an indication that the supplicant has been cast into prison, but the inference is questionable because darkness is such a general and archetypal image for adversity. The translation adds the adjective "bitter" to "foes" because the Hebrew *tsorerey nafshi*, literally "foes of my life," suggests implacability or the desire to kill the person.

144

For David.

Blessed is the LORD, my rock,

> Who trains my hands for battle,
>> my fingers for the fray.

My strength and my bastion,

> my fortress and my deliverer.

My shield in which I shelter,

> Who tramples down peoples beneath me.

1

2

---

1. *Blessed is the* LORD, *my rock.* From these opening words, this psalm shows a distinct generic kinship with the royal victory hymn that constitutes Psalm 18 (with the image of imperial conquest at the end of verse 2 suggesting that the speaker is a king). Hermann Gunkel once proposed that this poem was an "imitation" of Psalm 18, but, especially because some of the topics it touches on are unlike anything in Psalm 18, it seems more accurate to speak of certain citations from the earlier psalm woven into a different poetic context.

hands . . . fingers. Hands are the obvious body part to train for battle (in poetic parallelism, the more obvious or familiar term almost always occurs in the first verset) because the hand wields the sword. Perhaps the fingers refer to the pulling of the bowstring.

2. *My strength.* The Masoretic text has *ḥasdi*, "my kindness," which seems unlikely. This translation reads instead, with many scholars, *ḥosni*, "my strength."

tramples down. This is the most likely meaning of the verb *roded*, confused by most translations with *rodeh*, "to hold sway over." "Tramples" also accords better with the term used in the analogous verset in Psalm 18:48, "and He crushes [*wayadber*] peoples beneath me."

9 5

3   LORD, what is a human creature that You should know him,
          the son of man, that You pay him mind?
4   The human is like unto breath,
          his days like a passing shadow.
5   LORD, tilt Your heavens and come down,
          but touch the mountains, that they smoke.
6   Crack lightning and scatter them,
          send forth Your bolts and panic them.

---

3. *what is a human creature that You should know him.* This whole line is strongly reminiscent of Psalm 8:6. The meditative theme of this and the next verse seems a little out of keeping with a victory psalm but may be justified as an expression of humility on the part of the royal speaker: What is man, king or commoner, that he should be worthy of such glorious beneficence from God?

4. *The human is like unto breath.* The Israeli scholar Gershon Brin has made the ingenious proposal that the previous verse and this one allude punningly to the first three generations of humankind: 'adam ("the human," or "Adam"), hevel ("breath," or "Abel"), and ben 'enosh ("the son of man," or "Enosh"). In a pattern of intensification, this line moves from mere breath to something still more insubstantial, a passing shadow.

5. LORD, *tilt Your heavens and come down.* This verset cites Psalm 18:10.

6. *Crack lightning.* The Hebrew, using a cognate accusative, has a strong onomatopoeic sound, *broq baraq.*
     bolts. Lightning flashes, in a variety of ancient mythologies, are imagined as the arrows of the gods. This poem, like Psalm 18, reflects an ancient Near Eastern poetic tradition about warrior gods.
     panic them. The reference is to the enemies of the king.

Send forth Your hand from on high,   7
> redeem me and save me from the many waters,
> > from the foreigners' hand,
whose mouth speaks falsely,   8
> and whose right hand is a right hand of lies.
God, a new song I would sing to You,   9
> on a ten-stringed lute I would hymn to You.
Who grants rescue to kings,   10
> redeems David His servant from the evil sword.
Redeem me and save me from the foreigners' hand,   11
> whose mouth speaks falsely,
> > and whose right hand is a right hand of lies.

---

7. *Send forth Your hand.* This is a characteristic move of biblical literature—first "send forth" in the sense of shooting bolts of lightning, then the identical verb in a different, positive sense of reaching out to help. Thanksgiving for victory merges here with a prayer for (further?) help.

the many waters. Or "the mighty waters," an archetypal image of death constantly invoked in Psalms.

8. *a right hand of lies.* Because this is parallel to speaking falsely, many interpreters understand this as raising the right hand to pronounce a false vow—perhaps, if the military context is relevant, in a treaty declaration.

11. *Redeem me and save me.* This line repeats the last two versets of verse 7, either as a refrain or through scribal duplication.

12   While our sons are like saplings,
>   tended from their youth;
>   our daughters, like corner-pillars
>   hewn for the shape of a palace.

13   Our granaries are full,
>   dispensing food of every kind.
>   Our flocks are in the thousands,
>   ten thousands in our fields,

---

12. *While.* The initial subordinate conjugation *'asher*, which has a variety of functions, is ambiguous, and there is a sudden leap from the plea to be rescued from lying enemies to this idyllic vision of fine sons and daughters and abundant flocks that concludes the poem. Some scholars have inferred that this is a different poem tacked onto the victory psalm, though it can be argued that peace and prosperity conventionally follow the king's military triumphs in biblical poetry.

like corner-pillars / hewn for the shape of a palace. The pillars at the corners of a building were often the site of carved ornamentation, so the simile probably invokes this architectural feature as an image of the exquisite shapeliness of the young women.

13. *in our fields.* The noun *ḥutsot* typically means "outside areas" in an urban context.

THE BOOK OF PSALMS 144:14

Our cattle, big with young.
                    There is no breach and none goes out,   14
                              and no screaming in our squares.
Happy the people who has it thus,   15
                    happy the people whose God is the LORD.

---

14. *There is no breach and none goes out.* There are divergent interpretations of
what this line refers to. Because of the immediately preceding reference to
abundant flocks, it is likely that what the poet has in mind is the safe enclosure
of the flocks. There is no breach in the fences that pen in the flocks—hence
"none goes out" (a feminine verb, perhaps because the Hebrew for flock, *tso'n*,
is feminine).

   and no screaming in our squares. The obvious reference is to cries of terror
or anguish in time of war. The idyllic picture of flourishing sons and daughters
and multiplying flocks is completed by this image of secure, untroubled peace.
The psalm that began by thanking God for the gift of victory in battle concludes
with a vision of the reign of peace.

145

1 A David song of praise.
> Let me exalt You, my God the king,
> > and let me bless Your name forevermore.

---

1. *A . . . song of praise.* This is the only psalm so designated. The Hebrew term *tehilah* yields in rabbinic Hebrew the plural *tehilim*, which is the set title in Hebrew for the Book of Psalms. Although psalms of supplication are actually more numerous in the canonical collection, the assumption of post-biblical Jewish tradition was that the purpose par excellence of the poetry of psalms was to praise God. This assumption accords with the view of the ancient editors, for the last six psalms, beginning with this one, are all psalms of praise. It should be said that even the psalms of supplication very often contain elements of praise.

    Let me exalt. The Hebrew *'aromimkha* shows an initial *aleph*, marking the beginning of an alphabetic acrostic. *Nun*, the fourteenth letter of the alphabet, is missing, so the psalm has twenty-one verses instead of twenty-two. But most of the ancient translations as well as a text of this psalm found at Qumran and also one medieval Hebrew manuscript have a verse for *nun*. "Trustworthy [*ne'eman*] is God in all His ways, / and faithful in all His deeds." The evidence strongly suggests that this line was in the original psalm and somehow was dropped in the tradition of scribal transmission that became the Masoretic text. The mode of the verbs here should be noted. Previous English translations usually render them as simple future verbs. But the suffix *ah* of several verbs in the second versets (verses 1, 2, and 5) indicates a jussive or optative mode ("let me," "may I"), and this translation registers that nuance.

    my God the king. Divine kingship is the leading topic of this song of praise, with a special emphasis on terms of kingship in the central lines of the psalm, verses 11–13.

ב   Every day let me bless You,
            and let me praise Your name forevermore.   2

ג   Great is the LORD and highly praised,
            and His greatness cannot be fathomed.   3

ד   Let one generation to the next extol Your deeds
            and tell of Your mighty acts.   4

ה   Of the grandeur of Your glorious majesty
            and Your wondrous acts let me treat.   5

ו   And the power of Your awesome deeds let them say,
            and Your greatness let me recount.   6

ז   The fame of Your great goodness they utter,
            and of Your bounty they joyously sing.   7

ח   Gracious and merciful is the LORD,
            slow to anger, great in kindness.   8

---

2. *bless . . . praise.* In keeping with its generic purpose, the psalm abounds in synonyms for praise. The Hebrew verb *halel*, "praise," is cognate with the noun *tehilah*, "song of praise." The poet does not appear to make distinctions among the synonyms (exalt, bless, extol, praise). In keeping with this deployment of synonymity, there is a prevalence of semantic balance between versets, without much sign of the pattern of intensification from first verset to second generally characteristic of biblical poetry. Perhaps this poetic style was felt appropriate for this doxological rehearsal of God's virtues as king of the world.

6. *let them say, / . . . let me recount.* The switch from third-person plural to first-person singular is disorienting, and some scholars emend the second verb to read "let them recount." It is quite possible, however, that the received text in shuttling between persons reflects the intention of the poet, which would be to weave his own voice of praise with the universal chorus of praise.

8. *Gracious and merciful is the LORD.* This whole line is a citation of the pronouncement of the divine attributes in Exodus 34:5.

9   Good is the L<small>ORD</small> to all,
            and His mercy is over all His creatures.   ט

10   All Your creatures, L<small>ORD</small>, acclaim You,
            and Your faithful ones bless You.   י

11   The glory of Your kingship they say,
            and of Your might they speak,   כ

12   to make known to humankind His mighty acts
            and the grandeur of His kingship's glory.   ל

13   Your kingship is a kingship for all time,
            and Your dominion for all generations.   מ

14   The L<small>ORD</small> props up all who fall
            and makes all who are bent stand erect.   ס

15   The eyes of all look in hope to You
            and You give them their food in its season,   ע

16   opening Your hand
            and sating to their pleasure all living things.   פ

17   Just is the L<small>ORD</small> in all His ways,
            and faithful in all His deeds.   צ

18   Close is the L<small>ORD</small> to all who call Him,
            to all who call to Him in truth.   ק

19   The pleasure of those who fear Him He performs,
            and their outcry He hears and rescues them.   ר

20   The L<small>ORD</small> guards all who love Him,
            and all the wicked He destroys.   ש

21   The L<small>ORD</small>'s praise let my mouth speak,
            and let all flesh bless His holy name
                forevermore.   ת

---

9. *Good is the* L<small>ORD</small> *to all.* In keeping with the theme of God's kingship, the perspective of this psalm is universal rather than national. God's beneficent dominion extends over all living creatures, and "all flesh" (verse 21) praises Him.

21. *The* L<small>ORD</small>*'s praise.* The psalm that began with the generic rubric of "praise" (*tehilah*) neatly concludes by highlighting the same term.

146

Hallelujah.
  Praise the LORD, O my being!   1
      Let me praise the LORD while I live,   2
          let me hymn to my God while I breathe.
  Do not trust in princes,   3
      in a human who offers no rescue.
  His breath departs, he returns to the dust.   4
      On that day his plans are naught.
  Happy whose help is Jacob's God,   5
      his hope—for the LORD his God,

---

1. *Praise the* LORD. Although this psalm has a certain kinship with the thanks-giving psalms, it is more precise to view it as a psalm of praise because it is a general celebration of God's benevolent qualities rather than the personal expression of gratitude for having been saved from some plight.

2. *while I breathe.* The literal sense of the Hebrew *be'odi* is "while I still [am]."

3. *who offers no rescue.* The literal meaning is "who has no rescue."

4. *to the dust.* Literally, this reads "to his soil," with a probable allusion to Genesis 3:19, "till you return to the soil." The continuation of the passage in Genesis emphasizes "dust," *'afar*. Here and in Genesis, the clear reference of the phrase is to death.

  his plans. The Hebrew *'eshtonot* appears only here, but it is related to a ver-bal stem in Jonah that means "to think" or "to reflect." The use of this word is one of several linguistic indications in the poem that this is late-biblical Hebrew.

6   maker of heaven and earth,
                    the sea, and of all that is in them,
                            Who keeps faith forever,

7   does justice for the oppressed,
                    gives bread to the hungry,
                            the LORD looses those in fetters.

8   The LORD gives sight to the blind.
                    The LORD makes the bent stand erect.
                            The LORD loves the righteous.

9   The LORD guards sojourners,
                    orphan and widow He sustains
                            but the way of the wicked contorts.

10   The LORD shall reign forever,
                    your God, O Zion, for all generations.
                            Hallelujah.

---

9. *sojourners . . . orphan . . . widow.* Repeatedly in biblical literature, these are the exemplary instances of the vulnerable and the disenfranchised in society who are in need of special protection. The "sojourner" is a resident alien.

sustains. The verb 'oded appears only here and in Psalm 147. In modern Hebrew, it means "to encourage," which could conceivably be its meaning here. But it probably is derived from the adverb 'od, "still" (as in the declined form 'odi in verse 2 that has been commented on). In that case, the likely sense is to enable someone to persist, or to sustain someone.

the way of the wicked contorts. Again and again in biblical imagery, a straight or level way is a secure way to go. A crooked way—one in which, let us say, there are hairpin turns—is the antithesis, the just deserts of the wicked.

147

Hallelujah.   1
   For it is good to hymn to our God,
        for it is sweet to adorn with praise.
   Builder of Jerusalem, the Lord,   2
        Israel's scattered ones He gathers in.
   Healer of the broken-hearted,   3
        He binds their painful wounds.

---

1. *to adorn.* Following a proposal by the Israeli linguist Yehosua Blau, this translation understands *na'awah* not as an adjective but as an infinitive verb (parallel to *zamrah*, "to hymn") meaning "to adorn" or "to embellish."

2. *Builder of Jerusalem.* This epithet is evidence for the composition of the
psalm in the fifth century BCE, after the rebuilding of Jerusalem. The gathering
in of Israel's scattered ones in the second verset is a reference to the return
from exile (and the verb used, *kanes*, is a late-biblical term). The strengthening
of the bars of the city gates in verse 13 is another allusion to the rebuilding and
refortification of Jerusalem. It is the gratitude for this national restoration that
is the particular reason for praising God in this psalm.

3. *Healer of the broken-hearted.* Although the specific reference is to those who
had suffered the despair of exile, the general nature of the formulation points
to an embracing celebration of God's benevolent compassion and prepares the
way for the comprehensive praise of God's cosmic greatness in the next line.

4   He counts the number of the stars,
                to all of them gives names.
5   Great is our Master, abounding in power,
                His wisdom is beyond number.
6   The LORD sustains the lowly,
                casts the wicked to the ground.
7   Call out to the LORD in thanksgiving,
                hymn to our God on the lyre,
8   Who covers the heavens with clouds,
                readies rain for the earth,
                        makes mountains flourish with grass,
9   gives the beast its food,
                to the raven's young who call.

---

4. *He counts the number of the stars.* In Genesis 15:5, God invokes the stars as an instance of that which cannot be counted, but of course He is able to count them.

   to all of them gives names. This is a neat illustration of the heightening or intensification of an idea in the second verset of the poetic line. God not only can count the multitudinous stars but actually gives a name to each one of them.

5. *His wisdom is beyond number.* The literal sense is "His wisdom has no number." The use of the term "number," *mispar,* pointedly follows God's counting the number of the stars in the preceding line.

8. *covers the heavens with clouds.* After invoking God's mastery over the starry spaces, the poet moves to "heavens" in the sense of sky, then downward to earth where God's providential care is manifested in rainfall, the growth of verdure, and the providing of food to all creatures.

Not the might of the horse He desires,   10
    not by a man's thighs is He pleased.
The Lord is pleased by those who fear Him,   11
    those who long for His kindness.
Extol, O Jerusalem, the Lord,   12
    praise your God, O Zion.
For He strengthens the bars of your gates,   13
    blesses your children in your midst.
He bestows peace in your land,   14
    He sates you with choice wheat.
He sends down His utterance to earth,   15
    quickly His word races.
He pours forth snow like fleece,   16
    scatters frost like ash.

---

10. *Not the might of the horse . . . / not by a man's thighs.* This is a transitional verse. The horse belongs to the realm of nature, like the raven's young of the preceding verse, but "the might of the horse" refers to man's use of the horse in battle. From here, the line moves on to the power of the warrior concentrated concretely in the muscles of his thighs (with perhaps as well a metonymic glance at his sexual power). All this brings us back to the historical situation for which the psalm was composed: Israel has been returned to its land not through any feat of arms but because it faithfully revered its God.

12. *Extol, O Jerusalem, the Lord.* In the concluding movement of the poem, the restored city is apostrophized and exhorted to join in the praise of God that has been taken up by its inhabitants in verse 1 and verse 7.

15. *His utterance . . . His word.* Although it cannot be excluded that both these terms refer to God's commands to Israel, which are explicitly mentioned in verse 19, the context of the next several lines suggests that what is in view here is God's bidding to nature, which He rules absolutely.

16. *scatters frost like ash.* This verset is the alliterative jewel in this splendid evocation of winter in the hill country of the Land of Israel. The Hebrew is *kefor ka'efer yefazer.*

17   He flings His ice like bread crumbs.
                In the face of His cold who can endure?
18   He sends out His word and melts them,
                He lets His breath blow—the waters flow.
19   He tells His word to Jacob,
                His statutes and laws to Israel.
20   He did not thus to all the nations,
                and they knew not the laws.
                        Hallelujah.

---

18. *He lets His breath blow.* Although the noun *ruaḥ* could also mean "wind," the anthropomorphic vividness of God's melting the ice and snow by blowing on them makes "breath" the more likely sense here.

148

Hallelujah. 1
  Praise the Lord from the heavens,
      praise Him on the heights.
  Praise Him, all His messengers, 2
      praise Him, all His armies.
  Praise Him, sun and moon, 3
      praise Him, all you stars of light.

---

1. *Praise the Lord from the heavens.* One of the most majestic of these six concluding psalms of praise, the poem expresses a grand cosmic vision, beginning with the heavens and the celestial beings, then moving down to the earth and to humankind, as all created things are enjoined to praise the Creator.

2. *His messengers . . . His armies.* The "messengers" (*mal'akhim*) are the "angels" of traditional translations—not to be thought of as wingèd figures with haloes but as perfectly anthropomorphic beings whose function it is to carry out God's sundry instructions and to serve as a celestial entourage to God the king. Though "armies," when they are located in the heavens, usually are the stars, here they appear to be synonymous with "messengers," the messengers conceived as God's battalions.

3. *sun . . . moon . . . stars.* This marks the beginning of a poetic reprise of the creation story in Genesis 1. It continues with the "utmost heavens," "the waters above the heavens," "sea monsters," "deeps," and the "crawling things" and "wingèd birds" in the following verses.

4   Praise Him, utmost heavens,
        and the waters above the heavens.
5   Let them praise the LORD's name,
        for He commanded, and they were created.
6   And He made them stand forever, for all time.
        He set them a border that could not be crossed.
7   Praise the LORD from the earth,
        sea monsters and all you deeps.
8   Fire and hail, snow and smoke,
        stormwind that performs His command,

---

4. *utmost heavens.* The literal sense is "the heavens of the heavens," a characteristic Hebrew way of forming a superlative. This designation recurs elsewhere in biblical literature and indicates the uppermost reaches (or top level) of the heavens, above which it was thought that there were waters (these appear here in the second verset).

6. *He set them a border that could not be crossed.* Although the noun *ḥoq* in other contexts means "precept" or "law," it can also mean "border" or "limit." The cosmogonic setting here, with primordial waters held in check, strongly argues for the sense of "border." Behind this image lies the old Canaanite myth of the conquest of a sea god, but it has been thoroughly integrated into a monotheistic conceptual framework. Thus, in the next line, "sea monsters" (*taninim*) and "deeps" (*tehomot*), both terms that are associated in Canaanite tradition with the cosmogonic adversaries of Baal, are called on to praise YHWH.

7. *sea monsters.* These are the *taninim* of Genesis 1:21.
    deeps. This is the plural of *tehom,* the deep over which God's breath hovers in Genesis 1.

8. *smoke.* The Hebrew *qitor* usually means "smoke," though some scholars argue that here it has the sense of "fog." It is hard to determine how fluid these meanings might have been, but *qitor* elsewhere is the product of burning.

the mountains and all the hills,   9
          fruit trees and all the cedars,
wild beasts and all the cattle,   10
          crawling things and wingèd birds,
kings of earth and all the nations,   11
          princes and all leaders of earth,
young men and also maidens,   12
          elders together with lads.
Let them praise the LORD's name,   13
          for His name alone is exalted.
                    His grandeur is over earth and the heavens.
And may He raise up a horn for His people,   14
          praise of all His faithful,
                    of the Israelites, the people near Him.
                    Hallelujah.

---

11. *leaders of earth*. The Hebrew *shoftim* means either "judges" or "leaders," but
the parallel with "kings" makes the judicial sense less likely.

13. *His grandeur is over earth and the heavens*. This verse nicely recapitulates the
movement of the entire poem.

14. *And may He raise up a horn*. Some scholars, with an eye to the cosmic perspective of the poem, think this verse of national blessing is an editorial addition, a kind of epilogue to the psalm proper. But it is possible that the poet felt
that a brief prayer for the well-being of the people was an appropriate coda to
the celebration of the cosmic God.
     praise of all His faithful. The prefix *lᵉ* usually means "for" or "to," but another
common function is to indicate ownership (as on countless ostraca that archaeologists have found), and that is its likely sense here. The praise of God belongs
to, is the proper obligation of, His faithful people. In any case, it should be
noted that the psalm, which began with the verb "praise" (*halel*) concludes with
the noun "praise" (*tehilah*).

149

1 Hallelujah.
  Sing to the LORD a new song,
    His praise in the faithful's assembly.
2 Let Israel rejoice in its Maker,
    Zion's sons exult in their king.
3 Let them praise His name in dance,
    on the timbrel and lyre let them hymn to Him.
4 For the LORD looks with favor on His people,
    He adorns the lowly with victory.

---

1. *Sing to the* LORD *a new song.* The idea of a "new song" is highlighted in several psalms. In a sense, this is a kind of self-advertisement of the psalmist, as if to say "here is a fresh and vibrant psalm that you have never heard before." In this case, the newness of the song is manifested chiefly in the strong emphasis of this psalm of praise on a glorious military victory.

2. *its Maker.* The Masoretic text oddly has a plural noun here.

4. *He adorns the lowly with victory.* The "lowly" in this poem does not refer to an abject social class, as it usually does elsewhere, but to the people of Israel, once brought low by its powerful enemies but now granted victory through God's favor. *Yeshuʿah*, which is regularly represented in this translation as "rescue," here seems to carry the triumphalist nuance of "victory" because of the lines that follow.

Let the faithful delight in glory,   5
            sing gladly on their couches.
Exultations of God in their throat   6
            and a double-edged sword in their hand,
to wreak vengeance upon the nations,   7
            punishment on the peoples,
to bind their kings in fetters,   8
            and their nobles in iron chains,

---

5. *sing gladly on their couches.* The "couches" have bothered some interpreters, but the proposed emendations are unpersuasive. It might mean that the daytime celebrations of God's greatness through dance and song and musical instruments will continue into the night. If this psalm is late (the dating is a little uncertain), the couches could conceivably refer to the couches on which revelers reclined at feasts, as reflected in the Book of Esther.

6. *Exaltations of God in their throat / and a double-edged sword in their hand.* This line vividly carries over the idea of a temple celebration of God with song and dance to an image of warriors going out to battle joyfully praising God. There is a punning link between the two versets in the Hebrew because the term for "double-edged sword" is literally "a sword of mouths," so the line moves from throat to mouth.

7. *to wreak vengeance upon the nations.* Attempts to anchor this prospective vision of a great military triumph in a particular historical context have been unavailing. Indeed, some interpreters have proposed that the victory evoked is intended for an eschatological future.

8. *fetters . . . iron chains.* The "fetters" (*ziqim*, a shortened form of the more usual *'aziqim*) are handcuffs. The "chains" would be for the feet or to bind prisoners in a line by their necks. Both possibilities are depicted in Mesopotamian bas-reliefs.

9   to exact from them justice as written—
                    it is grandeur for all His faithful.
                         Hallelujah.

---

9. *to exact from them justice as written.* The reference could be to a canonical text, such as the promise of victory over the nations if Israel is loyal to its covenant that one finds in Deuteronomy. It could also refer to some notion of a divine book of destiny, an idea that occurs in several ancient cultures.

150

Hallelujah. 1

    Praise God in His holy place,

            praise Him in the vault of His power.

    Praise Him for His mighty acts, 2

            praise Him as befits His abounding greatness.

    Praise Him with the ram-horn's blast, 3

            praise Him with the lute and the lyre.

---

1. *Hallelujah.* The ancient editors, having chosen to represent the Book of Psalms as above all *tehilim*, songs of praise, by concluding the collection with six psalms of praise, now climactically set at the end this psalm that begins and ends with "hallelujah" (which of course means "praise God") and repeats the verb *halel*, "praise," in each verset of the poem for a pointed total of ten times.

His holy place, / . . . *the vault of His power.* There is a harmonious concordance between the "holy place"—the temple below and the heavens above—both conceived as sites of God's habitation.

3. *the ram-horn's blast.* The catalog of musical instruments that begins with this phrase is another way in which this psalm is a fitting culmination to the entire collection. The psalms have prominently featured singing with orchestral accompaniment. Here at the very end, we have a grand roll call of the instruments—wind, strings, and percussion—that are used to create this music.

4 Praise Him with timbrel and dance,
   praise Him with strings and flute.
5 Praise Him with sounding cymbals,
   praise Him with crashing cymbals.
6 Let all that has breath praise Yah.
   Hallelujah!

---

4. *strings.* The Hebrew *minim* is related to the Ugaritic *mnm* and also to the rabbinic *nimim*, both of which refer to strings. Though it could possibly be the name of a particular stringed instrument, the precise identification of which eludes us, it may well indicate the general class of stringed instruments.

flute. Although the term ʿ*ugav* has been applied to the organ in modern Hebrew, it probably is some sort of straight flute, as the archaeological evidence from Egypt suggests.

5. *sounding cymbals . . . crashing cymbals.* In all likelihood, these are not two different percussion instruments but two different sounds produced with the same instrument, the second louder or more penetrating than the first.

6. *Let all that has breath praise Yah.* Appropriately, the psalm and the book conclude on a note of universalism: Not Israel alone but every living thing is exhorted to praise the God of all creation. From this grandly resonant conclusion, one can see how the Book of Psalms has spoken to people through the ages across the borders of nations, languages, and sectarian divisions.

FOR FURTHER READING

Alter, Robert. "Forms of Faith in Psalms," in *The Art of Biblical Narrative*. New York: Basic Books, 1985.

    An attempt to trace the connections between poetic form and the expression of religious experience through the close reading of a number of different psalms.

Fisch, Harold. "Psalms: The Limits of Subjectivity," in *Poetry with a Purpose*. Bloomington: Indiana University Press, 1988.

    Part of a larger argument about the distinctiveness of biblical poetics, this chapter proposes ways in which Psalms swerves from the dominant Western model of lyric poetry in keeping with a compelling agenda of the monotheistic faith.

Flint, Peter, and Patrick Millers, ed. *The Book of Psalms: Composition and Reception*. Leiden: Brill Publishers, 2005.

    A collection of essays, some of them technical, that affords a representative spectrum of recent scholarly discussions of Psalms.

Gillingham, C. E. *The Poems and Psalms of the Hebrew Bible*. Oxford: Oxford University Press, 1994.

    The last third of this book is devoted to a scrupulous overview of the various approaches to Psalms and to a scrutiny of its genres and characteristic poetic devices.

Gunkel, Hermann. *The Psalms: A Form-Critical Introduction*, translated by Thomas M. Horner, Philadelphia: Fortress Press, 1967.

    A classic statement, initially written in German in the early twentieth century, of the analysis of Psalms as a system of distinct poetic genres.

Kraus, Hans-Joachim. *Psalms: A Commentary*, translated by Hilton C. Oswald, two volumes. Minneapolis: Augsburg Publishing House, 1988.

    This carefully discriminating philological commentary, first published in German in 1978, is still the best available scholarly analysis of Psalms, though it is sometimes too quick to emend the text and has a tendency to conclude its discussion of particular psalms with an odd little Christological flourish.

Kugel, James. "Topics in the History of the Spirituality of the Psalms," in *Jewish Spirituality from the Bible through the Middle Ages*, edited by Arthur Green. New York: Crossroad, 1988.

    This essay provides a well-informed, useful summary of the various ways in which Psalms has been thought of over the ages and into the period of modern scholarship.

Mowinckel, Sigmund. *The Psalms in Israel's Worship*. Oxford: Blackwell, 1962.

    This book is the central articulation of a once highly influential approach to the sundry psalms that sought to identify them as expressions of specific cultic settings.

Sarna, Nahum. *Songs of the Heart: An Introduction to the Book of Psalms*. New York: Schocken Books, 1993.

    This book consists of a series of close readings of selected psalms. It provides some nice perceptions of the texts and their relation to ancient Near Eastern contexts, though at times the interpretations reflect an apologetic view.

ROBERT ALTER is the Class of 1937 Professor of Hebrew and Comparative Literature at the University of California, Berkeley, where he has taught since 1967. He is a member of the American Academy of Arts and Sciences, the American Philosophical Society, and the Council of Scholars of the Library of Congress, and is past president of the Association of Literary Scholars and Critics. He has twice been a Guggenheim Fellow and has been a Senior Fellow of the National Endowment for the Humanities, a Fellow at the Institute for Advanced Studies in Jerusalem, and Old Dominion Fellow at Princeton University.

Alter has written extensively on literary aspects of the Bible. His twenty-two published books include two prize-winning volumes on biblical narrative and poetry and award-winning translations of Genesis and of the Five Books of Moses. He has also written widely on the European novel from the eighteenth century to the present, on contemporary American fiction, and on modern Hebrew literature.

Alter was honored with the 2008 *Los Angeles Times* Book Prizes' Robert Kirsch Award for lifetime achievement. His translation of *The Five Books of Moses* won the PEN Center USA Literary Award for Translation and the Koret Jewish Book Award for Translation.